SEÁN MACENTEE: A POLITICAL LIFE

In memory of my father.

New Directions in Irish History is a series initiated by the Royal Irish Academy National Committee for History, which showcases the work of new scholars in Irish history. The series reflects the most up-to-date research, inclusive of all historical periods and with a broad inter-disciplinary approach.

FIRST TITLES IN THIS SERIES

Seán MacEntee
A Political Life
Tom Feeney

The Glory of Being Britons
Civic Unionism in Nineteenth-Century Belfast
John Bew

SEÁN MACENTEE
A Political Life

TOM FEENEY
University College Dublin

IRISH ACADEMIC PRESS
DUBLIN • PORTLAND, OR

First published in 2009 by Irish Academic Press

44 Northumberland Road,
Ballsbridge,
Dublin 4, Ireland

920 NE 58th Avenue, Suite 300
Portland, Oregon,
97213-3786, USA

www.iap.ie

British Library Cataloguing in Publication Data
An entry can be found on request

978 0 7165 2912 5 (cloth)

Library of Congress Cataloging-in-Publication Data
An entry can be found on request

Printed by Biddles Ltd., King's Lynn, Norfolk

Contents

List of Plates

1. MacEntee, c. 1914 when he left Belfast.

2. MacEntee, taken on his arrival in Dartmoor prison, in June 1916. This photograph later appeared in *Hue and Cry* when he was 'on the run' in 1920–1.

3. Disembarking the *Munster* at Kingstown, behind his 'chief', Éamon de Valera, 18 June 1917.

4. Sinn Féin activists returning from the East Clare by-election, photographed outside the Imperial Hotel, Lisdoonvarna. MacEntee is seated beside Arthur Griffith, 13 July 1917.

5. Addressing an election meeting, c. 1918.

6. The speakers and organising committee at the Archbishop Mannix protest meeting, Cardiff. MacEntee is in the front row, centre, 5 September 1920.

7. MacEntee and his wife Margaret, early 1920s.

8. The first Fianna Fáil parliamentary party. MacEntee (fifth from left, back row) is among forty-two Fianna Fáil TDs returned at the June 1927 general election.

9. MacEntee addressing the Fianna Fáil árd fheis in the early 1940s. Seated is Dr Conn Ward, his parliamentary secretary.

10. Members of the first Irish delegation to the Council of Europe, Strasbourg, including MacEntee (third from right), William Norton (centre, Tánaiste and Minister for Social Welfare), James Everett (far left, Minister for Posts and Telegraphs) and Frank Aiken (third from left), September 1949.

11. Portrait taken around at the time of the infamous budget of 1952.

12. De Valera's last cabinet, 1957.

13. At home in Leeson Park. c. 1940s.

14. John F Kennedy, president of the USA, being presented with the freedom of

the city of Dublin by Alderman Seán Moore, lord mayor, in St Patrick's hall, Dublin Castle in the presence of the government, 28 June 1963.

15. MacEntee, his wife and two grandsons, with President Éamon de Valera at Áras an Uachtaráin, presenting a copy of *Episode at Easter*, 7 April 1966.

16. Presentation to MacEntee by the Dublin South-East constituency party, to mark his retirement from politics, November 1969. Photographed with him are the Taoiseach, Jack Lynch and David Harris, chairman of the constituency party.

17. At a reception to mark the retirement of James Patrick Beddy from the Industrial Credit Corporation, set up by MacEntee as Minister for Finance in 1933, August 1972.

18. Proudly wearing military service medals, c. 1970s.

19. Attending a meeting of the Council of State in December 1981. MacEntee, then ninety-two, is seated between Liam Cosgrave and Siobhán McKenna. The other members include President Patrick Hillery, Garret FitzGerald, Jack Lynch, Charles Haughey, Tom O'Higgins, John O'Connell and Barry Desmond, 22 December 1981.

All photographs reproduced by kind permission of UCD archives.

List of Abbreviations

ACC	Agricultural Credit Corporation
AOH	Ancient Order of Hibernians
ATGWU	Amalgamated Transport and General Workers' Union
BMH	Bureau of Military History
C na G	Cumann na nGaedheal
C na P	Clann na Poblachta
DD	Dáil Debates
DORA	Defence of the Realm Act
ERP	European Recovery Programme
ESB	Electricity Supply Board
FF	Fianna Fáil
FG	Fine Gael
GAA	Gaelic Athletic Association
GNP	Gross National Product
GPO	General Post Office (Dublin)
ICC	Industrial Credit Corporation
IDA	Industrial Development Authority
IMA	Irish Medical Association
IRA	Irish Republican Army
IRB	Irish Republican Brotherhood
ITGWU	Irish Transport and General Workers' Union
ITUC	Irish Trade Union Congress
KC	King's Counsel
LRP	Land Reclamation Project
MP	Member of Parliament (House of Commons, Westminster)
NAI	National Archives, Ireland

NDF	National Development Fund
NLI	National Library of Ireland
PWA	Pure Water Association
RIC	Royal Irish Constabulary
SPI	Socialist Party of Ireland
TD	Teachta Dála (Member of Dáil Éireann)
UCDA	University College, Dublin, Archives Department
UDC	Urban District Council
UVF	Ulster Volunteer Force
WUI	Workers' Union of Ireland

Acknowledgements

This book began life as a PhD dissertation undertaken under the supervision of Mary E. Daly in the School of History and Archives, University College, Dublin (UCD). My principal academic debt is to her. As well as being an exacting and scrupulous judge of history, her insight and appreciation of the context and detail of many of the policy decisions advocated or opposed (more often the latter) by MacEntee in government provided me with an eminently dependable sounding board for some of my more tentative conclusions. Other invaluable academic support and guidance came from Ronan Fanning, in whose tutorials I was fortunate enough to end up as a callow first year Arts student and whose encouragement has been forthcoming ever since. Susannah Riordan and Diarmaid Ferriter, in my final year, were responsible for a truly inspiring course on the history of independent Ireland, which, more than anything, led to my pursuance of a postgraduate degree in history. While tutoring in the school of history, I was given much generous and helpful support – both moral and academic – by members of staff. In particular, I would like to extend thanks to Richard Aldous, Tadhg Ó hAnnracháin, Eddie Coleman, David Kerr, Michael Laffan, James McGuire and Ivar McGrath as well as to Eiriol Townsend. My tutor colleagues and fellow researchers were always a source of friendship and cooperation during good days and bad. Special mention in this regard to Deirdre Bryan, Clara Cullen, Coleman Dennehy, Aoife Duignan, Marnie Hay, Carole Holohan and Niamh Puirséil. I also wish to acknowledge the financial assistance provided by the Irish Research Council for the Humanities and Social Sciences, the Lord Edward FitzGerald Bursary and the Albert Lovett Memorial Fund.

I was fortunate enough to interview many prominent people who knew MacEntee both personally and professionally. In this regard, I would like to thank Máire Cruise O'Brien – whose memoir gave a very intimate and vivid portrayal of life in the MacEntee household – Garret FitzGerald, Liam Ó Murchú, T.K. Whitaker and the late Paddy Hillery and Michael B. Yeats. Kevin Burke of St Mary's, Belfast provided helpful information on MacEntee's primary education. Paul Bew, Deirdre McMahon and Eunan O'Halpin offered valuable advice on earlier drafts of the material, for which I am grateful, as well as responding to general queries and generously granting practical assistance. Many others recommended sources and provided ideas in the course of this research, including Marie Coleman, Anne Dolan, Lindsey Earner-Byrne, Margaret Ó hÓgartaigh, Peter Martin, Gary Murphy, William Murphy and Ann de Valera.

I wish to acknowledge the staff of the various libraries and archive departments consulted over the past few years. In the UCD library, Avril Patterson was particularly helpful. Special mention must go to the staff of the National

Archives in Bishop Street for their unending good humour when delivering yet more files for my perusal. Seamus Helferty and all the staff in the UCD Archive Department were most helpful in assisting me with my research and providing the photographic material that makes up the plate section of the book. Their professionalism and unfailing courtesy is much appreciated. Lisa Hyde at Irish Academic Press was a very enthusiastic, patient and accommodating editor from the beginning. Family and friends indulged me by not asking too many questions about the research, allowing me the time and space required to complete the task. Michael and Florence Gavin were a fantastic help in this regard. My mother Evelyn and my brother Mick have always been unconditional in their support and encouragement. My heartfelt gratitude to Blánaid, her generosity and love sustained me through every stage of the process; and to Euan and Freya whose presence in my life has made it infinitely more rewarding, not to mention eventful. This book is dedicated to the memory of my father, John Feeney, who would undoubtedly have approved of its subject.

Tom Feeney
Dublin, July 2008

Introduction

My life has been fairly eventful and seldom boring, indeed not at all boring.

Seán MacEntee, 29 March 1969

In the summer of 1974, the octogenarian veteran politician, Seán MacEntee enlisted the help of his grandsons to begin sorting and filing his voluminous collection of personal papers which were stored in wooden boxes in his garage. The collection included a substantial number of government memoranda spanning the years 1932–65; correspondence conducted throughout a political life that extended from 1918 until 1969 and many other personal items. His long life, in the words of Michael Mills, had been 'woven from the fabric of modern Irish history' and here was the documentary evidence.[1] Two documents in particular caught his attention, taking him somewhat by surprise. The years had been kind to his agile mind and the sight of the discoloured pages sparked a vivid memory of two occasions, both in their own way critical junctures for his country. One was an original letter dated 8 June 1917 from Lord Mounteagle to the Belfast solicitor Tom Alexander, requesting his assistance to ensure that MacEntee be included in a proposed amnesty for Irish political prisoners serving in England for their part in the Easter Rising of the previous year. The second was a letter dated 17 February 1938 to the Taoiseach, Éamon de Valera, in MacEntee's own hand, dealing with differences in the Fianna Fáil cabinet regarding a proposed financial agreement with the United Kingdom government. MacEntee, gratified by the contents of his discovery, recorded in his diary with evident satisfaction that he had 'set out [his] position without reserve'.[2] In fact, throughout a long and distinguished political career, Seán MacEntee rarely failed to set out his position without reserve.

Biographies of Irish politicians, with the exceptions of a number of taoisigh, are relatively rare.[3] Similarly, there is no real tradition of former Irish cabinet ministers recording their memoirs.[4] The comparative lack of serious academic research on the lives of Irish cabinet ministers can be attributed, in part, to the fact that, as George Colley acknowledged, 'politicians are not required to commit their thoughts to paper in the same degree as civil servants'. T.K. Whitaker, arguably the most eminent and respected public official to have served the state, elaborated on this point, suggesting that their 'role is to decide rather than to argue and they relate to officials orally rather than in writing'.[5] These observations are generally true, but when assessing the political career of Seán MacEntee many such axioms can be discarded. Indeed MacEntee's written contribution to the public life of independent Ireland is considerable. Fortunately for the researcher, his collection of private papers, into which he assiduously delved in that summer of 1974, afford a unique insight into his undisclosed mindset as well as providing a comprehensive account of his publicly declared outlook. This capacious collection reflects MacEntee's insatiable interest in all aspects of government policy, not merely those for which he bore ultimate responsibility.[6] The collection also complements the official government files in the National Archives which, when viewed *in toto*, convey the full force of his ministerial thinking. 'It is from the minutes and oral discussions,' according to Whitaker, 'in which these views are expressed, rather than from White Papers or other means of commending policy decisions to the public, that a judgement could best be formed of the "quality of the thought that informs public policy".'[7] Oral discussions, alas, can only be related by recollection, itself an unreliable tool, but the prolific minutes that MacEntee wrote to officials and colleagues survive as an eminently dependable testament to his political perspective.[8]

The post-revolutionary generation of Irish state-builders, of which MacEntee was an integral member, was in many ways *sui generis*. It bequeathed a compelling legacy to future politicians, which was distinguished by a scrupulous regard for the highest standards in public office; a staunchly upright accountability to the electorate it served; a rigorous vigilance over the public purse and an unswerving dedication that may perhaps never be repeated. That most of those involved were 'politicians by accident', to borrow Liam Skinner's well-worn phrase, explains in part why this was so.[9] Furthermore, it distinguished itself for its unusual longevity; and, in Fianna Fáil in particular, its exclusivity. That so few individuals maintained so inordinate an influence on the shape of Irish public policy for the best part of four decades is remarkable and deserving of considerable investigation. These men were chiefly: Éamon de Valera, Seán Lemass, James Ryan, Frank Aiken and Seán MacEntee. Others, such as Seán T. O'Kelly and P.J. Ruttledge, for example, were intrinsic to the foundation of the party and contributed much to the state. Nevertheless, the aforementioned group, to a man, were active during the revolutionary period 1916–22 and remained active in political life, shaping the legislation of the state right up to the 1960s. Whatever one may think of what Tom Garvin has called the 'Fianna Fáil school of revisionist history' – which can be summarised as the assumption by that party of the legitimate inheritance of a teleological nationalist tradition – its importance in the formation of public policy in independent Ireland cannot be overstated.[10]

Seán MacEntee served in every Fianna Fáil administration from 1932 to 1965; firstly as Minister for Finance between 1932 and 1939 and again from 1951–4; as Minister for Industry and Commerce 1939–41; as Minister for Local Government and Public Health 1941–8; as Minister for Social Welfare 1957–61 and finally as Minister for Health 1957–65. He was Tánaiste from 1959 to 1965. In all, MacEntee was a minister in nine Fianna Fáil administrations that lasted a total of twenty-seven years. This study will recount his considerable contribution to politics and public life in independent Ireland, bearing in mind Maurice Cowling's important caveat:

> [O]ne has to convey the involvement in the compulsions and uncertainties of the [political] system which was characteristic of the whole of a politician's public life. For this purpose, biography is almost always misleading.

His refraction is partial in relation to the system. It abstracts a man whose public action should not be abstracted. It implies linear connections between one situation and the next. In fact connections were not linear. The system was a circular relationship: a shift in one element changed the position of all others in relation to the rest.[11]

Moreover, in analysing MacEntee's political life, certain important disclaimers must first be made. Any work that attempts to gauge public policy development through the prism of an individual member of government must rely on selectivity in the first instance and on an appreciation of not only the historical context in which the protagonist operated [Cowling's political system], but also recognition of the responsibilities imposed by his membership of a political party. Furthermore, it would not be possible, given the limitations on space, to document every significant issue to which MacEntee contributed; nor is it feasible to record every policy measure upon which he exerted a decisive influence. As enduring and as prominent a role as MacEntee's, therefore, must be assessed on the merits and importance of the measures to which he contributed over the *longue durée*. Accordingly, the public policy issues that form the basis of the following assessment of MacEntee's considerable political career are what this writer regards as his enduring legacy to the political life of independent Ireland.

An appraisal of MacEntee's involvement in Irish public life is made all the more urgent in view of the somewhat one-dimensional figure that has emerged from a variety of works that touch either directly or indirectly on public policy formation in the period. A definitive history of the Fianna Fáil party has yet to be written but Richard Dunphy's work is invaluable for its analysis of the party's evolution to being the most successful in the state.[12] Dunphy is interested in the 'political changes – the strategic and tactical choices, conscious or otherwise – which were effected [by the party] in order to reproduce "political stability"'.[13] In presenting this thesis, Dunphy regards MacEntee, in the main, as a conservative reactionary. This satisfies Dunphy's overall project, which is to relate how Fianna Fáil's enduring political hegemony was contingent upon a move to the right, which was facilitated by the presence of personalities such as MacEntee. This biography shares features common to Dunphy's analysis in its conceptual framework, which, given that it is primarily interested in the individuals involved, attests to what Garvin has termed a 'manipulative interpretation'. Such interpretations emphasise the manufactured quality of the party and the role played by the various personalities in shaping its character.[14] Another 'manipulative interpretation' is provided by Paul Bew and Henry Patterson, who have examined Seán Lemass's role in the advent of 'modern Ireland'. This work limits itself exclusively to a portrayal of Lemass at the expense of any considered treatment of others in the cabinet, including MacEntee.[15] While the current study takes issue with some of their conclusions, it acknowledges the debt that it owes to their style and aims.

By far the most sustained analysis of MacEntee that views him, *inter alia*, as a key member of the 'forces of resistance', is J.J. Lee's *Ireland 1912–1985: Politics and Society*, perhaps the most authoritative and definitive history of twentieth-century Ireland. Lee's work delivers a steadfastly withering verdict on MacEntee's performance as a member of government, largely based on his defiance of many policy initiatives instigated or espoused by Lemass. In fact MacEntee's political style is very easy to caricature. The artificial bombast that he could wilfully manufacture on demand should be read as latter day 'shock and awe' politics, designed principally to grab the attention of whoever comprised his target audience. It was a style that was honed after many years of political combat and which was made possible by a scathingly sardonic tongue that never failed to rouse a reciprocal retort. Although his rather supercilious manner often overshadowed his contribution to debate, insofar as this is what tended to be reported in the press and was how the opposition liked to represent him, it did not always eclipse the substance of his argument which was often articulated forcefully and prudently.

MacEntee's remarkable career is noteworthy both for his enduring prominence at the coalface of Irish politics and his political longevity but, apart from using his role as evidence of Lemass's progressiveness, it is time to pay his particular contribution to the political life of the independent state the attention it deserves. Indeed MacEntee's career is often contrasted directly with the man regarded by many as the major influence behind the making of 'modern Ireland'. Historians have often viewed the evolution of the Fianna Fáil party as a struggle between these two ministers of very different political sensibilities. As Dunphy has rightly acknowledged: 'it is a major mistake to treat Fianna Fáil in power as an undifferentiated monolith', a point most cogently exemplified by the MacEntee–Lemass dialectic.[16] Undeniably, de Valera's cabinets contained forceful personalities with their own strongly held views, even if, in the end, they routinely bowed to the wisdom of their chief. It would also be mistaken to regard MacEntee as an archetypal Fianna Fáil minister. In fact, in many ways he was untypical of the anti-intellectual culture that often pervaded the party. This biography examines the contribution of a Fianna Fáil cabinet minister outside that domi-nant nexus of Éamon de Valera and Seán Lemass and is therefore indispensable to a full appreciation of the policy dialogue within successive Fianna Fáil cabinets and to a thorough reassessment of the dynamics of their decision making.

NOTES

1. M. Mills, 'MacEntee's fruitful career', *Irish Press*, 26 May 1976.
2. MacEntee Papers, UCD Archives [Hereafter UCDA] P67/815 (8), diary entries for 26 and 30 July, 1974.
3. See, for example, E. Magner, 'Seán Moylan: Some Aspects of his Parliamentary Career' (Unpublished MA thesis, UCC, 1982); B. Farrell, *Seán Lemass* (Dublin, 1991); J. Horgan, *Seán Lemass: The Enigmatic Patriot* (Dublin, 1997); T.P. O'Neill and the Earl of Longford, *Éamon de Valera* (Dublin, 1970). In recent years, this trend has begun to be redressed. For examples see M. Manning, *James Dillon: A Biography* (Dublin, 1999) and J. Horgan, *Noel Browne: Passionate Outsider* (Dublin, 2000).
4. Exceptions to this rule include N. Browne, *Against the Tide* (Dublin, 1986); G. FitzGerald, *All in a Life* (Dublin, 1992); T.F. O'Higgins, *A Double Life* (Dublin, 1996); G. Hussey, *At the Cutting Edge: Cabinet Diaries 1982–87* (Dublin, 1990) and B. Desmond, *Finally and in Conclusion: A Political Memoir* (Dublin, 2000).
5. T.K. Whitaker, *Interests* (Dublin, 1983), p.163.
6. For example, see MacEntee's reaction to the reorganisation of the defence forces during the mid to late 1930s in UCDA P67/190–96; for MacEntee's views on the Constitution of 1937, see UCDA P67/183–7; for MacEntee's correspondence relating to partition and Northern Ireland, see UCDA

P67493, P67/514, P67/520. Also, for a rare occasion when a cabinet minister attempted to influence de Valera on external affairs, see a letter from MacEntee dated 18 March 1932 in UCDA P67/94, recommending a 'more vigorous diplomatic policy in the Department of External Affairs'. The letter also considers the possibility of Ireland acting as a catalyst in the development of a European bloc to neutralise British influence on the continent.

7. T.K. Whitaker, 'The finance attitude', *Administration*, 2, 3 (1953–4), pp.61–6.
8. For example, for MacEntee's views on Fianna Fáil land policy, see UCDA P67/108; and for his views on agricultural policy, see UCDA P67/271.
9. L. Skinner, *Politicians by Accident* (Dublin, 1946).
10. J.M. Regan, *The Irish Counter-Revolution, 1921–1936* (Dublin, 1999), p.xiv.
11. M. Cowling, *The Impact of Labour, 1920–24* (Cambridge, 1971).
12. R. Dunphy, *The Making of Fianna Fáil Power in Ireland 1923–48* (Oxford, 1995).
13. Ibid., p.311.
14. See T. Garvin, 'Theory, culture and Fianna Fáil: a review', in M. Kelly, L. O'Dowd and J. Wickham (eds), *Power, Conflict and Inequality* (Dublin, 1985), pp.171–86.
15. P. Bew and H. Patterson, *Seán Lemass and the Making of Modern Ireland 1945–66* (Dublin, 1982).
16. R. Dunphy, 'The enigma of Fianna Fáil: party, strategy, social classes and the politics of hegemony', in M. Cronin and J.M. Regan (eds), *Ireland: The Politics of Independence, 1922–49* (Hampshire, 2000), p.72.

1

Belfast Child

Seán MacEntee (John Francis McEntee) was born on 23 August 1889 at 42 Mill Street Belfast, home to the family business – McEntee's Public House – 'not a mile from the Falls Road' and in the shadow of the 'Black Man', the local term for the forbidding statue of the Presbyterian divine Dr Henry Cooke.[1] His father's public house occupied a large corner site at the intersection of King Street. The area derived its name from the nearby Manor Mill and had been home to one of the first meeting places for Catholics in the city. The local Catholic church of St Mary's, the first in the city, had stood in nearby Chapel Lane since 1783. Mill Street was also home to the lying-in hospital during the Famine and many immigrants from neighbouring counties settled there.[2] By the beginning of the twentieth century, the area was a mixture of private dwellings and small commercial enterprises such as grocery shops, butcher shops and public houses. The family home was 'an old many-storied building, very comfortable'[3] which in 1901 housed two servants, James and Mary McEntee and their six children: John Francis, James, Mary (May), Margaret (Meg), Charles Owen and Edward. A seventh child, Joseph, was born two years later; four others had predeceased him in infancy.[4] James McEntee was then forty-four years of age and was a respected and established member of the Belfast Municipal Council as well as a successful merchant who at one time had owned three public houses including the famous Crown Bar.[5] It is unclear when he first came to Belfast but the family was always made starkly aware of its Monaghan roots. His family had owned land in the townland of Annyalty from about the beginning of the seventeenth century, and some of his ancestors were buried near the village of Ballinode, a few miles from the county town. James McEntee's three brothers emigrated to America; one going to California, one to the Yukon and one to the mid-west, although family legend had it that 'he had two brothers, each over six feet tall, both of whom emigrated to Canada and ended up owning the Biltmore hotel in New York.[6] It is likely that James's father, Francis McEntee, was part of the large influx of Catholics who settled in Belfast in the immediate post-Famine period.[7] In 1860, there were eight separate premises occupied by McEntees in the Smithfield ward, one of which was occupied by Francis McEntee at 42 Hercules Street.[8]

The name, which can be spelled MacEntee or McEntee, is the anglicised form of the Irish name Mac an tSaoi, which is translated 'son of the sage'. The family had always been McEntees; it wasn't until after 1916 when he was a republican prisoner in England that Johnny McEntee became Seán MacEntee, adopting what perhaps he felt was the closer form to the original Irish patronymic.[9] By then he was fully engaged in the republican movement and had become something of a *cause célèbre* among family and friends. Indeed his siblings were used to their eldest brother being the centre of family life. His daughter has described him as 'an exceptionally self-assured and autocratic eldest brother, who evolved into a national hero'.[10] Notwithstanding his pre-eminent position in the family, he spoke little of his childhood and the impression given to his own family in later life was of a 'stern and cold' environment. His father cared much about appearances and was always immaculately presented: 'He wore waxed moustaches, striped trousers with a dark waistcoat and jacket, a gold watch-chain, wing collar and bow-tie, or even a stock, and, of course a bowler hat.'[11] Legend also had it that he had lost two of his premises playing cards. Whether this is true or not, the McEntees were relatively well-off; the eldest son later recalled that 'money was never tight. We could always go to the old man and ask for £5 any time we wanted.'[12] When James McEntee's first grandchild was born in 1922, there was champagne on the house all night.[13] MacEntee's mother, Mary Owens, also originally from a Monaghan family, 'was an exquisite … Edwardian doll with a whim of steel under a nervous, retiring exterior'.[14]

Nationalist politics dominated life in the household and as a very young child MacEntee undoubtedly witnessed the same contested attitudes recorded by James Joyce's alter ego Stephen Dedalus in *A Portrait of the Artist as a Young Man* surrounding the Parnell split. As with Joyce, MacEntee's father was an unyielding supporter of Parnell. He had also been a member of the Fenian Brotherhood prior to the 'New Departure'.[15] As well as nationalist politics, the young Seán MacEntee cultivated other interests which may have prevented the former from consuming him altogether. For example, he became a member of the Gaelic League but never joined the republican boy scouts, Na Fianna, nor did he join the Irish Republican Brotherhood (IRB) as his father had, despite the vibrancy of both movements – not to mention their proximity to his Belfast home – in the first decade of the twentieth century. Home life, which he later described as 'a virtual university library', also fostered a strong interest in literature, particularly the works of Carleton, Dickens, Edgeworth, Scott and Spender as well as nationalist tracts by writers such as Fintan Lalor and Canon Sheehan.[16] He was a member of the Ultonian Club and the Ulster Literary Theatre where he encountered a range of political and religious opinion, including many Protestants and agnostics who described themselves as nationalists. Founded in 1901 by a Quaker, Bulmer Hobson, the Ulster Literary Theatre presented the work of northern playwrights and was recognised as 'the centrepiece of the north's contribution to the [literary] renaissance'.[17]

Formal education for Seán MacEntee began three weeks before his fourth birthday, when he entered St Mary's primary school in Divis Street on 1 August 1893.[18] The school consisted of four classrooms and had been home to the first Christian Brothers community in the city when Brothers Louis Caton, Thomas Neaton, Alipius Maguire and John Ennis arrived in November 1866.[19] From here MacEntee entered St Malachy's College. Founded in 1833 it was the first Catholic college of secondary education established in Ulster and the third oldest Catholic school in Ireland.[20] The college was founded as a seminary for the diocese of Down and Connor and in the early years most of the pupils had no other ambition than the priesthood. Distinguished past pupils of the college included Charles Russell, Attorney General in two Gladstone cabinets, and Eoin MacNeill, future Chief of Staff of the Irish Volunteers, who in 1881 went there as a boarder.[21] Despite being a naturally bright student, MacEntee was denied a university education, the reasons for which are not altogether clear, but which left him with an enduring bitterness. His father's aforementioned profligacy may have something to do with it but as his own daughter noted in her memoir: 'Middle-class materialistic families at that time did not necessarily value higher education.'[22] Living in Belfast, it may also have been a more natural step to pursue a professional education, which he duly did, qualifying as an electrical engineer from the Belfast Municipal College of Technology. After completing his engineering course, he joined the staff of the Belfast Electricity Works as a pupil-engineer, and after three years became engineer-in-charge of one of the sub-stations attached to that undertaking.

The McEntee family, heavily influenced by the predilections of its eldest son who had turned twenty-one in August 1910, subscribed fully to the cultural revival.[23] In 1911, that year's census return was filled out completely in Irish despite the fact that no member of the family was proficient in the language. Indeed the cultural revival in Ulster, as elsewhere, had not been confined to literature. Cultural nationalists encouraged the promotion of Irish language, art, sport and other activities such as lace-making. Bulmer Hobson himself had embraced the Irish language and the development of Irish sport.[24] Clubs promoting cultural activities were also breeding grounds for political activism. One such organisation, in which Hobson again played a leading role, was Cumann na nGaedheal. Founded by the Dublin journalist Arthur Griffith in September 1900, Cumann na nGaedheal became an umbrella organisation for literary, athletic and political groups advocating advanced nationalism. Its main goal was the de-anglicisation of Ireland. In 1903 Hobson presided over the inaugural meeting of the Henry Joy McCracken branch of Cumann na nGaedheal at the Foresters' Hall in Mill Street, yards from McEntee's public house and later home to the Irish Volunteers in Belfast.[25] The work of Hobson in the early years of the twentieth century built upon the activities of individuals such as Alice Milligan, who in 1895 had opened a reading room in Belfast inviting donations of books of 'national character'. Milligan's purpose was to break down 'the forces of intolerance, ignorance and bigotry, which kept Ulster apart from the rest of the country'.[26] Milligan was also responsible for the journal *Shan Van Vocht* which included contributions from prominent nationalists in the city such as Francis Joseph Bigger, James Connolly and Alice Furlong. The paper's main achievements were to provide cultural nationalists with political focus during the events of the 1798 centenary commemorations and to consolidate the Gaelic League as a major organisation in the north.[27]

That commemorative summer of 1898 also provided MacEntee with his first 'conscious contact with the realities of [the] North-Eastern problem'. In most parts of the island the Rising was commemorated reverently and peacefully. In Belfast it was otherwise. The committee formed to arrange commemoration of the Rising in the city chose 6 June for the ceremony, which was to take the traditional form of a procession, with bands and banners, through the main thoroughfares of the city. To MacEntee, writing sometime later, it 'was an occasion that any Presbyterian might glory in but the great grandsons of the men who had fought at Antrim or at Ballynahinch and Saintfield would have no part in it'.

> The 1798 Rising in Antrim and Down, they held to be a Protestant rising. It belonged to them and their tradition; and that 'teagues' and 'fenians' should combine to celebrate it was not to be endured. So, wherever the procession had to touch on the periphery of Protestant territory, the more bellicose of them gathered in their hundreds, maybe thousands, to stone the procession.
>
> As always the assault upon the 'papishes' was carried from the streets into the factories, the mills and the shipyards. Gradually, however, the ferocity of the pogrom abated, bigotry became quiescent, and 'papishes' and their ilk, 'rotten protestants' were allowed back to their jobs – on sufferance – to await the next Orange celebration; wondering whether it was going to be a quiet 'twelfth' or a wild one, whether they would get through the summer without being driven from their job.

It was in this confrontational environment that MacEntee's politics were formed. Like all those immediately around him, he readily described himself as a nationalist and a home ruler: 'By family tradition and parental influence it was unthinkable that I should be otherwise.'[28] It was undoubtedly this influence that prevented him from becoming involved with the small but growing band of separatists in the city, as James McEntee had become a close associate of Joseph Devlin, the Irish Party MP after 1906. Nevertheless it is somewhat surprising that he remained outside this group given the close links nurtured by separatists with the cultural movement. A prime example of this was the group of veteran Fenians who had started the National Literary Club in 1898 and was responsible for organising one of the first branches of the Gaelic League in Belfast, Lios na bhFiann. The literary society was used as a recruiting ground and cover for the activities of the IRB. Indeed the club used the same premises as the Gaelic League and was also responsible for the formation of the Mitchel Hurling Club.[29] As well as the cultural activities of Belfast Fenians, there was also a vibrant group of younger separatists in the city organised by Bulmer Hobson and Denis McCullough. McCullough, the son of a Catholic publican and IRB member, was the senior member of a group of young radicals which also included Seán MacDermott, whom he swore into the IRB in 1906. In 1901, as a seventeen-year-old, McCullough had been sworn into the Brotherhood at the side door of a pub on the Falls Road by an inebriated senior member. Disillusioned by the moribund state of the organisation, he managed to take control of his father's ageing circle and was instrumental in establishing another in the city in 1904, meeting at his family home at 12 Divis Street and later in Grosvenor Road.[30] In 1907, McCullough and Hobson formed the Dungannon Clubs, another recruitment agency for the IRB, which printed a paper called *The Republic*. The club met in two rooms in the top floor above Tom Finnegan's chemist shop in Royal Avenue. Seán MacDermott and Cathal O'Shannon were also members.[31] Hobson and

McCullough not only targeted traditional nationalist enemies such as the RIC and the British Army in their pamphlets but also criticised and lampooned the Irish Parliamentary Party. They 'also arranged lectures and debates ... both for propaganda purposes and to help raise money ...' Among those invited to give lectures were the labour leaders Jim Larkin and Tom Johnson. The primary subjects discussed at club meetings included the value of an abstentionist policy as opposed to attendance at Westminster, the relief of emigration and the revival of native Irish industry.[32] On a few occasions, speakers from the club debated with supporters of Joe Devlin on the policies of physical force versus constitutionalism. According to one of its members, 'the Devlinite opposition in these debates were men of mature years, and, as a result, Bulmer Hobson was strongly of the opinion that no converts to the policy of physical force could be made amongst grown-up men and he encouraged us all to concentrate on attracting the youth to our movement.'[33] Needless to say, the young Seán MacEntee was ripe for persuasion to Hobson's arguments but family loyalty probably meant that he resisted its lure.

There were, however, good reasons for MacEntee to keep faith with the Irish Party in the first decade of the twentieth century. The end of the Victorian era had witnessed the first flowering of a newly effective and organised political nationalism in Belfast. The defeat of the Second Home Rule Bill in 1893 had made nationalists in Belfast all the more determined to fight against discrimination in public employment, and the period saw a re-emergence of political and ethnic conflict in the city.[34] According to one historian, the 'Victorian era closed in Belfast upon two communities intransigent in their politics; intolerant in their religion; inured to the violent ethic; trusting neither the English parliament to promote their interests, nor the Irish Executive to protect their safety'.[35] The 'delicately balanced' constituency of West Belfast, created by the Redistribution Act of 1885, promised political advancement for a well-organised nationalist candidate. So too did changes to local government. Before 1897 representation on Belfast Corporation bore little resemblance to the demographics of the city. While the Catholic population of the city stood at 25 per cent at the turn of the century, from a high of one-third in the mid-nineteenth century, only three Catholics had sat on the Town Council before that year.[36] Aspiring Catholic councillors were hampered by the £10 municipal franchise and the ward alignment by which the corporation in 1837 and 1853 had dispersed the Catholic and Liberal vote. These obstacles were removed in 1896 when Westminster forced the council to accept the predominantly Catholic areas of Falls and Smithfield as two of its fifteen wards in its Boundary Extension Bill.[37] Under the Extension Bill, ten new wards were created and the number of councillors was increased from forty to sixty.[38] The extension came at a propitious time for the Catholic community, which had seen a considerable expansion in organised social activity, mainly through the efforts of the bishop of Down and Connor, Dr Henry, who in 1896 had opened a Central Catholic Club to provide the Catholic commercial class with a 'bulwark of defence against the strong hostile influences with which they [found] themselves confronted'.[39]

In the 1897 elections to the Belfast Municipal Council, the Catholic

Association, also founded by Bishop Henry, and the local branch of the Irish National Federation selected candidates for each of the so-called Catholic wards. The nominees of the association were 'Catholic' candidates while those of the federation were 'Irish Nationalists'. James McEntee stood as one of the Catholic nominees, probably more due to political differences with those in the federation than any desire to stand on a purely Catholic platform. According to contemporary accounts, the election was fought with 'great bitterness'. The veteran land campaigner, Michael Davitt, enlisted by the federation to champion its candidates, proclaimed that 'religion should not be allowed to enter into municipal contests, and that although they respected Dr Henry as the bishop of the diocese they would not tolerate his interference with the free judgement of the people'.[40] The battle lines were clearly drawn, the Catholic clergy running an equally vigorous campaign on behalf of the association candidates. In the end there was a clear winner: all the Catholic Association candidates were returned while not one of the Irish National Federation candidates proved successful. In Smithfield, James McEntee polled 1,158 votes, twenty-six shy of the overall winner and fellow association nominee, Dr O'Connell, with a third Catholic candidate, James McLorman, filling the final vacancy.[41] The defeated federalists spuriously claimed that the result signalled a vote against home rule.

This schism in nationalist politics in Belfast was healed by the emergence of Joe Devlin. With his victory in West Belfast in the 1906 general election, the city finally had a nationalist MP. Devlin's success can be attributed to his shrewd use of the political machinery of the Ancient Order of Hibernians (AOH), a tactic which invigorated Ulster nationalism and at the same time defeated the Catholic Association's efforts to establish a clerical party in Belfast. After Devlin's election to Westminster, the AOH experienced even more rapid growth. A membership of 10,000 in 1905 had by 1909 expanded to 60,000.[42] On the surface, it was a social society, offering members of like-minded views something to do without an overtly political programme, but in practice it was 'thoroughly political'. By the time of Devlin's election, James McEntee had switched his allegiance to the Irish Party despite the misgivings of his son:

> My father was a supporter and close friend of [Joe Devlin], and I certainly was not opposed to him. But I wasn't in any of the official Irish Party organisations. I was perhaps inclined to be critical of the party. I know now that I underrated the odds it had to contend with in its dealings with the Liberal Government of the day. But I was a very close reader of the more radical nationalist journalists like the 'Irish Peasant' and 'Irish Freedom' and 'Sinn Féin'.

Despite this interest, MacEntee was still not tempted to join the proponents of this 'new nationalism', nor did he become part of the Hibernian society, preferring the more cerebral attractions of the Gaelic League. The latter organisation 'offered a narrower range of activities and an image which was more highbrow and (in the opinion of Cardinal Logue) more wholesome'.[43] The Gaelic League also introduced MacEntee to an alternative economic message, one which he found instantly appealing:

[Arthur] Griffith's theme that so long as we failed to build up our manufacturing industries we would remain a one-armed people appealed to me. I
saw all around me in Belfast, which was then a thriving industrial city, the
extent to which it was possible, even though all the raw materials were
imported, to compete in all the world markets. Belfast had then two ship-
yards and one of these was the largest shipyard in the world and built the
largest ships in the world. It had also the largest tobacco factory in the
world, as well as the largest rope factory and, of course, the mastery of the
linen trade. All these industries were based on imported raw materials. So,
though I was far from agreeing with Griffith's attitude towards trade unionism and social problems generally, I was in full agreement with his industrial policy.[44]

In fact the young MacEntee's attitude 'towards trade unionism and social
problems generally' found a greater influence in the shape of James Connolly,
who he saw lecture in North Street in the winter of 1910.[45] Connolly was then
organising the Irish Transport Workers' Union in Belfast with some associates,
including Cathal O'Shannon and Jim Larkin.[46] 'I was so impressed by his
earnestness, his reasoning, his manifest conviction and driving force, that before
I left the hall I had myself enrolled in the Socialist Party of Ireland.' This did not
mean, however, that MacEntee was a socialist convert; rather that he recognised
in Connolly a passion and sincerity that was perhaps missing in mainstream
nationalist politics:

I was not converted to Marxism, nor had I ceased to be a fervent nationalist. It was simply that here was a man who was concerned about the dire
poverty of the mass, especially the nationalist mass, and who was striving
to do something about it. It seemed to me to be better to work with him
than to wait, prayerfully, for Home Rule to come and change it all.

Until 1914, when he left Belfast, MacEntee worked in the Socialist Party carrying out administrative chores and cutting his teeth in public speaking. Later he
cited the 'conditions under which our people lived in Belfast' as the principal
motivation behind his political activity. He described the working class of the
city as:

... the most depressed and exploited stratum in the community. In the
Belfast mills most of the workers, especially females, were paid as piece
workers. There was too a lot of what were called half-timers employed;
children of tender years of age went, alternately, one day to school and the
next day to the mill. The mills in those days started up at half past six in
the morning and worked through the day until six o'clock in the evening
for six days of the week. Many of the working class women in Belfast at
that time did not wear shoes and neither did even more children.

He maintained that 'one could not live in Belfast and not be conscious of these
things generally. It was perhaps because of this that the first, in fact the only,
political organisation that I became associated with in Belfast was the Socialist

Party of Ireland.'[47] The membership of the Belfast branch of the SPI was small. Activists met in Danny MacDevitt's workshop in Rosemary Street where a small coterie of trade unionists was also endeavouring in adverse circumstances to build up a political labour movement in Belfast. Every afternoon a few of them were likely to gather to exchange gossip, or to discuss some trades council manoeuvre, or whatever other affair might interest them. When time and work permitted, MacEntee often made his way to MacDevitt's to listen to several of the more prominent trade union officials. Connolly sometimes dropped in 'but always on business, never for badinage. Being only a neophyte in the [party] my contacts with Connolly and, at that time, with Tom Johnson were limited and superficial.'[48]

By his own admission MacEntee had never been an 'out-and-outer' in nationalist terms. He fully believed that the attainment of home rule was 'a prerequisite for the social and economic progress of the nation'. It would take the circumstances of war and the accommodation of unionist opposition to the Home Rule Bill by the Westminster government in the form of an amending bill to dilute his faith in this belief. 'It was only when it became clear, as it did very early in the war, that Redmond could not extract a reasonable measure from the British that the opinion grew and became general that parliamentary action had failed. We were diverted to another course by force of circumstances, by what was happening in the world around us. Other peoples were fighting for freedom: why not we?' This disillusionment with parliamentary action was compounded by the possibility of conscription being applied to Ireland, as was being mooted before 1916. MacEntee later maintained that conscription was not a factor in bringing about the 1916 Rising. He believed that this was determined long before. 'What made it possible was that so many people like myself had come to the conclusion that something had to be done to justify our existence as a nation and that the 1914 war provided the chance.' For MacEntee to arrive at this conclusion, it was first necessary for him to leave the family home and to plough his own political furrow away from the uniquely partisan political *milieu* that prevailed in his native city.

EPISODE AT EASTER

In January 1914, MacEntee left Belfast to take up a position with the Dundalk Urban District Council as assistant engineer on a salary of £100 a year.[49] His reasons for moving to Dundalk were strictly professional; he wished to have some experience in a works with diesel engines – which were just then being commercially developed – whereas the ones in Belfast were steam driven.[50] As it turned out, his move to Dundalk determined the course of the rest of his life. Had he stayed in Belfast, it is likely that he would have gone to war as did many of his contemporaries and friends. That he did not meant that he could devote his extracurricular energies to the reorganised Irish Volunteers, which ultimately resulted in his involvement in the 1916 Rising. This involvement in turn led to his sentencing to penal servitude for life, in itself an admission card into the upper echelons of political nationalism in the post-Rising period. Prison brought him into close contact with many of the future leaders of the independence movement, including Éamon de Valera, Austin Stack and Harry Boland. Involvement in the Rising also gave participants a morally superior claim to political office exemplified by MacEntee's parachuting into the constituency of South Monaghan in the 1918 general election.

The political situation as he found it in Dundalk was altogether different to that which he had been accustomed in his native city. There he was confronted with a stark choice:

> Coming from the stronghold of Ulster unionism where nationalists had to fight unitedly for their rights against odds of three to one, the political situation, as I found it in Dundalk, was somewhat dis-edifying. There it did not suffice to be an Irish nationalist, one had to be a nationalist of one of other of two rival dispensations. You either followed John Redmond and abhorred Tim Healy; or you followed Tim Healy and abhorred John Redmond. If you happened to be a follower of Arthur Griffith, you were 'an extremist', a visionary, a dreamer.[51]

Although Devlin's talismanic success in the 1906 general election had much to do with the fact that, for MacEntee's generation, 'Republicanism never really took hold in Belfast',[52] it would be wrong to assume that Dundalk provided a more fertile ground for advanced nationalism in 1914. In fact, the republican faction in Belfast under McCullough, although small, was better organised than anything that Dundalk had to offer. Republican activities in the town were almost singularly the work of one individual, Paddy Hughes, a fellow employee of MacEntee's at the Dundalk UDC. Hughes was a rate collector and a serial supporter of separatist organisations. He was described by one contemporary as 'the father of republicanism in Dundalk'.[53] He was the chairman of Sinn Féin in the town since 1910 and was well known due to his organisation of a group to protest on the accession of King George V. At least one onlooker was impressed enough by Hughes's defiance to join the party:

> The ten men took up position on the ground flag stones of the '98 monument facing the courthouse and continuously interrupted the sheriff by singing patriotic songs and shouting 'to hell with the king' etc. Things became so bad that the sheriff interrupted reading the King's proclamation to read The Riot Act to legalise the order he had decided to remove opposition. Having done so the RIC were ordered to 'fix bayonets' but the charge never took place; the explanation given afterwards being that the men stood on private property and could not be removed. I witnessed this scene and joined Sinn Féin that week.[54]

Hostility to Sinn Féin principally came from the AOH – the strong arm of the Irish Party – which was well supported in Dundalk and in north Louth generally.[55] The local press – in particular the *Dundalk Democrat* – was also supportive of Redmond and largely unsympathetic to Sinn Féin. According to one early recruit of the organisation, Hughes's efforts in recruiting were unsuccessful: 'Although … we did create an interest amongst the people in a general way that, later, when the National Volunteers were organised, helped to swell the ranks.'[56] The bad feeling between Sinn Féin and the AOH was temporarily suppressed by the formation of the Irish Volunteers at the Young Ireland athletic grounds in February 1914. For some members of Sinn Féin, cooperation with the 'Hibernians' was too much to bear but MacEntee and Hughes became willing members, despite residual tensions between the rival groups. The new organisation's paper, *The Irish Volunteer*, reported a successful beginning to the Volunteers in Dundalk, with Hughes sharing the same platform as the AOH representatives. The latter told the inaugural meeting that the object of the Volunteers was 'to secure and maintain the rights and liberties common to all the people of Ireland', quoting the official manifesto which had been launched in Dublin's Rotunda Rink on 25 November 1913. After Hughes delivered a short address accentuating the unity of purpose being displayed, noting that representatives of every national organisation in town were present, 'several hundred men enrolled'.[57] Many of the Dundalk Volunteers remember a membership of three hundred to four hundred people in the early honeymoon period.

MacEntee also joined the original committee of the organisation mainly due to his friendship with Hughes and James Brennan, who was an accountant in the electricity works.[58] He later attributed his joining the Volunteers to 'mounting resentment in my mind, and in the minds of all those whom I knew' at the course of political developments since the Home Rule Bill had been introduced in 1912.[59] In particular, what exercised MacEntee was the possible partition of the country given the trenchant opposition to home rule in Ulster, illustrated most forcefully by the signing of the Solemn League and Covenant in September 1912 and the rapid development of an Ulster Volunteer Force (UVF) from January 1913, the latter being the most immediate exemplar of its nationalist counterpart. The UVF quickly became a formidable challenge to the Liberal government following its landing of 25,000 firearms in April 1914. Redmond's earlier attempts to dismiss Ulster intransigence as bluff became increasingly hollow, and the Irish Party was forced to accept Asquith's amending bill in May dealing separately with the province and providing for individual counties to opt out of home rule for six years. In July the Buckingham Palace conference, convened to work out an exclusion formula, lasted three days before deadlock was ruefully admitted. There were no winners: the bill, although placed on the statute book thereby fulfilling nationalist aspirations, included the exclusion amendment, thereby securing Ulster's veto and, in principle, the partition of the island. This, more than anything, troubled northern nationalists such as MacEntee. To him, the exclusion compromise meant that 'government by consensus or government by franchise was abandoned', being replaced by 'government by force of arms'. By joining the Irish Volunteers, MacEntee's ultimate aim was to prevent partition.

The history of the Irish Volunteers in Dundalk mirrors that of the organisation in other towns and cities all over Ireland. Conceived by its leading lights – Eoin MacNeill, The O'Rahilly and Bulmer Hobson – as a defensive bulwark against conscription, the Volunteers were given relatively free reign to drill and recruit by the government's passivity towards the Ulster Volunteers. Overall recruitment was slow until the Curragh Incident in March, when it reached almost 100,000 nationally. In Dundalk the new influx of recruits doubled the overall membership. Volunteers engaged in drills and training exercises in 'The Rink' and also in the adjoining athletic grounds under the supervision of drill instructors that were, more often than not, ex-British Army men. Other activities included collecting money for, and attempting to procure, arms whenever available. Typically, drilling exercises were carried out with hurleys and wooden guns but some rifles were available through the Hibernians and the IRB.[60] Membership of the Volunteers in Dundalk, as elsewhere, was drawn mainly from the respectable working class or skilled workers. The leadership, however, came from the business community: one former member recalled how the 'people behind the Volunteers were men of substance in the town' and how the majority were 'supporters of John Redmond'.[61] When Redmond formally gained control of the Volunteers in June 1914, the numbers in the organisation swelled even more. This event, though a bitterly divisive one within the Volunteer leadership, probably did not unduly perturb MacEntee. Although, by his admission, he tended to be 'critical of the [Irish] Party', he was inclined towards supporting a united nationalist movement. His position had not changed since 1910 when, in his own words, he was not an 'out and outer': 'Everyone, whether he thought Redmond was a strong leader or a weak leader, whether he thought, or not, that Griffith's policy of abstention would be more effective than agitation and propaganda in the British House of Commons, felt that the attainment of Home Rule was a prerequisite for the social and economic progress of the nation.'[62] Indeed MacEntee's views at this time were also Eoin MacNeill's who had 'no personal ambition, no idea of doing other than support the party'.[63]

The most notable achievement of the Volunteers was the landing of a shipment of badly needed arms from Germany in July 1914. Arriving in Howth on 26 July – two days after the breakdown of the Buckingham Palace conference – the *Asgard* carried 900 rifles and 29,000 rounds of ammunition. It was a daring expedition and the decision to land in daylight proved both provocative and fateful. The Dublin Metropolitan Police, alarmed at the thought of 'a body of more than 1,000 men armed with rifles marching on Dublin', attempted with military aid to disarm the Volunteers as they made their way towards the city. A mêlée ensued when they approached the Volunteers on Malahide Road, leading to random shots being fired. As the troops returned along the quays they were abused and pelted with stones by the largely hostile crowd. Their response was to fire at the crowd at Bachelors' Walk, leading to the deaths of four civilians. The dead quickly became nationalist martyrs and provided the subject for MacEntee's first written contribution to a political periodical: an essay entitled 'The Messengers' in the 8 August issue of the *Irish Volunteer* under the pseudonym Laurence Keeran. He began by eulogising the spirit of the fallen victims in typically pious and verbose terms – 'Their poor lifeless bodies, the earthly caskets of their so great souls may lie lacerated and bloody from the murderer's bullets in the houses of sorrow, but still they are not dead' – but proceeded to offer a more militant response to their deaths:

> Too long have we been slothful. A few years of a novel ease and prosperi-
> ty have fattened up our souls; a comfortable complacency has drugged our

spirits: we have been content, many of us, to leave to the few the work that all should be up and doing. It is true some one hundred thousand men are enrolled in the National Army, it is true some ten or twenty thousand pounds have been subscribed for their equipment – but what are one hundred thousand men or twenty thousand pounds to a nation whose five hundred thousand able sons ought to be drilling and arming? ... Now is the day, now is the hour to prove ourselves fit for freedom. The great ones who have gone beckon us down the path, perchance the bloody path that leads us to immortality. Come! Too long have we been quiescent – too long have the scales of justice been weighted against us, too long has blind and fatuous denial been our portion: let us plead no more for our rights; let us demand them. And if we be refused, why then a good strong hand to the sword and let the stern arbitrament of war settle the question for ever.

The very notion of five hundred thousand Irishmen drilling and arming to prove themselves fit for freedom was shattered by the split in the Irish Volunteers, precipitated by Redmond's Woodenbridge speech on 20 September in which he announced that it was the duty of Volunteers to enlist and fight in the European War. Four days earlier, he issued a public call for recruits to an Irish brigade to go to the front. Again MacEntee, unlike the original Volunteer leadership, was inclined to support Redmond. He applied for a commission to the newly created Irish division, the 16th, and but for a delayed response would have experienced at first hand 'the stern arbitrament of war', albeit in a far different context to the one envisaged in 'The Messengers'. In Dundalk, tensions within the Volunteers had already come to the surface well before Redmond's pledge of support. In August a rumpus broke out when the Volunteer band escorted the garrison in Dundalk to the railway station on their departure to France, leading to Hughes taking his supporters out of the Volunteers. The numbers that followed him were small and the rifles the Volunteers had before the split were controlled by the Hibernians.[64] MacEntee decided at this time to leave the Volunteers altogether. He saw no future in a band of thirteen men attempting to face down extreme hostility in the town by turning their back on the 'leader of the nation'. Hughes also saw little point in carrying on, and shortly after the split in Dundalk the Irish Volunteers ceased to be active.

MacEntee's concern regarding the 'Ulster question' prompted a second contribution to the *Irish Volunteer* in October 1914. In a six-verse poem entitled 'To the Garrison in Ulster', MacEntee outlined the historical divisions between the communities of the province:

Race of our race, your kindred they,
Who crossed the narrow Irish sea
With torch and sword to burn and slay,
And confiscate by King's decree.
The land the Lord had giv'n our sires,
And they for Him had held in fee:
A truth so sacred faith requires,
How could they yield it manfully
To your black flag?

The aspiring young poet went on to assert the similarities rather than the differences between the rival groups by reminding Ulster unionists of their own republican heritage:

> Race of our race, and your kin, too,
> Were Drennan, Munro, Orr and Rowan,
> McCracken, Neilson call to you,
> This land hath made you all her own;
> As she hath made the Viking Dane,
> The Norman Duke, your patriot sires,
> Spurn her not now! When once again
> She in her nationhood aspires
> To raise her flag.

The final verse pointed to a somewhat improbable, if romantic, future when both nationalists and unionists would be united in nationhood:

> Brothers in arms, as one, we too
> Shall knit together bone and bone,
> Sinew and sinew, and renew
> Our strength in Ireland's, so her own
> Shall be revived in her,
> And she in them – a burning light
> She to the nations yet shall flare,
> Come! To this end, in Hell's despite
> We'll raise our flag.[65]

A few weeks after this poem was published the first convention of the Irish Volunteers was held in the Abbey Theatre in Dublin. MacEntee's name was not among the list of delegates present although Paddy Hughes did attend, representing Dundalk.[66] Some time in early 1915, MacEntee met Paddy Hughes in the town square in Dundalk and was told that he and some friends were thinking of reorganising the Volunteers and needed help. Without hesitation MacEntee agreed and was made adjutant to the battalion.

Notwithstanding the enthusiasm of its members, efforts to reorganise the Volunteers in Dundalk did not receive much support from the people in the town and was met by active opposition from the AOH. In fact at the inaugural reorganisation meeting held in Dundalk Town Hall and attended by twenty people, the Hibernians 'surrounded the hall and attacked people trying to get in'.[67] One witness recalled how 'Archie Heron, who came down from Dublin to address the meeting, was attacked by the Hibernians and ... could not get into the meeting. The business of the meeting had to be dropped, as it became a riotous affair, with scrapping all over the place. We had to beat a retreat from the back of the hall into houses in Shambles Lane, and the Hibernians followed us, and threatened to break into the houses and take us out.'[68] After the riot at the town hall, the Volunteers set up headquarters at the Boyle O'Reilly Hall in Clanbrassil Street where drill practice and meetings were held. Lectures on military matters were occasionally provided by prominent Volunteer officers from Dublin including Seán MacDermott, Seán Tobin and Major John McBride.[69]

MacEntee later recalled that there were about one hundred members by the middle of 1915[70] but that 'there was a growing tendency, a growing support for the Volunteer movement. There was a growing, a very rapidly growing, disillusionment with the situation in which the Irish Parliamentary Party found itself at Westminster, where it was completely impotent and where it appeared that [John] Redmond, having shot his bolt ... they had no longer paid any attention to him. Due to that, throughout the country it wasn't visible, but underneath there was a great deal of seething discontent. Desire for a change.'[71] Despite this unseen desire for change, MacEntee was evidently getting itchy feet, frustrated that the movement appeared to be drifting rather aimlessly. At the end of the year he came very close to emigrating, applying for the post of assistant electrical engineer to the government of Malta, which he was duly offered. In the meantime, however, the fact that a 'rising' was contemplated before the end of the war was conveyed to him, presumably by Hughes. He decided not to go to Malta and withdrew his application.[72] In January 1916, Hughes became officer in charge of the Dundalk Volunteers and also had control of the Volunteers in the whole of Co Louth and the counties of Monaghan, Cavan and Meath. He was also a member of the Executive Committee of the Irish Volunteers and despite not being in the IRB was directly responsible to headquarters for the large area over which he had control.[73] By not going to Malta and by devoting all his energies to re-organising the Volunteers in Dundalk, MacEntee had made a deliberate choice, the consequences of which were clear to him: 'Perhaps, at that particular period, from 1915 to 1916, there was a determination that one had to fight and one had to die, whether it was going to be at home rather than somewhere else. Now I think that was one reason why the Volunteers really were very enthusiastic and devoted and zealous, in trying to train themselves, so that they would be a disciplined force.'[74]

The message that a rising was being contemplated was probably relayed to Hughes after the IRB supreme council met in Clontarf Town Hall in mid-January 1916 to fix the date for the Rising.[75] By early February, a message that armed action would begin on Easter Sunday reached the Fenian hierarchy in the United States. There is wide testimony that rank-and-file Volunteers knew that something was happening and the large-scale mobilisation on St Patrick's Day, when 1,400 Volunteers assembled in Dublin and 4,500 elsewhere, was an obvious pointer.[76] One authority has noted that 'the intensification of preparations was unmistakeable'.[77] As part of these preparations, members of the Volunteer hierarchy paid visits to towns around the country in order to attract new recruits and to boost the morale of the existing units. Among those who visited Dundalk to give lectures and talks on military tactics were Seán MacDermott, Seán Milroy, Piaras Beaslaí and Archie Heron. Seán Tobin also came on a few occasions and addressed meetings in the Boyle O'Reilly Hall. Tobin also held a meeting of the IRB at the Neptune hotel in Blackrock where he disarmed all the old men of the IRB.[78]

If Tobin's mission in Dundalk was part of a wider campaign by the IRB to procure as many arms as it could lay its hands on before Easter, MacDermott's presence in the town – on 16 March he delivered the Robert Emmett commemoration

lecture – was to have a greater impact on the local Volunteers. In response to a
direct request made to him, a temporary commander was sent from Dublin at the
beginning of April to 'knock into shape the local units'. The new commander
was Donal O'Hannigan (Dan Hannigan), a cooper by trade, and a 'trained military man [who] put us through a severe course of training practically every night
up to the rising'. The arrival of O'Hannigan did not reflect any ill-feeling
towards Hughes among the men who still regarded him 'as the O/C that we
looked up to'. But Hughes's lack of sufficient military training meant that capable back up was required.[79] MacEntee described O'Hannigan as 'master of
everything that a competent regimental sergeant-major should know about the
role of the combat infantryman'.[80] MacDermott met O'Hannigan shortly after his
visit to Dundalk and issued him with instructions. O'Hannigan was informed
that he would be taking charge of the Louth–Meath–south Down–south
Armagh–south Monaghan area. The total number of Volunteers under his command was 1,337, the biggest unit being Dundalk with about 270 men, a figure
that was testimony to the indefatigable efforts of Hughes and MacEntee in the
first half of 1916. MacDermott duly supplied O'Hannigan with a list of the IRB
men in the area as well as information about local leaders. He was told that
Hughes 'although not an IRB man, was absolutely dependable to the last'.
MacDermott's opinion of MacEntee was that he was 'a very capable man and
that, though he had applied for a commission in the British Army some considerable time previously, he believed he was all right'. He added that O'Hannigan
could use his own discretion about using him and if he was satisfied could 'promote him to any appointment' that was necessary.[81]

Two weeks before the Rising, O'Hannigan travelled to Dundalk where there
was a muster parade of the Volunteers. He contacted Paddy Hughes, who introduced him to MacEntee. That evening the Volunteers were put through their paces
by their new commander to give him some idea 'of the standard they had reached
in training'. On the following Tuesday morning O'Hannigan called to see Pádraig
Pearse at his school, St Enda's in Rathfarnham. Pearse went through the plans for
the Rising in the presence of Seán Boylan, another IRB man who had raised the
Dunboyne company and who was to come under O'Hannigan's command. Pearse
gave O'Hannigan his orders: he was to mobilise the Volunteers from the area at
Tara in Meath on Easter Sunday at 7 p.m. On completion of mobilisation he was
to read the proclamation of the Irish Republic and then march via Dunshaughlin
on Blanchardstown where he would contact Seán Boylan and the Dunboyne men.
They were to seize the railway at Blanchardstown and cut the line there to prevent the English artillery coming from Athlone. The Fingal battalion (5th Dublin
brigade) was to make contact on their left flank and the Kildare men were to come
in on the right. The Wicklow and south County Dublin area was to be on the right
side of them again. In this way they would form a ring around the city. The ring
would extend from Swords via Blanchardstown – Lucan – Tallaght and from
there across the hills to the sea. All units forming this line except the Fingal battalion were to come under O'Hannigan's orders when established.[82] Boylan, however, 'did not hear from O'Hannigan again until after the rebellion had started',
although he had expected to.[83] When events began on Sunday, it came as a com-

plete surprise to Boylan to learn from Volunteer headquarters that he was responsible for mobilisation at Tara. On Monday, thinking everything was off, he went with his brother to Fairyhouse races.[84]

Similar misunderstandings plagued the efforts of O'Hannigan's men in Dundalk and many other Volunteer companies outside the capital. A week before the Rising O'Hannigan attended a meeting of the Volunteer Executive Council at Éamon Ceannt's house at which he pointed out that 'Tara was a very inconvenient place for mobilisation, but Pearse said that for historical reasons Tara was all important and he wanted the proclamation of the Republic read there'. At a further meeting with Pearse at St Enda's, O'Hannigan was instructed to call a meeting of the Volunteers in the area for the town hall for Good Friday night and to bill him to speak at the meeting: 'He said it would be most unlikely that he would be there but that in this way I would get all Volunteer officers to Dundalk and be able to give them the necessary instructions for mobilisation etc.' Pearse was to send three despatches to O'Hannigan on Friday by three different routes. Receipt of these would mean confirmation of the plans but the newly installed commandant was not to tell volunteers of the Rising but 'of a very important route march on Sunday'. Pearse also stressed that O'Hannigan would have to be discreet in choosing the persons he would inform regarding these plans.

Notwithstanding MacDermott's note of warning, O'Hannigan's impression of MacEntee was instantly favourable. Having called to see him at the electricity works, he concluded that 'the man was genuine and could be trusted with any mission'. On the Wednesday before Easter, all Volunteers in the town and Dundalk area were mobilised. They moved out to the country and practised attack and defence tactics, exercises which O'Hannigan described as 'very successful'. Before leaving Dundalk, O'Hannigan received a despatch from Eoin O'Duffy, then an engineer in Monaghan County Council, that he had a considerable quantity of explosives and was placing them at his disposal. O'Duffy, however, failed in his attempts to access the explosives. On Easter Saturday O'Hannigan again sent for the explosives and O'Duffy promised to forward them on Sunday morning but they never arrived. The Volunteers were left to their own ingenuity to augment their limited arsenal of weapons. MacEntee was instrumental in this, procuring some lead from 'the power house' which was moulded into slugs for the cartridges.[85] In total, the Dundalk Volunteers had about twenty to twenty-five shotguns, many of which had been purchased by individual recruits. They had no rifles but intended to commandeer over a hundred Lee Enfield rifles belonging to the National Volunteers which were stored in Ardee.[86] All the rifle drill was carried out two weeks before Easter under O'Hannigan's supervision.[87]

On Good Friday night at 8 p.m. the scheduled meeting at which Pearse was to speak was held in the town hall. In Pearse's absence, O'Hannigan addressed the Volunteers where he announced that a route march for all units would be held on Sunday morning and that 'all men [were] to carry arms and equipment and ammunition and three days' rations. No indication was given to them of what was afoot. Instructions would be given later as to assembly areas and lines of march. Volunteers were to remain and see their officers after the meeting.'[88] At the conclusion of the meeting O'Hannigan held a meeting of local officers which included MacEntee, Paddy Hughes, Paddy McHugh and Jemmy Toal. O'Hannigan told them that 'we were definitely striking on Sunday evening and explained to them how serious this would be for all of them'. He further explained 'that if anyone of them felt that they were not in a position to go on, they were at liberty to withdraw at this stage'. At this point MacEntee stood up in salute and asked to see O'Hannigan privately. He informed his military superior that he had applied for a commission in the British Army and, it being delayed, in the meantime had read T.D. Sullivan's famous book *Speeches from the Dock* which 'changed his whole outlook': 'He was now prepared to go the whole hog in the service of his country and to stand or fall by the Irish Volunteers.' O'Hannigan told MacEntee that he was aware of his application but that he trusted him implicitly. MacEntee, apparently relieved by O'Hannigan's response to his closely guarded secret, asked his commandant if he could sleep in his room for the next two nights, 'a privilege he would appreciate, as he said we might never see each other again'. After this private summit, the two men returned to the meeting where O'Hannigan gave out the necessary instructions: 'All information given them was secret and not to be conveyed to the men or any other person outside themselves.'

MacEntee's confession to O'Hannigan had patently been difficult and indicated his lack of conviction over which course to take at the time of the split in the Volunteers. Whatever of the reasons he gave to O'Hannigan about his change of heart, MacEntee later insisted that his commitment to the Volunteers rested on the question of Ulster: 'As the time went on it was clear that the war was going to last, that Mr Redmond's policy had failed and there was no assurances at that time there would be any form of government which would embrace the whole 32 counties. There was a growing mood of discontent about the leadership and the policy for which the Irish Party stood'; discontent that was undoubtedly fuelled to some degree by his choice of reading material.[89] MacEntee's personal loyalty to his comrades, particularly Paddy Hughes, was also a significant factor in this regard. MacEntee did in fact know the Rising was planned for Easter Sunday before meeting with O'Hannigan. On the previous day he had told another Volunteer, Arthur Greene, that 'if something would not happen soon he was getting "fed up"'. Greene interpreted this as MacEntee's way of telling him that mobilisation was going to happen on Easter Sunday.[90] That afternoon Paddy Hughes had paid MacEntee a visit at his office in the electricity works: '"Mac," he said, "the time has come!" His eyes glittered with excitement, though his voice was quite cool and steady. "We are to march with full equipment and make Tara on Sunday night." "You're not making fun Paddy?" said I, my heart pumping wildly, but he would say to me, "it's for Ireland Mac, it's for Ireland".'[91] That night MacEntee went to Belfast 'to bid goodbye' to his family and 'to buy surgical bandages and first aid satchels, some ordnance maps, a pair of binoculars, a prismatic compass and such other items of an officer's paraphernalia as I could afford'.

If this account is accurate, MacEntee knew more about the planned rising than the organisation's Chief of Staff Eoin MacNeill. The military committee, dominated by the IRB, which had been carefully planning the Rising for months, had deliberately kept MacNeill in the dark to prevent any interference with the mobilisation and went further by detaining Bulmer Hobson who the conspirators believed was more likely than MacNeill to take effective action against them.[92] When MacNeill did get wind of what was happening his response was to issue a curt order to all units which he placed in the Sunday newspapers: 'Volunteers completely deceived. All orders for special action are hereby cancelled, and on no account will action be taken'. The impact MacNeill's countermanding order had on the Rising has been contested. Maureen Wall, for example, argued that the countermanding order 'stopped no Volunteer, who was anxious for war, from participating in the Rising'.[93] This assertion may well be true but what is also true is that MacNeill's order threw O'Hannigan's plans into confusion and disarray, in turn making Seán MacEntee's experiences during Easter week all the more fascinating. These experiences were published in 1966 in MacEntee's memoir of the Rising, *Episode at Easter*, from drafts which he started to write in Crumlin Road Jail in August 1917. According to one reviewer, MacEntee's account 'tells his story with both clarity and charity', providing 'a valuable account of an episode of Easter Week which deserves to be better known'.[94] Another reviewer regarded its greatest merit as 'the stamp of sincerity which it unmistakeably bears'.[95]

Mobilisation of volunteers began after early mass in Dundalk on Easter Sunday. The Dundalk contingent was over 160 strong when it moved off at around 9.30 a.m. towards Ardee in order to seize the Redmondite rifles. MacEntee was asked to select six Volunteers to remain behind to seize the rifles after the main body had left the town. The reason for this arrangement was that, according to orders, the Louth battalion was to occupy the village of Slane where there was an important bridge across the Boyne at 7 p.m. on Easter Sunday evening and to hold the bridge until detachments from Monaghan, Armagh, Tyrone, Down and Antrim had joined O'Hannigan's men, which was to concentrate on Tara, and were then to blow it up.[96] MacEntee had made all the arrangements to seize the rifles, when at about 4 p.m. on Sunday afternoon he received by two separate routes two despatches signed by Eoin MacNeill: 'Volunteers completely deceived – all orders for Sunday cancelled'.

> Naturally MacNeill's despatch upset everything. I suspended the attempt to seize the rifles, and in order to prevent Hannigan acting at Slane went off in pursuit of him; I caught him just as the Volunteers were on the outskirts of Slane at about 6 o'clock in the evening. After discussion we sent messengers to Dublin, asking for confirmation of MacNeill's despatch, since Hannigan and the rest of us were unwilling to act except on [Pádraig] Pearse's direct orders. Meanwhile we waited in Slane until 2 a.m. on Monday morning. It was a terribly wet night.

O'Hannigan next called a council of the officers and said he wanted a responsible person – one who would return – to proceed to the city for verification of the order. MacEntee immediately volunteered to go: 'If you draw me a plan of the city, setting out where you want me to go, I guarantee to get to Dublin and to come back if I am alive.' O'Hannigan made a brief sketch of the city, directing him where to go when he got there. It was decided that he should ride to Drogheda, catch the mail that passed through there, get to Dublin, find Pearse, report to him and receive his instructions. MacEntee's journey to Dublin in the early hours of Easter Monday was fraught with danger; his efforts to reach the train at Drogheda with his co-rider Tom Hamill were captured in a particularly vivid passage of his memoir:

> There was a strong head wind blowing, beating the heavy rain into our faces and almost blinding us. Our raincoats were soaked, and streams of water poured off them and down our legs and ankles. The mud, thin and liquid, was inches deep on the road, and as our wheels splashed through it, they cast up a lavish spray that no mudguard could intercept. It was dark too, almost impenetrably dark and I could scarcely see Tom though he was no more than twenty yards ahead of me. And it was lonely.[97]

As they approached the station at almost 3.45 a.m., MacEntee instructed Hamill to ride on ahead and leave him to follow:

> When I reached the foot of the steep hill that leads to the station, I could see him pedalling vigorously to the top. That hill was still before me, and the station clock showed three forty-five. The slope was a climb to break one's heart, but I climbed it at last; and carrying my bicycle on my shoulder, I rushed through the station entrance and down some stairs to the platform. As I ran, I could hear Tom's voice shouting, 'Wait! Wait! Here's some other poor devil like myself.' And then, in a tone of the most genuine commiseration, 'God help him!' The guard had blown his whistle, but the driver gave me an extra second; I flung my bicycle on the platform and scrambled into the train.

The rest of MacEntee's story had a nightmarish quality to it, as mishap after mishap seemed to thwart his best efforts to carry out orders. Having successfully reached Dublin and made contact with James Connolly (who recognised him from his Belfast days) and Pádraig Pearse at Liberty Hall, he missed his return train and did not manage to get back to Dundalk until early evening on Monday. By this time, O'Hannigan's force was reduced to twenty-eight men. At about 4 p.m., as O'Hannigan's men, 'looking sadly footsore, weary and bedraggled', reached Lurgan Green near Dundalk, MacEntee arrived in a motor car he had commandeered in Ashbourne. He had a despatch from Pearse which read 'Dublin is in arms. You will carry out your original instructions.' O'Hannigan duly declared to all present, including the RIC, 'that a Republic had been proclaimed, and that headquarters of the Republic had been established at the GPO in Dublin'.[98] He addressed the police, telling them that they were now his prisoners. Soon after, a farmer called Patrick McCormick came towards Sergeant Wymes, who had been following the party throughout and who O'Hannigan was forced to threaten with a revolver to make him surrender his arms and documents, accusing MacEntee of having wounded him with a revolver. MacEntee claimed it was an accident caused by the farmer's refusal to obey Volunteer orders and to fend off an attack by McCormick's horse whip. MacEntee was unrepentant: 'I did it as a matter of duty. Ireland is proclaimed a Republic, and you must stand or fall by that fact.'[99] After all the travails he had suffered over the previous twenty-four hours, he now felt an electric sense of liberation: 'A strange feeling of independence and exhilaration possessed me … We were soldiers of the free Irish nation. A yoke seemed lifted from my shoulders.'[100]

The group, turning back towards Tara, then proceeded towards the village of Castlebellingham, where another ten unarmed RIC men were captured. On their approach to Castlebellingham, having commandeered a number of cars returning from Fairyhouse races,[101] O'Hannigan remained in front with the advance guard placing MacEntee, Paddy Hughes and Paddy McHugh in succession 'so that if anything happened me they would assume command in that order'.[102] MacEntee's derring-do mission to Dublin had evidently impressed O'Hannigan enough to elevate him to second in command, taking charge of the main body of Volunteers. O'Hannigan's decision was to prove fateful for MacEntee. At Castlebellingham, MacEntee ordered his men to watch over some prisoners assembled in the village green and to 'See that your revolvers are properly loaded and be ready to obey me'.[103] Another RIC man, a Constable McGee, approached on a bicycle. He was ordered to dismount and was placed with the other captured RIC who were then standing against an iron railing in the centre of the village. Another passing car was stopped, which to everyone's surprise contained British Army staff officer Lieutenant Robert Dunville who was 'exceedingly angry at being held up and refused to get out of his car'.[104] One of the Volunteers recalled Dunville's amazement 'to see a youth like me with a gun ordering him about … the whole police garrison of Castlebellingham were standing in line as our prisoners along with a British Army Staff Officer.'[105] Dunville was not searched by his captors, MacEntee recalling that there had been no time to search him as O'Hannigan had ordered them to move on. He also recalled what happened next:

> To ensure as far as possible that no mishap would occur, I now took charge of the prisoners myself and ordered the men who had been guarding them back to their cars. Keeping the prisoners covered, I then backed towards my own car which was the last in line. I had just turned to enter it, had mounted the footboard and was stepping into the car, when a shot rang out, I jumped back at once and looked towards the prisoners.[106]

As far as MacEntee was aware nobody had been injured by the shots, and as 'most of our cars had already left the village and were moving along towards Dunleer; I could not stop them, nor turn back to find out whether the officer [Dunville] had been seriously wounded or not'.[107] In fact Dunville had only sustained a minor injury but the shots had killed Constable McGee. Frank Martin, one of the three men court-martialled along with Seán MacEntee for the 'murder' of Constable McGee, was apparently closer to the incident than MacEntee. He remembered Lieutenant Dunville 'jeering and abusing us … There was intense excitement at the time, mainly caused by Lieutenant Dunville's antics.' He could not, however, explain what caused the shooting.[108]Another Volunteer,

Paddy McHugh, was even closer than Martin. At the signal for the convoy to move off, MacEntee withdrew the guard on the prisoners and ordered McHugh to cover the prisoners from the last car:

> I took up position on the running board of the car and I covered the prison-ers with the rifle I carried. As the guard was being withdrawn and MacEntee's back being turned, the staff officer [Dunville] whom I had cov-ered made a move that appeared to me as if he was attempting to draw a gun. I immediately called on him to put up his hands. He did not obey. I called again and he again ignored my call. I called no more but fired, and, to my amazement, the RIC man at the other end of the line of prisoners fell. Another shot rang out, and I called out to cease fire. What happened has never been fully explained. The RIC man who fell on the road was killed by a charge of buckshot fired from a shotgun and the staff officer who fell to the ground as we were leaving the village was shot through the lung with a .303 bullet.[109]

When giving this statement to the Bureau of Military History in May 1952, McHugh was described by his interviewer as a reliable witness: 'a most intelli-gent man' with 'a good memory'. He was convinced that the shooting was a mis-take: 'The man who fired the shot from the shotgun has never admitted the mis-take or the accident or whatever his motive was so it will now probably remain forever his secret. I feel convinced that the RIC man was killed accidentally. His death as it happened was regretted sincerely by all in charge of the Volunteers.'[110] At his court-martial in June, MacEntee also stated his regret over the shooting, affirming that 'the constable received no abuse from him, and he lamented his death; the constable was his fellow countryman, discharging his duty'.[111]

Late that evening the convoy arrived in Tara. According to MacEntee, 'there was such an air of romance and grand adventure about that drive through the night'. The romance soon dissipated, however, when they reached their histori-cally significant location and found no other detachments. The Tara force had in fact been sent home earlier that day after hearing of the countermand from Seán Boylan.[112] It was then that some of O'Hannigan's men lost faith and set off back for Dundalk. MacEntee was not among them; he had decided to go to Dublin and to report to Connolly what had occurred. By his own admission, his apparent bravery and purpose were offset by the mistakes he committed on the way: near Dunboyne he rested for some minutes beside a stream, took off one boot to bathe a foot, and dropped asleep from exhaustion; when he came to he pushed on, crawled under a hedge and fell asleep once again. He eventually passed through the British lines on Wednesday afternoon, making his way down to Sackville Street (O'Connell Street). To the young Volunteer from Belfast, unfamiliar with the city, the scene that greeted him there was magnificent to behold:

> The whole of O'Connell Street was filled with sunshine, but empty of peo-ple. It might have been in the early morning of a Sunday in summer. Half way down the street rose the massed bulk of the GPO, the citadel of the Irish Republic. In the morning sunlight its dark grey stone shone with

something of the lustre and texture of polished metal, and its walls rose in rugged strength to defy the might of England. High up on its roof floated two flags; a green flag with white letters, the flag of the Workers' Republic; the other a tricolour of green, white and orange, fronting the bullets aimed at it from Findlater's Church. It was a truly moving sight; such rich, bright green, such deep, living orange![113]

By this time, his blood was stirred sufficiently for him to want to join the action. He fell in with a detachment of Volunteers[114] that was holding the block bounded by O'Connell Street, Earl Street, Abbey Street, Marlborough Street and Marlborough Lane. He later found out that his new comrades were very doubtful of their northern friend, thinking he was possibly a spy.[115] Eventually the group was compelled to evacuate its station and 'after a particularly hot time in the neighbourhood of Marlborough Street'[116] succeeded, in the early hours of Thursday morning under heavy fire, in reaching the GPO. After another short sleep in his new quarters, MacEntee duly reported to Pearse and Connolly what had befallen the Louth detachments. At first he felt isolated in his new surroundings. He had met Pearse before on Easter Monday and knew Connolly 'well enough to know that he knew me and we knew each other', but to the other leaders and to the Dublin Volunteers, he was a stranger. His first task was to report to Tom Clarke, who, having heard that he was an electrical engineer, suggested that he assist two other Volunteers who were busy trying to get 'some juice from the telephone to try to get a signal from the Post Office'.[117]

MacEntee arrived in the GPO just in time to experience the beginning of the British bombardment on Friday afternoon and once it had started it was not long before the roof of the building was in flames. MacEntee recalled the scene inside the building:

Now there was a good deal of activity – the first noticeable thing about it was that each window on the ground floor was manned and that there were changes of guards periodically, they were strengthening the defence of the Post Office … the roof was ablaze for part of that period, but there wasn't any sort of desire to get away … it was still fairly close tight discipline.

On Friday evening MacEntee was in the detachment led by The O'Rahilly which, having evacuated the GPO, filed into Henry Street with the aim of taking possession of the Williams and Woods factory in Parnell Street and 'to hold that position until the main body came up'.[118] Turning into Moore Street, the column came under heavy gun fire: 'Up the street we rushed, men falling as we went, and the farther we went the more men fell; our group was melting away like straw in a flame.' MacEntee was one of the lucky ones, finding cover at dusk in a 'new brick building' in a laneway adjacent to Moore Street. The following day, the Volunteers were struck by the stillness which greeted them, a stillness they feared might portend a further assault! At 'about three o'clock in the afternoon' they heard voices outside. To his amazement and apparent devastation, MacEntee was met by two Volunteer officers, one of whom was Pádraig Pearse's brother, Willie; the other was a Captain Breen who was holding a white flag.

MacEntee reportedly ran to the two men, and, 'breaking down with emotion', asked Pearse, 'Has it come to this?'[119] Only yards down the street the surviving headquarters forces had reached the limits of their endurance. Dr James Ryan, a future cabinet colleague of MacEntee's, who was in charge of the medical unit, had run out of supplies, including morphine for the severely wounded James Connolly. While he was changing Connolly's dressings at midday on Saturday 29 April, Connolly had told him that Pádraig Pearse, as President of the Provisional Government of the Irish Republic, had gone to arrange surrender terms.[120] Less than a week after it had begun, the Rising was over.

The captured Volunteers were marched down Sackville Street to the Rotunda Gardens, 'and there in the open, in a space where there was scarcely room for us to stand, we were compelled to spend the night in bitter cold'.[121] The next morning they were marched through the streets to Richmond Barracks in Inchicore, encountering on the way 'jeering mobs, spitting and wanting to tear us asunder for the damage we'd done to the city'. MacEntee remained here until his deportation to Stafford Prison on 1 May. Fortunately for him, coming from Belfast and Dundalk, he was not familiar to the Dublin detectives so his time spent in Stafford 'enabled the heat to cool a bit' and may have saved his life.[122] By that time, the British authorities had executed all seven signatories of the proclamation read by Pearse shortly after noon on Easter Monday. In addition, all the commandants of the Dublin outposts were executed, except for Éamon de Valera, commandant of the 3rd Dublin city battalion, who always maintained that his court-martial and sentence on 8 May had been late enough to prevent his execution.[123] Two men (James Connolly and Seán MacDermott) were in fact executed after de Valera's death sentence had been commuted to penal servitude for life. Both were signatories of the proclamation and had been in the GPO. After hearing of these executions, MacEntee 'had very little hope' that he would escape the same fate, as the British prime minister, H.H. Asquith, had promised in the House of Commons there should be no more executions, with the exception of the two remaining signatories of the proclamation and the man responsible for the Dundalk and Castlebellingham affairs.[124]

Courts martial proceedings in 1916 were brisk but, according to McConville, 'did adhere to rough standards of elementary justice': 'A great deal of discretion was given to the authorities with respect to procedure, and a distinction was drawn by them between a Field General Court Martial (the form for all the early trials) where legal representation was not allowed, and a General Court-Martial, at which it was.'[125] Again luck was on MacEntee's side; his general court-martial took place in Richmond Barracks on 9–10 June where he was represented by Henry Hanna, KC. Defence counsel had been arranged by John Gore, solicitor, whose services had been secured by MacEntee's parents on 26 May.[126] By that time, MacEntee was back in Richmond Barracks where he was being held along with his co-accused, Frank Martin, Denis Leahy and James Sally. At their meeting, James McEntee told Gore 'that he would wish the boy to be well defended and would pay the costs and that I was to employ good counsel'.[127] The next day, Gore visited MacEntee at the barracks where they conferred for over four hours. He later conveyed his thoughts on the case to Dan McMenamin, an Irish Party

MP who was friendly with James McEntee. Gore explained 'that having fully gone into the matter I feared very much that the charge against the prisoner was a very grave one, and I thought at least two of the parties charged would be found guilty of murder in the first degree'. On 1 June Gore received copies of the charge sheet and of the depositions taken at the preliminary examinations at Richmond Barracks. Subpoenas were duly sent to two individuals whose cars had been commandeered by MacEntee at Lurgan Green and who were willing to testify as to his courtesy towards them.

The other three prisoners from Dundalk were represented by a solicitor from the town who informed Gore that they would not consent to have Henry Hanna as counsel, preferring Parnell's political nemesis, T.M. Healy, to act instead. The trial began on Friday 9 June at Richmond Barracks before Lord Cheylesmore and twelve other officers.[128] All four were accused of the murder of Constable David McGee at Castlebellingham on 24 April 'while waging war against the king', and the attempted murder of Lieutenant Robert Dunville of the Grenadier Guards on the same occasion.[129] Prosecution evidence at the court-martial revealed more about MacEntee and his role in the Volunteers. One RIC officer testified that he had searched MacEntee's lodgings in Anne Street, Dundalk on 17 May. He found a number of incriminating papers and documents, one of which gave details of a proposed Volunteer meeting in the Dundalk Town Hall on Easter Sunday to discuss ways in which Ireland could reach independence. Other documents found included what the officer described as 'Sinn Féin news-papers, such as the *Spark* and the *Volunteer*' and a Volunteer training manual. Most ominously for MacEntee was the discovery of correspondence with two of the executed leaders, James Connolly and Pádraig Pearse, as well as a reply from the War Office to MacEntee's application for a commission which the prosecu-tion regarded as evidence that he was intending to spy in the British Army.[130] All of the witnesses called by the prosecution placed MacEntee at the scene armed with a revolver and stated that it was he who issued orders to the Volunteers. Acting Sergeant Patrick Kiernan, who was stationed at Castlebellingham, was one such witness. Describing what happened when he heard the first shot, Kiernan corroborated MacEntee's version that he had given a command for the Volunteers to move off but to keep the prisoners covered. As the Volunteers made their way to the waiting car, 'Lieutenant Dunville was hit by a bullet, which passed through one side to the other, going through his lungs and he fell first. Almost immediately Constable McGee was hit, and he fell and died within a couple of hours.[131] The implication was clear, both men were hit by the same shot.

When the defence opened its case on MacEntee's behalf, the accused read a prepared statement denying the charge of murder.

He was not a murderer and the term was loathsome to him. If he had been guilty of the murder of this poor man he should have known it, and, to show the Court that he had no connection with the incident, he never knew of the constable's death until he was charged with it at a preliminary inquiry at Richmond Barracks. In obedience to the order of his commander, he stopped the constable, and searched him. He took from him an envelope, which he brought to his commander. The constable received no abuse from him, and he lamented his death; the constable was his fellow countryman, discharging his duty.[132]

MacEntee also denied the charge of giving assistance to the king's enemies: 'Anything he did was done out of love for Ireland, and not to assist the King's enemies in any way.' He affirmed that to him foreign governments were the same and that if he had to choose 'out of two evils he would choose the lesser', opining that England had done much in recent years to improve his country. To the charge of participation in the rebellion, MacEntee pleaded guilty. He admitted that for some months he had been an active and enthusiastic Volunteer: 'First of all, being an Irishman, he thought that the economic and industrial future of the country could only be assured by such government as was enjoyed by the Empire's free Dominions.' He recognised the Home Rule Act as such a measure and, 'taking a note from the book of his fellow citizens in Belfast, who were ready to make a display of force against that Act, he was a Volunteer because, being an Ulsterman, and knowing the history of his province and of his country, he knew how Catholic and Nationalist Ireland looked up to Protestant and Unionist Ulster for much that was noblest and grandest in Irish history'. He saw in the promise of the amending bill 'a proposal whereby Ulster should be cut off and separated from the Ireland which he loved, and in such issue he was obliged to disavow the hope which he cherished, that one day in this land the old religious feuds should be forgotten, and that North and South, which now very much misjudged each other, should unite and work harmoniously together for the good of their common country'.

The court-martial also heard testimony from a number of prominent Belfast citizens, including Alderman John McGrath and T.E. Alexander, who stated that their car had been commandeered by the Volunteers as they returned from Fairyhouse races and, but for MacEntee, they 'would have behaved badly' towards them. Perhaps the most significant contribution on MacEntee's behalf was made by the Irish Party MP, Joe Devlin, who said he had known him since he was a boy: 'He has always been upright and honourable in his character – hard working and estimable in every respect.'[133] Other character witnesses were provided by the treasury solicitor for Ireland, Joseph Donnelly, who had also known MacEntee as a child and who affirmed that 'his character had always been excellent', and MacEntee's boss at the electricity works, Percy Alfred Spalding. Spalding described MacEntee as 'a young gentleman of education and intelligence'. He also stated that MacEntee had been granted leave for Easter week but had expected him to return to work on Easter Monday. Apart from these testimonials, MacEntee's case was also helped by the evidence provided by Patrick Byrne, a publican from Castlebellingham. He submitted that MacEntee did not fire at Constable McGee and that he knew the man who had. At the inquest into the constable's death, both Sergeant Kiernan and Byrne had named Paddy McHugh as the man who fired the fatal shot. McHugh's response to this accusation was given in his statement to the Bureau of Military History thirty-six years later: 'The usual verdict in such cases and with such evidence was given – a charge of murder against me. My name and a very good description of my appearance was [sic] inserted in the *Hue and Cry*, an official police publication.'[134]

At the conclusion of the trial MacEntee was brought to Kilmainham jail and remained there with the three other Dundalk Volunteers until after sentencing on Wednesday, 14 June.[135] Years later he recalled the moment when the verdict was read:

> Just after exercise one day we were all paraded before the commandant of the prison, who appeared with solemn ceremony accompanied by sergeant majors, guards and another red-tabbed, brass-hatted officer, who proceeded to read most portentously: 'Denis Leahy, Francis Martin, James Joseph Sally and John Francis MacEntee – you have been charged etc.' for about five minutes during which 'waging war against His Majesty' 'aiding the enemy' 'endangering the lives of his majesty's loyal subjects' frequently occurred, ending up with – 'You, Denis Leahy, have been found guilty and sentenced to death, you Francis Martin have etc and been sentenced to death … You John Francis MacEntee have etc and sentenced to death.'

By the time this verdict had been read out, MacEntee had already 'made up my mind … that I was certainly for it'. The 'greatest shock' he got was when the officer, after reciting that the general officer commanding had confirmed the finding of the court, went on to say that he had commuted it to penal servitude for life. This was not an uncommon occurrence during the long drawn-out series of trials brought about by the Rising. Of the ninety sentences of death imposed by the courts martial, all bar fifteen were commuted – usually to penal servitude for life.[136] At the age of twenty-six years, MacEntee now faced the prospect of a life in prison in an English jail, a fate which he found infinitely more appealing than the alternative and one that would catapult him into a long and successful political life.

NOTES

1. The address of MacEntee's family home has been given as both 47 King Street and 42 Mill Street. The King Street address is in fact the one on his birth certificate. This is explained by the location of the pub at the intersection of both streets. When referring to his home, MacEntee often referred to the McEntees of King Street.
2. M. Patton, *Central Belfast: A Historical Gazetteer* (Belfast, 1993).
3. M. Cruise O'Brien, *Same Age as the State* (Dublin, 2003), p.33.
4. NAI, 1911 census returns.
5. Cruise O'Brien, *Same Age as the State*, p.33.
6. Ibid., p.34. The founder and owner of the Biltmore hotel was John McEntee Bowman (1875–1931), a Canadian-born businessman who may well have been the son of an Irish emigrant. See also *Time*, 4 March 1929.
7. MacEntee's school friend Padraic Gregory claimed during the 1918 general election campaign that the family had been forced to leave Monaghan because of its association with 'the 67 movement'. There is good reason to believe that because Gregory was appealing to the radical republican constituency in the county, that he may have embellished this slightly. See *Dundalk Democrat*, 14 December 1918.
8. National Library of Ireland [NLI], Griffith's Valuation, Belfast 1860, Parish of Shankill, Smithfield Ward.

9. UCDA P67/18 (41) Seán MacEntee to Reverend Sister Grace Miriam, 21 June 1966.
10. Cruise O'Brien, *Same Age as the State*, p.36.
11. Ibid., p.34.
12. UCDA P67/773 (6), Interview with Seán MacEntee by Harlan J Strauss, research fellow, Department of Political Science, University of Oregon at the Shelbourne hotel, 22 March 1972.
13. Cruise O'Brien, *Same Age as the State*, p.33.
14. Ibid.
15. UCDA P67/ 793, Copy letter from MacEntee to Seamus McCall, April 1952.
16. M. McInerney, 'Seán MacEntee: republican leader', *Irish Times*, 22 July 1974.
17. C. Morris, 'In the enemy's camp: Alice Milligan and *fin de siècle* Belfast', in N. Allen and A. Kelly (eds), *The Cities of Belfast* (Dublin, 2003).
18. Information supplied by Mr Kevin Burke, principal of St Mary's school, Belfast.
19. *Christian Brothers' Jubilee Souvenir Magazine* (Belfast, 1916).
20. Dr P. Rogers, 'St. Malachy's College Belfast, 1833–1933', *Collegian*, 1933.
21. M. Tierney, *Eoin MacNeill: Scholar and Man of Action, 1867–1945* (Oxford, 1980), p.5.
22. Cruise O'Brien, *Same Age as the State*, p.34.
23. MacEntee's daughter has recalled that 'there was never any doubt but that my father was the [family] favourite'. Cruise O'Brien, *Same Age as the State*, p.32.
24. M. Hay, 'Bulmer Hobson: The Rise and Fall of an Irish Nationalist, 1900–16' [Unpublished PhD thesis, UCD, 2005], p.25.
25. Ibid., p.47.
26. Quoted in Morris, 'In the enemy's camp'.
27. Ibid.
28. UCDA P67/805, Handwritten account of early political experiences, January 1978.
29. Bureau of Military History [hereafter BMH] WS 279, Seamus Dobbyn.
30. R. Lynch, *The Northern IRA and the Early Years of Partition, 1920–1922* (Dublin, 2006), p.10.
31. BMH WS 183, Liam Gaynor.
32. BMH WS 916, Denis McCullough.
33. BMH WS 183, Liam Gaynor.
34. S.E. Baker, 'Orange and Green: Belfast, 1832–1912', in H.J. Dyos and M. Wolff (eds), *The Victorian City: Images and Realities* (London, 1973).
35. Ibid.
36. Hepburn, 'Belfast 1871–1911: work, class and religion', in *Irish Economic and Social History*, vol. X (1983).
37. Baker, 'Orange and Green'.
38. *Irish Times*, 26 November 1897.
39. A.C. Hepburn, *A Past Apart: Studies in the History of Catholic Belfast, 1850–1950* (Belfast, 1996), p.131.
40. *Irish Times*, 26 November 1897.
41. *Irish Times*, 27 November 1897.
42. A.C. Hepburn, *A Past Apart*, p.161.
43. Ibid., p.163.
44. UCDA P67/795, Transcript interview by Tony Meade with MacEntee in the *Kerryman* newspaper, 29 March 1969.
45. Ibid.
46. See D. Nevin, *James Connolly: A Full Life* (Dublin, 2005), p. 380.
47. Ibid.
48. UDCA P67/805, Handwritten account of early political experiences, January 1978.
49. *Irish Times*, 3 January 1914.
50. UCDA P67/ 793, Copy letter from MacEntee to Seamus McCall, consisting of biographical material supplied at McCall's request as background for a series of articles in the *Express*.
51. Quoted in Cruise O'Brien, *Same Age as the State*, p.35.
52. M. McInerney, 'Seán MacEntee: republican leader', *Irish Times*, 22 July 1974.
53. BMH WS 238, Arthur Greene, Member of the IRB Dundalk, Sergeant Major Irish Volunteers, Dundalk 1916.
54. UCDA P67/41, Patrick McHugh, BMH WS 677.
55. UCDA P67/27, Hugh Kearney, BMH WS 260.
56. Ibid.
57. *The Irish Volunteer*, 7 March 1914.
58. UCDA P67/43(1), Bureau Statement of Seán MacEntee, WS 1052 (18 December 1954).
59. UCDA P67/776 (11), Transcript of MacEntee interview filmed by the BBC in July 1972.

60. UCDA P67/25, Frank Martin, member of the Irish Volunteers, Dundalk BMH WS 236.
61. UCDA P67 28, Arthur Greene, BMH WS 238.
62. UCDA P67/795, Transcript interview by Tony Meade with MacEntee in the *Kerryman* newspaper, 29 March 1969.
63. Quoted in C. Townshend, *Easter 1916: The Irish Rebellion* (London, 2005), p.53.
64. UCDA P67/27, Hugh Kearney, WS 260.
65. *The Irish Volunteer*, 3 October 1914.
66. BMH WS338, Francis McQuillan.
67. *The Irish Volunteer*, 31 October 1914.
68. BMH WS 338, Francis McQuillan, member of the IRB/Irish Volunteers, Dundalk.
69. BMH WS 232, Thomas Hamill.
70. This would appear from other witness accounts to be an overestimate. See, for example, BMH WS 260, Hugh Kearney.
71. UCDA P67/776 (11), Transcript of an interview filmed by the BBC in July 1972.
72. UCDA P67/ 793, Copy letter from MacEntee to Seamus McCall [journalist], consisting of biographical material supplied at McCall's request as background for a series of articles in the *Express*.
73. BMH WS 260, Hugh Kearney.
74. UCDA P67/776 (11), BBC interview, July 1972.
75. Townshend, *Easter 1916*, p.122.
76. Ibid., p.124.
77. Ibid.
78. BMH WS 238, Arthur Greene.
79. See BMH WS 236, Frank Martin and BMH WS 260, Hugh Kearney.
80. S. MacEntee, *Episode at Easter* (Dublin, 1966), p.64. At the instance of Tom Clarke and Seán MacDermott, O'Hannigan had taken up employment as a land steward in Maryboro where he organised a circle of the IRB. Having returned to Dublin to work in the Guinness factory, he rejoined the Teeling circle of the IRB in Parnell Square and became an IRB recruiter.
81. Ibid.
82. Ibid.
83. BMH WS 212, Seán Boylan. See also Townshend, *Easter 1916*, p.222.
84. Townshend, *Easter 1916*, p.222.
85. BMH WS 238, Arthur Greene.
86. UCDA P67/ 793, MacEntee to McCall.
87. BMH WS 238, Arthur Greene.
88. BMH WS 161, Donal O'Hannigan.
89. UCDA P67/776 (11), BBC interview, July 1972.
90. BMH WS 238, Arthur Greene.
91. UCDA P67/43(1) BMH WS 1052, Seán MacEntee (18 December 1954).
92. Townshend, *Easter 1916*, p.137.
93. See M. Wall, 'The plans and the countermand', in K.B. Nowlan (ed.), *The Making of 1916* (Dublin, 1969).
94. UCDA P67/20 (1), Review of MacEntee, *Episode at Easter* by T.P. O'Neill.
95. Ibid. Review by Donal McCartney.
96. UCDA P67/ 793, MacEntee to McCall.
97. MacEntee, *Episode at Easter*, p.81.
98. BMH WS 161, Donal O'Hannigan.
99. *Sinn Fein Rebellion Handbook*, published by the *Weekly Irish Times* (Dublin, 1917), pp.109–12. Proceedings of Court Martial of John McEntee, 9 June 1916.
100. BMH WS 1052, Seán MacEntee.
101. Two occupants of cars commandeered by MacEntee were members of the Belfast Corporation who knew his father and provided favourable testimony at MacEntee's subsequent court martial.
102. BMH WS 161, Donal O'Hannigan.
103. *Dundalk Democrat*, 10 June 1916.
104. MacEntee, *Episode at Easter*, p.111.
105. BMH WS 677, Paddy McHugh.
106. MacEntee, *Episode at Easter*, p.111.
107. Ibid., p.112.
108. BMH WS 236, Frank Martin.
109. BMH WS 677, Paddy McHugh.
110. McHugh was subsequently accused of delivering the fatal shot to Constable McGee: 'At the inquest held on the shot policeman, a Sergeant Kiernan, RIC who knew me personally, swore that I was the

man who fired the fatal shot. The sergeant's evidence was corroborated by a civilian witness named Byrne, a local publican, who also knew me. The usual verdict in such cases and with such evidence was given – a charge of murder against me. My name and a very good description of my appearance was inserted in the *Hue and Cry*, an official police publication.'

111. Quoted in Townshend, *Easter 1916*, p.224.
112. Ibid.
113. The flag that flew alongside the tricolour to which MacEntee referred was a 'one-off creation' – 'using the traditional golden Irish harp on a green ground', the words Irish Republic were in fact painted in gold and not white. The flag of the Workers' Republic, 'The Starry Plough', flew, not on the GPO but across the road on the Imperial hotel. See Townshend, *Easter 1916*, pp.159–60.
114. The detachment comprised Gerard Crofts, Frank Thornton and Ned Boland, a brother of Harry and Gerald.
115. UCDA P67/793, MacEntee to McCall.
116. It was here in Marlborough Street that MacEntee first met his future departmental secretary, J.J. McElligott.
117. UCDA P67/776 (11), Transcript of BBC interview, July 1972. The other two Volunteers were Jack Plunkett, brother of Joseph, and Fergus O'Kelly, with whom MacEntee later started a consultancy firm.
118. MacEntee, *Episode at Easter*, p.160.
119. Ibid., p.163.
120. Townshend, *Easter 1916*, p.245.
121. MacEntee, *Episode at Easter*, p.166.
122. Seán MacEntee: republican leader', *Irish Times*, 22 July 1974.
123. D. Ferriter, *Judging Dev* (Dublin, 2007), p.28.
124. UCDA P67/ 793, MacEntee to McCall.
125. S. McConville, *Irish Political Prisoners* (London, 2003), p.431.
126. UCDA P67/2, 17 July 1916, John Gore, solicitor, 6 Cavendish Row, Dublin to James McEntee; statement of costs in relation to the court-martial of John McEntee.
127. MacEntee's total legal costs amounted to £48.3.2.
128. *Dundalk Democrat*, 10 June 1916.
129. *Irish Times*, 12 June 1916.
130. M. McInerney, 'Seán MacEntee: republican leader', *Irish Times*, 22 July 1974.
131. *Dundalk Democrat*, 10 June 1916.
132. Ibid., 17 June 1916.
133. Ibid.
134. BMH WS 677, Paddy McHugh.
135. UCDA P67/793, MacEntee to McCall.
136. McConville, *Irish Political Prisoners*, p.433.

2

Soldier of Destiny

The 1916 Rising was undoubtedly the defining event of Seán MacEntee's long life, as it was in a more symbolic way for a generation of Irish nationalists. Had he not been in Castlebellingham on Easter Monday when Constable McGee was shot and killed or among the GPO garrison when the rebels surrendered, he would not have met, and become one of, the future leaders of political nationalism in Ireland. To him, the Rising was inevitable 'whether it was right or wrong': 'There was no stopping it. I was all for it personally. It was the only action to take at the time. For me to think anything else would be to make my whole life's work unreal or false.'[1] After the Rising, 122 men and one woman were sent to penal servitude and a further eighteen to ordinary imprisonment.[2] Many more participants were interned without trial, including future leaders such as Michael Collins and Arthur Griffith. Indeed for many of the convicted rebels, prison became 'war by other means' and after they were released under the general amnesty of June 1917, a significant number of them, including MacEntee, went on to almost consummate the aims of the Rising through their involvement in the Sinn Féin party and the Irish Volunteers. Prison was also where MacEntee formed his closest political allegiances and in the Civil War that followed the signing of the Anglo-Irish Treaty of 1921, his personal relationships with the respective leaders did much to define the course he would take during that conflict.

Of course, his most enduring political allegiance was to Éamon de Valera with whom he was politically associated for almost sixty years. When de Valera died in 1975, MacEntee wrote to his personal secretary conveying the genuine and heartfelt esteem in which he held his former leader: 'I firmly believe that our Chief was among the best and godliest of men. I cannot recall one unjust thing, nor even an unkind one that he consciously did. He was rectitude and integrity personified; and he evoked, though maybe not in an equal intensity, those qualities in others. He set a standard in public conduct and private behaviour that those around him were led by his example to emulate.'[3] MacEntee first encountered his 'Chief' in the summer of 1916 within the confines of Dartmoor Prison in Devonshire, to where he was sent after his court-martial. De Valera was the last surviving Dublin commandant of the Rising, a position which provided him with 'huge political opportunities ... in terms of leadership'.[4] On the evidence of those who were incarcerated with him, it was an opportunity that he seized with much gravitas. The presence of the Irish convicts had, in fact, created difficulties for the prison authorities in England who saw no difference between them and other criminals. The political situation, however, demanded that the Irish be treated more sensitively as public opinion became increasingly more sympathetic to the Easter rebels. If anything, de Valera's actions amplified this conflict of interest between the prison commissioners and the politicians by his constant agiation for political status and his continual observation of military etiquette in prison. One example of de Valera's defiant attitude to the prison authorities occurred on the morning Eoin MacNeill joined the rest of the prisoners in Dartmoor. De Valera reportedly stepped out from their ranks and, facing the Volunteers, called the men to attention. According to Robert Brennan, 'From the moment he gave the salute to McNeill [sic], Dev was our unquestioned leader.'[5]

Due to the lateness of his court-martial, MacEntee was one of the last prisoners to arrive in Dartmoor. The journey was made somewhat easier as the officer in charge of the escort belonged to the same regiment as a school friend from Belfast who a few days previously had been in charge of the party which brought Austin Stack to the same prison. MacEntee's friend had asked the officer to treat the prisoners decently, which he duly did.[6] On his arrival, MacEntee (convict q 221), was photographed for inclusion in the rogues' gallery. Before taking the picture, his neck was adorned with a muffler, and placed on his head was 'a very dilapidated cap', which made him appear somewhat tougher than he was in reality.[7] Apart from the Dundalk Volunteers, Frank Martin and Denis Leahy, MacEntee did not know any of the other prisoners. The climate of Dartmoor was bleak, and 'before August was out conditions were already becoming wintry'.[8] Frank Thornton remembered the rules in Dartmoor being very strict: 'Talking [was] strictly forbidden, and, during exercise in the prison yard, two paces had to be kept between each prisoner when walking around the ring.'[9] It wasn't long, however, before the prisoners acquired the art of being able to talk to each other without moving their lips. The main body of the party was detailed to the bag-making shop, and it was here in July that MacEntee first 'spoke' to de Valera.

> Because of the vigilance of the warders, we were not in a position to converse freely, but we did manage to maintain a fairly coherent exchange of views. As I had lived in Belfast virtually all my life, I knew something of Northern politics and Northern politicians. De Valera, on the other hand, knew them only by repute and what he had heard of them had not impressed him. He was surprised indeed, that I had so much that was good to tell about 'wee' Joe Devlin. Though his views mellowed later, he was then firm in the conviction that the trouble there was due to British guile and nothing else. It was a view with which I did not agree.[10]

The daily routine at Dartmoor was unforgiving. Prisoners were called every morning at 4.30 a.m. Their first task was to clean their cells, polish all the tin-ware, fold all blankets and roll them, and have everything ready for inspection by 5 o'clock. At about 5.30 they were served breakfast – 'a pint of skilly and a dark, nearly black loaf, but you could get all the water you wanted to drink.'

After breakfast, the cells were inspected and, at 7 a.m., the doors were opened. The first order issued was every man to stand to his door. Then the order was given: 'Two paces forward, right and left turn, quick march, and off we went for our daily routine.' At 4.30 prisoners were back in their cells where they were served with 'a magnificent tea – a pint of shell cocoa and another black loaf'. Everyone had to be in bed by 8 p.m. when 'lights out' was sounded. 'The only occupation we had when we were locked up was reading the bible or walking up and down the cell, but this had to cease by 8 o'clock.'[11] The harshness of the regime took its toll on the prisoners and before long 'a spirit of real revolt had set in and, in actual fact, the prisoners were ready for anything'.

Again de Valera was at the forefront of this dissent. His technique, according to McConville, was to carefully pick an issue, take an action which broke the rules, be punished and respond to the punishment with further and more widespread breaches.[12] De Valera's carefully choreographed campaign had its effect. Between August and October, sixty-five Irish prisoners in Dartmoor complained persistently, while the remaining Irish convicts in Portland prison did not lodge a single complaint. De Valera's disobedience resulted in him being transferred to Maidstone in October along with 'his lieutenants' Richard Hayes and Desmond FitzGerald. After the release of the Irish internees in November and December 1916, it was decided to concentrate the remaining prisoners in Lewes Jail in Sussex. Lewes was described by one of the prisoners as 'a beautiful place after the experience of Dartmoor. The cell floors were of wood and there were hot water pipes and, though they were never hot, they looked good.'[13] Concessions were also made, by the more genial governor of the prison, Major R.A. Marriott, to the prisoners such as supplying them with writing materials, increasing their visit and letter allowances and allowing them to associate and talk freely 'as long as good order was maintained'. This particular concession led to Eoin MacNeill giving a series of lectures on ancient Irish history as well as Irish language lessons to MacEntee, Con Donovan and Robert Brennan during exercise.[14] The more relaxed conditions in Lewes only strengthened the prisoners' resolve to rebel at every opportunity. This rebellion reached its peak in early June 1917. The authorities having refused to grant prisoner-of-war status, the prisoners responded by carrying out a campaign of destruction leading to the intervention of the military, which satisfied de Valera's original objective:

> [I]t wasn't long before we drove a 'coach and fours' through all their rules and regulations, resulting in a general breakdown in control at Lewes. A council of war was formed and Éamon de Valera was appointed leader [commandant]. A demand was made for treatment as prisoners of war, but, under the guise of 'negotiations' they [the prison authorities] succeeded in getting us back into our cells, and refused to unlock our doors on Sunday morning to let us out to mass. The singing of 'God Save Ireland' by Bob Brennan on Sunday was the signal for the general smash up of the prison. I have never seen a job so thoroughly carried out. The prison was literally

pulled to pieces, brick by brick, holes were bored in the walls and in the floors, and a regular line of communication existed from one end of the corridors to the other. This went on for a number of days, during which we were being fed through a square hole which carried the lighting for the cell. Subsequently, bringing in reinforcements of warders, firemen and policemen, they smashed down the walls and hosed us out of our cells.

The prisoners were removed to different locations, thirty each at Parkhust and Portland, twenty-eight at Maidstone and thirty-one remaining in Lewes. MacEntee was among the group sent to Portland.

The mutiny at Lewes was partly prompted by the favourable political situation in Ireland. In April one of the Lewes prisoners, Joe McGuinness, had been selected to run as a Sinn Féin candidate in the South Longford by-election. The unexpected victory in February of Count Plunkett in North Roscommon had given a timely fillip to the radical nationalist agenda, which activists had attempted to build upon by forging a united movement. Sinn Féin became an umbrella organisation for the many separatist factions that had existed before the 1916 Rising. In order to give the movement greater moral authority and to harness the apparent goodwill towards the Easter rebels, Michael Collins, one of the released internees and a rising star in the movement, championed McGuinness's candidature against the wishes of his military superiors. De Valera's initial response was also disapproving. In a memorandum composed on Easter Sunday, he impugned the old Sinn Féin policy of Arthur Griffith (including his dual monarchy model), which he argued tended 'to alienate a number of Irishmen'. De Valera feared that if the candidate were to be defeated and the prisoners were to be identified formally with this policy 'it would mean the ruin of the hopes – not to say the ideals – which prompted our comrades to give the word last Easter'.[15] This suspicion of Griffith and more moderate opinion in general was shared by the Volunteer leadership. Despite de Valera's misgivings and the almost unanimous decision by the prisoners to reject the proposal, McGuinness's name was put forward by their freed comrades in Dublin. The Sinn Féin activists ran on a separatist platform, and on issues such as McGuinness's status as a prisoner and the legacy of the Rising. In the end the strategy worked but by a margin of a mere thirty-seven votes.

In June, the British Prime Minister, David Lloyd George, summoned the Irish Convention, which was designed to represent all factions in the country and to placate American opinion. In order to create a mood of goodwill and to give the convention a better chance of succeeding, the British government decided to release the remaining Irish prisoners. MacEntee's life sentence had barely lasted a full year. When rumours began circulating in early June that the prisoners were to be released, a personal petition for his inclusion in any amnesty was made on MacEntee's behalf by Thomas Spring Rice, Baron Mounteagle of Brandon, grandson to a former Chancellor of the Exchequer. Spring Rice had attended the second day of MacEntee's court-martial and formed a very favourable opinion of him after hearing his testimony. On 8 June he wrote to the chief secretary, Henry Duke, describing MacEntee as 'an exceptionally high-minded man': 'I venture to plead, therefore, that if the Lewes prisoners are any of them amnestied, that he will not be discriminated against, as, though on the bare facts it might appear that he was guilty of deliberate murder, I believe any impartial man, who heard the whole case, and observed his personality and demeanour during the trial, would share my conviction that he was not morally guilty.'[16] His fears were not realised; MacEntee disembarked the Dublin Steampacket Company's boat *Munster* at Kingstown (Dun Laoghaire) behind his chief on the morning of 18 June 1917.[17] De Valera's deference to Volunteer etiquette was observed to the last, giving the men orders to disembark in military formation.

> As the boat came alongside it was seen that the stern deck was crowded with men – gaunt-featured, unshaven, and close-cropped for the most part, and dressed in shoddy, ill-fitting clothes. Eagerly they took stock of the lit-tle crowd on the pier, and with equal interest the latter searched amongst the passengers for familiar faces. A ripple of cheering rose and more hats and handkerchiefs waved in the hot sunlight. Greetings were flung across the narrow strip of water between the vessel and the pier. Then suddenly, as if at a given signal, the released men broke into 'The Soldier's Song'.[18]

The enthusiasm of the crowd at Kingstown was nothing compared to the recep-tion awaiting the released prisoners at Westland Row. Crowds had gathered in the early hours anticipating the prisoners' arrival at the North Wall but rumours that the *Munster* was to come in at Kingstown prompted an exodus to Westland Row. From here the released prisoners were carried out on to the open brakes outside the station and escorted through the city by a huge crowd of people to Fleming's Hotel in Gardiner Place where, after a 'royal feast', de Valera's candi-dature in the upcoming East Clare by-election was ratified.[19] MacEntee's father was at Westland Row to meet him, anxious that his son would look the part, bringing a new three-piece suit.[20] In the afternoon they met in Exchequer Street, where a document for presentation to the American government was prepared. It was written on a sheet of Irish linen and signed by all the returned prisoners pres-ent.[21] Afterwards the released prisoners moved on to the Mansion House where a group photograph was taken by Keogh Brothers of Dorset Street.

The released Volunteers' triumphant return demonstrated that they were the natural leaders of the separatist movement which had been flourishing in their absence. Confirmation of just how strong the movement had become was pro-vided by the East Clare contest, which was brought about by the death at Messines on the Western Front of the Irish Party leader's brother, Major Willie Redmond. Before leaving for Clare to participate in the campaign, MacEntee paid a visit to his parents' home in Belfast. According to the police report, 'At 12.35 a.m. on 19 June, a large but orderly crowd met him on arrival and accom-panied him to his father's house at 42 Mill Street where both McEntee [sic] and local suspect Denis McCullough addressed the crowd, but did not make use of any disloyal or seditious language.' The same police report also noted the advance of the separatist movement in the city: 'For some months past the local Sinn Féiners have been extremely active in propaganda work and their numbers and influence have increased very considerably. They seem to have got hold of the younger members of the Nationalist community.'[22] Among these new recruits were MacEntee's brothers, Joe, Eddie and Charlie. MacEntee was disappointed, however, to find a lack of unity among republicans in Belfast. He wrote to MacNeill a month later, informing him that he 'found a certain amount of friction and a want of cohesion among the several sections of them', and requested the 'services of yourself, de Valera and – as has been suggested by a couple of the men here – the Count and perhaps the Countess [Plunkett] to give them a good straight talking to: such as might secure a more agreeable spirit among them'.[23]

Belfast seems to have been in the minority in this respect. According to Laffan, the timing of the prisoners' return was perfect: 'They found a united, efficient and energetic party awaiting them. If the unification of Sinn Féin had been delayed until after the release of the prisoners, it is virtually certain that Griffith, Plunkett and others who had been active in early 1917 would have been discredited.'[24] The self-confident defiance displayed by de Valera in prison was also on show at the hustings in Clare. He told audiences that 'you have no enemy but England, and you must be prepared to fight against England', and 'although we fought once and lost, it is only a lesson for the second time'.[25] MacEntee also adopted a militant tone, telling a meeting in Drogheda on 22 July that if people 'wanted freedom they must be prepared to fight for it – by constitutional means if those means could be successful; if not, by any means that would give them victory. He called on the women to help and to be ready to give up their husbands and their brothers in this cause if necessary.'[26] The rebellious tone of the Sinn Féin candidate struck a chord with the young people and the local newspaper in Clare, making de Valera's victory widely anticipated, even though the margin (5,010 votes to his rival Patrick Lynch's total of 2,035) was more than expected. Another Sinn Féin victory followed in August when William T. Cosgrave, another ex-internee, was returned in Kilkenny. MacEntee did not play any part in the Kilkenny election, owing to his arrest on 6 August at his home in Belfast.[27] His Drogheda speech had attracted the attention of the local constabulary and he was charged under the Defence of the Realm Act (DORA), leading to a return to prison – this time in Crumlin Road Jail – where he began writing his memoir of 1916. While in Crumlin Road, MacEntee, along with Philip Monahan, resisted the attempts of their fellow prisoner, J. J. Kelly, to start a hunger strike. De Valera and MacNeill visited Belfast to express the view that a hunger strike was not necessary.[28] Somewhat ironically, at his court-martial in September MacEntee was defended by T.J. Campbell, who would later stand against him in the 1918 general election.

MacEntee was released in time to attend the Sinn Féin convention held at the Mansion House in October. In the meantime, he continued to make seditious speeches, telling a meeting in Monaghan on 7 October that 'the independence for which they were fighting was re-baptised in blood, the blood of O'Rahilly and

Pearse and the other men of Easter Week'. He asked those present to be like them and to adopt their principles, and said an Irish Republic would be the most befitting memorial they could give those men.[29] That an Irish Republic was the ultimate objective of the reconstructed Sinn Féin party was still in some doubt, however. A week before the convention, Griffith had held talks with de Valera in a Grafton Street café, where they arranged that the former would not contest the election for the position of president.[30] This led to de Valera's unanimous coronation in the Mansion House and greatly furthered the agenda of those advocating a republican policy. Griffith, in the course of proposing de Valera, described him as a 'man of cool judgement, in whose judgement I have absolute confidence'.[31] There was some dissent at the meeting, however. When Eoin MacNeill's name was put forward for a place on the National Executive Countess Markiewicz strongly objected, considering it her 'duty not only to the memory of the dead, but to the men and women who remain behind to work under the leadership'. MacEntee immediately objected on a point of order to MacNeill's name being singled out and argued if 'one of the names of those nominated is allowed to be discussed we are entitled to discuss every name on the list'. In the end both Griffith and de Valera defended MacNeill as 'an honest man who acted as a good Irishman', leading to his election to the executive with by far the most votes of any candidate. Indeed the released prisoners were well represented on the twenty-four-man executive; MacEntee succeeded in getting 342 votes, two more than Michael Collins and Ernest Blythe, who attracted the lowest number of ballots. MacEntee's other contribution to the convention was to propose a resolution that 'all nations be asked at the Peace Conference to sanction Ireland's claim to independence according to President Wilson's dictum'.

The Mansion House meeting regulated the political structures of an organisation that had transformed itself since the beginning of the year, helped in no small measure by the release of the prisoners in June. The following day, a separate convention was held in Croke Park, home of the Gaelic Athletic Association (GAA), to give a formal structure to the military arm of the movement. A sign of just how closely the political and military wings were interrelated was that almost all of the delegates at the Volunteer convention had been present in the Mansion House.[32] Again, de Valera was elected president and a National Executive was appointed. This comprised delegates from all four provinces, each group of provincial delegates electing its own members, and six others from Dublin who would comprise the Resident Executive. MacEntee was elected as one of the four Ulster members which also included Joe O'Doherty (Donegal), Paul Galligan (Cavan) and Eoin O'Duffy (Monaghan).[33] After the convention, MacEntee returned to Belfast and continued to foster a united spirit among republicans, organising for Arthur Griffith and Eoin MacNeill to address party meetings during November and December.[34] His long-term future was still somewhat uncertain despite his evident enthusiasm for politics. In September he had written to the Irish National Aid Association seeking financial support in order to attend university.[35]

Sinn Féin activists had little time to think about other things, however. The
party had decided to contest the South Armagh by-election to be held in January
1918, even though there were only eight party branches in the constituency and
Joe Devlin's AOH was particularly powerful there. The election saw MacEntee
in direct opposition to Devlin, his father's long-term associate and the most
prominent character witness at his court-martial. While MacEntee complained
that the older generation in the constituency was Redmondite, advising the
young men 'not to plough, sow or reap for fathers who would be so base as to
betray Ireland', Devlin appealed to the people's sense of gratitude towards the
Irish Party.[36] MacEntee's entreaties to the electors of South Armagh were made
in the absence of the Sinn Féin candidate, Dr Patrick McCartan, who had been
sent to America to highlight Ireland's plight to President Wilson. South Armagh
was to be a minor setback to Sinn Féin's onward march to electoral hegemony,
the Nationalist candidate, Patrick Donnelly, winning by a clear margin of 2,324
votes to 1,305. Any hope the victory may have lent the Irish Party was false,
however; a few weeks later, John Redmond died and was succeeded by his
deputy of eighteen years, John Dillon.

After the setback in South Armagh, de Valera embarked on a twelve-day
organising tour in Ulster beginning on 8 February, enlisting the help of local
knowledge in the form of MacEntee. Indeed MacEntee recalled being very close
to de Valera at that time as he shared platforms in counties Donegal, Derry and
Tyrone.[37] Both men continued to advocate physical force. At a meeting in
Raphoe, County Donegal on 13 February, MacEntee said that 'England was
never so near defeat as now, and urged the Irish Volunteers to drill and arm so as
to give her a knock-out blow at the earliest opportunity'. Meanwhile at Castlefin
on 13 February, de Valera said that physical force defeated the tithe laws and
won the Land Acts: 'England is in a critical position and if the Volunteers take
their chance at the right time they will rid Ireland of English tyranny.'[38] England
had other uses for the Volunteers, however. After the Bolshevik surrender at
Brest-Litovsk, one million German soldiers were moved to the Western Front.
The most attractive solution to the crisis for the British government was to
extend the Military Service Bill, operational in Britain since 1916, to Ireland.
According to one historian of the period, the Conscription Crisis was significant
because it 'changed the challenge to the authorities from open defiance of large
groups of Volunteers led by men who often invited arrest, to secret preparation
for military conflict by a small group of dedicated Volunteers'.[39] The conscription threat fulfilled the worst fears of those in Lloyd George's cabinet who had
warned against it. The RIC inspector general's report for April noted that 'the
Irish Volunteer movement has naturally gathered impetus from the general dread
of conscription'.[40] It was not only the Volunteers who had become exercised by
conscription; the Irish Party and the clergy also united in opposition to its introduction. In Belfast during May, a series of meetings was held outside the various
Catholic churches for the purpose of signing an anti-conscription pledge with
Devlin the principal speaker at the most important of these. In the face of nation-

alist intransigence, the British government decided to postpone the implementation of the military service law and at the same time exact retribution on those it held responsible for the failure of the measure. On the night of 17–18 May seventy-three prominent Sinn Féin members were arrested on the pretext that a German agent had been arrested off the coast of County Clare. In Belfast, apart from MacEntee, Denis McCullough and Robert Haskins were arrested and on the following day another Belfast activist, Dr Russell McNabb, was arrested in Cavan.[41] If anything, the arrests strengthened the position of the radicals in the party such as Harry Boland and Fr Michael O'Flanagan, who replaced the more moderating influence of people like Arthur Griffith.

Like MacEntee, Griffith had been deported to Gloucester Jail where he was to spend the best part of the next year. Among the other internees in Gloucester were Denis McCullough, Desmond FitzGerald and Thomas Dillon. The prison regimen in Gloucester was nothing like that in Dartmoor or Lewes. Internees were allowed to receive mainstream Irish newspapers and they corresponded freely with the outside world, albeit under the watchful eye of the censor. In July, Denis McCullough wrote to his wife, describing the conditions:

> Every Saturday the water is more or less hot, so practically everybody goes out to the bath on that morning. We get back about 6.30 and get a clean towel every morning. Then we have a few minutes to complete dressing, when the signal is given for morning prayers by our chaplain (Pierce McCann) about 6.45. Immediately afterwards breakfast comes in at 7 o'clock and we divide up into our usual groups, e.g A Griffiths [sic] and Joe McGuinness; Desmond FitzGerald and Dr Dillon; Jas Dolan and Pearse [Pierce] McCann; Ginger, Tom Hunter and myself. Seán McEntee [sic] and Jos McBride dine by themselves in their own cells. Seán used to take his meals with FitzGerald and Dillon, but after a little altercation we had one day he broke off and retired to his solitary state.[42]

Unfortunately the cause of the altercation with Dillon and FitzGerald was never revealed. Most of MacEntee's own postal correspondence was concerned with the publication of his poetry and his prospects of being nominated as a Sinn Féin candidate at the general election. Once the Representation of the People Bill had been enacted in February it was likely that a poll would take place before the end of the year.[43] Throughout September rumours and counter-rumours swept the prisons concerning the ratification of candidates for the election. One of the difficulties facing the Sinn Féin standing committee was that it had to come to some accommodation with Labour, which was threatening to contest some fifteen seats.[44]

Harry Boland had been assigned the task of placating the Labour interest as well as being chief broker in the selection process. What concerned MacEntee most was not *if* he would be nominated but *where* he would be nominated. For example, he rejected any attempts to make him stand in his native city. McCullough wrote to his wife on 1 September asking her 'to write to Mr P

Whelan, Coroner, Monaghan for me. Seán Mac absolutely refuses to allow his name to go forward for the Belfast job, but would accept one down there if offered to him.'[45] MacEntee's reluctance was based on his intimate knowledge of Joe Devlin's strength in West Belfast; Devlin routed de Valera in the ensuing contest, proving that MacEntee's political instincts were already maturing. The first batch of candidates was selected on 12 September, prompting more anxiety in Gloucester. McCullough, evidently bitter that de Valera had been chosen for Belfast, wrote: 'Seán Mac and myself were not good enough for Barney and his friends, and as he could not have it for himself, he saw to it that we wouldn't get the chance. We are good enough to do this kind of thing though, apparently.' MacEntee's hopes rested on him being selected in one of the Monaghan constituencies but by mid-September this looked unlikely. A local businessman, Bernard O'Rourke, was the favourite for the position but doubts were expressed in some quarters as to his suitability: 'Many share the opinion that his past record as a staunch advocate of the constitutional movement and the Irish Party may render his candidature a trifle distasteful to the republican advocates.'[46] On 28 September, the local newspaper the *Dundalk Democrat* announced the selection of 'Mr Shaun McEntee [sic] as Sinn Féin candidate for South Monaghan'. Indeed the news came 'as a surprise to many in Carrick who are not "in the know" of Sinn Féin activities'.[47] News of his selection was slow to reach MacEntee. On 4 October, McCullough wrote: 'Seán MacE was a bit disappointed over that place I think, especially as a rotter of neither brains or importance got it, through the influence of his brother, a curate and our "friend" Fr O'Daly.' It was not until the end of that month that MacEntee wrote to his father to relay the good news: 'I received this morning an official intimation from Henry Boland that I have been sanctioned as official candidate for South Monaghan at the General Election. I will reply accepting the nomination, though how one is to fight an election cooped up in prison passes my comprehension.' Despite his handicap, MacEntee proclaimed himself 'sanguine of success'.[48]

One month before the election, MacEntee received a progress report from his father whose optimism was somewhat guarded: 'We are doing fairly well here but I cannot say we will win.'[49] As the candidate was still interned, his father had enlisted the support of as many friends and family as were available, including MacEntee's school friend Padraic Gregory who paid tribute to him 'as the son of a man who devoted much time to the welfare of the Catholics of Belfast'. MacEntee's opponent, his former barrister, T.J. Campbell, quoted MacEntee's court-martial testimony to make his case: 'Being an Irishman, he thought that the economic and industrial future of his country could only be assured by such government as was enjoyed by the Empire's free dominions, and he (Mr. McEntee) recognised that the Home Rule Act was such a measure.'[50] The Redmondite local newspaper described the scene on polling day:

> South Monaghan election was one of the most hotly waged of the Irish election battles. In one day the Nationalists held as many as seven open-air

meetings. A feature of the election was the ceaseless activity of many clergy in the constituency who canvassed indefatigably for Sinn Féin. On polling day an army of Sinn Féin motor cars from Cavan and elsewhere was let loose on the constituency. Bodies of strange men equipped with bludgeons and hurley sticks appeared on the scene. Squads of these peaceable pilgrims collected about polling stations where their presence intimidated aged Nationalists.[51]

Indeed the presence of the clergy was one of the most salient features of the election recalled by MacEntee sometime later: 'When I was introduced as a political figure to the county I met many priests, indeed, I believe, more priests than laymen.'[52] Meanwhile, as the priests busied themselves campaigning, MacEntee 'returned each evening to [his] plank bed and fibre mattress undisturbed and unperplexed by those reflections which tend to afflict an ambitiously active candidate with insomnia'.[53]

The poet Patrick Kavanagh remembered 1918 as being 'more than a mere election. It was a battle of the New Ireland versus the old men and the servitude.'[54] MacEntee was returned with 7,524 votes to Campbell's 4,413. After the election, the victor wrote to his election agent, F.M. Duffy, in Carrickmacross to express his gratitude 'not only for the personal honour you have done me, highly indeed though I value that, but far above and beyond all personal considerations for the manly and patriotic part which through the exertions of her truly patriotic people South Monaghan has taken in the present great resurgence of the Irish Nation'.[55] The great resurgence to which MacEntee referred was the devastating victory won by Sinn Féin in the general election, which one historian has described as 'an upheaval in Irish politics comparable to that of the Parnell landslide in 1885'.[56] In total, the party won seventy-three seats (sixty-eight candidates were successful, five having represented more than one constituency) to the Irish Parliamentary Party's six. Less than a month after the election, on 21 January 1919, the newly elected Sinn Féin MPs carried out their intention of establishing a native Irish parliament, Dáil Éireann. Few of its members were in a position to attend. MacEntee, still confined in Gloucester, had succumbed to the influenza epidemic which swept the world between the spring of 1918 and early 1919. Thomas Dillon was the first internee to fall ill in October, followed by Denis McCullough, who blamed the governor of the prison for bringing it in.[57] By January 1919, twenty-eight men had been afflicted and had been removed to a nursing home; one of the men, Pierce McCann, also an elected MP, died.[58]

After his release in the spring of 1919, MacEntee was appointed vice-brigadier of the Belfast brigade of the IRA [previously Irish Volunteers] as the country descended, in the words of the RIC, into violence and lawlessness. With Joseph McKelvey and Seán O'Neill, he was responsible for organising the IRA during the Belfast pogroms of 1920–1. Despite his position on the executive of the IRA, MacEntee did little, if any, active service. This is borne out by a letter from Richard Mulcahy, chief of staff, to the Minister for Defence, Cathal

Brugha, in April 1921. Responding to a memorandum from MacEntee advising Brugha to modify instructions to the northern officers, Mulcahy disregarded the advice 'owing to his total disassociation with any Volunteer work' and 'otherwise his pacifist views generally'.[59] MacEntee abhorred the violence that he witnessed in Belfast and was grateful when de Valera summoned him back to Dublin to assist in the negotiations with Joseph Devlin which led to the Anti-Partition Pact of 1921, by the terms of which Sinn Féin and the Nationalist Party joined hands in fighting the elections in the new northern state. In the course of these negotiations, MacEntee got caught in what was one of the 'hottest ambushes' he had ever experienced: 'We took cover while the bullets hopped all around the street and I must say that, though it was probably his first experience of the kind, Devlin was as cool as could be.'[60] All this time MacEntee had been 'on the run'; his description and photographs, with the offer of a substantial reward, appeared in *Hue and Cry*.[61] He later explained how he had evaded capture:

> I grew a tooth-brush moustache, took to wearing a bowler hat and by padding one shoulder of my coat, lowering the heel on one of my boots and adopting a stick for walking purposes, contrived to look like a victim of the Great War that I was able to move around Belfast fairly freely even when the search was keenest. At this time I rarely slept more than three or four nights in the same house. But generally contrived, however, to get a billet somewhere in a Unionist neighbourhood – much too respectable to harbour a republican and therefore more or less free from the nocturnal activities of the RIC and military raiding parties who visited my home weekly.

Though MacEntee had been selected as one of the republican candidates for West Belfast in the Northern election, de Valera retained his services in Dublin in order to organise a special propaganda department for northeast Ulster. Together with some hand-picked staff, he published *The Unionist*, advocating 'the preservation of the ancient unity of Ireland'.[62]

While in Gloucester, MacEntee had been corresponding with his future wife, Margaret Browne, whom he had met in 1917 at a Sinn Féin *céilí*.[63] They cemented their friendship after a subsequent meeting in Denis McCullough's house. Like her future husband, Margaret Browne had been involved in the 1916 Rising, having been commissioned by Seán MacDermott to bring the signal for the insurrection to Galway in 1916.[64] She had been a teacher but her 'national activities' compelled her to resign, becoming assistant secretary of the Belfast Boycott Department under Joseph MacDonagh. Her flat in Parnell Square had also been used for HQ work by Michael Collins, Rory O'Connor, Piaras Beasley, Gearoid O'Sullivan, Tom Cullen, Liam Tobin and others. They decided to get married before MacEntee went back to Belfast to speak during the last few days of the elections. The ceremony took place behind locked doors on 18 May 1921 at 7 p.m. in the University Church in St Stephen's Green. Two of the bride's brothers officiated and Austin Stack was MacEntee's best man. The guest list, which included Michael Collins, was a who's who of the revolution. As Joe

MacDonagh put it subsequently at the wedding supper, 'There's about £50,000 worth of high treason here.' The happy couple spent their honeymoon, first in the Marine Hotel in Sutton and then in Belfast where MacEntee was billed to speak at a final republican rally before the election.[65]

The elections were necessitated by the British government's passing of the Government of Ireland Act, 1920 which proposed to establish parliaments in Dublin and Belfast with powers of self-government. While the act did not satisfy the aspirations of Sinn Féin, it provided unionists with their own particular version of home rule. Partition of the country, the very thing that MacEntee had joined the Volunteers to prevent, now came into existence in spite of the continuing IRA violence. By the summer of 1921, both the IRA and the British government were ready to negotiate a truce. MacEntee saw opportunity in the peace, attempting 'for the third time since 1917 to resume practice as consulting engineer'.[66] He and a former 1916 comrade, Fergus O'Kelly, opened an office in Nassau Street. Having got his offices going, he was 'beginning to build up a nice practice' when politics again intervened. The Anglo-Irish Treaty of 6 December 1921 divided the Sinn Féin party and the IRA, resulting in the Civil War of 1922–3. The Treaty was debated in the Dáil over the course of fifteen days between 14 December and 7 January when a vote was taken to endorse its terms. MacEntee was almost a singular voice during the Treaty debates in drawing attention to the partition issue. He had been part of a specialist Sinn Féin committee to prepare the plenipotentiaries for the London talks with Lloyd George's government.[67] Despite this, the party had paid little attention to the Ulster question over the years, and was now ready to defer to the terms of a boundary commission to resolve the matter. It would not be the last time that MacEntee adopted the minority view: 'I have heard some say that they will vote for this Treaty because it is not a final settlement. But I am voting against it because I believe it will be a final settlement, and it is the terrible finality of this settlement that appals me.'[68]

MacEntee became deeply disillusioned after the ratification of the Treaty, which was compounded when it was indicated to him by a deputation from his constituency that because of his opposition, he would have to resign his seat in South Monaghan.[69] When Michael Collins, as Commander in Chief of the Free State Army, attacked the republican garrison in the Four Courts on 28 June, MacEntee decided to join up with the 'irregular' forces. As in 1916, he found himself defending a post office, this time in Marlborough Street through which on 5 July the main body of republicans was evacuated from the Hammam (now Gresham) Hotel where Cathal Brugha made his last stand: 'After he had ordered his men to surrender and seen them all off the premises, Brugha ran out of the building, gun at the ready, and was instantly shot down. He died that evening in the Mater Hospital.'[70] Having made his way home to 60 Pembroke Street, MacEntee was asked by Tom Barry's wife, Leslie, to take charge of an attempt to tunnel in to Mountjoy Jail to secure the escape of the republican leaders – including Barry, Rory O'Connor and Liam Mellows – imprisoned after the surrender at the Four Courts.

[A]fter making all the plans and securing what materials and equipment I could I started on the job with a picked squad of men. We started our work in a house in Glengariff Parade, into which we had smuggled ourselves, tools and men, at night. Matters went alright for about 30 hours and we had sunk a shaft deep enough to allow us to pass under the prison wall and had begun our tunnel when the Free State troops under the command of Commandant Joe O'Reilly – subsequently Mr Cosgrave's personal 'Aide' – swooped down on us. They had a couple of armoured cars and machine guns and we were, apart from that, greatly outnumbered. As the rest of the men were being taken out I saw a chance and slipped under the flooring of the house, where I covered myself with earth. I just heard the cars moving off, I thought, when I heard someone shouting 'Where's MacEntee?' and they stopped and back again came O'Reilly and the others searching for me. I was eventually discovered, brought to Kilmainham and afterwards to Gormanstown [sic], where I regret to say I remained for the rest of the Civil War.[71]

MacEntee's eventual release from internment in Gormanston in the spring of 1923 was facilitated by the mayor of Wexford, Richard Corish, who refused to pay the contractors of a street lighting scheme for the town until the planning engineer had passed the work as satisfactory.[72] This allowed MacEntee out on parole, which he broke after Desmond FitzGerald secured his safe passage to France where he spent a second, and more authentic, honeymoon.[73]

After the Civil War, MacEntee could not resist the lure of politics and was again elected treasurer of Sinn Féin along with Cathal Brugha's widow, Caitlín. It was a difficult time for republicans; de Valera remained in prison until the summer of 1924 and many of their leaders had been killed in the Civil War. MacEntee too found the new political dispensation difficult. He was unsuccessful in the general election of August 1923 and in the by-election of 1924. Nevertheless, de Valera placed much faith in his abilities. He wrote to MacEntee in advance of the December 1924 by-election to persuade him to assume responsibility for a Sinn Féin organising committee, in the face of evident hesitation on MacEntee's part, stating that he 'felt more and more loth to abandon the idea of having the Committee under your direction. The work you have outlined for the Committee is the work we are all waiting to have done. I realise, of course, the magnitude of the task involved. Could you not hold on for a while and set it going on the right lines, and prepare an understudy to take your place after a while?'[74] When the special conference convened at the Rotunda on 9 March 1926 to discuss the motion put down by de Valera to allow republican representatives to attend the Dáil if the oath of allegiance were removed, MacEntee spoke in its favour, extolling the virtues of his chief:

For over four years now we have been engaged in a losing battle. What some may say is four years in the life of a nation? It may be nothing, but it may be as significant as a century. In the two years of black '47 and 48 the

English came nearer to conquering this country than ever before. And the same might be said of the single month of August in 1914. From the day in June, 1917, that Éamon de Valera, a prisoner whose sagacity, whose fore-sight, whose courage had forced the gates of England's prisons and won freedom for himself and his comrades; from that day that he came back their chosen leader to become the leader of the Irish people, to that day in June 1921 that he Proclaimed President of the Irish Republic and said in the Mansion House of the first city of the English Pale, to receive the Commander-in-Chief of the British who came to negotiate a truce at his hands, was but four years. Four years, nothing some will say in the life of a nation, yet in those four years this nation, under this man's guidance, came nearer to the crowning victory than it had ever done in all the long centuries of warfare and of suffering that had preceded.[75]

When the motion was defeated, MacEntee's loyalty to de Valera resulted in him becoming one of the founding members of de Valera's new party, Fianna Fáil, inaugurated two months later in the La Scala theatre 'when the crowd over-flowed on the street outside. So massive and enthusiastic was the response it seemed as if some unspoken call had been answered.'[76]

FIANNA FÁIL

The party that de Valera led away from Sinn Féin in 1926 became, in a relatively short time, a rigorously disciplined and meticulously organised group that was committed to achieving electoral success. Indeed what made Fianna Fáil a potent and effective opposition was its unwavering discipline.[77] At its inaugural árd fheis, the party leader outlined the quality he wanted above all from each member of the nascent organisation: 'The first thing we want is loyalty to our cause ... we want a proper *esprit de corps* in our ranks so that the enemy will not find anything ... in order to disintegrate us.'[78] And although the party did well to harness the sup-port of the republican malcontents who shared its detestation of the oath of alle-giance, it also enlisted a large constituency dismayed by the social and economic policies of the Cumann na nGaedheal government.[79] The party's publicity depart-ment issued 'Notes for speakers' which attempted to delineate the Fianna Fáil position on a number of issues. Particular stress was given to social and econom-ic policy.[80] At the foundational meeting of the party on 16 May 1926 at the La Scala theatre in Dublin, seven aims of the organisation were announced, which included: 'To make the resources and wealth of Ireland subservient to the needs and welfare of all the people of Ireland'; 'To make Ireland, as far as possible, eco-nomically self-contained and self-sufficing'; 'To establish as many families as practicable on the land', and 'To carry out the Democratic Programme of the First Dáil'.[81] This emphasis on social and economic policy was one of a number of defining differences between the respective approaches of Fianna Fáil and the government party, Cumann na nGaedheal. Of course, the principal difference between the parties remained the enduring, and often violently contentious, one concerning the Free State's constitutional relationship with Britain. In fact, it could be said that economic policy was informed by this very consideration. While the Cumann na nGaedheal government's preference was for free trade, underpinned by a maximisation of agricultural incomes, relying almost exclusively on the British market, Fianna Fáil resorted to the axioms of economic nationalism favoured by Arthur Griffith. Cumann na nGaedheal policy, meanwhile, was more in line with the strategy adopted by John Redmond and John Dillon in 1915 for a home rule administration.[82] In order to prevent a flight of capital to the British money market, Cumann na nGaedheal adopted an extremely conservative monetary policy designed to keep income tax rates lower than those pertaining in the United Kingdom, and to keep public spending to a minimum.[83] This policy resulted in a heavy reliance on regressive taxation, the most important of which were customs and excise duties on standard items such as beer, spirits and tobacco. According to one historian, Cumann na nGaedheal's budgetary policy helped to consolidate the Civil War division by favouring the classes that had supported the Treaty at the expense of the poorer sections of the community from which the republicans drew much of their strength.[84] In contrast, Fianna Fáil committed itself to a programme of industrial development, and the success of the party's strategy was reflected in its electoral performance between 1927 and 1933, when a rapid rise in its support can be discerned in urban working-class constituencies.[85] That is not to say that the party courted a class-conscious electorate. Its appeals to that stratum of Irish society were made from a desire to embrace an anti-class platform which would appeal to that more nebulous constituency: the 'plain people of Ireland'.

From October 1927, when the party entered the Dáil, Seán Lemass vigorously provided the theoretical justification for the party's economic principles.[86]Although Lemass is justifiably regarded as the most important figure in the development of the party's economic thinking, the issue was far too important to be left to one individual alone. MacEntee, de Valera, James Ryan and Hugo Flinn contributed strongly to debates on social and economic policy in the Dáil.[87] Unsurprisingly, the guard of unanimity slipped occasionally and subtle differences in political philosophy, as well as economic policy, appeared but scarcely to the extent that they would later when the party entered government. Richard Dunphy has illustrated that there existed limitations to Fianna Fáil's radicalism, and that inconsistencies emerged in its position, notably on the issues of private property; the role of the state; the role of banking and financial institutions; and finally, on taxation.[88] However, Dunphy's synopsis confuses the notion of radicalism as an end in itself with the ultimate goal of the party which was to attain power in order to advance policies it saw as being in the national interest. He regards the party's failure to address coherently its attitude to taxation, for example, as amounting to 'an important contradiction within Fianna Fáil'. This contradiction was personified, according to Dunphy, by the contrasting approaches of Lemass and MacEntee: 'It is the persistent tension between MacEntee's conservatism and the greater political astuteness and opportunism of

Lemass which was to condition both the achievement and limitations of Fianna Fáil ...'[89] Again, this is a somewhat reductive assessment, which presupposes that Fianna Fáil's radicalism would define its achievement. It is a premise not uncommon in much of the writing on the political accomplishment of Fianna Fáil.[90] The point does, however, draw attention to the difference in emphasis – as well as providing a rather superficial appraisal – of the individual political philosophies of Lemass and MacEntee.

Dunphy is certainly right to assign considerable importance to taxation. Taxation policy was a central, and perhaps even a sensitive, issue for Fianna Fáil before it entered Dáil Éireann. An election advertisement for Cumann na nGaedheal during the September 1927 campaign was unambiguous about what it saw as Fianna Fáil's intentions if successful. It doubted the party's ability to get support in raising a new national loan and maintained that 'Fianna Fáil won't borrow the money, because they cannot. They can only get it by imposing heavier taxation on the Irish people.'[91] In a campaign dominated by questions of security, and by Fianna Fáil's fealty to the very instruments of the state it wished to serve, it is telling that the taxation issue was regarded as a potential Achilles' heel. The theme of promoting a stable political environment in which investors might repose full confidence was one which the government exploited and one it clearly felt made Fianna Fáil vulnerable.[92] In turn, Fianna Fáil used the unemployment problem to counter accusations of radicalism and communism by stressing that by tackling unemployment they would also be tackling potential unrest and subversion.[93] The party was also keen to display its support of socially ameliorative measures. Once inside the Dáil, Fianna Fáil supported a number of motions that sought to tackle the causes and relief of unemployment. One such motion put down by the Labour deputy Daniel Morrissey maintained 'That the [Government] measures ... for the relief of unemployment are insufficient and ought to be extended immediately'.[94] Fianna Fáil nominated speakers to contribute to upcoming Dáil motions in party meetings, and at the standing committee meeting of 18 October 1927, it was decided that '"the Chief" would speak first [indicating the magnitude of the motion], followed by Lemass, Hugo Flinn and Tom Derrig and any others who might like to speak'.[95] MacEntee accepted this invitation and contributed freely to the ensuing debate. Whereas the government response (as articulated by the Minister for Finance, Ernest Blythe) was very much in keeping with Department of Finance orthodoxy: 'If we expend money for the relief of unemployment on works that are not fully economic or fully remunerative, then we are placing a burden on industry and we are necessarily causing unemployment in some other direction', the opposition deputies viewed the matter as a trenchant indictment of the government's economic policies and as an opportunity to expound their own economic imperative, namely protectionism or economic nationalism.[96]

De Valera used the debate to outline a major shift in economic thinking from a potential new government, and to commit his party to an important social policy axiom: 'We stand firmly on the principle that it is the duty of a modern state under modern conditions to see that work is available for those willing to work.'[97] This view was endorsed by the wider Fianna Fáil organisation. During the second árd fheis, one of the resolutions ratified was: 'That ... Fianna Fáil affirms that it is the duty of the state to provide employment under proper conditions, for all its citizens who are able to work, and to provide maintenance for those it cannot provide with work'.[98] The subtlety of the discrepancy between party hierarchy undertaking and grassroots' aspiration barely concealed the fact that Fianna Fáil was now providing the electorate with a more national alternative to the Labour Party (Labour had won less than a quarter the number of Dáil seats attained by Fianna Fáil in the September 1927 general election: thirteen to fifty-seven).[99] During the June 1927 general election Labour had dismissed Fianna Fáil's economic programme as consisting 'only of a few items taken without acknowledgement from the programme of the Labour Party'.[100] Labour did not argue with the content of Fianna Fáil's programme; rather, it doubted that the programme would be executed. It was an argument that was bound to fail. As one commentator has put it: 'The Labour Party complained that FF [sic] had stolen its policies. That was to miss the point. F[ianna] F[áil]'s appeal lay not in this or that piece of social or economic policy, but in identifying itself as the only realistically "national" party. By attempting to compete with F[ianna] F[áil] a Labour Party, which could never hope to appeal to the large constituency of petty bourgeois radicalism that existed in the countryside, hopelessly caricatured and thus ultimately vindicated the F[ianna] F[áil] approach.'[101] MacEntee also used the motion on unemployment to castigate the government's apparent inadequacies on the social policy front, while announcing his party's own plans; but, intriguingly, his attack focused on the issue of excessive taxation. Echoing Blythe's stated distrust of unremunerative expenditure, he made explicit the difference between Fianna Fáil's policy and that of the government:

> We stand for the cutting down of unreproductive expenditure, but we do not want some person to say: 'Oh, you want to reduce the old age pensions.' We do not stand for that. We believe that public money spent to enable the citizens to maintain themselves according to a decent standard will be productive in the end. We believe that all the money spent on social services and on public health will be better in the end, because a healthy nation is a wealthy one.[102]

MacEntee went further, suggesting the establishment of an independent commission (i.e. one not populated by civil servants) to look into economies in the public service; that the 'monetary policy of the Government should be framed so as to place Irish capital at the disposal of Irish enterprise'; and that a development commission be set up to consider the 'whole question of national development ... so that whatever money is expended will provide the greatest amount of employment'. MacEntee's contribution to the debate enunciated some of Fianna Fáil's core economic beliefs at this time. While Lemass had largely concentrated on the quantifiable benefits of economic nationalism in the form of tariff protection,

MacEntee derided the government's lack of an independent fiscal policy. This was a more emphatic expression of economic nationalism, and possibly an approach more likely to appeal to the visceral anti-British element of the party's grassroots, than Lemass's more careful distinction between Irish and foreign-owned industry. MacEntee insisted that, while some foreign capital was welcome, it 'has [also] been a menace to the peaceful development and advancement of other countries'.[103] For a country to develop peacefully, in MacEntee's opinion, it did not need foreign capital and the attendant cultural and political links that it brought with it. Those political links certainly had a strong resonance for Irish nationalists who, as Meenan has noted, long held as 'an article of faith that Ireland had been over-taxed under British rule and that the country could be administered more cheaply under native rule'.[104]

De Valera, too, called for the establishment of a body to look into the financial affairs of the state. Like MacEntee, he visualised it as a body of apolitical economic experts.[105] On 16 November 1927, the government duly set up a committee on the relief of unemployment. W.T. Cosgrave, President of the Executive Council, outlined its terms: 'To consider and report as to the steps that might be taken for the immediate relief of unemployment, regard being had on the one hand to the need for avoiding any undue strain on the resources of agriculture and industry, and on the other to the fact that the continued existence of abnormal unemployment involves in itself a severe economic loss'.[106] In December 1927, the Fianna Fáil leadership failed to disguise its scepticism when it wrote to all TDs and cumainn seeking suggestions for local schemes which could be put before it: 'We do not believe that the committee was appointed to deal seriously with the unemployment problem, but we consider it important they should not be in a position to report that nothing can be done or that no practical schemes were brought to their attention.'[107] In the event, the terms of the committee proved restrictive and handcuffed any thoughts of alternative and innovative ideas being put forward to government. Its first interim report, which appeared in January 1928, failed to investigate the causes or the exact level of unemployment and ruled out proposals that it considered matters of government policy.[108] This failed to satisfy Fianna Fáil, and calls continued from the opposition benches for a committee to examine, not only unemployment, but the general economic position. Cosgrave acquiesced by setting up an all-party committee of the Dáil on 5 December 1928 to 'inquire into the general economic situation in Saorstát Éireann' and 'To report how best, having regard to the relative contribution which might reasonably be expected by way of taxation or otherwise from the various sections of the community, the economic situation may be improved and additional employment provided'.[109] Somewhat predictably, the committee's ship ran aground after a short time, principally over the issue of tariffs on wheat, and reflected, according to Fanning, 'the widening gulf between free traders and protectionists following Fianna Fáil's entry into the Dáil'.[110]

Fianna Fáil's strong commitment to social development was also apparent on a number of occasions during the party's time in opposition. One such instance involved a private member's bill put down by deputy Tadhg Murphy in regard to what he described as the 'inadequate' provisions made for widows and orphans, requesting the Executive Council to prepare and present a report upon schemes of insurance and estimates of the cost.[111] MacEntee was eager to support the motion 'on behalf of Fianna Fáil' and in so doing to promulgate the party's faith in state action: 'It is the duty of the state to redress that inadequacy, and in doing so not to do violence to the self-respect and the feelings of those whose necessity or poverty compels them to have recourse to public relief ...'[112] He quoted liberally from the principal recommendations of the Commission on the Relief of the Destitute and Sick Poor, established by the Minister for Local Government and Public Health in 1925, and which reported in 1927. Social policy provision or, more precisely, the lack thereof, also allowed 'the Republican Party' to revisit its revolutionary credo, while exposing the ruling party's abandonment of such aims. As MacEntee put it in the Dáil: 'This is a motion ... most of us on both sides of the House and on the Labour benches are already committed by public declarations, which we made over eight years ago – public declarations which I hope we all regard as binding and which we will take at least the first step to honour.'[113] In fact, the new party had a ready-made stockpile of rhetorical armour that it was keen to utilise at every opportunity. Fianna Fáil speakers, both inside and outside the Dáil, alluded with impunity to the Democratic Programme of 1919; to the 1916 proclamation; and to the speeches of James Connolly and Arthur Griffith. MacEntee made it clear that the amount being expended by the government on the social services was not only inadequate, it gave the impression that Ireland cared less for its citizens than other developed countries did for theirs: 'Practically every important country in Europe [has] increased their national expenditure upon social services within the past three or four years. I am sure that nobody in this House will advocate that we should have less care for our citizens than those states have.'[114]

If it was its consistency and unanimity in opposition that made Fianna Fáil an effective voice in the Dáil from August 1927, MacEntee, more than any of his colleagues, generously used the stick of taxation policy to beat the government. This was invariably linked to government wastefulness in administration, particularly in regard to the salaries of senior civil servants and the public service in general. Dunphy postulates that MacEntee's attacks on the government's taxation policy were ideologically motivated, and that they created a contradiction between Fianna Fáil's commitment to increase social services and to involve the state in the provision of employment. But speeches attacking the alleged extravagance of the Cosgrave government were an important and frequently utilised part of the Fianna Fáil arsenal, as well as providing continuity with nationalist economic assumptions expressed by both Sinn Féin and earlier by the Irish Parliamentary Party.[115] Whether MacEntee's repeated attack on the government's taxation policy came from an ideological standpoint or merely was another rhetorical arrow cannot be assessed without considering fully his performance in government. It is, however, an important distinction between his approach and that of Lemass. In June 1928, MacEntee reiterated the party's opposition to the government's economic policy: 'We feel that the present position of the country and the tax-paying community is such that unless some very significant allevia-tion of the burdens imposed upon them is granted, that industry will be unable to thrive, will be unable, in fact, to survive …'[116]

MacEntee was more dubious than many of his Fianna Fáil colleagues about the principle of state intervention. If, as one commentator has asserted, 'Lemass's primary assumption was that individuals constitute themselves first as part of a national grouping and only on this basis can economic policy be eval-uated',[117] MacEntee's primary assumption was that individuals had a communal responsibility independent of, and paramount to, the state's responsibility to them. One example during his time in government reinforces the point. Reacting to strikes in the state-owned sugar company in 1937, MacEntee believed that 'if the state on behalf of the people opened the sugar factories it has an equal right, and indeed a duty, the moment *they cease to serve the needs of the people fair-ly*, to close them also' (emphasis added).[118] He contended that strikes in a nation-alised industry were 'unpatriotic and unfair' and that there was 'no just reason' that those involved should be employed by the state again. Similar rhetoric would be used by MacEntee as Minister for Industry and Commerce in the first two years of the Emergency, when a series of strikes threatened certain essential services.

During the 1932 election campaign, MacEntee returned to the issue of waste and high taxation. He claimed that the government stood for 'taxation before economy' and that Fianna Fáil stood for 'economy before taxation'. Again Lemass, possibly being more alert to the likely effect of Fianna Fáil's social pro-gramme, was forced to qualify such attacks in order to leave the door open to increased taxation: '… having saved every possible penny and if there was still a deficiency, then, only, should be considered the imposition of additional taxa-tion'. Lemass was also committed to relieving unemployment through state works. He told a meeting in Wynn's Hotel, Dublin in 1931 that protection, an independent currency and a state housing policy could absorb a significant ele-ment of the unemployed.[119] Despite such subtle differences in the economic pri-orities of two of the more important figures in the party, Fianna Fáil's great strength in opposition lay in its vigorous unanimity, its slightly constitutional subversiveness and its monolithic repetition of its position on state sovereignty. The party's National Executive was made up of Lemass, MacEntee, Seán T. O'Kelly, P.J. Ruttledge, Gerry Boland and de Valera.[120] De Valera, endorsing the reappointment of his colleagues at the 1928 árd fheis, spoke glowingly of their aptitude and ability: 'They possess the attributes that constitute the right type for work of this kind. They are men of independent opinion in council, and then, when any decision is arrived at, they are loyal in carrying it out.'[121] This proved to be a characteristically astute reading of their personalities; but whether their independent opinions would be voiced while the party was singing from the same opposition hymn sheet was a moot point. MacEntee was also one of two honorary treasurers (with James Ryan) as well as party whip in the Dáil, while Lemass and Boland were the honorary secretaries of the party. In September 1927, Fianna Fáil set up special committees shadowing the various government departments. The committees were designed to 'give close study to the work of the different Government departments with a view to drafting a detailed policy for the party regarding each department, and compiling a dossier of all the relevant facts, figures and quotations necessary to sustain the case for [its] policy'.[122] Initially there was much overlapping of personnel between these committees: MacEntee, for one, was a member of both the committees on Industry and Commerce and Justice. He did not become a member of the Finance committee until December of that year, joining Ryan (who was chairman), de Valera, Lemass, P.J. Little (vice-chairman), Tomás Derrig, M.J. Kennedy, Thomas O'Reilly, Ruttledge and Flinn as full-time members. A long discussion took place on financial policy at this meeting and it was decided to broaden the committee's membership to include the chairmen of all other committees and the party whips. This decision amounted to early recognition by the party of the importance of Finance and the need to co-ordinate the various committees' activities with Finance, as would be the case in government.

Early in 1928 the special committees were reorganised further.[123] Their resultant shape bore a striking resemblance to the departments of government after March 1932. MacEntee became the chairman of the Finance committee, Ryan moved to Agriculture, Frank Aiken to Defence, and Lemass remained in Industry and Commerce. It was also decided that the chairmen of the special committees would provide a written report of business coming up for discussion in the Dáil concerning their respective areas of interest. It had been customary for the leader of the opposition to give party policy on a particular question in the Dáil, leaving the other members of the party to argue the finer points. Each chairman of the various committees would now shadow his government counterpart during debate. De Valera's shadow cabinet also undertook to formulate party policy in their specialised area. Thus, when Fianna Fáil assumed power the party had a ready-made cabinet which should, in theory, have been on top of its collective brief. MacEntee's position, however, was slightly atypical. Because Lemass generally took up the argument relating to most socio-economic issues, MacEntee, more often than not, had to defer to his younger colleague. The idea of a specialist shadow cabinet in no way made the allocation of ministries a *fait accompli*. None of the ministers knew of their portfolios before being appointed. MacEntee, for one, was not disappointed. He said in later life: 'I was glad to be Minister for Finance; it would have been my own choice.'[124]

MacEntee entered Merrion Street as one of the key figures in Fianna Fáil. He had acted as party whip and had served the party's National Executive from its inception. Along with Ryan, Lemass and Boland, he undertook key administrative functions as Fianna Fáil became accustomed to life inside the Dáil. He had a significant role to play both opposing government policy and formulating his own party's response. His political rhetoric endorsed his party's economic nationalism. Espousing shibboleths of that particular credo, with some considerable vigour, he maintained resolutely that Ireland was overtaxed under British rule, that foreign capital was morally and culturally degrading and that the administration of government was wasteful and extravagant. These arguments had the weight of nationalist history behind them, having been enunciated by everyone from the Repeal movement in the first half of the nineteenth century, to the Irish Parliamentary Party under Parnell and Redmond, to Michael Collins, who had demanded the repayment of £400 million in overtaxation during the Treaty negotiations of 1921.[125] To the public servants in the Department of Finance, however, MacEntee remained an unknown quantity with 'shady credentials', and his party's election thus posed the first real challenge to the supremacy of the department in government.

NOTES

1. M. McInerney, 'Seán MacEntee: republican leader', *Irish Times*, 22 July 1974.
2. S. McConville, *Irish Political Prisoners 1848–1922: Theatres of War* (London, 2003), p.509.
3. Éamon de Valera Papers, UCDA 150/3559. See also Ferriter, *Judging Dev*, pp.344–5.
4. Ferriter, *Judging Dev*, p.30.
5. R. Brennan, *Éamon de Valera: A Memoir* (Dublin, 1950), p.102. Frank Thornton recalled de Valera bringing the Volunteers to attention when Austin Stack and Con Collins arrived but surprisingly does not mention MacNeill. In a separate account of the same incident, Brennan included MacEntee in this group but this does not tally with the timing of MacEntee's deportation which was a number of weeks after MacNeill's. Also see UCDA P150/530, note on Thornton's memoir that reads: 'This account by Frank Thornton does not tally with the President's [de Valera's] recollection of the same event.'
6. UCDA P67/ 793, Copy letter from MacEntee to Seamus McCall, April 1952.
7. Ibid.
8. M. Tierney, *Eoin MacNeill: Scholar and Man of Action, 1867–1945* (Oxford, 1980), p.243.
9. BMH WS 510, Frank Thornton.
10. UCDA P67/479, 'De Valera: the man I knew' by Seán MacEntee published in *Iris Fianna Fáil* (party journal) in winter 1975 edition. Also see UCDA P67/479, Seán MacEntee, 'The aristocrat without any pretensions', *Irish Press*, 30 August 1975.
11. UCDA P67/45 and BMH WS 510, Frank Thornton.
12. McConville, *Irish Political Prisoners*, p.518.
13. R. Brennan, *Allegiance* (Dublin, 1950), p.115.
14. Ibid., p.119. See also UCDA LA1/G/150, Eoin MacNeill Papers, MacNeill to his sister Margaret, Woodtown Park, Rathfarnham, 26 March 1917.
15. Quoted in M. Laffan, *The Resurrection of Ireland: The Sinn Féin Party, 1916–1923* (Cambridge, 1999), pp.96–7.
16. UCDA P67/4 8 June 1917, Copy letter from Baron Mounteagle to Henry Duke, Chief Secretary for Ireland.
17. UCDA P67/6, Copy of the *Catholic Bulletin* (July 1917) includes an article, 'Events of Easter Week', giving short biographical accounts of some Irish prisoners, including MacEntee. He was described as 'one of the most highly gifted of the men connected with the rebellion. He was well known in Belfast and Dundalk, particularly in Irish Literary and Irish Volunteer circles. He possessed rare intellectual gifts, was an able and cultured speaker, and his poetry was of a very high order. His was a very lovable character, noted for courteousness and gentleness, but absolutely fearless where the honour of Ireland and her rights to full Nationhood were at stake.'
18. *Freeman's Journal*, 19 June 1917.
19. BMH WS 944, Michael Staines.
20. Cruise O'Brien, *Same Age as the State*, p.62.
21. UCDA P67/ 793, MacEntee to Seamus McCall, April 1952.
22. CO 904/103, Confidential police report as to the state of the city of Belfast for the month of June, 1917.
23. UCDA LA1/H/19 (20), Seán MacEntee, 42 Mill St, Belfast to MacNeill, 16 July 1917.

24. Laffan, *The Resurrection of Ireland*, p.107.
25. Quoted in ibid., p.110.
26. Police reports CO 904/23, Meeting at Drogheda, 22 July 1917.
27. *Weekly Irish Times*, 11 August 1917.
28. A. Quinlivan, *Philip Monahan: A Man Apart* (Dublin, 2006), p. 20.
29. CO 904/23, Meeting in Monaghan, 7 October 1917.
30. Laffan, *The Resurrection of Ireland*, p.117.
31. CO 904/23, Sinn Féin Convention held in the Round Room of the Mansion House, on Thursday and Friday, 25 and 26 October 1917.
32. F. O'Donoghue, 'Reorganisation of the Irish Volunteers, 1916–1917', *Capuchin Annual*, 1966.
33. R. Mulcahy, 'The Irish Volunteer Convention, 27 October 1917', *Capuchin Annual*, 1966.
34. CO 904/104, police reports for November and December 1917 in the city of Belfast.
35. National Library of Ireland [Hereafter NLI] Ms 24,357 (2), Papers of Irish National Aid and Volunteer Dependants' Fund. MacEntee to Irish National Aid Association, 19 September 1917.
36. Quoted in Laffan, *The Resurrection of Ireland*, p.124.
37. 'De Valera remembered', RTÉ Radio interview, 26 October 1983.
38. CO 904/105, police report for County Donegal, February 1918.
39. J. Augusteijn, *From Public Defiance to Guerrilla Warfare: The Experience of Ordinary Volunteers in the Irish War of Independence, 1916–1921* (Dublin, 1996), p.85.
40. CO 904/105 Inspector General's report for April 1918.
41. CO 904/106, police report for city of Belfast, 1 June 1918. MacEntee later claimed that his arrest was due to the fact that he 'had been very actively engaged in organising the Volunteer opposition to Lord French's conscription proposals'.
42. UCDA P120/54 (5), Denis McCullough Papers, McCullough to his wife, Agnes, 7 July 1918.
43. Laffan, *The Resurrection of Ireland*, p.151.
44. D. Fitzpatrick, *Harry Boland's Irish Revolution* (Cork, 2003), p.107.
45. UCDA P120/54 (5) Denis McCullough Papers, McCullough to his wife, Agnes, 1 September 1918.
46. Quoted in T. Dooley, *Inniskeen, 1912–1918: The Political Conversion of Bernard O'Rourke* (Maynooth Studies in Local History, 2004), p.54.
47. *Dundalk Democrat*, 28 September 1918.
48. CO 904 Box 164, First report of the correspondence of the Irish Internees covering July–October 1918. MacEntee to James McEntee, 31 October 1918.
49. CO 904, Letter from James McEntee, 89 King St, Belfast, 25.11.18.
50. *Dundalk Democrat*, 14 December 1918.
51. *Dundalk Democrat*, 21 December 1918.
52. UCDA P67/772, MacEntee to Rev. L. Marron, PP, Latton, Castleblayney, County Monaghan, 24 March 1966.
53. UCDA P67/773 (4), MacEntee to Erskine Childers, November 1970.
54. Quoted in Dooley, *Inniskeen, 1912–1918*, p.54.
55. CO 904, MacEntee to Duffy, 31 December 1918.
56. Laffan, *The Resurrection of Ireland*, p.164.
57. UCDA P120/54 (13), McCullough to his wife, Agnes, Thursday 17 October.
58. G. Plunkett Dillon, *All in the Blood: A Memoir of the Plunkett Family, the 1916 Rising and the War of Independence* (Dublin, 2006), p.272. See also Cruise O'Brien, *Same Age as the State*, p.29.
59. Mulcahy Papers UCDA P7/A/17 (175), Letter to the M/D [Minister of Defence, Cathal Brugha], 7/4/21.
60. UCDA P67/ 793, MacEntee to Seamus McCall, April 1952.
61. He was then described as 'of light, active build, with sallow complexion, colour of eyes uncertain'. The photographs were the same ones taken on his arrival at Dartmoor. UCDA P67/793, MacEntee to Seamus McCall, April 1952.
62. Ibid. Jimmy Good, then of the *Freeman's Journal* and subsequently of the *Irish Independent*, was editor and Aodh de Blacam, Fr O'Flanagan and Seán Lester were among the principal contributors to the paper.
63. The following is the full list of those he corresponded with during his time in Gloucester: James McEntee (father); Edward and Charles McEntee (brothers); Miss A. Mullen, Park Street, Monaghan; Miss K. Murphy, 8 Harriet Street, Lettercliffe, Sheffield; Miss Margaret Browne, 60 Pembroke St, Dublin; Miss Claire Lavery, 45 Mary Street, Belfast; Rev. T O'Mahony, Blackrock College, Dublin; Rev. J. Hassan, St Mary's Presbytery, King Street, Belfast; Mrs Ed Byrne (sister), Coalisland, County Tyrone and Miss Nancy [Wyse] Power, 21 Henry Street, Dublin.
64. BMH WS 322, Margaret Browne.
65. His entertaining account of their trip to Belfast can be found in UCDA P67/ 793, MacEntee to Seamus McCall, April 1952 and Cruise O'Brien, *Same Age as the State*, p.42.

66. UCDA P67/793, MacEntee to Seamus McCall, April 1952.
67. J. Bowman, 'Sinn Féin's perception of the Ulster question: autumn 1921', *Crane Bag*, vol. 4 (1980), pp.50–6.
68. *Dáil debates*, vol. 3, cols 152–8, 22 December 1921. See also M. Wall, 'Partition: the Ulster question, 1916–26', in T.D. Williams (ed.), *The Irish Struggle, 1916–26* (London, 1966).
69. UCDA P67/52 (2). See, for example, telegram from John Coleman, Castleblayney, 22 December: 'Unanimous voice in Monaghan wants ratification of the Treaty. Peace and good will not war. Support their views.'
70. M. Hopkinson, *Green Against Green: The Irish Civil War* (Dublin, 1988), p.124.
71. UCDA P67/793, MacEntee to Seamus McCall, April 1952. See also UCDA P67/773 (1), MacEntee to Tomás Uasal Ó Dochartaigh, September 1969 in relation to a biography of Cathal Brugha.
72. Cruise O'Brien, *Same Age as the State*, p.71.
73. Information supplied by Dr Garret FitzGerald.
74. UCDA P67/82, Éamon de Valera, 23 Suffolk Street to MacEntee, 22 Nassau Street, 7 October 1924.
75. Ibid.
76. MacEntee profile by Michael McInerney, *Irish Times*, 23 July 1974.
77. See E. O'Halpin, 'Parliamentary party discipline and tactics: the Fianna Fáil archives, 1926–32', *Irish Historical Studies*, xxx, 120 (November 1997).
78. Fianna Fáil archives [hereafter UCDA P176] UCDA P176/701.
79. The oath of allegiance was prescribed in article 4 for all elected members of the Irish Free State parliament. 'Faith and allegiance' had to be sworn primarily to the constitution; fidelity to the king was sworn by virtue of common citizenship with Britain and membership of the commonwealth. Following the Electoral Amendment Act, 1927, de Valera reluctantly led Fianna Fáil into the Dáil. One of the party's key linchpins throughout its years in opposition was its objective of removing the oath at the earliest possible convenience.
80. R. Dunphy, *The Making of Fianna Fáil Power in Ireland* (Oxford, 1995), p.86.
81. Fianna Fáil, *A national policy outlined by Éamon de Valera, delivered at the inaugural meeting of Fianna Fáil at La Scala Theatre, Dublin, May 1926* (Dublin, 1927). See UCDA P176/23 for material relating to the founding of Fianna Fáil and on policy pamphlets issued by the party.
82. E. O'Halpin, 'Politics and the state, 1922–32', in J.R. Hill (ed.), *A New History of Ireland, VII: Ireland, 1921–1984* (Oxford, 2003), p.113.
83. T.K. Daniel, 'Griffith on his noble head: the determinants of Cumann na nGaedheal economic policy, 1922–32', *Irish Economic and Social History*, vol. 3 (1976). See also J.W. O'Hagan, 'An analysis of the relevant size of the government sector: Ireland 1926–52, *The Economic and Social Review*, vol. 12 (1980), p.25.
84. Daniel, 'Griffith on his noble head'.
85. See H. Patterson, 'Fianna Fáil and the working class: the origins of the enigmatic relationship', *Saothar*, vol. 13 (1988).
86. See, in particular, NLI, Frank Gallagher Papers, MS 18,339. This document, written sometime in 1929/30, was perhaps the fullest expression of Lemass's faith in the protectionist system.
87. See B. Farrell, *Seán Lemass* (Dublin, 1981), p.29.
88. Dunphy, *The Making of Fianna Fáil Power*, p.103.
89. Ibid., p.9.
90. See also K. Allen, *Fianna Fáil and Irish Labour: 1926 to the Present* (London, 1997).
91. *Irish Times*, 1 September 1927.
92. P. Buckley, 'The Electoral Policies of Fianna Fáil, 1927–32' (Unpublished MA thesis, UCD, 1984), p.76.
93. See National Archives of Ireland [hereafter NAI], Taoiseach files S5972 on public demonstrations regarding unemployment in 1929.
94. *Dáil debates*, vol. 21, col. 378, 26 October 1927. Morrissey later joined Fine Gael.
95. UCD P176/452, 18 October 1927.
96. *Dáil debates*, vol. 21, col. 388, 26 October 1927.
97. Ibid., col. 396.
98. UCDA P176/351.
99. B.M. Walker (ed.), *Parliamentary Election Results in Ireland 1918–92* (Dublin, 1992).
100. Buckley, 'The electoral policies of Fianna Fáil', p.35.
101. Patterson, 'Fianna Fáil and the working class'.
102. *Dáil debates*, vol. 21, cols 809–12.
103. Quoted in Buckley, 'The electoral policies of Fianna Fáil', p.120.
104. Quoted in J.W. O'Hagan, 'An analysis of the relative size of the government sector', pp.17–35.
105. Ibid., p.127.

106. *Dáil debates*, vol. 21, cols 1391–2, 16 November 1927. See also NAI DT S5553 for minutes of meetings, etc.
107. Quoted in W. Murphy, 'In pursuit of popularity and legitimacy: the rhetoric of Fianna Fáil's social and economic policy, 1926–34' (Unpublished MA thesis, UCD 1998), p.28.
108. Buckley, 'The electoral policies of Fianna Fáil', p.123.
109. R. Fanning, *The Irish Department of Finance, 1922–1958* (Dublin, 1978), p. 201.
110. Ibid., p.202.
111. *Dáil debates*, vol. 28, col. 480, 17 October 1928.
112. Ibid., col. 487.
113. Ibid., col. 490.
114. Ibid., col. 492.
115. UCDA P67/345 (1). In early 1927, MacEntee was reported as saying 'The present government, which is extravagant and wasteful, would continue spending on the same lavish scale for a year or two, if allowed, until it and the people who subscribed to it found themselves in the bankruptcy court.' And during the 1932 election campaign, de Valera attacked what he regarded as the excessive salaries of civil servants, stating that 'no man was worth more than £1,000 a year'. Point seven of the Fianna Fáil election manifesto also promised to 'Take the necessary powers to eliminate waste and extravagance in public administration'.
116. *Dáil debates*, vol. 24, col. 250, 7 June 1928.
117. B. Girvin, *Between Two Worlds: Politics and Economy in Independent Ireland* (Dublin, 1989), p.83.
118. Quoted in Dunphy, *The Making of Fianna Fáil Power*, p.182.
119. Girvin, *Between Two Worlds*, p.85.
120. UCDA P176/355.
121. UCDA P176/742, 26 October 1928.
122. UCDA P176/452, Minutes of standing committee, 6 September 1927.
123. Ibid., 24 February 1928.
124. *Irish Times*, 24 July 1974.
125. See L. Kennedy, *Colonialism, Religion and Nationalism in Ireland* (Dublin, 1996), p. 46.

3

Guarding the Nation's Purse Strings

On 9 March 1932, following the first change of government in the Irish Free State, the new President of the Executive Council, Éamon de Valera, appointed his cabinet. It contained few surprises. The majority of the new ministers had been political allies of de Valera since the Civil War of 1922–3, if not before, and had been founding members of Fianna Fáil in 1926. De Valera did not consult his colleagues before their appointment; rather, he allocated the portfolios on his understanding of their particular interests.[1] Many of the new ministers had in fact been well prepared for their new roles by a period of five years in opposition when they were given a specialised brief and were expected to shadow their government counterpart in debate. Seán MacEntee was given perhaps the most prestigious government portfolio: Finance. Since the foundation of the state, and particularly after the enactment of the Ministers and Secretaries Act in 1924, the Department of Finance was widely regarded as the 'boss' department, controlling all government spending and acting as watchdog over other departments. Senior personnel in that department were invariably the brightest minds in the fledgling state apparatus, and Finance tended to attract the cream of the new recruits.[2]

This chapter is the story of MacEntee's performance as Minister for Finance from 1932 to 1939. These years were not only markedly turbulent and controversial years in Irish political history, but were also singularly turbulent and controversial years in international economic history. With Séan Lemass, the Minister for Industry and Commerce, and Dr James Ryan, the Minister for Agriculture, MacEntee formed a triumvirate of arguably the most capable ministers in the cabinet. Finance, however, promised to be an arduous portfolio, given the rapidly deteriorating international economic outlook and, more pertinently, the government's commitment to a raft of new policies. What did these policies reveal about the new government party? Did Fianna Fáil change markedly once it attained power and how consistent and unanimous was the party in implementing its programme?

FINANCE

By the time Fianna Fáil formally entered Dáil Éireann, the Department of Finance had established its pre-eminence as the 'boss' department. Indeed, Finance's status had its roots in the very foundation of the new state. On 16 January 1922, the British authorities officially handed over the reins of government to Michael Collins as Chairman of the Provisional government of the Irish

Free State.[3] On the following day, the Provisional Government allocated individual portfolios, with Collins himself taking charge of Finance. Collins' department was officially designated 'Finance and General' and was assigned the five Treasury departments hitherto operating in Ireland as well as two of the twenty-five departments of Irish government and nine of the seventeen branches of United Kingdom departments then functioning in Ireland.[4] The significance of the changeover was that it transferred more than just the apparatus of the government machinery; with it came long ingrained attitudes and assumptions conditioned by the Treasury's hegemonic status in government. This status had, if anything, been copper-fastened by the application of the Whitley Report to the administrative departments of the civil service in the aftermath of the 1914–18 war. The reorganisation that ensued from the acceptance of these reports culminated in the permanent secretary of the Treasury having the added role of permanent head of the civil service.[5] From the very beginning of the infant state, the Department of Finance displayed a strong willingness to co-ordinate the workings of the different departments of government which it contended, using the British system as its guide, was merely a regularisation of procedure. The presence of officials such as H.P. Boland, who had been schooled in the British system, ensured that the Treasury's influence would remain strong. One young Irish official recalled how Boland 'wanted us to become civil servants on the English model', referring to a particular dress code and recommending that editorials in the London *Times* be studied for literary style.[6] It is important to point out, however, as the historian of the department has done, that the Irish officials 'did not necessarily conceive of themselves … as applying an old system to their new, Irish circumstances; rather they were working a new, almost radically modern, system'.[7] That they thought of it in this way 'gave the initial structure and organisation of the Department of Finance a durability it otherwise might not have possessed'.

Another factor that contributed to the department's prestige was its personnel. From 1919, in the First Dáil, Michael Collins had been responsible for financial affairs, and on the setting up of the Provisional Government he held on to this brief as well as becoming the chairman of the government. The power and influence that came with this added responsibility, along with the reverence in which he was held by his supporters, reinforced the department's primacy.[8] After Collins's death in August 1922, W.T. Cosgrave assumed both roles on a permanent basis, having deputised for the latter since July when military duties forced Collins's absence.[9] Moreover, the officials entering the department tended to be the cream of their generation. Joseph Brennan and J.J. McElligott, both trained in the British civil service, went on to become secretaries of the department and, thereafter, the first and second governors of the Central Bank respectively. It is scarcely stretching the point to suggest that McElligott and Brennan had more of a cumulative influence on the development of the new state than many of the ministers who subsequently passed through the corridors of the department's Merrion Street offices. If McElligott became the *éminence grise* of Irish public policy, at least for the period of unbroken Fianna Fáil rule between 1932 and 1948, Brennan's reputation, too, was arguably enhanced by the accession of

Fianna Fáil to power.[10] He was frequently consulted on economic issues and was appointed to a number of important chairmanships by the new government.[11] Such respect shown towards the longer established civil servants went some way to easing the working relationship between de Valera's government and its new officials, a relationship which, before 1932, was characterised by suspicion and disdain.[12] One former civil servant has described how 'the senior men' in Finance feared their new minister 'might have leanings towards some of the unorthodox [economic] views that were surfacing at that time'.[13] Any such fears were soon allayed. MacEntee, in fact, formed a close relationship with his civil servants and, according to the same source, was a 'pillar of orthodoxy by the end of his period as Minister for Finance'.[14]

IN GOVERNMENT

The general election took place on 16 February 1932 in a tense and frenzied atmosphere. It produced a record turnout of 75 per cent.[15] Fianna Fáil won 72 seats, just short of an overall majority, but was able to form a government with the support of the Labour Party. Its election manifesto promised radical change: removal of the oath of fidelity; retention of the land annuities owed to Britain; organisation of manufacturing industry to meet the needs of the community; preservation of the home market; and encouragement of self-sufficiency in food supplies.[16] In his maiden speech to the Dáil as leader of Labour, William Norton outlined the social programme he expected from the new government. It included work or maintenance for 80,000 unemployed men and women, the construction of 40,000 houses, pensions for widows and orphans and the regulation of food prices.[17] Fianna Fáil had, in fact, already given a commitment to create 85,000 extra jobs in industry and to introduce pensions for necessitous widows and orphans.[18] Significantly, however, the party did not promise increased expenditure; rather, it vowed to reduce taxes and to make substantial economies in administration without reducing the social services.[19]

The assumption that Lemass was synonymous with Fianna Fáil's economic programme remained unhindered by MacEntee's appointment as Minister for Finance. A month after taking office, the party's champion, the *Irish Press*, was triumphantly announcing that Lemass's new economic policy would be revealed within a matter of days but, intriguingly, as Horgan has observed, it never appeared.[20] Instead, an economic policy committee was set up comprising Lemass, de Valera, James Ryan (Minister for Agriculture) and the Minister for Posts and Telegraphs, Senator Joseph Connolly.[21] MacEntee was not part of the original committee but was added in September (a time lapse that was probably prolonged by his absence through illness during late July and early August and to the lack of cabinet meetings held due to the Ottawa conference). The committee wasted little time in delineating the government's avowed desideratum. In its early meetings, it recommended heavy additional expenditure on roads and housing which the Executive Council subsequently endorsed. At its very first meeting on 16 May (attended by de Valera, Lemass and Connolly), it was agreed that a grant of £1 million would be provided for road making and that 'allocations from the grant be not conditional on local authorities bearing any part of the cost of the schemes'.[22] While it could well be the case that MacEntee's well-known aversion to large expenditure precluded him from the committee, such analysis is no more than speculation. The establishment of a 'cuts committee', moreover, in keeping with the party's pre-election vow to streamline the cost of government, promised to ease any budgetary difficulties that might have arisen from the government's new commitments through a reduction of the salaries of public servants.[23]

MacEntee's exclusion from the delegation that travelled to the Imperial Economic Conference in Ottawa, however, combined with his late entry onto the economic committee, has been cited as evidence of de Valera's intention to diminish the influence of the Department of Finance.[24] The point should be made, however, that de Valera, too, was missing from the Ottawa delegation when, as Minister for External Affairs, he might have been expected to attend.[25] Moreover, it is patently clear that Finance's role, as seen by the new president, was not one of policy development – that would come from the executive arm of government. The greater concern of de Valera's party with issues of social and economic policy undoubtedly made life more difficult for Finance, but there is little evidence that its powers were diluted in real terms. Nonetheless, de Valera was keen to have a more balanced chain of command within his cabinet, an arrangement that was reflected at all levels in the administration and this, allied to the number of new proposals being sanctioned by cabinet, probably meant that Finance's advice was not being sought – given the desire to expedite policy – where once it would have been. Indeed, enthusiastic colleagues of the Minister for Finance complained that 'legislation proposals were being held up by the Department of Finance', although they were unable to isolate specific cases.[26] This was perhaps more symptomatic of the lack of administrative experience of the new cabinet and of the fact that the department remained politically suspect to the government. In this respect, Finance's cause was scarcely furthered by the department's enduring association with the British Treasury, which had been reinforced during the Cumann na nGaedheal administration by the presence of a number of officials who had come to Dublin Castle on secondment. Their hostility towards the new government was probably best encapsulated by the declaration made by one official in July 1932 that the resulting trade (economic) war 'ought to be sufficient to achieve the desired object of discrediting and leading to the downfall of Mr de Valera's government'.[27] De Valera's strategic objectives – both domestic and international – were, therefore, conditioned by many considerations.

MacEntee's first few months in government certainly constituted a political baptism of fire. His illness in late summer was, according to one observer, due to fatigue and overwork: 'He wanted to see the files; he wanted memoranda on this, that and the other. In no time the presses in his room were chock-full of files and, being busy otherwise with meetings and interviews, he could barely find time in the early afternoon to run round to the Shelbourne Hotel for a sandwich and a glass of sherry, his favourite drink. The result was that he cracked up quite early on. I remember the shock of being told ... that he had been taken ill and had three doctors with him. I rushed out to Ballyboden [Willbrook Road] where he lived, to find that he had gone into a nursing home.'[28] This was probably not surprising given MacEntee's inexperience and the fact that a budget had to be prepared in less than three months from taking office, a task made more onerous by the worsening economic conditions which had necessitated a supplementary budget in November 1931. The new minister was presented with a memorandum by his officials in April outlining the gravity of the crisis and what it would mean for Fianna Fáil's stated objectives:

> The position ... is that the national income of the Saorstát has fallen seriously in recent years while, on the other hand, the real burden of taxation has been seriously increased. The situation cannot be remedied merely by increasing taxation; and it must not be overlooked that an attempt to find £3 million by new taxation would seriously interfere with the consumption of many commodities which are at present a source of very substantial revenue. Moreover, there are certain contingencies which, from the point of view of the Exchequer, must be kept in view ... the estimates to which reference is made ... make no provision for the increased expenditure contemplated on old age pensions or on other social services, on unemployment relief, housing, public health schemes, etc.[29]

The change of government did little to alter the view of the financial position held by the mandarins in Merrion Street, or as Fanning has put it: 'The same men continued to give the same advice.'[30] One thing to which the officials were not accustomed was the minister's prolix writing style; at lunchtime on budget day, while they busily set about pruning his speech, MacEntee enjoyed an early afternoon viewing at the Grafton Street cinema.[31] The budget itself represented the first major statement of economic policy by Fianna Fáil in government. In it, MacEntee outlined the new government's priorities: 'We shall have to secure rigorous economies in the existing administrative machine, and we may have to borrow. One thing, however, we shall not do. We shall not cut the social services, and we shall also, as far as may be possible, suit the burden to the back.'[32]The resulting budget was unashamedly redistributive. Contrary to MacEntee's opposition soundings, the standard rate of income tax was increased from three shillings and six pence to five shillings; corporation profits tax was also increased; £2.5 million was designated for unemployment relief through grants, local loans and public works; and housing schemes were to be financed to the extent of £5 million.

The budget also provided Fianna Fáil with an opportunity to begin the process of protecting Irish industry. The thrust of this policy derived from Lemass's department: 'My position would,' admitted MacEntee 'have been a hopeless one if the need of the revenue and the policy of the Minister for Industry and Commerce had not chanced to coincide.' Needless to say, the wishes of Finance and the policy of the Minister for Industry and Commerce rarely coincided thereafter. Many of the new duties, such as those on musical records, entertainments and outdoor sports activities including horse racing and greyhound coursing, indicated the spartan conditions prevailing, but the officials responsible for the measures contented themselves that 'in a period of national crisis like the present there can be no doubt that [they are] fully justified'.[33] Reaction to the party's first budget ranged from the ecstatic – the *Irish Press* – to the downright hostile – the *Irish Times*. The latter ran an editorial the day after the budget which ended with this apocalyptic thought: 'Even if Fianna Fáil's first Budget proves to be also its last, the injury to the nation's welfare and prospects must be almost irreparable.'[34] A similar view came from John J. Horgan, the somewhat incredulous and hyperbolic Irish correspondent of the British periodical *Round Table*: 'If a Glasgow Communist and a die-hard tariff reformer were merged into a single personality and, having somehow managed to escape certification, became Minister of Finance [sic] in the Irish Free State, the result would probably be somewhat similar to the budget introduced in the Dáil ... by Mr Seán MacEntee.'[35]

Looking back some time later on his first budget, MacEntee proudly boasted that '[it] was the very first Keynesian budget in this island'.[36] While MacEntee was certainly no Keynesian, and this assessment was a retrospective one, the budget he introduced in the Dáil on 11 May 1932 did reflect some of the English economist's beliefs at this time. Keynes said as much when he delivered a lecture in April of the following year at University College, Dublin: 'If I were an Irishman, I should find much to attract me in the economic outlook of your present government towards greater self-sufficiency.'[37] His endorsement, however, came with the following words of warning for the new government: 'I should ask if Ireland – above all if the Free State – is a large enough unit geographically, with sufficiently diversified natural resources, for more than a very modest measure of national self-sufficiency to be feasible without a disastrous reduction in a standard of life which is already none too high.'[38] MacEntee, too, did not attempt to diminish the difficulties facing the state's finances but ended his speech on a note that offered some solace: 'The country is on the eve of a great change, and great changes cannot be brought about without great sacrifices. We are waging a war on hunger and unemployment, and the price of victory is a happy and contented people ... But what we are asking for now in this year of crisis and difficulty, we confidently believe will be returned to them a hundred-fold in the years to come.'

More great changes were to take place which would lead, inevitably, to greater sacrifices. The government's decision to withhold land annuities owed to the British government under the Land Acts of the late nineteenth and early twentieth century resulted in punitive action. On 12 July the British government, strongly influenced by the Treasury and the Dominions Secretary, J.H. Thomas, imposed special duties of 20 per cent on the major Irish exports to Britain: live animals, bacon, pork, poultry, butter, cream and eggs.[39] De Valera's government responded in kind and thus began what became known as the 'Economic War'. This financial dispute has been routinely blamed for the problems encountered by Irish farming throughout the 1930s but it served a number of purposes for de Valera, most of them undeniably political rather than economic. It allowed Fianna Fáil to play the 'green card' once more: the party accused the British government of trying to destroy the democratically elected Irish government by economic warfare and charged the opposition party with full complicity in this. The dispute was also a valuable component in securing a return to power for the party in a strengthened position in January 1933, when de Valera called a general election on MacEntee's advice. Facing a revolt from Labour deputies on public service pay cuts, MacEntee advised de Valera that the only solution was to go to the electorate, a decision which was regarded at the time as political suicide but resulted in the party gaining more than 50 per cent of the poll.[40] Perhaps most significantly, the Economic War established an unchallengeable rationale within the government for the promotion of its economic plan. It also proved that given the choice between economic and nationalist objectives, the latter took priority, at least for de Valera. This was not altogether the case for other members of the cabinet, however. Despite sharing 'a pragmatic, conciliatory approach towards the two pillars of de Valera's policy, Anglo-Irish relations and partition', both Lemass and MacEntee indicated their unease early on.[41] MacEntee advocated an early settlement of the dispute in a speech to the Dublin Chamber of Commerce in December.[42] Lemass's response to the worsening trade figures, and by extension to the dispute itself, was contained in what has been described as 'a revolutionary memorandum'. In it he advocated the establishment of a permanent Board of Trade that would have the power to impose import quotas and export bounties on a large number of items and to be supervised by the Department of Industry and Commerce. He sought a radical review of the state's economic and financial policy and argued that a resolution of the Economic War was not enough to alter the crisis.[43] Lemass suggested the 'abolition of the Board of Public Works and the creation of a Ministry of Public Works organised on the lines of an ordinary Department of State but financed by a grant-in-aid *free from the obligation to get Department of Finance sanction for its schemes*' (emphasis added).[44]

Both ministers were to be disappointed: Lemass's most radical proposals were either shelved or simply not approved and the Economic War intensified as de Valera, who was also Minister for External Affairs, dominated the cabinet on all matters relating to Anglo-Irish affairs.[45] If nothing else, Lemass's memorandum created waves of disquiet in MacEntee's department. If implemented, Lemass's plan, in the words of Fanning, 'would have necessitated a permanent shift in the balance of power between government departments, much larger powers being devolved upon Industry and Commerce (and, to a lesser extent, Agriculture) at Finance's expense'.[46] That it was not reinforces the point that de Valera had little intention of altering the basic administrative functions of government as inherited from Cosgrave's regime. Given the radical nature of Lemass's proposals, Finance was, unsurprisingly, lukewarm in its response. The secretary of the Department, J.J. McElligott, opposed everything in it save for two specific proposals: that the emergency duties be abolished, thus facilitating a resolution of the Economic War, and that public expenditure be reduced 'in every possible direction'.[47] Herein lay the seeds of a sharp divergence of approach between the two most important government departments where economic and financial policy was concerned and constituted the first significant act of a long-running battle for supremacy in this area. Both departments were in full agreement that the dispute with Britain was potentially disastrous for the farming community, and by extension the welfare of the wider economy, but the reaction to the impending crisis went a long way to defining the ideological posture of each.

The following week (14 November), Lemass submitted a further memorandum to the government. It made two specific proposals: that legislation be introduced to prevent landlords from ejecting *bona-fide* unemployed for non-payment of rent where the family income did not reach a specified limit; and a 'second and major proposal' that all unemployed over eighteen years should receive a weekly payment subject to a means test 'somewhat on the lines recently recommended by the British Royal Commission on Unemployment Insurance'. MacEntee's response was to request McElligott's 'immediate observations' before the matter was discussed at the next meeting of the Executive Council. The subsequent minute is significant, according to Fanning, for what it reveals of the principles which McElligott believed should inform financial policy at a time of such economic hardship.[48] It argued that, far from extending relief to the unemployed, the government should 'reduce it drastically'. The argument advanced by the most senior official in the Department of Finance established a template for all future debates on the level of public expenditure and provision of relief, and questioned implicitly some of the governing party's core economic principles.[49]

Much of McElligott's case was conditioned by what T.K. Whitaker later termed 'the finance attitude', which can roughly be distilled by the author's claim that 'Being at the centre, we have to cope with the wants not of one department but of all and our function is not to select the most meritorious and clap these on the taxpayer's back but, rather, to see that as few as possible emerge as new burdens on the community.'[50] The changed political and economic circumstances patently meant that McElligott's exhortations had to be made more forcefully than hitherto, but such resistance from a source that was indelibly associated with the previous administration was unlikely to test Fianna Fáil's resolve in implementing its programme for government.[51] MacEntee's summary of the situation played down the seriousness of Lemass's claims and attributed the worst effects to the Economic War (a tactic that was routinely used throughout the duration of the inter-governmental dispute).[52] Nevertheless, at its meeting of 18 November, the Economic Committee agreed that a committee be set up 'to examine the proposals for a weekly cash payment to unemployed persons, to prepare a detailed scheme for putting them into effect, and, if the proposals are considered impracticable, to devise an alternative scheme for the relief of the unemployed'.[53]

The committee reported to cabinet the following May and favoured Lemass's scheme over the alternative of relief works.[54] Lemass subsequently prepared the heads of a bill which would see all unemployed persons between the ages of eighteen and seventy, who were not maintained by their families or who left employment voluntarily or through misconduct, in receipt of unemployment assistance. In MacEntee's absence, the Executive Council approved the heads, modifying slightly Lemass's proposals on rates of assistance.[55] When the

Minister for Finance did return he admitted, in a handwritten note to one of his officials, Arthur Codling, that he was not in a position to comment because he had not seen 'the proposals of the Minister for Industry and Commerce ... nor the Interim Report of the Committee'.[56] This note was proffered by the minister in a casual and unselfconscious way but provides a revealing insight into the *modus operandi* of the new cabinet and its disregard for the normal apprehensions of a government vis-à-vis financial procedure. That the scheme was to be administered by Industry and Commerce through the same machinery of unemployment insurance does not fully explain why MacEntee's observations on the proposals were not sought at this sensitive stage in the framing of the legislation.

This did not mean that Finance would not have some influence on the eventual essence of the bill, however. A final draft was submitted by Industry and Commerce in September 1933, which anticipated increased costs of £1.9 million which they proposed be met by £250,000 from the Unemployment Insurance Fund, a reduction of £700,000 in the agricultural grant with the state meeting the balance.[57] While Agriculture bemoaned the reduction in its grant, Finance argued that the state contribution was excessive and called for 'drastic overhauling of the proposal to reduce the cost to £1 million'.[58] De Valera's preferred solution to problems of legislative drafting, the increasingly ubiquitous cabinet committee, was consequently called into action. It comprised all ministers directly concerned by the proposals: MacEntee, Ryan, Lemass and O'Kelly. Further reductions in unemployment assistance rates payable to recipients and to changes in the means test were subsequently agreed and the legislation came into effect in April 1934. The advent of what opposition spokesman, Paddy McGilligan, called a 'dole policy' has rightly been regarded as one of the great advances in social policy legislation under the Fianna Fáil government. The relative ease of its passage through cabinet to legislation would scarcely have been possible without a general concurrence by senior ministers on the principle of unemployment assistance. Finance's acquiescence can also be attributed to its undisguised abhorrence of relief works, despite this being the remit of the Office of Public Works, itself part of the Department of Finance. McElligott's argument that 'it cannot be denied that it is cheaper to maintain somebody out of work than to maintain him in work when the work itself has no economic value' remained the department's guiding principle in relation to this issue; and although his minister shared a belief, widely held among politicians of all hues, that relief works offered some psychological advantage, he also recognised their inherent drawbacks.[59]

MacEntee's illness during the late summer of 1932 came at an inopportune time for Finance as it coincided with a rash of legislation being put on the statute book in the Dáil, as well as the outbreak of the Economic War. On 29 July, de Valera was authorised to perform the duties of the Minister for Finance.[60] At the cabinet meeting of 2 August, an order was made advising the governor general to signify the king's assent to the Old Age Pensions Bill, 1932 which was passed by both houses of the Oireachtas on 28 July; the Housing (Financial and Miscellaneous Provisions) Bill was passed in the Oireachtas on 3 August, and the Finance Bill was passed on the following day. The Old Age Pensions Act, 1932 removed many of the restrictions which had previously disallowed aged and blind persons from receiving a pension.[61] The Housing Bill, too, had been approved in May. This was a highly ambitious measure that dramatically increased the scale of the housing programme from the previous government's target. Subsidies were also increased from the provisions of the previous year's act from 40 to 66.6 per cent for so-called slum clearance housing and from 15 to 33.3 per cent for other local authority housing.[62]

Having consolidated its position by an overall Dáil majority in the January 1933 election, Fianna Fáil was now unencumbered by its reliance on the support of the Labour Party to proceed with the implementation of its economic programme. Launching this programme, de Valera stressed the importance the government attached to relieving the worst manifestations of the economic malaise affecting the community: 'In our first Budget we provided in all some £2,500,000 for housing, public works and relief schemes. On these works 33,000 persons are now employed, not counting over 5,000 on work under the ordinary road grants. We propose to continue, and, if possible, to increase the number of workers on these schemes while the need for them remains.'[63] Despite McElligott's stated aversion to 'new' expenditure, MacEntee's budget of 1933 provided a total of £2,806,000 for employment schemes. This complemented the Unemployment Assistance Act introduced by Lemass. The budget also repeated the grant (at an estimated cost of £100,000) for free milk to necessitous children made in 1932 and supplemented this with a further grant of £25,000 for the provision of native fuel in needy homes 'where such fuel is not usually available'.[64]

The government's commitment to relieving unemployment was not open to question but there can be discerned in 1933 a perceptible shift in emphasis regarding its attitude towards responsibility for job creation. De Valera was reported in the *Irish Press* in January distancing the government from sole accountability for the task of creating new jobs: 'Mr de Valera said that when a reasonable time had been given to private enterprise to avail itself of its opportunities, the Government would then take stock and if they found that private enterprise was not doing the work of making the nation self-sufficient, the Government might then decide that the State should step in and do its part; but they hoped that would not be necessary.'[65] MacEntee told the Dáil in his budget speech that 'within the limits set by the resources of the community, the Government of a Christian State ought to provide maintenance for all citizens who may be in want', but he absolved the government from blame if its intentions were not realised: 'This Government does not accept the contention that it is in any way responsible for the prevalence of unemployment … unemployment was rife before it took office, concealed and cloaked over by an ingenious system of preference, but widespread and prevalent everywhere.'[66] The stark reality of being in government, and the political liability this entailed, meant that promises of future state involvement in the economy would be undertaken less lightly. It may also have prompted some reflection in the Minister for Finance as to the wisdom of the government's approach.

Irrespective of the additional expenditure, MacEntee was able to report a surplus on the budget for the second successive year in his 1934 budget speech when payments, (such as the purchase of 500,000 Ordinary Shares in the new state sugar company) 'which beyond question are not normally chargeable against revenue', were accounted for. The surplus, according to the minister, was 'a convincing testimony to the financial and economic strength of our people' and a vindication of the government's policy as 'every single tax heading contributed its quota'.[67] More cynical observers could have pointed out that the surplus was almost entirely accounted for by the retention of the land annuities.[68] Yet the government was still prepared to row back on the income tax increases of 1932 by reducing the standard rate to four shillings and six pence (a victory for MacEntee), which brought it to the same level then pertaining in Britain, and to decrease taxes on tea and home-grown tobacco in an attempt to lower the cost of living. Failure to locate alternative export markets meant that the government could do little to arrest the decline of agricultural incomes and, in turn, strengthened its desire to encourage native industry. Irrespective of MacEntee's sanguinity, Finance remained notably pessimistic about the economy's prospects, particularly as a solution to the Economic War was nowhere in sight. Industrial growth was also having little impact on 'the most endemic features of the economy'. MacEntee outlined the government's long-term plans to 'replace as large a portion as possible of present expenditure on unemployment maintenance on socially remunerative work' and announced that a committee was to be set up to 'consider the extent to which it is practicable to devise a scheme of useful and desirable public works with a view to reducing expenditure on Unemployment Assistance to a minimum'. The rising costs of Unemployment Assistance continued to be a major problem for Finance, and MacEntee's budget declaration reflected the government's vacillation on the putative advantages of public works. The other major piece of social legislation announced by MacEntee concerned non-contributory pensions for widows and orphans (at a cost of £400,000 per annum) which he described as 'a great measure of social amelioration'.

As well as the impetus supplied to industry through budgetary measures, new state companies, such as the Sugar Company (1933), the Turf Development Board (1934) and Aer Lingus (1936), were set up to provide much needed infrastructure and to accelerate the industrialisation drive. Native entrepreneurs were encouraged by the financial assistance provided by the Trade Loans (Guarantee) Act and by the restrictions on foreign control put in place by the Control of Manufactures Acts in 1932 and 1934.[69] The number of tariffs imposed also continued to rise exponentially, and by 1936 over 1,900 were in operation. Predictably, industrial production grew rapidly due in large part to the policy of protection and the building activity occasioned by the government's housing plans. Although there is no statistical evidence available, the total population probably rose in the first half of the decade, as emigration to the US was restricted. Total industrial employment grew by an impressive 35–40,000 (representing a growth rate of 25 per cent) from 1932 to 1936 but, despite this, unemployment remained stubbornly high.[70] At its peak in January 1936, the numbers entitled to benefit reached 145,000. Yet in his budget of that year, MacEntee was in ebullient mood over what he called the 'extraordinary improvement in economic conditions' which was largely facilitated by the 'coal-cattle pact' agreed with the British government in December 1934.

Interestingly, he felt that the most striking feature about his budget was 'the formulation of a definite programme to deal with unemployment', which again consisted of relief works and an employment fund costing £2,500,000. What he failed to mention was the sum advanced by the exchequer (£1,675,000) was less than it had been in 1932/3.[71] Many commentators condemned as unwarrantably excessive the comparatively high tax yield (£3,883,000 more than 1931/2) announced in the budget but it was justified by the minister because: 'it has been wisely spent in improving the condition of the people. Practically all of it has been devoted to the extension and improvement of the social services, including education and housing, whereon the aggregate actual expenditure last year was £3,695,000 more than 1931/32.' This sum was still far too much for some. An editorial in the *Irish Times* commented: 'We do not believe that the Free State can afford all this expenditure on social services; but we realise that if the people demand such luxuries they must be ready to foot the bill.'[72] As we shall see below, what the budget did not reveal was that MacEntee had almost completely lost faith in the efficacy of public works as a long-term solution to unemployment and, despite his cheery presentation of the budget, was now convinced of the need to reduce overall government expenditure significantly.

Social welfare increases and the government's attempt to mitigate the negative impact on agricultural incomes brought on by the Economic War accounted for a sharp rise in the growth of the public sector under Fianna Fáil despite the party's pledges to reduce public expenditure. The percentage share of the government sector in national product rose from 23.6 in 1926/7 to 30.4 in 1933/4. This figure had stabilised at 29.7 per cent on the outbreak of war in 1939. O'Hagan's analysis of the size of the government sector apportions 41.6 per cent of the total increase to agricultural subsidies in the form of export bounties required due to the effects of the Depression and the Economic War; 23.3 per cent to payments to the Land Commission and the remainder to the transfers for old age and unemployment benefit as well as the cost of the government's housing schemes.[73] The expenditure figures clearly demonstrate that the priority of policymakers during the various Fianna Fáil administrations of the 1930s was to fulfil the promises of extensive social amelioration made in opposition. Needless to say this approach came at a considerable cost to the exchequer.

The economic displacement occasioned by such policies was, however, becoming more difficult to reconcile with the political culture preached by Finance (and still widely accepted), which valued, above all else, the principle of budgetary equilibrium and a curtailment of public spending. It was left to the Minister for Finance to square this particular circle and it was this conundrum that increasingly troubled MacEntee during his term in the department. During a debate in the Dáil in December 1937 on the government's general economic and financial policy, MacEntee responded to opposition criticism of its taxation policy by adverting, in typically colourful fashion, to the necessity of its imposition, but also provided a concise expression of his own political principles which stressed that anything the community was given by government would result in it ultimately being burdened by the costs:

It is ... just as iniquitous to tax sugar as it is to tax wheat; but the fact of the matter is that civilised communities cannot get on without some form of indirect taxation. Of course, we know that ... Deputy Cosgrave has funny ideas about this question of taxation. I remember when he was sitting here on these benches as the responsible head of the Government in this country, he got up and told us that if the farmer did not take sugar, and did not take tea, and did not smoke, and did not drink, and did not wear boots, and did not wear clothes, he need not pay any tax at all. In fact, if he were to run around in a state of nature, he would be as happy as Adam in the Garden of Paradise ... We have got to consider the hard facts of life, and so long as we have to provide for the education of the youth of this country, so long, in short, as we have to provide for those who are out of employment in this country, so long as we have to provide for the preservation of the public peace in this country, so long as we have to meet, even upon the present limited scale, the necessities of defending this country, so long as we have to provide a Civil Service and the whole organisation of the State in this country, we shall always have to put on taxes which will hit every element and every individual in the community. If a person is in the community, and gets the benefits and advantages of the community, he has also got to bear the burdens and disabilities, too.[74]

The politics of dependency and of paternalism, of which Dunphy speaks, was indubitably the result of a government that underestimated the limits of what it could achieve given the political and economic climate in which it operated.[75] In other words, it may have been too ambitious too soon. The limits imposed by this political and economic culture also served to bring to the surface internal party divisions that had been submerged by the party's enthusiastic quest for power. To fully understand the Fianna Fáil performance during the 1930s, and to explain the political and economic dialectic created within the cabinet, it will be necessary to explore such divisions.

'A CYPHER AND A SCAPEGOAT'?

MacEntee commented in later life rather cryptically that disagreement in any de Valera cabinet 'never emerged in any formal way', but in many ways the cabinet as it emerged during the 1930s was, in Tom Garvin's phrase, 'pre-political': it had to explore its differences in power. Lemass's great interest in socio-economic issues, and his dominance in this area, placed the Department of Finance on the defensive almost from the outset.[76] One practice that caused most distress to MacEntee and his department was the government's continued use of public works to alleviate unemployment. In 1934, he appointed an inter-departmental committee on public works, which had the intention of reducing the costs of unemployment assistance while also attempting to secure what they described as 'useful and desirable public works'. The chairman of the committee was MacEntee's parliamentary secretary, Hugo Flinn. A total of five reports were presented to government by the committee and while they led to an increase in the level of public works, they failed to convince policymakers, least of all MacEntee, that they provided an adequate and worthwhile alternative.[77] The department's main objection to the works was that they offered poor value for money. MacEntee was, however, willing to overlook the prohibitive costs of an experimental scheme of road works recommended by the Office of Public Works (OPW) in order 'to improve the moral [sic] of the unemployed'.[78] His occupational concern with design and order also convinced him of the potential of the scheme. During his 1934 budget speech he complained of the 'heaps of litter and rubbish, mountain roads often impassable, flowers along the roadside ... towns without design and almost without ornament ... few agreeable buildings, few public gardens, few spacious streets or delightful squares'.[79] Furthermore, as Cousins argues, MacEntee appears to have developed a good relationship with his parliamentary secretaries and to have given them considerable scope.[80] Therefore, he was willing to let Flinn explore the possibility before finally acceding to the case put forward by McElligott. The minister's mind was sufficiently made up by the time it came to presenting the committee's third interim report, which MacEntee forwarded to the Executive Council in April 1936. Rejecting this report, which recommended an extension of public works programmes – optimistically suggesting that 'competent advice' should be sought on the possibility of funding a considerable portion by loan – he reminded his cabinet colleagues of the negative conclusions of the committee's second report on public works; conclusions which he regarded as 'of paramount importance in approaching consideration of any scheme of public works':

(1) A special scheme of public works provides no permanent solution to the unemployment problem and, even during its continuance, makes little contribution towards the training of the young in skilled occupations.
(2) No extensive special scheme of public works can be devised which will not include a high percentage of works of little or no economic value.
(3) Unemployment Assistance cannot be reduced by means of special schemes of public works without an overall increase of expenditure and, therefore, of taxation, which, in the opinion of the Committee, may have serious adverse effect on industrial and agricultural activity and, in the long run, intensify the unemployment problem.[81]

As we have seen, MacEntee played up the significance of the government's efforts to solve unemployment in his 1936 budget speech but was, by this time, cautioning the cabinet against reliance on this particular palliative and of the increasing costs involved. In contrast, Lemass described public works as the second line of defence against unemployment, behind industrial development but before unemployment assistance.[82] MacEntee articulated further his feelings on large-scale public works in a memorandum nine days later. This was a more comprehensive statement that revealed MacEntee's thoughts on the government's entire approach to economic policy. Reviewing the options open to the government to raise the required finance, he argued against an increase in taxation as well as a resort to borrowing. On taxing the community, he contended that this would come 'largely from the wage-earning classes who in the normal course would expend immediately on purchases the amount which it would now have to hand over to the State in the form of taxes'.[83] He also felt that some reduction in corporation profits tax was overdue and that industrial incomes in the Saorstát were over-taxed compared to similar incomes in Britain. Borrowing should also be ruled out because: 'A loan of any magnitude at this stage … apart from its tendency to raise interest rates for future issues … may interfere to a serious extent with endeavours to secure capital for future development.'[84] Future development would be threatened further, he reasoned, because the 'burden of unproductive expenditure inevitably compels a reduction in social services in later years'. MacEntee concluded by defining the role of government with regard to unemployment as he saw it:

> A Government which, in addition to pursuing a sound budgetary policy calculated to inspire confidence, takes special measures to foster and encourage industrial and other development goes much further to solving the problem than one which contents itself with the carrying out of large scale relief works, many of which, in practice, are of no permanent economic value.

On 1 May 1936, the government decided to allocate £2,500,000 for unemployment relief works during the 1936/7 financial year; £250,000 of that would be funded by borrowing and £825,000 by local authorities, with the remainder coming from the exchequer.[85]

In July of the following year, Fianna Fáil was returned to office once more but by then MacEntee's position in Finance was causing him serious concern. In a letter to de Valera, written some time after the election, MacEntee revealed that it was with doubt and hesitation that he decided to run in the election at all and that he was persuaded by an unnamed colleague to do so.[86] Soon after the election, de Valera approached MacEntee to ask him whether he still wished to move from Finance. MacEntee indicated a preference for Industry and Commerce or Local Government and Public Health 'with a certain reservation'. Whether he simply wanted to move to a department which he felt was benefiting from the spoils of the government's economic policy is unclear; what is clear is that he was tired of being undermined in Finance. Accordingly, he complained to de Valera about cabinet approval for schemes of large expenditure. In this way the minister felt he was a 'cypher, except when the bill had to be paid at which time he might be permitted to figure in the more active role of a scapegoat'.[87]Despite his protestations over the government's proposed public works schemes, a programme had been provisionally adopted in February 1937 which involved an increase of £150,000 on the figure 'set aside in recent years for relief works'.[88] His response to this development reiterated many of the points he had made in his memorandum of the previous April, but on this occasion he was more forthcoming with alternatives. He recommended the establishment of a 'Special Employment Fund' of £2 million for the purpose of financing the new works, made up of the 'proceeds of existing taxation which otherwise would be appropriated to a reduction therein'.

Another guide to the minister's disenchantment was advanced to cabinet in November 1937. A memorandum entitled 'Notes on general economic position' prepared by McElligott, revealed a department at the end of its tether.[89] A resolution of the Economic War was, by now, imperative, in the department's view, which was articulated in a strikingly petulant tone: 'It is suggested that the Government should make up its mind whether a genuine effort is going to be made forthwith to settle the dispute or whether we are going to maintain our policy of passive resistence [sic] ... no Government Department and no farmer or business man can plan ahead with so many major uncertainties.' Under the heading 'General Considerations' it asserted, if it wasn't patently clear already, that 'it is essential to disabuse people that this is a land flowing with milk and honey'.[90] The electorate certainly did not need to be disabused of this notion; the net emigration figure for the first six months of 1937 showed a big rise to 26,000, yet the numbers receiving unemployment benefit or employment at the state's expense remained unchanged at an estimated 138,841. In the 1937 general election, Fianna Fáil had emphasised its achievements in improving housing and the social services, but admitted that unemployment was its chief concern.[91] An earlier draft of the Finance memo (not revealed to cabinet) is noteworthy in that it anticipated many of the points made by the majority report of the banking commission, which was candidly critical of much of the government's economic programme since 1932:

> The maximum chances of employment are given in the country where the national income is maximised and Irish agricultural and other problems should be viewed from this standpoint. In agriculture we are pursuing two mutually contradictory policies; endeavouring to promote production and to settle the maximum number of people on the land ... The present policy of land division means less production, more deadweight debt and surplus population that can not find employment on the land or emigrate.

On 9 November, the minister submitted this memorandum with a covering note that sought to clarify his position: 'In the opinion of the Minister for Finance the conclusions enforced by the notes are:- (1) The need for securing freer and more profitable access to our principal external market. (2) The need for the strictest economy in regard to governmental expenditure under all heads and for avoiding either fresh commitments or the extension of existing commitments. (3) The need to avoid any further legislative or other measures which might tend to increase our internal costs of production and distribution.' Although the memorandum was circulated to individual ministers and the item came before the cabinet on 21 January, it was decided to defer discussion of it to some later date due presumably to the impending Anglo-Irish talks which ultimately resolved the Economic War.

'The 1938 general election,' notes Dunphy, 'is generally held to have marked a peak in Fianna Fáil's electoral fortunes, and to a turning-point in the party's social profile, heralding the onset of conventional, conservative, bourgeois politics, albeit sometimes tempered by nationalist fervour.'[92] He disputes this view somewhat, however, by drawing attention to 'the limited nature of the radicalism of the preceding period'. What undermines both the generally held view, and Dunphy's qualification, is the fact that the recurring and increasingly alarmist noises from the Department of Finance reached a crescendo between 1937 and 1939. If the party's perceived 'turn to the right' occurred at this time, it would have represented a victory for that department but Finance's concern grew audibly during the immediate pre-war period. This concern can be largely attributed to the publication of the majority report of the banking commission in 1938, the conclusions of which Finance was both sensitive to and disposed to agree with. It can also be attributed to the potential implications of war on the Irish economy. Moreover, such analysis misapprehends the very essence of Fianna Fáil's appeal. In fact, the party never claimed to be sectional or base its policies on class differences, nor was it ever likely that it would become a prisoner of its own rhetoric. The measures it introduced during the 1930s represented a major redistribution of the community's resources but this should not be deemed incongruent with MacEntee's overriding concern for 'the country and the taxpayer', which was entirely compatible with Fianna Fáil's national profile and its concern with that maltreated but ultimately aspirant constituency: 'the plain people of Ireland'.

The growth in public expenditure as detailed above was, by 1938, causing great anxiety to the Department of Finance. It was also the ostensible reason MacEntee composed another resignation letter that year. In it he foresaw a bleak outcome for the coming financial year:

> [W]e are facing a deficit upon the present year's budget of all but £2,000,000, do not over-emphasise the need for a drastic and immediate reduction in expenditure if our country is to escape the fate of France and New Zealand. As Minister for Finance I have a duty to the country and the taxpayer to enforce that reduction and if I fail therein to relinquish office.[93]

The letter not only indicated that MacEntee was openly at loggerheads with members of the cabinet but also that he felt that both he and his department were being undermined by the direction of government policy:

> It has been clear to me for some time past that my continuance in office as Minister for Finance is incompatible with the views which you in the first instance as head of the government, and, I believe, a majority of the cabinet hold in regard to public expenditure. I have not concealed from you or them my opinion that we are spending excessively and that our present policy ... is injurious to the State and the community. On occasions, this difference of opinion has been carried almost to the point of resignation, but I have carried on in the hope that experience would teach its own lesson and as the ill-effects of the policy which hitherto we have pursued manifested themselves in rising costs, increasing employment, higher taxes, and diminished resources; a more prudent and provident spirit would inform our counsels when proposals involving public expenditure, and therefore increased burdens for our already over-burdened people were under consideration.

Seán T. O'Kelly chaired government meetings from 7 September to 4 October 1938. O'Kelly had in fact viewed McElligott's note on the economic situation and had claimed to have been in agreement with much of it.[94] The cabinet minutes blandly reveal that 'Approval was given to the White Paper of Estimates of Receipts and Expenditure for the year ending 31st March, 1940, submitted by the Minister for Finance.'[95] What they don't reveal, however, is the frustration it caused MacEntee: 'Those members of the Government who are not disposed to agree … and I seem to be in a deadlock which, I at least know, is not to be resolved by hours of fruitless wrangling such as has preceded practically every budget that I presented since Fianna Fáil took office.'[96]

MacEntee's duty to the country and the taxpayer informed another resignation letter which took issue with a number of resolutions approved by the cabinet relating to the 1939 budget.[97] The letter was composed after the minister was overruled at cabinet, having recommended that the decision taken to increase income tax be reversed and that the provision for employment schemes be reduced by £300,000.[98] He strongly objected to the refusal of the cabinet to resist an increase in taxation: 'The Minister for Finance feels that this course is neither politic nor justifiable, and presses very strongly for a review of the position', and furthermore, argued that any increase in income tax would have 'an adverse effect on the unemployment situation'.[99] The budget he grimly presented to the Dáil on 10 May 1939 duly raised the standard rate of income tax, and the total increase in government expenditure amounted to £1,497,000.[100] The dead-weight liabilities[101] of the state increased by 48.3 per cent in the year from March 1938 to April 1939, a statistic which the minister could not conceal his displeasure at reporting. What marked this budget speech as extraordinary was the frequency with which the minister revealed his own counsel relating to the public finances, even when that counsel contradicted the very measures he was introducing:

> As I have said so frequently in relation to public spending, economy is a virtue that is often preached but seldom practised. I have no doubt that when I finish today I shall be criticised for placing additional burdens on the people. I shall be told that in the year 1931–32 the total revenue amounted to £25,496,419, of which £21,286,000 came from taxation; whereas in the year which has just passed it amounted to £31,884,000, with £25,987,000 from taxation; while for the current year we are going to get from taxation – but it is too soon to go into that just now. The point is that all these millions are taken from the taxpayer for one purpose and for one purpose only, and that is to pay for the public services which the people, in so far as their representatives here in this Dáil speak for them, demand.[102]

Tensions in the government, it could be argued, had existed from the beginning but the clearest evidence of division emanates from the period after 1936. During the 1938 Anglo-Irish talks, MacEntee wrote to de Valera pointing to a fundamental breach in cabinet unanimity. Pressing for a resolution of the talks, MacEntee regarded the position taken by some within the cabinet, particularly the Minister for Lands and the Minister for Posts and Telegraphs (namely Gerry Boland and Oscar Traynor) as one which 'has destroyed the only basis on which a cabinet can last: that upon agreement on the essentials of policy and a pervading confidence that the policy having been stated will be accepted by all'.[103] Clearly divisions in the cabinet were not solely between Industry and Commerce and Finance, and were not always about differences in economic policy. Nevertheless MacEntee, for the most part, subscribed to the 'essentials of policy' and was willing to accept it. Often when Finance did demur on issues of policy, as in the case of public works, a compromise was struck, thereby minimising the potential expenditure involved. Accordingly, it would be unwise to overstate the importance of MacEntee's resignation letters. While one cannot doubt their sincerity, there is considerable anecdotal evidence to suggest that the minister was somewhat thin-skinned and was prone to dramatic flourishes in response to adverse policy decisions. Their timing and regularity, however, does convey something of the attitude of the Department of Finance towards government policy, particularly after the publication of the report of the Banking Commission in the autumn of 1938.

THE BANKING COMMISSION

Perhaps the episode that best illustrates Seán MacEntee's relative isolation within the Fianna Fáil cabinet and the degree to which the party was compromised in pursuing its redistributive social and economic policy was the publication of the Majority Report of the Commission of Inquiry into Banking, Currency and Credit (Banking Commission) in August 1938. The report was the most far-reaching examination of Irish economic policy since the foundation of the state, and was the most forceful expression of the political credo of the Department of Finance. As we have seen, publication of the report coincided with a period of uncertainty for MacEntee in Finance and provided him with eminent justification for espousing the orthodox line favoured by his officials. The commission was appointed by the Minister for Finance on 20 November 1934, and had the following terms of reference:

> To examine and report on the system in Saorstát Éireann of currency, banking, credit, public borrowing and lending and the pledging of State credit on behalf of agriculture, industry and the social services, and to consider and report what changes, if any, are necessary or desirable to promote the social and economic welfare of the community and the interests of agriculture and industry.

The expansive nature of those terms reflected the breadth of Fianna Fáil's ambition as a new party of government and served as a trenchant example of its conviction to oversee the implementation of the socially conscious agenda upon which it had been elected. Despite the propitious timing of the report for the government, in the aftermath of the successful conclusion of the Anglo-Irish financial agreements in the spring of 1938, and Fianna Fáil's election triumph of that year, the report was strongly critical of the government's economic record and cautioned against further demands on public borrowing to finance its obligations. It also blamed government policy for the continuing depressed nature of domestic industry and agriculture, and the high unemployment figures. The majority report was accompanied by three minority reports, each with its own particular agenda. The first and third minority reports were motivated by a combination of Catholic social teaching and experimental economic strategies that involved the expansion of credit facilities and the assumption of credit control by the government or by a state agency. Two of the three minority reports were dismissed as insignificant by MacEntee, mainly on the assertion that they were fundamentally misconceived and misguided – if well-intentioned – schemes that disregarded economic realities.

Prior to 1932, Fianna Fáil regarded the banking fraternity in the Saorstát with contempt and suspicion. While in opposition, MacEntee held what he described as a 'clique' directly responsible for some of the root causes of the economic difficulties being experienced by the state. Fianna Fáil did, however, have an early opportunity to voice its concerns about this system when a government-sponsored Banking Commission, chaired by the American economist Henry Parker-Willis, reported on 31 January 1927. Indeed the party viewed the findings of this commission with disdain, which should not be surprising given that its membership – with the exception of the chairman and one Department of Finance official – was comprised wholly of representatives of the commercial banks operating in the state.[104] Moynihan has noted that the 'first and fundamental conclusion' of the report, which was subscribed to in writing by all except J.J. McElligott and Andrew Jameson, Director of the Bank of Ireland, 'was that whatever was done in the Saorstát should be done in such a way as to avoid "for the present" any serious breach with the currency, banking and trade system of Great Britain'.[105]

Predictably, those findings found little sympathy in Fianna Fáil, whose own economic programme was designed with altogether different goals in mind. The nationalist agenda to which the party subscribed sought to revive a culture which, it argued, had been weakened by British conquest and to sever economic links with Britain. The report drew an indignant response from the party's *Weekly Bulletin*, which anticipated an altogether more penetrating inquiry into the subject:

> The Banking Commission that is needed in Ireland is the Commission whose terms of reference would be to examine how the people of this island might be freed from the grip of this league [of bankers]. The evidence it would need is not the evidence that would be given by the high priests of the financial craft. The aim of these will always be to maintain their own domination, and to hide the secrets of the craft from the plain people whom they exploit.[106]

Another view of the Parker-Willis commission was provided by the Fianna Fáil spokesman on industry and commerce, Seán Lemass, who concentrated his attack on the maintenance of parity with sterling. He regarded it as 'apparent that the commission had devoted a greater portion of its energies to devising ways and means of keeping Irish financial interests permanently subservient to those of England ... The people should not allow themselves to be fooled by green pound notes, as they had been deceived by green pillar-boxes and green uniforms.' 'The report of the Banking Commission,' concluded Lemass, 'was only another stone in the gigantic edifice of fraud which was being built around the Irish people.'[107]

This rhetoric fitted neatly with the party's self-image as one representing the 'plain people' exploited by business or bureaucratic interests. The other main pillar of the party's self-image, namely antipathy to English interests in Irish affairs, was seized upon gratefully by Lemass. MacEntee was another prominent party spokesman who was highly critical of the banking system. He accused the banks of 'bleeding the Irish farmer, crushing Irish industry, investing Irish money abroad, [and] jeopardising it in British securities'.[108] Such criticism, while certainly exaggerated, was not completely unwarranted. The Parker-Willis Commission was loaded with banking interests whose *raison d'être* was, if anything, to underpin the existing arrangements which meant that a central bank was deemed unnecessary, as was the need for a domestic Irish money market. As Cormac Ó Gráda has noted: 'The Parker-Willis inquiry ... proposed the creation of an institution [the Currency Commission] responsible for a domestic currency backed one-hundred percent by sterling notes, short-maturity British government securities or gold as the only fundamental change required.'[109]

Accordingly, Fianna Fáil gave a commitment in its election manifesto of 1932 to investigate the financial institutions. At the party's árd fheis (held on 8/9 November), a resolution was adopted that 'with a view to providing better credit facilities for Irish industries and securing the freedom of this country's finances from foreign control, a central bank, controlled by the government be established'.[110] The advent of Fianna Fáil power, therefore, remained something that the banks felt they had good reason to fear. It is perhaps unsurprising then, that representatives of the commercial banks formally embodied in the Irish Banks' Standing Committee should harbour deep misgivings as to what lay in store for them. Such was their apprehension, that MacEntee, in the course of correspondence and discussions with the chairman of the Irish Banks' Standing Committee, Sir Lingard Goulding, deemed it necessary to allay such fears by assuring him that 'any alteration in our existing arrangements ... would be made only after a searching investigation by a competent body'.[111] The new government had good reason not to alienate the banks unduly: between 1929 and 1933, wholesale commodity prices, expressed in gold, declined by about one-third and raw material prices by 50 to 60 per cent. In September 1931, the National Government in Britain was forced to abandon the gold standard; indeed, the unexpectedness of Britain's decision was one reason advanced by the proponents of banking reform. MacEntee advanced the argument to de Valera in January 1933 that to gratuitously offend what he called 'monied interests' might help in creating an atmosphere of distrust and, in the course of counselling the Taoiseach that the 'present time is ... not favourable for an inquiry of this kind', painted a somewhat alarmist vista by claiming that 'There seems to be a distinct danger that interests which are not friendly to the Government may succeed ... in creating an atmosphere of distrust in the stability of our currency, and thereby jeopardise the success of our plans for financing Government obligations.'[112] His pessimistic advice was undoubtedly conditioned by the fact that the banks had often taken a bleak view of the government's creditworthiness.[113] De Valera was also cautioned by one of his economic advisers, Professor Timothy Smiddy, against taking precipitate action against the banks.[114] In March 1933, Smiddy wrote to de Valera to advise him of the benefits of a stable banking organisation.[115]

By the time the government was ready to appoint a commission of inquiry, the radical rhetoric of opposition had been abandoned in favour of a more politic approach.While the government did not actively court banking interests per se, it did make certain to remain on cordial terms with the Currency Commission, a body set up on the recommendation of the Parker-Willis commission and chaired by the former secretary of the Department of Finance, Joseph Brennan. Brennan's stock rose considerably after Fianna Fáil took office despite MacEntee's later description of him as 'an extraordinarily able, if sometime difficult, civil servant'.[116] He accompanied the government delegation to the Imperial Economic Conference in Ottawa, was appointed to the chairmanship of a Commission of Inquiry into the Civil Service later in the same year and would become the government's choice to chair the Commission on Currency, Banking and Credit. In September 1933, de Valera met Brennan with the aim of satisfying himself on a number of issues, all of which would eventually be considered by the Banking Commission, including: whether the banks were pressing farmers unduly for repayment of loans; what should be done to secure an expansion of bank credit for the stimulation of industry; whether the banks should take a direct part in industry; and whether the tie with sterling was in the best interest of the country.[117] Brennan expressed his belief that the existing arrangements did not prejudice anybody or exert undue pressure and maintained that the real problem lay in safeguarding public confidence.

Given the prevailing economic circumstances, courting the banks was an example of Fianna Fáil's early grasp of *realpolitik*. In a letter to de Valera outlining the provisional terms of reference of the commission, MacEntee indicated that it was now time to forgive and forget where the banks were concerned. One of the reasons he put forward to justify the new commission was: 'In view of the widespread and often unjustifiable criticism which has been levelled at the banks, particularly over the past five or six years ... it is desirable to anticipate public opinion in this matter and to set up such a commission as is now proposed.'[118] A Finance memorandum, further outlining the government's intentions vis-à-vis the commission, was sent to de Valera's office on 6 April. It revisited briefly the conclusions of the first banking commission of 1926 and attributed its short shelf-life to the changed economic conditions, and to the economic imperatives of the Fianna Fáil administration: 'The expansion of state activity involving as it does increased taxation, expenditure and borrowing necessitates a restatement of the tentative conclusions reached some time ago.'[119] What is striking about this memorandum is its confluence with the social and economic objectives of Fianna Fáil, which, given McElligott's own fiscal predilections, can only be attributed to MacEntee's early influence on the department:

> The Government is committed to a policy of extensive and intensive development of the national resources and to the removal of existing social evils

such as inadequate housing. This policy will necessitate borrowing on a large scale over a period of years … it would seem to be in the best interests of the banks as a whole that the present practice of banking in the Irish Free State should be re-examined by a body whose competence and impartiality would not be open to question and whose views would command respect.[120]

This statement would seem to point to an unwarranted optimism on the part of the government as to the collective ability of the proposed expert body. It also begs the following question: did the establishment of a body of experts to deal with what were, ostensibly, the key economic questions facing the community mean that the government felt ill-equipped to deal with them itself? Or did it simply illustrate the government's desire to gain as many points of view as were available without jeopardising its overall economic goals? It is likely that any attempt at structural change to the monetary system without the sanction of a commission would have posed innumerable difficulties for the government. De Valera admitted some time later that he was willing to set up a central bank without waiting for the commission because 'he was convinced the country needed it' but that he was persuaded to appoint the commission before taking any action.[121] Again it is worth stressing that he, and the people who advised him thus (primarily MacEntee), could not have anticipated that the commission would take almost four years to complete its task or that its recommendations would leave the government in such a compromised position.

SANE VIEWS AND CONSTRUCTIVE WORK?

Although the majority report was signed by sixteen of the twenty-one commissioners, one of its signatories, J.P. Colbert, advised later that 'One must not … exaggerate the degree of agreement reached amongst the members of the commission' given 'the unusual number of Addenda, Reservations and Appendices'.[122] Colbert himself signed the majority report with a reservation on the economic and financial situation, questioning the limitation of dead-weight debt proposed by the report, and argued that the existence of substantial external reserves permitted an increase in that debt for the purposes of aiding agriculture and industry and for house building.[123] He was responding specifically to the report's overriding preoccupation with the increase in the national debt: 'The large and continuous expansion of the burden of dead-weight debt is one of the most serious matters which we are called on to review.'[124] The report's review led to the following conclusions:

There are two considerations of special importance in this connection. In the first place, heavy loan expenditure of an unproductive character has a tendency, while it is being incurred, to weaken the economic and financial stability of the country, and especially to place a strain on the balance of payments. From comments made elsewhere in this report it is clear that the Free State is not in a position to take any increased risk in this matter.

Secondly, increase of the annual net debt charge consequent upon an increase in the volume of dead-weight debt threatens to create a serious position for the budget of the future. The task of balancing the budget must be more difficult according as the proportion of fixed charges in it rises. Expenditure on services that can expand or contract according to varying views of needs of Government policy will always be reasonably suscepti- ble of control, but expenditure to cover debt charges or other contractual obligations of the State, such as pensions, affords no scope for ministerial discretion.[125]

The commission also compiled a wealth of statistical material and data, which proved an invaluable aid to a full appreciation of the economic health of the state. National income had increased in real terms by 15 per cent between 1926 and 1938, but the price indexing system revealed that the Irish cost of living was 12.2 per cent higher than its equivalent in Great Britain, and that Irish prices were 10.4 per cent higher despite real wages being the same in both countries. Per Jacobsson, one of the external experts appointed, interpreted these figures as being condemnatory of government policy. He had consistently argued for no increase in the dead-weight debt and for a balanced budget throughout the com- mission's sittings. Having studied the monetary policies of the Swedish govern- ment in the early 1930s, he had little faith in budget deficits, regarding them as counter-productive to industrial development. The report also described capital being readily available for industry but that there was no 'disposition to invest [it] in domestic enterprises'. Perhaps the most important recommendations of the majority report were concerned with state borrowing and the borrowing power of the semi-state bodies. Predictably, it maintained that such borrowing required restrictions and advised that the volume of state borrowing and lending 'should be reduced from year to year at such a rate as general financial circumstances permit'. It also counselled that 'care should be taken to examine various govern- ment proposals with more regard to their possible monetary and financial reac- tions'.[126]

When the reports were finally published on 9 August 1938, the Minister for Finance drew attention to the debt position and pointed out that it had been altered by the financial agreement concluded in April 1938 with the United Kingdom, as a result of which the net dead-weight debt had been reduced from £37.3 million on 31 March 1937 to £12.7 million the following year.[127] Yet despite the minister's efforts to downplay the debt position, this became one of the most controversial aspects of the majority report. It had unequivocally called for budgets to be balanced and for this debt to be checked: 'No increase whatev- er beyond the existing volume of net dead-weight debt should be permitted, and that volume should be reduced from year to year at such rate as general financial circumstances permit.'[128] Furthermore, it was this recommendation which attract- ed most attention in the Dáil once the report was finally debated in July 1939, prompting a long discussion on the most appropriate ways of relieving unem- ployment and financial distress and which revealed the fundamental difference between the majority report and at least two out of the three minority reports.[129] In that debate, the government's policy was justified and defended by de Valera and other party spokesmen, but, privately, real differences had emerged within Fianna Fáil over the prospect of reducing its economic commitments.

MacEntee had clearly become exasperated by the rise in the public debt, and regarded the Banking Commission's diagnosis as a validation of his department's attitude. This put him on a collision course with much of his party. The *Irish Press* probably gauged the mood of most within Fianna Fáil when it advised: 'While giving due weight to the recommendations of the report, [the government] must maintain a policy of their own.'[130] It was to be some time, however, before the government made public its true feelings on the matter, a delay that was no doubt exacerbated by the lack of unanimity within the cabinet. In a speech in September, the new party deputy Erskine Childers warned that 'Fianna Fáil must strenuously resist the temptation to offer a defiant attitude to the general findings', although it 'might ... be possible to effect a compromise by not taking at 100 per cent value some of the more conservative strictures of the report'. In other words, the party should retain a certain political leeway without attempting any real change in the financial system.[131] The party's chief whip, P.J. Little, informed MacEntee in November that his colleague Seán O'Grady had requested that a party meeting be convened 'as soon as possible' to consider the reports (majority and minority) of the Banking Commission.[132] It is unclear whether the meeting was ever convened, but it did prompt MacEntee to request a memorandum on the pros and cons of each recommendation, based on a note prepared by McElligott earlier that month, which sought a decision from the government with the following objectives:

(a) that the currency link with sterling at the existing parity should be maintained;

(b) that the powers and functions of the Currency Commission be extended to render it capable of acting as a Central Bank and that the constitution should be suitably amended;

(c) that the system of consolidated bank notes should be terminated and that the existing consolidated bank notes will be redeemed over a period of 15 years;

(d) that the proposals about Banking institutions maintaining deposits in the High Court and taking out licences through the Minister for Finance be accepted;

(e) that, in the main, the recommendations in regard to the public finance, budgetary deficits, and treatment of dead weight debt should be followed. The amount of Deferred Charges Account might be raised from the £2,000,000 recommended by the Commission to £4,000,000 and the period of repayment of advances from this Account from 7 years to 10 years.[133]

Although the minister made it clear that he agreed 'generally with these suggestions', he wasn't yet ready to press the government for action.

Brennan found the government's silence on the matter disturbing enough to warrant a visit to MacEntee in December. During the meeting, Brennan betrayed his anxiety regarding the fate of the commission's main proposals and the future of the Currency Commission. Again, MacEntee was non-committal:

> The Minister stated that he had been unable so far to give more than a cursory reading to the Reports and that he had had no opportunity of discussing them with his colleagues ... While he personally felt sympathetic towards the points of view of the Majority on many of the matters dealt with in their report, he had, as stated, not yet studied the reports with sufficient thoroughness to be able to form final opinions. He thought the first step would be to deal with the Minority Reports.[134]

The minister's explanation to Brennan was somewhat disingenuous. MacEntee had certainly formed some definite opinions on all four reports by mid-summer and had circulated some of them to his government colleagues in July. In a memorandum dated 15 July, MacEntee allowed his own interpretation of the majority report's criticisms of certain features of government policy to be known. He rejected, for example, the report's criticism of the provision of credit for agriculture and industry, and in particular to criticism of a number of state organisations including the Electricity Supply Board (ESB), the Agricultural Credit Corporation (ACC) and the Industrial Credit Corporation (ICC).[135] On the issue of state borrowing and lending, MacEntee was more circumspect:

> The necessity for the Commission's recommendations is dependent on the validity of its criticisms, concerning which the Minister is not at present prepared to express an opinion. The whole subject is very intricate and involves as an incidental feature the financing of the Government's programme with regard to housing, land division and industrial development, and some time must elapse before it will be possible to complete the examination of the ... Report on these matters and to tender to the Government advice regarding its recommendations.[136]

Moreover, contrary to what he had told Brennan in December, MacEntee had by then already effectively dismissed the minority reports.

Robert Barton, chairman of the Agricultural Credit Corporation and one of the majority report's signatories, was also mindful enough of the minister's predicament when he wrote to MacEntee: 'Our conclusions may raise more controversy than enthusiasm but for you at any rate they will not increase the difficulty of balancing budgets or of answering the propagandists of untried panaceas and worn out inflationary schemes. In these days a Finance Minister who can say "well the charge of losing the people's savings cannot be laid at my door" has gained an enviable reputation.'[137] Such supportive sentiments were not forthcoming from within the government, however. It was his scrutiny of the minority reports, specifically Minority Report I, which was signed by Alfred O'Rahilly and the trade unionists William O'Brien and Seán P. Campbell, and Minority Report III, signed by Fianna Fáil TD Peter O'Loghlen, which formed the basis upon which MacEntee would advocate governmental acceptance of the majority report. It was his contention that these reports contained so little to recommend them, and that Minority Report II, which was signed by Professor Busteed, had broadly agreed with the majority in most respects that there was no practical alternative. O'Loghlen's report – which included recommendations for the abandonment of the fixed parity with sterling and the establishment of an Economic Development Commission, whose activities would be financed with money issued by the Currency Commission and of a Foreign Exchange Committee whose functions would include the determination of the rates of foreign exchange – was more politically pressing. It had the tentative approval of de Valera and had materialised in the form of a resolution at the party's árd fheis: 'That the control of the volume of currency and credit, at present the monopoly of a private trading interest, should be placed in the hands of a national monetary authority'.[138] In his report, Professor Busteed also made the call for a national monetary authority with wide-ranging powers.

Finance responded to the O'Loghlen resolution by drawing attention to the apparent discord between the minority reports, while succinctly questioning their economic basis:

> The árd fheis may rest assured that the Minority Reports also receive full consideration. It has to be appreciated, however, that there is no body of views common to all three Minority Reports and that the Minority Reports differ quite considerably among themselves ... There is, however, a common idea underlying the first and third Minority reports that credit can and should be regulated so as to secure social improvement. There is general sympathy with the desire for social uplift which appears to have actuated many of the observations in these Minority Reports; but it is considered that attempts to secure this end merely by reforming the monetary and banking system are fundamentally misconceived ... A 'magic formula' for economic and social progress had yet to be found.[139]

The departmental appraisal of the reports in question was specifically designed for its audience and, therefore, concealed the contempt both the minister and his officials held for them. Much of this contempt derived from the self-publicity engineered by both O'Loghlen and O'Rahilly for their respective agendas in the national press and, perhaps more pertinently, the fact that those agendas found a sympathetic home in publications that would typically be well-disposed to the government.[140] This derision was given full expression in a 136-page rebuttal of the main features of the minority reports, with O'Rahilly's report given extensive scrutiny:

> What the Government looked for from the members of the Banking Commission – Professor O'Rahilly and his colleagues with the rest – was not the formulation of a social programme (which the Government itself can do quite competently) ... but, so far as such is possible, a carefully worked out plan ... Professor O'Rahilly and his colleagues have failed even to attempt such an examination and the windy polemics of the section of their report which they have entitled 'Social Conditions' are no compensation for that failure.[141]

This dissection of the O'Rahilly document also highlighted the similarities between it and a Labour Party publication, entitled *Labour's Constructive Programme for an Organised Nation*, which had been written early in 1938. This association, in the minister's analysis, rendered the document unpardonably political:

> We should be treating this matter too lightly if we regarded it merely as marking the Labour Party's retreat from Moscow under the leadership of the Napoleonic Professor. It is of deeper significance. It betrays the fundamental dishonesty which permeates the Minority Report No 1 and which renders that document intrinsically worthless as an aid to the solution of our problems. It is clear that those who have signed it have not approached these problems with judicial and scientific minds, concerned only to discover the truth in regard to them and to propound solutions based upon the results of their research, but have abused their membership of the Commission by availing of it to make tendencious [sic] statements on behalf of a particular political party, making their report no more than a political pamphlet.[142]

In the absence of any official government response to the commission's findings, the Finance memorandum, written in response to the minority reports, along with the Dáil debate of July 1939, serve as the main sources from which to gauge individual ministerial verdicts upon them; and from which to infer what was being discussed in the corridors of power. MacEntee's views on the social obligations of the government, and how each report had dealt with them, are certainly indicative of his separation from the main body of opinion in his party, and although Fianna Fáil displayed an instinctive unanimity in the Dáil, there was a distinct difference in the emphasis and tone of the Minister for Finance's statements and those of the Taoiseach and his cabinet colleagues. When it came to the minority reports' evaluation of the relative merits of public spending in the overall economic programme, MacEntee characteristically preached caution: 'In relation to public expenditure, whether for housing or other socially desirable public purpose, there is an optimum rate which cannot be exceeded except at the risk of grave social injury.' The minister also refuted a suggestion by the third minority report that inflationary expenditure would only become detrimental (through price rises) once employment creation ceased by citing examples in other economies: '[I]t is well-known that, after a brief favourable reaction to the initial spending, large expenditures upon public works programs have of themselves failed to effect any sustained improvement in the employment position, as is evidenced by the experience in Germany in 1933 and 1934, and in the USA in 1934, 1935 and 1936.'

The example of Germany was utilised again when MacEntee came to consider the third minority report, signed by Peter O'Loghlen, but written by Bulmer Hobson, Rev. Edward Cahill, SJ and Mrs Berthon Waters (who styled themselves The League for Social Justice). Using quotations from Hjalmar Schacht, former president of the Reichsbank in the Weimar Republic, who was described in the memorandum as 'a practical financier', MacEntee derided what he called 'Consumer Credit' systems. He also attacked James Meade, the economist who was cited in O'Loghlen's report.[143] MacEntee contended that the proposals endorsed by Meade would involve 'the usurpation of all individual rights in labour and property and the mass regimentation of human beings in all their needs and desires'. As we shall see below, this concept was to become something of a mantra to MacEntee, and was clearly considered by him to be the most potent argument against what he regarded as fiscal recklessness. After his appointment as President of the Reichsbank in 1923, Schacht had been associated with the suppression of currency separatism and the choking off of revived inflationary tendencies by a severe policy of credit restriction in April 1924.[144] Throughout the whole Banking Commission debate, both interdepartmentally and in the Dáil, Schacht was used as a talisman for MacEntee and his Finance officials.[145]

The Dáil debate in question did not occur until July 1939, over a year after the report had first been submitted to government. The debate moved beyond the terms of the Banking Commission and, over three days and many lengthy speeches, covered all aspects of the economic and financial position of the state. MacEntee's own contribution lasted three and a half hours. He made it clear from the beginning that he was keen to sing from the same hymn sheet as his colleagues in defending the government's record and in questioning the majority report's conclusions. He contended that, due to the ending of the Economic War and the financial agreement with the United Kingdom government, much of the statistical material compiled by the commission was obsolete. He was also keen to remind his audience of the government's autonomy in deciding whether to pursue the report's recommendations: 'I am not going to take, and I am certain my colleagues in the Government, and the members in the House, and the general public, are not going to take the members of the Banking Commission as working under the afflatus of Divine inspiration.' Despite this, the minister's analysis reiterated many of the arguments that had been advanced in his denunciation of the minority reports but, in keeping with his party's profile, he was also keen to indicate his general empathy with their efforts.

The minister's use of examples such as the New Deal of Roosevelt's America betrayed his genuine regard for the majority report.[146] For MacEntee, these examples provided the 'considered judgment of those who have had actual practical experience of the sort of policy which has been advocated in the Labour Party amendment'. Having examined the results of the policies of the governments of France and the USA, the minister moved on to Germany, which inevitably led to the invocation of his trusted friend, Dr Schacht, whom he quoted at length. MacEntee also used the example of New Zealand, whose expansionist policies he denounced for inducing 'an inflationary spiral' and for precipitating budgetary difficulties for the government, and whose economic experimentation he likened to 'totalitarian Germany'. The antithesis to this arrangement came down to his often stated political creed: that of governmental responsibility to the community:

> Are we to take it, from what the Deputy is saying, and from what was said last night, that we or any other Government are going to go to the people and ask them to entrust us with their savings and tell them: 'Do not forget

that there are gentlemen in the Dáil who may be sitting in the Dáil as a
Government five or ten years from now and, when faced with the unpleasant task of imposing taxation in order to meet the State's commitments to
you, their answer is going to be: "We have no responsibility for it; this
money was borrowed by another Government"'?

Indeed, MacEntee's entire case had been predicated upon the likelihood of an
impending European war and the impact it would have on imports, particularly
ones that yielded high taxation. He summed up a long speech, and perhaps his
most sustained justification for the attitude adopted by his department, by rein-
troducing Schacht and by stating some bald economic fundamentals: 'I will sum
up by saying once again that we have got to remember what Dr Schacht said, that
it is not the quantity of money as expressed by bank notes that counts; it is not
the rate of wages or the amount of income that matters, it is what goods can be
got for those bank notes and what goods can be purchased for those wages that
count.' The debate culminated with the most vivid expression of the Minister for
Finance's political credo; one by which he undertook his governmental duties
and which would inevitably lead him into conflict both in the Dáil and in cabinet:

> The money that lies in the banks belongs to the small farmers, the small
> shopkeepers and the small traders of the country. By all means, if we can
> find a profitable use for it, if we can induce these people to lend us that
> money for the purpose of building up the nation, let us take advantage of
> it. If we can use it in profitable production, if we can induce them to lend
> us the money for the purpose of providing more houses, for the purpose of
> settling more people on the land, for the purpose of developing our nation-
> al resources, by all means let us go out and induce them to lend this money
> to us but let us never forget that the moneys are not ours. They have only
> been lent to us and it does not matter whether that money was lent to our
> predecessors, or lent to us, or to our successors, a solemn obligation rests
> on this Assembly, so long as it lasts, to see that these moneys are paid back
> to those who lent them to us originally, to see that moneys entrusted to us
> are repaid to the people who lent them, together with a fair price for their
> use.

De Valera's contribution, too, was unusually long. His speech concentrated on
Fianna Fáil's economic imperatives since 1932 and the difficulties they faced,
and, as such, was the fullest declaration by the Taoiseach of his party's performance in this regard. De Valera's diagnosis did disclose some acute differences of
opinion with his Minister for Finance as well as with the majority report, such as
his comparative lack of concern over the fate of the state's external assets: 'The
capital that is in these factories and workshops is very much more valuable for
the nation than capital abroad, and if there has been any diminution of our external assets to give us that capital equipment and fit us for that production, it is a
good change.'[147] He also rejected very forthrightly the commission's criticism of
the government's role in the nation's economic problems, and he was unrepen-

tant regarding the policies it had pursued since coming to power: 'I, for one, would not change a tittle of the fundamental programme which we put before the people as our industrial programme when we got into office. I believe that that old policy, which we have been fortunate enough to be the people to put into practice, the policy of Sinn Féin, is fundamentally sound and there is nothing in this report that shows anything to the contrary.' He also justified the extent to which Fianna Fáil had invested in the social services despite the financial burden it had fashioned:

> [W]e had a duty to a section of the community, those who, under the exist-ing system and in the existing circumstances, were not able to work and to maintain themselves, and we developed certain social services for that rea-son. These services have added to the cost ... These things have to be met, but we still believe that these social services, notwithstanding the fact that they are, to the extent to which contributions have to be made by the indi-vidual in the way of taxes and so on ... a burden (it is a burden) which we ought to carry, which I believe we can carry and which I believe it is our duty to carry ...

As Dunphy has acknowledged, 'Fianna Fáil's political instinct was sharp enough to resist any attempt to tie its hands in the field of social spending.' De Valera's sympathy for O'Loghlen's report and his commitment to further social spending notwithstanding, Dunphy's laconic observation that 'there was no break with sterling' implicitly supports the notion that de Valera never seriously contemplat-ed far-reaching change and was not going to allow his government to be dictat-ed to by those seeking such change.[148]

Farrell's assertion that 'the recommendations [of the banking commission] appear to have had little real influence on either government policy or public dis-cussion' is generally true. He is also right in recording that 'Finance continued to use the Banking Commission's arguments in attempts to obstruct [Lemass's] policies.' The one recommendation that did have a significant influence on gov-ernment policy, however, was its proposal to establish a central bank. Farrell's analysis, therefore, that there was 'a long war of attrition by Finance against Lemass's efforts to establish an Irish central bank with real powers to control currency credit and investment' must be qualified.[149] In fact, Finance supported the government's moves in this regard, although it viewed powers of control in an altogether different way to Lemass. It concurred with the majority report, which had defined the principal duty of a central bank 'to maintain the integrity of the national monetary unit'.[150] It also maintained that '[central banks] should in particular endeavour as far as their domestic position would permit, take account in their measures of credit regulation of any tendency towards undue charge in the state of general business activities, that is, by a contraction or expansion of credit assist business by cheap money in a depression and holding back in a boom'.[151]

One of MacEntee's last acts as Minister for Finance was to submit a memo-randum to the government in August 1939 recommending that the existing cur-rency commission be wound up and that in its stead a central bank be established. The timing of the memorandum reflected a sense of urgency on the part of the government brought about by the impending war. MacEntee observed that in 'view of the growth of international tension, it has become desirable to have machinery which will enable some measure of effective control to be exercised, if necessary, over such important matters on the financial and economic side as remittances to and from this country, payments for essential imports, sale and purchase of foreign securities, regulation of capital issues etc, for all of which no statutory machinery at present exists'.[152] War conditions would necessitate control over external payments and the purchase and sale of foreign securities, duties which the Currency Commission was ill-equipped to undertake. Moreover, all four of the Banking Commission reports had recommended the establishment of a national monetary authority. By the time the cabinet had decided in principle that a central bank should be set up, MacEntee had left Finance.[153]

AN IMPECCABLY MONOLITHIC GOVERNMENT?

Fianna Fáil, under the leadership of Éamon de Valera, presented itself, according to Farrell, 'as a cohesive national party, united at grass-roots, regimented in parliament and impeccably monolithic in government; there was neither dissent or resignation'.[154] The truth is, however, that there certainly was dissent – though little of it was directed at de Valera personally – and there was, if we are to put any faith in the MacEntee correspondence, very nearly resignation. As Brian Girvin has noted, de Valera 'dominated the cabinet and party in terms of influence and prestige. He commanded the loyalty of his ministers, a position that allowed him to stamp his own authority on what otherwise might have been an unstable cabinet.'[155] At the beginning of a long debate on the appointment of the government in 1943, James Dillon claimed that: 'The first pre-requisite for membership of a government under Taoiseach de Valera is that you are a "yes-man".' De Valera, refusing to be goaded into an explanation of how he allocated ministries, protested that the cabinet was put forward as a team. This desire for balance, coupled with the government's economic prerogatives, placed MacEntee, as Minister for Finance, in an invidious position. Fianna Fáil's assertion of an interventionist social and economic policy challenged the sacred nostrums of his department.

At cabinet meetings, de Valera rarely allowed votes, waiting upon the arrival of consensus: 'No one dared oppose him, but he did not object to ministerial differences.'[156] These differences became acute after 1936, when political and economic stability had been restored somewhat, and it was de Valera's preparation for the 1937 constitution that allowed Finance to articulate most fully its desire to cement its primary place in government and to remind other government departments of their responsibilities. In a memorandum prepared by McElligott for his minister, the language employed by the official anticipates strongly MacEntee's own entreaties to de Valera in his series of resignation letters. McElligott complained that: 'It is not so much that financial considerations are forgotten as that they are completely ignored and if thought of at all they are dismissed as irrelevant and even impertinent.'[157] Finance even went as far as proposing – presumably in an effort to regain lost ground – that the Minister for Finance, under the

1937 constitution, should automatically be elected Tánaiste.[158] Unsurprisingly, de Valera rejected this request, but by making it the department cogently illustrated its besieged position. Similarly, MacEntee's numerous resignation letters offer an insight into his own embattled mindset. Some of these resignation letters, it should be noted, coincided with a turbulent period in the minister's personal life. His younger brother, Charles Owen, died in August 1938 and his father died some months later.[159] Over the course of the previous seven years, MacEntee had developed a close working relationship with his civil servants and respected their opinions and advice.[160] It should not be assumed, however, that MacEntee, having discarded the rhetoric of economic nationalism, now became a prisoner of his civil servants. Ó Broin's testimony bears witness to a very hard-working minister who was suitably well-informed on all issues that concerned his department.[161]

It may also be over-simplistic to regard MacEntee's tenure in Finance during the 1930s as an irrevocable move towards the climacteric of fiscal orthodoxy. His dislike of high taxation was well known by the time he entered office in 1932. That is not to say that he did not regard it as a necessary imposition if the government were to succeed in implementing its social programme. Indeed it must be concluded that MacEntee endorsed, in the main, Fianna Fáil's strategy. He was certainly ambivalent about the merit of public works, but many of his colleagues (with the notable exception of Lemass) shared this ambivalence. He supported the introduction of unemployment assistance; widows' and orphans' pensions; the extension of old age pensions; and the government's extensive housing programme, although he did not agree with the method of its financing. Cousins has demonstrated that this commitment to social policy was not motivated by any proto-Keynesian policy of debt-financed expenditure to boost the economy, rather to meet the needs of the most disadvantaged groups in the community.[162] If the cumulative effect of the measures 'represented a political rather than a coherent economic logic', it is clear that economic policymakers were compromised by the government's competing priorities. This was further complicated by de Valera's prioritisation of what may be called a 'coherent constitutional logic'. This led to some frustration for the Minister for Finance, which was most evident after the publication of the majority report of the Banking Commission, which repeated Finance's more apocalyptic warnings.

Indeed the reports of the Commission on Currency, Banking and Credit, 1934–8 reveal a significant truth about the government of the day, not only in its reaction to the reports but in how it conducted itself in framing the terms of reference and in appointing the commission. Most importantly, the cabinet's reception of them reveals the extent to which MacEntee had diverged from his cabinet colleagues on the fundamental economic questions that confronted the government. That a commission of such 'variegated character' (as *The Economist* described it at the time) could yield a majority report having sixteen of twenty-one signatories was not only testimony to the vitality of the prevailing economic philosophy but also of the sense of fear that the prospect of economic change and experimentation wrought in commercial and agricultural representatives, not to mention in those of the banks and the civil service. The minority reports, while displaying a more catholic approach (in both senses of the word), failed to mount a convincing challenge to this accepted wisdom which, in turn, made it more difficult for the government to execute any alteration to the system or indeed to fulfil the economic programme it began in 1932.

The 1939 Banking Commission debate, moreover, mirrored the debate (interdepartmental as well as public) on the occasion of MacEntee's last budget – which had again raised the rate of income tax – before he left the department for the first time. It was noted by one political opponent in the Seanad that the minister's 'Budget speech did not suggest he was at all happy about the State finances'.[163] However, as punitive and as grave as this measure was regarded by MacEntee, what he found most disturbing was the evident futility of the government's policy:

> In an effort to cope with unemployment we have increased tariffs, we have fostered tillage, we have subsidised dairying and pigs and livestock production, we have developed the sugar-making industry; we have raised the prices of agricultural commodities, we have shortened the working hours of the employed and given them holidays with pay, we have introduced quota restrictions and established virtual monopolies. We have more regimentation, more regulation, more control everywhere. And more unemployment.[164]

As an advocate of sound finance, MacEntee was gratified by the conclusions drawn by the majority report of the Banking Commission – a commission he had done much to establish and one in which he placed considerable faith – and was unafraid to use them in cabinet discussions on framing policy. The minority reports, while more in keeping with the general drift of the government's economic strategy, were never likely to win the confidence of a minister who required evidence of a scheme's infallibility before embarking on something novel. His unremitting questioning of that strategy and his innate distrust of social and economic regulation made it imperative for the viability of the government that he discontinue as Minister for Finance before the onset of war. The one recommendation of the majority report that did secure governmental approbation was its proposal to establish a national monetary authority with greater powers than the Currency Commission. This undertaking was also burdened with interdepartmental disagreement and a somewhat confused understanding of the anticipated body's main functions. Lemass's desire to ensure that the central bank would be considerably less toothless than the existing monetary machinery, and that credit regulation would be part of its remit, was opposed consistently by MacEntee. That Lemass secured the support of de Valera and a significant majority of the government on this point reinforces the impression that MacEntee was becoming increasingly isolated within the cabinet. Tom Garvin has recently surmised that MacEntee's 'outsider' status derived from his Belfast background.[165] That he 'formed a one-man loyal opposition inside the Fianna Fáil government' and that he unwittingly earned the unappealing soubriquet 'leader of the opposition' within de Valera's close circle may suggest a more deep-seated cause.[166]

Regardless from where this outsider status derived, MacEntee, by 1940 at the latest, had consistently questioned government policy enough to be seen as an irritant by those members of the cabinet who espoused it most vehemently. In 1940, he even had the temerity to impugn de Valera's precious agricultural policy of tillage farming, implicit in which was a condemnation of the Economic War, at the expense of commercial agriculture.[167] MacEntee's polemic included the suggestion that 'present government policy appeared to be opposed to, rather than directed to, the promotion of [agricultural] development, and ... that exports were necessary not for their own sake but only because people here wanted to consume coal, iron, timber, tin, gold, silver, cocoa, coffee, sugar and thousand[s] of other things, and that such exports depended on either a socialist or capitalist order of competitive efficiency'. The minister's contrariness was undoubtedly nurtured by a succession of interdepartmental squabbles, and in assessing his evolution from unreconstructed economic nationalist before 1932 to pragmatic developmentalist by 1940, it is perhaps possible to employ a perceptive description of Lemass's speeches in the same period – 'an interesting study in gradual political education' – as equally apposite to MacEntee.[168] That this education was fulfilled in the corridors of the Department of Finance should not be regarded as coincidental. While it may be going too far to suggest that, by the end of his tenure in Finance, MacEntee had lost sympathy for the government's economic objectives, it is indisputable that he had lost faith in the methods adopted by the government to oversee the execution of those objectives.

NOTES

1. D. McMahon, *Republicans and Imperialists: Anglo-Irish Relations in the 1930s* (London, 1984), p.21.
2. See Fanning, *Finance*, pp.537–48.
3. Two comprehensive accounts on the transfer of power are: J. McColgan, *British Policy and the Irish Administration, 1920–22* (London, 1983) and L.W. McBride, *The Greening of Dublin Castle: The Transformation of Bureaucratic and Judicial Personnel in Ireland, 1892–1922* (Washington, 1991).
4. See Fanning, *Finance*, pp.32–4.
5. Ibid., p.7.
6. L. Ó Broin, *Just Like Yesterday* (Dublin, 1986), p.81.
7. Fanning, *Finance*, p.8. See also Eunan O'Halpin, 'The civil service and the political system', *Administration*, 38, 4 (1991).
8. For a discussion of Collins' political legacy and his role in the setting up of Irish administrative functions, see J. Regan, 'Michael Collins: the legacy and the intestacy', in G. Doherty and D. Keogh (eds), *Michael Collins and the Making of the Irish State* (Dublin, 1998). For a discussion of Collins' performance in Finance, see A. McCarthy, 'Michael Collins – Minister for Finance 1919–1922', in idem.
9. Regan suggests that Finance's dominance can also be attributed to the lack of expertise within the early cabinets: 'Save for Cosgrave's limited experience on the Finance Committee of Dublin Corporation, Cumann na nGaedheal Governments were devoid of financial expertise. Excepting the army estimates, finance was not discussed in cabinet and in this crucial sphere the Government was forced to rely on its senior civil servants.' See J.M. Regan, *The Irish Counter-revolution 1921–1936* (Dublin, 1999), p.147. It should also be noted, however, that Brennan left the department in 1927, owing to frequent disagreements with his minister, Ernest Blythe.
10. For character studies of both men see L. Ó Broin, 'Joseph Brennan, civil servant extraordinary', *Studies*, vol. 66 (1977), and *No Man's Man* (Dublin, 1982); 'Silhouette', 'J.J. McElligott', *Administration*, vol. 1 (1953); and Whitaker, *Interests*, pp.287–9.
11. His influence was most notable on the findings of the commission to inquire into the civil service, 1934 and on the majority report of the Banking Commission, 1934–38.
12. See T.M. Feeney 'Fianna Fáil and the civil service, 1927–37' (Unpublished MA thesis, UCD, 1999).
13. Ó Broin, *Just Like Yesterday*, p.97.
14. Ibid., p.100.

15. Walker (ed.), *Parliamentary Election Results in Ireland 1918–92*.
16. McMahon, *Republicans and Imperialists*, pp.4–5.
17. *Dáil debates*, vol. 41, cols 27–34, 9 March 1932; F.W. Powell, *The Politics of Irish Social Policy, 1600–1990* (New York, 1992), p.193.
18. *Irish Press*, 11 February 1932. UCD P176/744, The party had also vowed to introduce pensions for widows and orphans at its árd fheis in October 1930.
19. M. Cousins, *The Birth of Irish Social Welfare in Ireland* (Dublin, 2003), pp.56–7. This was very much in keeping with de Valera's contention that public servants were overpaid.
20. J. Horgan, *Seán Lemass: The Enigmatic Patriot* (Dublin, 1997) p.69.
21. NAI S6274, Minutes of the Economic Committee of the Cabinet.
22. Ibid.
23. The committee sought to establish how best to make 'the reductions necessary in the remuneration of the civil service, civic guards, teachers and the army', Fanning, *Finance* p.223. MacEntee was again excluded from the committee which consisted of O'Kelly, James Ryan and the Minister for Education, Tom Derrig.
24. See Fanning, *Finance*, pp.218–19.
25. Indeed it could be said that de Valera had a somewhat arcane and unusual method of choosing negotiating teams. He also left the Minister for Defence, Frank Aiken, out of the Anglo-Irish negotiations in 1938, when, it could be argued, he had a direct interest in the outcome.
26. Quoted in Fanning, *Finance*, p.225.
27. D. McMahon 'A transient apparition: British policy towards the de Valera government, 1932–5', *Irish Historical Studies*, vol. 22 (1981). For further British views on de Valera, see P. Canning, *British Policy towards Ireland, 1921–1941* (Oxford, 1985), pp.140–1.
28. Ó Broin, *Just Like Yesterday*, p.100.
29. NAI F43/2/32.
30. Fanning, *Finance*, p.223.
31. Ó Broin, *Just Like Yesterday*, p.99.
32. UCDA P67/127.
33. NAI F43/2/32.
34. *Irish Times*, 12 May 1932.
35. Quoted in T. Brown, *Ireland: A Social and Cultural History 1922–1985* (London, 1981) p.143. Horgan was also a defeated Cumann na nGaedheal candidate in the 1932 election.
36. *Irish Times*, 23 July 1974.
37. Published as J.M. Keynes, 'National self-sufficiency', *Studies* (June, 1933), pp.177–93.
38. Ibid., p.189.
39. McMahon, 'A transient apparition', p.342.
40. Profile of Seán MacEntee, *Irish Times*, 23 July 1974.
41. McMahon, *Republicans and Imperialists*, p.18.
42. See ibid., pp.104–5.
43. Quoted in Fanning, *Finance*, p.247.
44. NAI F200/25/37.
45. MacEntee later recalled that 'as Minister for External Affairs, de Valera was responsible for formulating that policy and you did not change that policy unless you had very good grounds for doing so … Nobody ever formulated foreign policy except de Valera.' Quoted in E. O'Halpin, 'Fianna Fáil on the high wire of foreign policy', in P. Hannon and J. Gallagher (eds), *Taking the Long View: Seventy Years of Fianna Fáil* (Dublin, 1996).
46. Fanning, *Finance*, p.245.
47. McElligott and MacEntee quickly formed a close working relationship in the Department of Finance. Their mutual respect may have come from a chance encounter in Easter week, 1916, but, in keeping with the strict code of practice laid down by government with respect to civil servants, they never met outside the office. See Whitaker, *Interests*, pp.287–9 and Cruise O'Brien, *Same Age as the State*, p.126.
48. Fanning, *Finance*, p.250.
49. Quoted in ibid., p.251.
50. T.K. Whitaker, 'The Finance Attitude', *Administration* (1953–4) pp.60–8.
51. De Valera was reported in the *Irish Times* on 6 January 1933 saying 'We knew that many of the officials in key positions in the State service were political and personal friends of our opponents, to whom many of them owed their positions. We knew that it was most improbable that, with their sympathies elsewhere, they could serve us and our opponents as loyally and enthusiastically as our opponents.'
52. NAI DT S. 6242B.

53. NAI S6274. There were two officials from Industry and Commerce included on the committee and one from Finance. See also M. Scanlon, 'The social policy of the first Fianna Fáil government, 1932–33' (Unpublished MA thesis, UCD 1979).
54. NAI F88/9/33.
55. Cousins, *The Birth of Social Welfare*, p.63.
56. Ibid.
57. NAI DT S.6242B; Also see Cousins, *The Birth of Social Welfare*, p.64.
58. Cousins, *The Birth of Social Welfare*, pp.64–5.
59. Quoted in ibid., pp.61–2.
60. NAI G2/9, Minutes of Sixth Executive Council, 29 July 1932.
61. Quoted in Murphy, 'In pursuit of popularity and legitimacy', p 37.
62. M.E. Daly, *The Buffer State: The Historical Roots of the Department of the Environment* (Dublin, 1997), p.220.
63. *Irish Times*, 6 January 1933.
64. UCDA P67/129.
65. Quoted in Murphy, 'In pursuit of popularity and legitimacy', p.34.
66. *Dáil debates*, vol. 47, col. 743, 10 May 1933.
67. NAI F43/2/34, Minister's budget statement.
68. McMahon, *Republicans and Imperialists*, pp.144–5.
69. See M.E. Daly, 'An Irish-Ireland for business? The Control of Manufactures Acts 1932 and 1934', *Irish Historical Studies*, xxiv, 94 (November 1984) and 'Government finance for industry in the Irish Free State: the Trade Loans (Guarantee) Acts', *Irish Economic and Social History*, vol. XI (1984).
70. M.E. Daly, 'The employment gains from industrial protection in the Irish Free State during the 1930s: a note', *Irish Economic and Social History*, vol. XV (1988), pp.71–5.
71. UCDA P67/130, Budget speech, 12 May 1936.
72. *Irish Times*, 13 May 1936.
73. O'Hagan, 'An analysis of the relative size of the government sector', pp.23–4.
74. *Dáil debates*, vol. 69, cols 2884–5, 17 December 1937.
75. Dunphy, *The Making of Fianna Fáil Power*, p.182.
76. That is not to say that Finance had its own way under Cumann na nGaedheal. That government's financing of the Shannon Scheme, in particular, was a cause of friction between the department and the cabinet. Fanning has recorded that 'By 1925–26 [Brennan] had become increasingly disillusioned by his inability to curb state borrowing powers and by his differences of opinion with his minister [Blythe], of which the Shannon Scheme is an outstanding example.' Fanning, *Finance*, p.190.
77. NAI DT S.11644, MacEntee, in a meeting with a delegation of the ITUC in January 1940, described the results of the committee's work as 'very disappointing'.
78. NAI DT S. 8786, Finance memo on public works, 15 April 1935.
79. Quoted in Daly, *The Buffer State*, p.187.
80. Cousins, *The Birth of Social Welfare*, p.69.
81. UCDA P67/111 (45). Memorandum dated 9 April 1936.
82. *Dáil debates*, vol. 51, col. 2553, 27 April 1934.
83. Ibid., 18 April 1936.
84. Ibid.
85. Daly, *The Buffer State*, p.193.
86. UCDA P67/121. Handwritten letter to de Valera, n.d.
87. Although there is no reply to this letter on file, MacEntee later confided to the *Irish Times* political correspondent Michael McInerney that 'Once or twice I may have reached the point of giving up and resigning, but Dev with his patience and realism resolved my difficulties.' UCDA P67/800, Correspondence with Michael McInerney, concerning four-part profile of MacEntee, June 1974.
88. UCDA P67/111.
89. NAI. F200/25/37.
90. Ibid.
91. Cousins, *The Birth of Social Welfare*, p.87; *Irish Press*, 1 July 1937.
92. Dunphy, *The Making of Fianna Fáil Power*, p.210.
93. UCDA P67/125, MacEntee to de Valera, n.d.
94. De Valera was absent from government meetings on 28 February 1939, 14 March, 21 March, 22 March and 24 March.
95. NAI, G3/2, Minutes of Second Government, 4 May 1939.
96. UCDA P67/133, MacEntee to de Valera. It is likely that such a discussion took place on 24 February 1939 when the estimates for the public services 1939/40 were submitted to cabinet by MacEntee.

97. UCDA P67/132, MacEntee to de Valera, 30 April 1939.
98. Ibid., 28 April 1939.
99. Ibid.
100. UCDA P67/331.
101. Dead-weight debt is debt incurred without leading to the creation of any specific asset from which the cost of the debt service can be met.
102. *Dáil debates*, vol. 75, 10 May 1939.
103. UCDA P67/155.
104. That official was J.J. McElligott; the secretary of the commission, J.L. Lynd, was also from the Department of Finance.
105. M. Moynihan, *Currency and Central Banking in Ireland, 1922–60* (Dublin, 1975), p.63.
106. UCDA P176/26, Fianna Fáil *Weekly Bulletin*, 24 January 1927.
107. UCDA P176/26, Fianna Fáil *Weekly Bulletin*.
108. Ibid.
109. C. Ó Gráda, 'Money and banking in the Irish Free State 1921–1939', Centre for Economic Research, UCD; working paper number WP92/3.
110. UCDA P176/746, 8/9 November 1932.
111. UCDA P67/105(2), MacEntee to de Valera, 23 February 1933.
112. UCDA P67/105.
113. C. Ó Gráda, *Ireland: A New Economic History 1780–1939* (Oxford, 1994), p.369.
114. The other adviser was John Busteed.
115. DT S2235 A, Smiddy to de Valera, 16 March 1933. De Valera continued to get Smiddy's views on the establishment of a central bank throughout 1932 and 1933. De Valera's confidence in Smiddy was based on the fact that he had examined the banking and currency situation for the Provisional government in 1922 and had suggested the establishment of a central bank. Smiddy, who had been the first Professor of Economics in University College, Cork, was in 1932 a member of the Tariff Commission and somewhat conveniently for the president had an office in Government Buildings.
116. UCDA P67/800, Correspondence with Michael McInerney, 1974.
117. Moynihan, *Currency and Banking*, p.184.
118. UCDA P67/105.
119. UCDA P67/105 (17), Finance memo, 6 April 1934.
120. Ibid.
121. Conversation between de Valera and Jacobsson, 1 November 1937, E.E. Jucker-Fleetwood, 'The Irish Banking Commission 1934–38 as seen by Per Jacobsson' *Quarterly Bulletin of Central Bank* (winter 1974).
122. J.P. Colbert, 'The Banking Commission in General', *Irish Monthly* (May 1939). There were four addenda, one note, two separate reservations and thirty-two appendices to the majority report.
123. Reservation I, majority report, pp.407–13.
124. *Majority Report of the Banking Commission*, para. 488. Brennan had already published his thoughts on the public debt position of the Irish Free State (up to 1934) in the *Journal of the Statistical and Social Inquiry Society of Ireland, 1935*. This paper had been read to the society on 18 January 1935 (during the course of the commission's sitting) and, interestingly, in attendance were J.C.M. Eason and Dr Per Jacobsson. Indeed Jacobsson congratulated Brennan on an 'excellent and instructive paper'.
125. Ibid., para. 489.
126. Quoted in Fanning, *Finance*, pp.358–9.
127. Moynihan, *Currency and Banking*, pp.221–2.
128. *Majority Report of the Banking Commission*, para 489.
129. *Dáil debates*, vol. 76, 6–7 July 1939.
130. *Irish Press*, 9 August 1938.
131. Quoted in Dunphy, *The Making of Fianna Fáil Power*, p.176.
132. NAI F9/19/38, Little to MacEntee, 23 November 1938.
133. Ibid.
134. NAI F9/19/38.
135. NAI F9/9/38, Finance Memorandum, 15 July 1938.
136. Ibid.
137. Ibid., Barton to MacEntee, 8 August 1938.
138. NAI F9/19/38. De Valera told the Dáil in June 1939 that he accepted the social principles of the third minority report. See Moynihan, *The Speeches and Statements of Éamon de Valera, 1917–1973* (Dublin, 1980), p.404.
139. Ibid.

140. The memorandum called it 'unscrupulous propaganda'.
141. NAI DT S10612, Memorandum dated 17 April 1939.
142. Ibid.
143. Meade was an Oxford graduate who had been influenced by Keynes during the 1930s. He published *The Rate of Interest in a Progressive State* in 1933. In 1936, he wrote one of the first modern Keynesian textbooks, *An Introduction to Economic Analysis and Policy*. He was also the author of two world economic surveys for the European Intelligence Service of the League of Nations. He was awarded the Nobel Prize in 1977 with the Swedish economist, Bertil Ohlin. The authors of the third minority report had sent their proposals to Meade, who gave them qualified approval. For a further discussion on this memorandum and on the Finance attitude to Meade, see Lee, *Ireland 1912–1985: Politics and Society*, pp.563–7.
144. G.D. Feldman, *The Great Disorder: Politics, Economics, and Society in the German Inflation 1914–24* (New York, 1997), p.821.
145. MacEntee submitted memoranda to cabinet of speeches by Dr Schacht and the German Secretary of State, Brinkman dealing with aspects of German economic policy in May 1939. See UCDA P67/199.
146. Ibid.
147. Ibid., 7 July 1939.
148. Dunphy, *The Making of Fianna Fáil Power*, p.176.
149. Farrell, *Seán Lemass*, pp 48–9.
150. Majority report, p.224.
151. Ibid., p.237.
152. NAI DT S.2235 A, Finance memo on establishment of central bank, 28 August 1939. See also UCDA P67/108.
153. Ibid.
154. B. Farrell, 'De Valera: unique dictator or charismatic chairman?' in J.P. O'Carroll and J.A. Murphy (eds), *De Valera and his Times* (Cork, 1983).
155. B. Girvin, 'The republicanisation of Irish society', in J.R. Hill (ed.), *A New History of Ireland, VII: Ireland, 1921–1984* (Oxford, 2003), p.128.
156. T. Desmond Williams, 'De Valera in power', in F. MacManus (ed.), *The Years of the Great Test, 1926–39* (Cork, 1967).
157. Quoted in Fanning, *Finance*, p.274.
158. Ibid., pp.569–71.
159. *Irish Times*, 12 August 1938. See also Cruise O'Brien, *The Same Age as the State*, pp.33–6. Charlie McEntee had in fact followed in the footsteps of his older brother, becoming an engineer and setting up a consultancy in Dublin. He died in his parents' home on Ravenhill Road, Belfast after a short illness.
160. I have been unable to find any specific cases of disagreement between MacEntee and his officials. More often than not he accepted their counsel, but he presented it to government in a more palatable style than would have been the case if left to McElligott.
161. Ó Broin, *Just Like Yesterday*, p.100.
162. Cousins, *The Birth of Social Welfare*, pp.83–5.
163. *Seanad debates*, vol. 22, 1799–1800, 28 June 1939. The opponent in question was Sir John Keane.
164. UCDA P67/125.
165. T. Garvin, *Preventing the Future: Why was Ireland so Poor for so Long?* (Dublin, 2004), pp.32–3.
166. T. de Valera, *A Memoir* (Dublin, 2004), p.185.
167. UCDA P67/108. See also Garvin, *Preventing the Future*, pp.28–32.
168. Quoted in Neary and Ó Gráda, 'Protection, economic war and structural change: the 1930s in Ireland', *Irish Historical Studies*, xxvii, 107 (May 1991).

4

Emergency Politics

In September 1939, on the outbreak of what in Éire became known as the Emergency,[1] de Valera made his first significant cabinet reshuffle since Fianna Fáil had become a party of government.[2] The Taoiseach attributed the need for the reshuffle to the creation of two new ministerial posts: a Minister for Supplies and a Minister for the Co-ordination of Defensive Measures. He denied that the changes would in any way result in a change of policy: 'No change of policy is involved, as may be realised from the fact that the reallocation which has been made does not involve any change in the personnel of the Government as a whole, the members of which are collectively responsible for policy.'[3] Despite de Valera's attempt at buttressing the party's monolithic image, there were significant divisions within the cabinet, particularly in relation to economic policy. MacEntee's positive reception of the Banking Commission's main findings, combined with his mounting alarm at the budgetary strategy adopted by the party, demonstrated this quite clearly. However, the Taoiseach, buoyed by the successful conclusion of the Anglo-Irish negotiations of 1938, and the party's resounding electoral victory later that year, was keen to extend Fianna Fáil's political hegemony and saw in these events a powerful vindication of his party's performance. The triumphs of 1938 constituted an electoral apotheosis for Fianna Fáil; the party even won an endorsement from the once hostile *Irish Times*.[4] Nonetheless, a number of problems – namely, rising emigration and unemployment – threatened to undermine the government's complacency.[5]

The crisis brought by war was not a huge surprise to policymakers. As early as April 1938, the Department of Industry and Commerce had warned the government of the likely effect of a European war.[6] In particular, it drew attention to the enduring reliance of the state on Britain for goods, and warned that a high proportion of imports consisted of 'essential supplies ... which we cannot provide ourselves'.[7] MacEntee was also preparing for war: 'My drive through Europe in September 1937 had begun to make me doubt the future in Europe; and my doubts had been heightened by my interchange with Chamberlain during the 1938 negotiations.'[8] Accordingly, during March and April 1938 he sought advice from Joseph Brennan and Per Jacobsson regarding future policy if the international situation deteriorated.[9] Jacobsson warned MacEntee of the dangers of overexposure to sterling and suggested that investments be spread over gold bullion and dollar securities. Following the general election of June 1938, MacEntee met with Brennan and McElligott suggesting a gold reserve of £8 million to back the currency should war break out.[10] Both were opposed to his suggestion: Brennan because of the loss in income deriving from £8 million in gilt-edged securities, almost entirely British, and McElligott because of the loss to exchequer funds of its portion from the Currency Commission. MacEntee's powers of persuasion were enough to get both Brennan and McElligott to finally agree but 'great pressure was brought to bear' by de Valera, 'on whom it was being impressed by several influential persons that the gold purchase was an unnecessary expense'.[11] Ultimately, the matter was determined by MacEntee agreeing to let half the gold go, so when the war broke out, the state had accumulated £4 million in gold bullion.

War planning also preoccupied de Valera. In September 1938 he compiled a list of twelve matters which required urgent attention in the event of war. Of utmost concern to the Taoiseach were food supplies and external trade, followed by censorship and other security concerns.[12] The need to maintain supplies led to the rotation of ministries. Lemass's new responsibilities in the freshly created Department of Supplies left a significant void in his old department, a void that the Taoiseach reasoned somewhat unconvincingly would be best filled by the person who had most contact with it, namely the Minister for Finance.[13] If de Valera's justification for appointing MacEntee to Industry and Commerce appeared somewhat disingenuous, his calculations were certainly dictated by political expediency. They made political sense because MacEntee, as we have seen, was becoming increasingly isolated in Finance and probably welcomed the change to a department that did not bear the ultimate responsibility for the government finances.[14] Nevertheless, wartime conditions meant that MacEntee would have little respite from key policy objectives. He now bore the equally onerous burden of maintaining employment and productivity in the new circumstances. He would also have to contend with an upsurge in trade union disaffection, on foot of government policy to rationalise what it saw as their erratic organisation. All of these difficulties would make policy formulation less coherent and more reactive and made de Valera's claims of regime solidarity largely academic. What remained most noteworthy about the reshuffle is that it placed the cautious and painstakingly pedantic MacEntee in a department that had enjoyed a customary dynamism throughout the period of Fianna Fáil government under the vigorous stewardship of Lemass and the benign sponsorship of de Valera.

The industrial sector employed one person in six of the working population, and the demands on it to maintain employment and production throughout the war years would prove arduous. That task was made even more difficult by the shortage of essential raw materials, low fuel stocks, inadequate equipment and limited machinery. Considering his new role would be hamstrung by such limitations, McEntee's move has been interpreted as a demotion. It could, however, be interpreted in a more generous way. Given MacEntee's reputation as an uncompromising negotiator and someone who was accustomed to being in the front line when it came to presenting tough government measures, de Valera may well have seen him as particularly suited to his new brief. While the cost of living soared, wage levels had to be controlled by the government who dreaded above all the onset of inflationary pressures.[15] It was, therefore, an equally opportune time for the labour movement to capitalise on such conditions. Trade union membership, which had increased to 162,000 in 1939 from a figure of 95,000 in 1933, was predominantly industrial, and it was MacEntee's responsibility to deal with a constituency that had become increasingly politicised.[16]

INDUSTRY AND COMMERCE AND SUPPLIES

'The supply of essential commodities,' according to Fanning, 'was, and remained, the first national economic priority throughout the Emergency.'[17] In fact, this had been recognised by the government since the mid-1930s, and preparations had been underway since that time with a view to securing basic supplies in the event of war. Little was done before September 1938, however, when preparations were put on a more urgent footing by the setting up of a special branch of the Department of Industry and Commerce, known as the emergency supplies branch.[18] A deputy assistant secretary and other staff were withdrawn from the department to devote their full attention to this work.[19] Their principal duties were to make surveys of the foremost trades and industries in the country, and to undertake discussions with representatives of the various trades and industries as to the position that would arise in the event of an emergency. Five months later, that emergency arrived and Seán Lemass was duly appointed Minister for Supplies on 16 September. De Valera's decision to invest the responsibility for maintaining the country's supplies in Lemass 'marked a heightened plateau in his ministerial career'.[20] According to Horgan, Lemass's new position provided him with 'a degree of power and freedom of action he had never hitherto experienced'.[21] Financial control and normal administrative procedure were deemed less important under the new conditions. Lemass encouraged all officials concerned with policy formation to attend departmental conferences at which decisions were pushed through speedily, circumventing the standard administrative arrangements.[22] Lemass's *modus operandi* was certainly unconventional; it left no paper trail, so decisions could not be readily justified by appropriate memoranda.[23] The new department was staffed by the transfer on loan of officers from other departments, 'largely but not entirely' from the emergency supplies branch of Industry and Commerce, but also by a principal, D.P. Shanagher, from Finance.[24] John Leydon, the secretary of the Department of Industry and Commerce, also followed Lemass to Supplies.

The department that MacEntee inherited, therefore, had lost some of its key personnel. The new department secretary, R.C. Ferguson, was promoted from assistant secretary, while the other incumbent in that position, T.J. Flynn, remained in the department along with the deputy assistant, W. Maguire, who succeeded Ferguson as assistant.[25] Staff of the prices commission, set up under the Control of Prices Act, 1937, was also transferred to the new Department of Supplies. Lemass told the Dáil in March 1940 that the work of the Department of Supplies fell into three main divisions: supplies, distribution of supplies and prices.[26] Under Lemass, Industry and Commerce had been remarkably successful in promoting the government's industrialisation drive. Between 1932 and the outbreak of the Emergency in 1939, there was a significant rise in the numbers employed in industry.[27] For example, transportable goods employment grew at an

annual rate of 6.5 per cent in 1931–8. Total industrial employment has been estimated at 166,500 in 1938, but the difficulties of obtaining materials and fuel
imports during the war had a considerable impact.[28] This figure fell to 143,500 in
1943. While employment creation and industrial development remained Industry
and Commerce's main functions, Supplies was now responsible for co-ordinat-
ing and sometimes directing many of the activities of both Agriculture and
MacEntee's department. The Department of Supplies had become, in de Valera's
estimation, 'the central planning department of our economic life'.[29] The
Emergency Powers Act, which became law in September 1939, made provision
for 'securing the public safety and the preservation of the state in a time of war,
and in particular, for the maintenance of public order and for the provision and
control of supplies and services essential to the life of the community'.[30]

UNEMPLOYMENT AND EMIGRATION

One area where Lemass was less influential was in employment policy. The
employment branch of Industry and Commerce continued to be responsible for
all aspects of industrial employment. Indeed Lemass's move to Supplies had
taken him out of the loop of industrial development, not that there was much during the war.[31] MacEntee ruefully explained to the Dáil in May that, owing to the
war, a great number of the new industries being considered by his department
had little chance of materialising.[32] This bleak forecast drew a vigorous response
from the new minister. In July, he attempted to by-pass normal procedure in
implementing a new bill by seeking, by way of an emergency powers order, 'all
the powers in relation to the acquisition and development of mineral deposits'
and 'with the consent of the Minister for Finance, to acquire compulsorily minerals in private ownership and to work mineral deposits as a state enterprise'.
The memorandum did concede that MacEntee was hesitant about seeking such
powers but argued that they were essential 'to deal expeditiously with proposals
relating e.g., to the provision of fuel by acquiring and developing coal deposits
or of raw industrial materials by taking over of phosphate rock deposits'.[33]
Finance rejected the minister's request owing to the lack of any financial provisions in the draft order. Industry and Commerce responded by explaining that the
minister's initiative had been prompted by his anxiety to develop certain coal
deposits at Slieveardagh Mine with maximum speed and indicated, in a conciliatory fashion, that Finance sanction would be sought in regard to expenditure.
In the end, Finance objections led to the withdrawal of the emergency powers
order and the introduction of the Mineral Development Bill which allowed for
public ownership of the mine, something to which in other circumstances
MacEntee would not have been disposed:

> Left to development by private enterprise, experience has shown that there
> is a probability that the mineral deposits, such as they are, in the country,
> may never be developed. In the interests of the State it is important that such
> possibilities as there are should be fully explored and should be fully availed
> of. The development of the deposits which we have would give much-need-

ed employment, and the coal and other minerals which may be raised would help to feed essential industries with raw materials at a time when the flow of imports is for any cause interrupted ... There is, naturally, no desire to confiscate private property, but it is important that the efforts of the State or of private persons to develop mineral deposits should not provide the owners of deposits which may have lain dormant for years with the opportunity of demanding for their interests amounts which would make the exploitation of the deposits uneconomic.[34]

The passage of the Mineral Development Act witnessed one of the first examples of MacEntee's new-found determination to use the legislative powers of the state in pursuit of an amelioration of the wartime conditions. Concern for the state's capacity to generate its own fuel and power also governed the minister's decision to introduce the Electricity (Supply) (Amendment) Bill, 1940. The purpose of this act was to provide additional advances to the Electricity Supply Board to cover its estimated capital requirements to 31 March 1942; to ensure that the board had power to erect electric generating stations, using peat as fuel, and to make provision for the investment of the board's reserves.[35] The additional £4,000,000 advanced by the government provided for the erection of a peat-fuelled generating station near Portarlington, adjacent to Clonsast bog. In his estimates speech in 1941, MacEntee contended that the two largest accessions to positive employment had been in the production of food and the production of fuel.[36] The turf cutting campaign, he explained, had 'created an intense demand for labour suitable and available in the vicinity of bogs'.

MacEntee's more *dirigiste* thinking was also revealed by his introduction of the Emergency Powers (No. 93) Order, 1941, which increased allowances for dependents under the unemployment insurance acts, and a scheme for the distribution of vouchers entitling the recipients of unemployment assistance, as well as of old age and widows' and orphans' pensions, to weekly rations of milk, bread and butter.[37] There were also amendments made to the unemployment insurance and unemployment assistance acts enabling unemployment benefit or assistance to be paid in the case of alternating periods of employment and unemployment in a more flexible way. Such emoluments could only have a limited effect, however, as the department's efforts to prolong employment were heavily reliant on the cooperation and success of Lemass's department.[38] Creating employment and seeking new industrial development opportunities were ostensibly the main functions of the Department of Industry and Commerce under MacEntee's stewardship. Continuing difficulties in these areas, however, meant that other means of mitigating unemployment had to be sought, such as facilitating emigration to Britain. MacEntee conceded in the same debate that 'The policy of providing economic work by way of developing new industries and maintaining those recently established is meeting with almost insuperable difficulties and obstacles in present conditions.'[39] Indeed the prevalence of unemployment, particularly urban unemployment, and the palliatives required to assuage its worst effects, together with the need to control wage inflation, conditioned every public policy decision made by MacEntee as Minister for Industry and

Commerce. The prospect of acutely high unemployment was a constant preoccupation of the cabinet in the opening months of the war. On 19 October 1939,
in a statement to the Dáil on government policy, the recently appointed Minister
for Finance, Seán T. O'Kelly, set out to explain how the new circumstances
would affect the state's economic prospects. His appointment of an economy
committee in September 'to review all existing services and to report on the
economies which could reasonably be effected by their suspension or curtailment in the present emergency, and to make such other suggestions with a view
to retrenchment as appear feasible and desirable', indicated that those altered
conditions would have severe repercussions on the government's ability to sustain employment and ensure a continuation of trade.[40]

Opposition deputies immediately sought reassurances from the government
in this regard. William Norton, the Labour Party leader, interrogated the minister on the incidence of unemployment in the building industry, anticipating further distress caused by the possible return of emigrants from Britain.[41] He contended that the unemployment problem was significantly worse than the official
figures presented owing to the working of the employment period order; those
who were called for service in the army; and those who returned from Britain
and who found little advantage in registering for assistance. Much of Norton's
alarm was predicated on an expected deterioration of the supply position.
Lemass had attempted to reassure employers in this regard, urging them not to
pay off workers in any haste or panic until things became appreciably worse.
MacEntee conceded that there had been an increase in unemployment in the
building industry, which he attributed to seasonal factors; to a breakdown of
machinery; and to a shortage of raw materials. He was adamant, however, that it
was 'to a very small extent' due to a shortage of raw materials arising out of the
war.[42] Notwithstanding this, he remained attentive to the potential seriousness of
the matter if the required supplies became unavailable: 'The moment there is an
interruption of such supplies as the Minister [for Supplies] has been able to
secure, then we are going to be faced with an unemployment problem which I
quite frankly say will be insoluble so long as that particular interruption of supplies remains.'[43] With this in mind, any sudden influx of Ireland's prodigal children from Britain was not something that the minister felt his government should
be unduly concerned about:

> First of all our responsibility is to the people who have remained at home
> and not so much to the people who have returned home after a period of
> years away. Naturally they have to take second place. I will not say that in
> certain circumstances we will not help them, but I cannot take the view that
> they are entitled to take precedence over the others.[44]

MacEntee's lack of hospitality to returning émigrés indicated the seriousness of
the problem. One part of the government's strategy was the Derelict Sites Act,
1940, which gave local authorities power to acquire derelict urban sites compulsorily with a view to clearing them and which promised to provide a number of
projects. Another was the Construction Corps: 'a quasi military corps of young
single unemployed males, who would be employed on national projects'.[45]

Neither convinced MacEntee, mainly because they involved unproductive and costly schemes. De Valera, on the other hand, was seduced by the idea of replicating labour battalions based on the Civilian Conservation Corps in the United States to engage unemployed urban males and in October 1938 he instructed Hugo Flinn to make arrangements for a general preliminary investigation of such schemes.[46] Although de Valera continued to force the agenda on the project, MacEntee again demonstrated his lack of faith in the efficacy of relief works. He calculated the potential costs to be 'enormous' and was of the opinion that the scheme would provide 'no permanent solution to the unemployment problem'. But given de Valera's evident enthusiasm for it, he agreed to an experiment with one camp which would provide for about 180 youths. De Valera saw numerous benefits in the scheme. As well as creating work for a portion of the residually unemployed, it was hoped to instil a benign militaristic discipline in the youths, and to satisfy the growing scarcity of fuel. When an experiment at Clonsast bog yielded disappointing results, he regarded it as evidence of a 'general disinclination for work on the part of young unemployed men in the city'.[47]

In addition to the labour battalion scheme, de Valera had also issued Flinn with instructions 'to prepare a large scheme of public works available in an emergency for operation at very short notice, to deal with an anticipated large influx of Irish nationals from Great Britain, if and when the present position became absolutely critical'.[48] Flinn agreed to undertake the order but stated his opinion that the schemes of works 'could not be expected to have a high standard of economy'. The Taoiseach replied that 'in the event envisaged economy would have to go by the board; and broadly speaking the main consideration would be to deliver the goods'.[49] Such disregard for the general economy clearly differentiated the respective approaches of the Taoiseach and MacEntee.

That is not to say, however, that MacEntee failed to recognise the priorities of his new brief. In January 1940, he set up a meeting with representatives of the Irish Trade Union Congress (ITUC) to discuss unemployment. This meeting was in the context of a resolution passed by congress at its annual conference that called on the government to set up a commission 'with powers to enquire into all aspects of unemployment, and to recommend after consultation with the National Executive of the Trade Union Congress – how the unemployed may be absorbed in useful occupations, and further that industry be called upon to make greater provision to meet the needs of those who are denied the right to work'.[50] The minister assured the delegation that he would propose to examine the proposal 'very carefully and sympathetically'. The ITUC representatives, Sam Kyle and Senator Éamon Lynch, expressed their concern at the increase in unemployment and urged the government to seek 'a permanent solution to the problem'. MacEntee stressed that the personnel on any commission should be 'expert in most of the aspects of the unemployment problem'[51] and was at pains to defend the government's response to unemployment. However, looking at specific remedies such as housing, MacEntee expressed the view that 'in the city of Dublin, house-building has been ... a very grave and serious disappointment as a medium for providing employment'. The minister also failed to give any guarantees on the issue of increasing the amount of unemployment assistance and contended that the recent increases in the incidence of unemployment constituted 'a special type of unemployment' caused by people returning from abroad to counties such as Galway, Cork, Donegal, Mayo and Sligo. MacEntee also responded to a Labour Party motion on unemployment in November 1940 put down by Norton, by moving an amendment 'to inquire into and report upon the extent, cause, incidence, general character and other aspects of unemployment, and to make proposals in relation thereto'. Elaborating on the government's aspiration, he maintained:

> We have put down this amendment ... because we are satisfied that the more public attention is devoted to this problem, the more we can have an impartial investigation of it, the more it will be clear that it cannot be solved by any of the facile methods which are so often advocated from party political platforms.[52]

Furthermore, his reasons for dismissing some of the remedies advanced by Labour were entirely consistent with his views when Minister for Finance:

> We do not need to be very great economists, nor even to be expert bankers, to realise that if your productive processes depend for their financing upon the fact that people make savings, that men are prepared to deny themselves a temporary pleasure in order to have some security and some assurance for the future. The moment you begin to embark upon courses which, to their minds, endanger those savings, the whole basis of your productive structure begins to fall away. We have seen in other countries lavish expenditure, unjustifiable expenditure, optimistic expenditure upon this and that sort of undertaking, and all the time we have seen the standard of value in those countries gradually decline in terms of real value, until ultimately everything that the worker had saved, everything that he had got together by self denial and self discipline disappeared, and with it disappeared the character of the people.[53]

Such concern for the community's savings was to be put to one side, however, when, in February 1941, Industry and Commerce considered the unemployment position in the light of a new investigation which revealed that it was 'not possible to substitute native raw materials for the raw materials hitherto imported and used in our industrial processes (outside the food group), except to a very limited extent'.[54] The department 'took the gloomiest view as to the extent to which unemployment, particularly in industrial production, will develop in this country during the present year, if overseas supplies are cut off'; and the minister revised upwards, to almost 400,000, an earlier estimate of total unemployed figures made in July 1940. Even the possibility of such a drastic outcome clearly required some significant government consideration. To this end, MacEntee recommended that a committee comprising the government departments 'more intimately concerned with the various aspects of the matter' be constituted to 'investigate and report as to the extent to which it would be possible to provide employment for male workers upon such works of public utility as would make a minimum demand upon plant and materials normally required for productive industry'.[55]

The concisely named Committee on Emergency Production differed somewhat from the one envisaged by MacEntee. He had argued that the acute decline in industrial production, with the concomitant increase in unemployment, would produce 'a tendency towards panic with, no doubt, a disastrous fall in prices for farm produce'. This in turn could lead, MacEntee maintained, to a crisis of confidence in the currency. 'In matters of currency,' he reasoned, 'psychological causes are frequently more disastrous than actual economic causes.' Such an eventuality might involve 'an alteration during the Emergency period in the whole currency system, as what has to be achieved is, on the one hand, to maintain an adequate supply of food and, on the other, to put all members of the community on an equal footing and in a position to purchase, or be supplied with, the essentials of life'. McElligott's response to his former minister was to counsel resistance towards 'any reference to currency'. Ultimately Finance exerted enough caution for the question of currency control to be excluded from the committee's terms of reference and for the cabinet to reject MacEntee's proposal to prepare a general rationing scheme.

The alarming nature of the proposals advanced by a habitually cautious minister reinforced the notion that the relief of wartime unemployment required radical measures. One obvious way of mitigating its worst effects presented itself through increased migration to Britain. The exigencies of total war resulted in increased opportunities for Irish emigrants seeking work there. Enda Delaney has noted that the 'involvement of the state in the regulation of migration between Ireland and the United Kingdom [wa]s the most significant development of the wartime period'.[56] Similarly, it might be said that MacEntee's faith in state action was the most significant development in his political thinking during his time in the Department of Industry and Commerce. Prior to the outbreak of war in September 1939, there was no restriction on the movement of labour between Britain and Ireland. However, after that date all persons travelling to Great Britain were required to carry a valid identity card issued by the Department of External Affairs. This development ensured that the government remained acutely aware of emigration levels to Great Britain. After the fall of France in June 1940, the British government implemented further restrictions in movement, and in the same month set up a permit office in Dublin to consider applications for employment visas.

Throughout late 1940 and early 1941, a considerable amount of unofficial cooperation occurred between the British Ministry of Labour and National Service and the Department of Industry and Commerce.[57] In the wake of a flood of applications for visas in February and March 1941, MacEntee pressed the cabinet to reverse a decision taken in January of the previous year that employment exchange and branch employment offices should not be used for the purpose of bringing to the notice of workers the opportunities for employment in Great Britain.[58] He constructed a compelling case, arguing that employment in Great Britain would 'be of temporary duration and would, it is thought, last only so long as the conditions responsible for their unemployment in this country lasted', and that 'the Department [of Industry and Commerce] should not refuse them the facilities and assistance which they seek to earn their livelihood elsewhere'.[59] As well as providing a convenient antidote to unemployment, MacEntee argued that to facilitate large groups of potentially disgruntled unemployed in their desire to go to Britain would offset a significant menace to social order. To illustrate his point, MacEntee referred to a meeting of unemployed persons outside the Custom House and postulated that those who had convened the meeting were 'mainly concerned with the exploitation of the unemployed for their own purposes to which end the presence of an increased number of unemployed with the suffering that must accompany it would prove a welcome asset'.

MacEntee's entreaties posed a dilemma for the cabinet given the possibility of a labour shortage in Ireland at some future date. Indeed during the spring of 1941 newspapers and Dáil deputies were suggesting that the army should be deployed for agricultural work. Many farm labourers had either emigrated or were employed as turf-cutters.[60] The government would also invite public criticism if it were revealed that it had actively facilitated emigration to Britain. With this dilemma in mind, MacEntee informed the government that his department had received from the British a suggestion that might assuage the fears of the cabinet. The Department of Industry and Commerce would send particulars of the person looking for work to prospective employers. MacEntee regarded this as acceptable to public opinion because it involved no alteration to the existing machinery and would apply only to persons who had sought work on their own initiative. Its approval was also conditioned by the exigencies of the circumstances in which the government was operating: 'It is thought that if the Department's fears [relating to the unemployment problem in the event of supplies being cut off] ... were unfortunately realised the placing of Irish unemployed workers in employment in Great Britain would provide a very welcome mitigation of the difficulties at home.' The cabinet agreed to the recommendations subject to the Department of Industry and Commerce 'satisfying itself that persons going to Britain under these arrangements and who wish to return to this country will be facilitated and that such persons will be safeguarded against any obligations to join the British armed forces'.

One is forced to conclude that the department's desire to mitigate the 'difficulties at home' outweighed all other considerations, but that the nature of that employment was temporary and that those employed would, in all likelihood, return suggests that it was a practical contingency worth pursuing. MacEntee's own libertarian attitude to the problem should not be underestimated either. He was strongly of the opinion that workers who could not secure normal employment in Ireland during the Emergency should be facilitated to find it elsewhere. After some diplomatic squabbling, in June the Irish government duly received an assurance that migrants would not be subject to conscription and would be entitled to receive compensation for war injuries.[61] MacEntee's desire to see migrants facilitated also led to his proposal to cabinet to place the local offices of the Department of Industry and Commerce at the disposal of British agents recruiting workers for employment in Great Britain. He also resisted the suggestion of the interdepartmental conference of 11 June that recruitment of agricultural workers should be totally prohibited except in the congested districts and contiguous areas scheduled in the Third Employment Order, 1940.[62] And when Hugo Flinn, in his capacity as Turf Controller, wrote to MacEntee to relate his

view that 'there does not seem to be anything at the moment to be said for getting rid of people who could add to the wealth of the country and help to meet
what may be an overwhelming necessity in the matter of fuel by staying here',[63]
MacEntee responded by adverting to the moral prerogative: 'I say nothing of the
question as to whether we have any moral right to restrict the movement of these
people in search of a livelihood or to compel them, by the exercise of extraordinary powers which were taken for police purposes, to remain here and labour at
our command.'[64] To the Minister for Industry and Commerce, this was something
that deserved more emphasis in the debate: 'That aspect of this matter seems to
me to raise an issue of fundamental importance, which would require to be considered not merely in relation to the question of turf production, but in relation
to the social and ethical basis upon which our polity here has been declared to
rest.' Having considered the memorandum at its meeting of 24 June, the government decided that no embargo should be placed on the issue of travel permits to
migratory workers travelling to Britain for seasonal employment.[65] Instead, the
cabinet endorsed MacEntee's proposal, with the reservation that a travel permit
was not to be refused to any person unless it was clear that there was employment available to him in Éire producing food or fuel.[66]

Such reservations were deemed necessary, not only to avert a manpower
shortage in fuel or food production, but also because the government was sensitive to criticism of its emigration policy. The Department of External Affairs
advised the Taoiseach that such arrangements involved a 'disposition to facilitate' emigration rather than an outright impediment to the practice, and a British
official noted, after a discussion with his Irish counterparts later in July, that they
were prepared to cooperate on transferring labour to Britain, as long as this did
not expose the Irish government to criticism at home.[67] Criticism was forthcoming, however, notably from the Bishop of Galway, who was reported in the
Standard in August deploring the continuance of emigration.

> Those who go across [to Britain] leave their dependant here: they say they
> will send a few pounds each week to them. We know that story. But even
> if they do, what good is paper money if there is not to be fuel and food to
> buy, and how will there be food and turf if the producers have left this
> country? There is very little good in appealing to the country to grow more
> wheat and cut more turf if this emigration continues ... The first duty of
> Irishmen, whether they have capital or labour, is to their own country, and
> the duty of the Government is to control the movement of both in the inter-
> ests of the nation.[68]

The number of emigrants estimated by the Department of External Affairs for the
month of August 1941 was 15,000, with 450 new applications received every day.
Travel permits issued by the Department of External Affairs to persons apparently going to employment in Great Britain and Northern Ireland reached a peak of
almost 52,000 in 1942 and 48,000 in 1943.[69] These figures were recorded after
Lemass had returned to the Department of Industry and Commerce in August
1941 and despite his efforts to establish a more rigorous procedure for applications. From October, all persons applying for a travel permit were required to be

over twenty-two years of age and the role of recruitment agents for British employers was also curtailed. Direct recruitment was henceforth prohibited and the censor was instructed to ensure that no advertisements which offered employment outside the country were to appear in the national press.[70] Lemass also recommended to the government in September that 'with the exception of unemployed industrial workers and migratory labourers, all men resident in rural areas ... should be refused travel permits' on the understanding, however, that unemployment assistance should be made available all year round for rural dwellers as it was for urban dwellers, and that a reserve pool of labour be formed.[71] This proposal was forthrightly rejected by Finance who argued, à la MacEntee, that from both 'moral and economic points it is preferable that workers should be allowed to obtain employment outside the country than that they should be compelled through circumstances outside their control to remain in idleness at home'.[72]

Delaney has noted the degree of unease within the Irish political and administrative elite about the migration of Irish workers to Britain in 1941 and 1942.[73] Clearly, this unease was not shared by the Department of Industry and Commerce under MacEntee, who regarded it as a moral right. Finance advanced a similar line on the narrow grounds of cost, but there can be detected in MacEntee's appraisal of the issue a more fundamental reason. His approach to the question was intrinsically related to his strong libertarian philosophy, which also saw him championing the migrants' case after his move to the Department of Local Government and Public Health. In 1943, Local Government sought to solve a labour shortage in turf production by restricting emigration, suggesting that, in certain counties, migrants be required to work on bogs for a specified period in order to secure an exit permit. MacEntee scuppered this plan by announcing his opposition to 'further restrictions being placed on the natural right of persons to sell their labour where it will give maximum return'.[74] Also in 1943, in response to concerns raised by the British authorities, a scheme for delousing Irish emigrants at point of entry was proposed in order to eliminate louse infestation.[75] In the end, the government, through the Department of Local Government and Public Health, instituted a health embarkation scheme under which each migrant was examined and certified in Irish centres before leaving the country. To carry the scheme out successfully, MacEntee sought further funding from Finance for public health measures to combat infectious diseases.[76] Despite initial opposition, funding was duly secured after a group of senior civil servants, including J.J. McElligott, accompanied the Chief Medical Officer, James Deeny, to inspect the working of the scheme. The secretary of the Department of Finance was so overcome at the sight of the process that he 'had to be taken outside and revived in the fresh air'.[77] McElligott's subsequent intervention ensured that Finance's position on the matter was reversed, and a bill to increase levels of public health was proceeded with.

McKee has cogently argued that 'since Fianna Fáil had tended to portray the Emergency as a period when "democracy was on trial" ... that unemployment represented a tangible and pervasive indictment of the new state, something whose removal would conclusively legitimise the cause of Irish sovereignty'.[78]

Never had Fianna Fáil come close to fulfilling this deeply-rooted objective, and now that calls for its eradication became louder, it was forced to confront the issue head on. 'The establishment of the Construction Corps,' Daly argues, 'and the difficulties in devising a relief works programme for Dublin highlighted the need for a more coherent approach towards planning for employment.'[79] Emigration to Britain, no matter how temporary, clearly provided one superficial solution, but the disruption to the state's supplies made a coherent and enduring remedy unattainable. Furthermore, it was estimated that postal and money orders from emigrants, during the six months ended February 1942, averaged £275,000 per month or £3.3 million a year – a figure that was £2.6 million in excess of the pre-war figure, and one that considerably eased the burden of maintaining the number of families that were left fatherless during that time.[80]

ORDER 83: THE WAGES STANDSTILL ORDER

Continuous shortage of essential goods threatened the economy of the state in other ways too. Unlike Britain, Ireland had a vested interest in sustaining demand while Britain's domestic economic policy was designed to encourage savings in order to help finance the war. Britain's rationing system was part of this policy whereas Ireland risked a price-wage spiral which would force up the price level and precipitate demands for compensatory wage increases, a demand which constituted the second major challenge facing the new Minister for Industry and Commerce. When introducing his Supplementary Budget of 1939, the Minister for Finance, Seán T. O'Kelly, made a far-reaching and controversial declaration on the position of wages and earnings during the war:

> The war has resulted in increases in the prices of many essential commodi-
> ties and, before it ends, further increases are unfortunately probable. These
> increases will bear heavily on every class and there will be a strong temp-
> tation to demand a corresponding increase in wages, salaries and profits. If
> such demands were successful, the effect would be to increase prices still
> more and to give occasion for new demands. In that way an artificial price
> structure would be built up which would inevitably collapse at the end of
> the war, if not before, leaving behind widespread unemployment and
> depression. The government feels it has a duty to do everything in its
> power to avert such a development and is determined to set its face against
> the efforts of any class to obtain compensation for the rise in prices at the
> expense of the community. Action to the same end is in contemplation with
> regard to all classes of public servants and, if the war continues for a long
> time, the Government may be forced to adopt more drastic measures.[81]

In June 1940 the Department of Finance followed this general statement by urging the government to 'set its face against the concession of increased wages in order to meet higher costs of living'.[82] The official cost of living index (July 1914=100) had risen from 174 in February 1939 to 218 in the same month two years later.[83] Consequently, the purchasing power derived from wages in industry and agriculture decreased substantially. In the same memorandum, Finance

indicated that the Department of Industry and Commerce appeared 'powerless in the matter' and that 'they [did] not consider that any of the tentative proposals which [Finance] put forward [were] feasible'.[84] These proposals included a standstill order being issued under the Emergency Powers Act or some special tribunal being set up to which all claims for increased wages had to be referred. McElligott also suggested the suspension of all conciliation trade board machinery for the period of the Emergency and that those employers' associations should be notified that concessions should not be given without the prior approval of the Minister for Industry and Commerce.[85]

The first step taken by the government in wage control, as promised in O'Kelly's speech, was to stabilise the cost of living bonus paid to civil servants, which was soon followed by a similar measure for officials of local government. While MacEntee supported wage control in principle, the responsibility for implementing such proposals did not rest easy on his libertarian shoulders. 'It is a new problem,' he remarked, ruefully, 'for a government to consider the fixing and enforcement of maximum wages and there are no precedents outside totalitarian states.'[86] Despite this, he was willing to concede that some increases had taken place, particularly in the case of tradesmen and labourers.[87] Industry and Commerce duly submitted that a general standstill order be made under the Emergency Powers Act, making it illegal for an employer to pay, or for a worker to strike, in support of an application for increased remuneration. The new order discomfited the minister enough however for him to warn the cabinet of the possibility of 'widespread and concerted opposition' to its imposition.

In October 1940 MacEntee's earlier proposals were diluted somewhat when it was decided that the standstill order should operate 'so as to prevent an increase in the remuneration of any employee and so stabilise the position existing at the date of making the order'.[88] MacEntee also told the cabinet that he had been considering a restriction of profits with a view to demonstrating the government's even-handedness where employers and employees were concerned. And in a further effort to assuage the hardship of the workers, he offered the view that restrictions be imposed on increases of rent for houses under a certain valuation, and the possibility of restricting the prices of gas or electricity might be explored. He also suggested the appointment of an interdepartmental committee to examine and report upon the possibilities of giving undertakings in respect of prices of essential commodities such as flour and sugar. The issue was thrown back to the cabinet later in the month; the committee felt that it was a matter of policy on which they could not adjudicate. After his examination of the interdepartmental report, MacEntee felt justified in acting, submitting that a statement should be made on behalf of the government that it would use all its powers 'to prevent for a period of at least six months any increase in the retail prices of flour and bread, oatmeal, butter, fresh milk, sugar, tobacco, rent, bacon, fresh meat, margarine, potatoes, jam, soap, candles, electricity, and rail, tram and bus fares'.[89]

Finance demurred at the possibility of food subsidies funded by the exchequer being introduced. MacEntee agreed, but wished to point out 'that the utmost should be done by way of giving undertakings in respect of retail prices to ensure general acceptance of the principles of the order'. No compromise was reached; the item was withdrawn from the cabinet agenda on 19 November pending further notice. It was withdrawn once again at the meeting of 10 December, but following suggestions for amendments to the order by the departments of Local Government and Public Health, Agriculture and Finance, MacEntee revised and reconsidered the position, facilitating government approval in February. This attempt at wage control demonstrated how difficult it was for the cabinet to impose arbitrary restraints on the operation of the economy, however much it might be aided by emergency powers or the moral authority bestowed by crisis.[90] The interval from the instigation of the debate in the summer of 1940 to the final cabinet decision of February 1941 was a considerable gap in wartime and provided a trenchant illustration of how solutions to inveterate problems proved obstinately unmanageable during the Emergency.

Such procrastination was undoubtedly irritating to some senior cabinet members, including MacEntee, who had made an earnest attempt to redirect government policy away from the politically aggressive act of wage restraint without some compensatory provision. The order was finally issued on 7 May 1941, under the Emergency Powers Act, 1939. It put a stay on any increases in remuneration from that date and removed legal protection from workers striking to enforce higher wages.[91] Any employer found guilty of granting a wage increase was liable to a fine of £100. The response of the trade unions was unanimous and swift. A special Trade Union Conference convened on 16 May to discuss the Trade Union Bill (see below) passed a motion protesting 'in the strongest possible manner against the operation of the Emergency Powers (no. 83) Orders, 1941' and called on 'the national executive to take appropriate action in connection therewith the Labour Party'.[92] The result of this was a motion in the Seanad made on behalf of Senators Lynch, Campbell and Foran seeking an annulment of the order. Senator Foran regarded it as 'the most reactionary order that has ever been put through this House since its inception'.[93] He also saw something fundamentally insidious in the government's attitude to the plight of the working class, and regarded the order as the culmination of an apparently definite effort on the part of the government to enslave the workers.[94] MacEntee responded by claiming that Labour indignation was the result of a misunderstanding of the order's purpose. He rejected the claim that 'it was an attack upon the standard of the workers of this country', stating that the government's real aim was 'to see, first of all, that the remuneration should stand at its present level'. The minister regarded anyone who attempted to evade the order as 'breaking the ranks': 'He is precipitating a panic which would inevitably lead to economic disaster for the whole of us and, therefore, all we are asking with regard to this order is that we should all at this moment, and for the next three or four or five months, as this crisis is building up, stand fast.'[95]

MacEntee tried to assure the Seanad that such opposition was misdirected, placing the responsibility for the increase in the cost of living on the propensity of those in 'sheltered industries, public utility undertakings and in other occupations … to dictate their own terms'. Though keen to stress that the order should not be regarded 'as part of normal government policy',[96] the general feeling that

vulnerable sections of the community were being victimised by government policy prevailed. Public opposition to the order, which comprised street protests,
mass meetings and calls for agitation in the labour paper, *Torch*, was coordinated at trade union level.[97] Having embarked on a *dirigiste* path as the course of the
Emergency worsened, the government was determined to face down these
attacks. In fact, the Emergency conditions, with the security alert that it offered,
persuaded the government of the need to impose greater controls over the entire
trade union movement, in order to limit the threat of strike action in essential
services. These concerns were largely conditioned by the climate of opinion that
had developed throughout the 1930s with regard to the unions. It was widely felt
that the power of trade unions was increasing, and that this power was being used
irresponsibly by elements within trade unionism. Chief among the suspects were
the numerous unions representing the construction industry. In an article in
Studies in December 1940, Rev. Cornelius Lucey, Professor of Ethics at
Maynooth and a future bishop of Cork, drew attention to the socially damaging
effects of the building strike of 1937.[98] Trade unions, too, were mindful of the
need for changes in their organisation. In 1936, the Irish Trade Union Congress
set up the Trade Union Commission to explore this very issue. Divisions
revealed in its 1939 recommendations were extensive enough to prompt Lemass
to warn them that if self-regulation proved impossible, the government would
act. The government did not anticipate such action until a strike by the municipal employees of Dublin threatened to spread to Dublin port, thereby imperilling
the all-important cattle markets.

'BILL'S BILL': THE TRADE UNION ACT, 1941

Moves to rationalise trade union organisation came about through the government's response to the threat of strikes in essential services at the height of the
Emergency. This threat first materialised on 26 January 1940, when the cabinet
considered how to handle the debilitating effects of the Dublin municipal strike
which threatened to escalate to other industries.[99] At this meeting, the cabinet
resolved to assist Dublin Corporation in resisting workers' wage demands.
MacEntee went further, following this up with a memorandum on 8 March,
informing the cabinet that he intended to write to the secretary of the Dublin
Trades Council referring to the events of the previous day in Dublin cattle market when threats were made by the council that cattle sold there would not be
shipped for export. MacEntee also indicated that he would warn the representatives of the Dublin Trades Council that the government would not acquiesce in
the extension of the municipal dispute to the port of Dublin and that it would ask
the Oireachtas for special powers to deal with the position should it arise. This
legislation would:

> [C]onfer special powers on the Government on the lines of the (British)
> Emergency Powers Act, 1920 (which made exceptional provision for the
> protection of the community in cases of emergency due to threat by any per-
> sons or body of persons of such a nature as to be calculated by interfering

with the supply and distribution of food, water, fuel or light or with the means of locomotion to deprive the community of any substantial part of the community of the essentials of life) and the statutory orders which may require to be made under such a measure if the Dublin Trades Council persist in its intention to take sympathetic action in relation to the Municipal Strike.[100]

The cabinet duly authorised the drafting of legislation as outlined in MacEntee's submission. Heads of the proposed bill were circulated to other government departments on 3 April, but the draft was withdrawn from the agenda of the government pending the response of the Department of Finance. This draft comprised MacEntee's principal motives for enacting the legislation, which were given their most explicit expression in a minute to his departmental secretary, R.C. Ferguson, on 17 March and which revealed the less varnished thoughts of the Minister for Industry and Commerce.

MacEntee outlined the problem at hand in the first paragraph of the minute as 'to so regulate the right to strike that it will not be exercised in an irresponsible or unjustifiable way'.[101] He felt that a previous draft by Ferguson had not fully dealt with that problem because it had not made any provision for penalising trade unions found guilty of irresponsible action through lightning strikes and, what is more, had not included the principle that the community could exact retribution on those trade unions or individuals who chose to engage in such a strike in an essential industry.[102] The minister was of the view that trade unionists who relied on physical strength in their everyday occupations naturally resorted to 'force and violence to secure their ends', and this he argued offered the potential of creating grave public disorder. Thus he cautioned against using the police and the army to enforce the proposed legislation, preferring sanctions that would be 'economic and not physical in character'. According to MacEntee, the trade unions had committed what he considered the greatest social evil: 'tremendous power ... without a due feeling of responsibility'. Governmental action was wholly justified, he continued, because trade union members were entitled under the existing legislation to do 'what no government would dare do, that is, at their own sweet will to paralyse our whole productive economy without any advertence whatsoever to the loss and suffering which may be inflicted upon other sections of the community and with no regard for the public interest'.[103]

MacEntee was so adamant that a measure of social retribution be included in the bill that he was willing to suffer delays in order for it to be implemented. The so-called 'irresponsible strike' was part of a two-pronged attack which also included what he called 'the unjustifiable strike', which was action taken against an arbitration settlement or the finding of some industrial court. This was another principle that the minister deemed imperative to the success of the bill: 'We cannot stultify ourselves by setting up industrial courts for essential undertakings or industries and permit the findings of those courts to be flouted.' The penalty proposed by MacEntee for unions whose members engaged in this type of strike was pecuniary. Furthermore, he proposed provisions excluding culpable individuals for stated periods from the benefits of the employment acts, unemployment assistance acts and 'other social measures'. He regarded it as important to 'utilise

1. MacEntee, c. 1914 when he left Belfast. (UCDA P67/914)

John Mc.Entee, M.P.

2. MacEntee, taken on his arrival in Dartmoor prison, in June 1916. This photograph later appeared in *Hue and Cry* when he was 'on the run' in 1920–1. (UCDA P67/915)

3. Disembarking the *Munster* at Kingstown, behind his 'chief', Éamon de Valera, 18 June 1917. (UCDA P150/533, Éamon de Valera Papers)

4. Sinn Féin activists returning from the East Clare by-election, photographed outside the Imperial Hotel, Lisdoonvarna. MacEntee is seated beside Arthur Griffith, 13 July 1917. (UCDA P67/916)

5. Addressing an election meeting, c. 1918. (UCDA P67/917)

6. The speakers and organising committee at the Archbishop Mannix protest meeting, Cardiff. MacEntee is in the front row, centre, 5 September 1920. (UCDA P67/918)

7. MacEntee and his wife Margaret, early 1920s. (UCDA P67/920)

8. The first Fianna Fáil parliamentary party. MacEntee (fifth from left, back row) is among forty-two Fianna Fáil TDs returned at the June 1927 general election. (UCDA P67/921)

9. MacEntee addressing the Fianna Fáil árd fheis in the early 1940s. Seated is Dr Conn Ward, his parliamentary secretary. (UCDA P67/924)

10. Members of the first Irish delegation to the Council of Europe, Strasbourg, including MacEntee (third from right), William Norton (centre, Tánaiste and Minister for Social Welfare), James Everett (far left, Minister for Posts and Telegraphs) and Frank Aiken (third from left), September 1949. (UCDA P67/926 (1))

11. Portrait taken around at the time of the infamous budget of 1952. (UCDA P67/928)

12. De Valera's last cabinet, 1957. (UCDA P67/929)

13. At home in Leeson Park. c. 1940s. (UCDA P67/932)

14. John F Kennedy, president of the USA, being presented with the freedom of the city of Dublin by Alderman Seán Moore, lord mayor, in St Patrick's hall, Dublin Castle in the presence of the government, 28 June 1963. (UCDA P67/938)

15. MacEntee, his wife and two grandsons, with President Éamon de Valera at Áras an Uachtaráin, presenting a copy of *Episode at Easter*, 7 April 1966. (UCDA P67/941)

16. Presentation to MacEntee by the Dublin South-East constituency party, to mark his retirement from politics, November 1969. Photographed with him are the Taoiseach, Jack Lynch and David Harris, chairman of the constituency party. (UCDA P67/942)

17. At a reception to mark the retirement of James Patrick Beddy from the Industrial Credit Corporation, set up by MacEntee as Minister for Finance in 1933, August 1972. (UCDA P67/944)

18. Proudly wearing military service medals, c. 1970s. (UCDA P67/947)

19. Attending a meeting of the Council of State in December 1981. MacEntee, then ninety-two, is seated between Liam Cosgrave and Siobhán McKenna. The other members include President Patrick Hillery, Garret FitzGerald, Jack Lynch, Charles Haughey, Tom O'Higgins, John O'Connell and Barry Desmond, 22 December 1981. (UCDA P67/950)

the present favourable condition of public opinion' to secure the acceptance of these principles.[104]

MacEntee's aggressive tone towards the trade unions was influenced to a degree by an address sent to him by C.P. McCarthy that drew attention to 'the very many' increases of wages granted to industrial workers since the war started.[105] McCarthy questioned whether this was something that was in the public interest: 'Quite definitely there must arise the question whether industrial or other groups are to be allowed complete freedom of negotiation with their workers without some supervision in the public interest.'[106] MacEntee had also expressed his own concern about the damaging effects of strike action in the Seanad in April, claiming that it was 'arousing public anger'.[107] It could be said, then, that the public interest was the defining concern underlying any legislation envisaged by the minister. This was certainly the way he justified it to the Dáil and to the public, but his antagonism towards the trade union constituency would suggest that he was doing more than that. As a relatively new incumbent in the Industry and Commerce portfolio, one is tempted to suggest that MacEntee was keen to establish an altogether different relationship between his department and the unions to the one overseen by Lemass – a relationship wherein there would be little doubt who was in control. It was, in some respects, a manifestation of MacEntee's desire to see ministerial authority accepted and respected by the interest groups within his sphere of influence. Moreover, the minister's *raison d'être* may have been constructed on a wilful avoidance of the facts pertaining to the prevalence of strikes which had been on the wane. In 1939, there was a total of ninety-nine disputes, while in the two previous years the average was 141. The number of working days lost in 1939 was 106,476 as opposed to a decade average of c. 200,000.[108]

The draft heads submitted to cabinet in April were an extension of the ideas outlined in MacEntee's minute to Ferguson.

> The legislation now proposed is intended to regulate the exercise of the right to strike so that it will no longer be possible with impunity to resort to the strike weapon (a) for political purposes (b) in an unjustifiable way or (c) in any arbitrary and irresponsible way. An individual may strike for any purpose no matter how arbitrary or unjustifiable, but the legislation proposed will deprive the individual embarking upon subversive, unjustifiable or irresponsible strikes of the protection of the law and the immunity from the social and economic consequences of his acts which he has hitherto enjoyed. It will give the government powers to deal with the situation which might be created by a subversive strike, and will provide the community with sanctions to be exercised against those who injure the common interest by irresponsible or unjustifiable strike action.[109]

The powers adverted to in the introductory paragraph amounted to giving the government authority to declare a state of emergency when such strikes threatened essential services or public utilities. It could also require employers to submit a register of their employees, who could be called upon by the minister to perform these services. Retributive action on the part of the community involved stripping such recalcitrants of their rights to social welfare benefits, denying them the right to buy goods – a peculiarly malevolent measure that reflected the minister's uncompromising approach – and dismissing, fining or imprisoning anyone who refused the minister's call for assistance. Part III of the bill dealt with arbitration procedures, while part IV required 'trade unions and "associations of persons, whether women or employers, whose objects include the fixing of wages and the negotiation of other conditions of employment" to lodge substantial deposits with the accountant of the Court of Justice and to comply with other conditions necessary to make the provisions of part I, II and III effective'.[110] Many of MacEntee's proposals resembled in form provisions of the British Emergency Powers Act, 1920 and the British Trade Disputes and Trade Unions Act, 1927, but the minister regarded it as a badge of honour that his proposals went further than any of these acts, opining that it was appropriate that the government should be empowered to 'take all and any steps it considers necessary to deal with the situation'.

The draconian nature of MacEntee's proposals was too much for the Fianna Fáil cabinet. It baulked at the likelihood of a challenge in the courts, a potentiality to which the Attorney General drew attention in his submission on the proposals.[111] Lemass, although agreeing with the principles of the memorandum, was keen to see the measure simplified to deal with lightning strikes in essential services only. The most damning criticism of the proposed measure, however, came from MacEntee's former department, Finance. In fact, McElligott regarded the proposals as 'of such a drastic nature … with consequences of a kind that could not readily be foreseen, that in considering them it is hardly practicable to divorce considerations of financial expediency from considerations of policy'.[112] The main impediment to the measure, he argued, was the likelihood of large-scale resistance to it.[113] Finance also feared that the bill might be challenged in the courts and become the subject of a costly referendum. It questioned whether the emergency powers legislation enacted in 1939 already gave 'the government adequate powers to deal with political strikes during the war emergency'. Perhaps the most sensible and valid point made by the Finance memorandum and one that was also counselled by MacEntee's officials was that 'the advisability might be considered of making an effort to get them accepted in their present, or even in a less drastic form, through negotiation'.[114]

In fact, contact had already been established between MacEntee's department and certain prominent figures in the labour movement. The minister's modified proposals in August, on imposing demarcation lines on unions, prompted his civil servants to seek trade union assistance.[115] Help came in the form of the senior trade unionist William O'Brien, general secretary of the Irish Transport and General Workers' Union (ITGWU), who had been the main agitator for reform within the movement, and who had been instrumental in seeking change through the Trade Union Commission.[116] Having failed in this, largely due to the vetoing of the proposed reform by those members of the commission representing the amalgamated trade unions, O'Brien was determined to explore alternative avenues and actively sought to co-opt governmental authority in order to see his plans come to fruition. Thus the government's proposed legislation, with its attendant desire for industrial amity during the Emergency, combined with insistent lobbying by the Fianna Fáil deputy Erskine Childers on behalf of manufacturers who desired legislative reform,[117] along with the consequences of O'Brien's struggle for supremacy with the Amalgamated Transport and General Workers' Union (and the Workers' Union of Ireland) – which he somewhat conceitedly expressed as the 'desire on the part of Irish workers to be in Irish unions'[118] – all contributed to the form of the Trade Union Act, 1941 and determined the deep hostility with which it was met. O'Brien's intervention effectively altered MacEntee's proposals to such an extent that the bill changed from being one specifically aimed at lightning strikes in essential undertakings to one that aimed at comprehensive rationalisation and regulation of the trade union movement, or, to borrow a phrase heard commonly during this time, it became 'Bill's bill'. O'Brien's initial communication with MacEntee's department had simply resulted in the incorporation of his recommendations from the Trade Union Commission, but in a series of meetings beginning on 23 September, he sought to influence further the shape of the legislation, forwarding 'in strict confidence' to the principal officer in the department extracts from a speech he delivered to the ITGWU in June, which warned that congress's inability to reform itself was 'a direct invitation to the government to interfere in their movement'.[119] That the government chose to do business with O'Brien, regarding him and the president of the ITGWU, Tom Kennedy, as 'the better elements of the Irish trade union movement', is undoubtedly significant and does suggest that the needs of the government coalesced to an extent with the needs of the ITGWU.[120] Endorsing O'Brien's recommendations, moreover, would not prove to be particularly difficult for a government ever vigilant to the cause of Irish sovereignty and to the nebulous position of the amalgamated unions whose leaders, in many cases, were based in England and Northern Ireland.

O'Brien and Kennedy were not the only members of the labour movement consulted by the government. On 19 November, the Labour Party deputy Michael Keyes addressed a meeting of the National Union of Railwaymen and informed it that the government had met with the Irish Trade Union Congress and members of the Labour Party regarding the proposal of new legislation. He outlined further that 'the government had not taken this step until it had given every opportunity to the trade union movement "to put its house in order"', confessing that this the movement had failed to do.[121] Although the cabinet was willing to indulge the ITGWU with further meetings wherein the union could review the progress of the legislation, MacEntee was disinclined to jettison his earlier proposals in their entirety, and despite O'Brien's protestations, persevered with the plan to force trade unions to lodge deposits with the High Court before they would be afforded protection under the Trade Disputes Act, 1906.[122] O'Brien continued to advise that the bill should concentrate on regulation and that it should be simplified so as to exclude the issue of lightning strikes altogether, which could, he suggested, be dealt with by a separate bill. In fact, the drafting of a second bill was expedited by a carpenters' strike in Limerick that had obstructed public authority building in mid-September, and which convinced the minister that the Trade Disputes Act should be suspended in the case of strikes affecting public enterprises or defence works for the duration of the Emergency. This legislation was drafted and printed but was postponed when the immediate crisis passed, because it was felt that its introduction in advance of the Trade Union Bill would hinder the passage of that measure. The final bill that emerged from the consultations with the ITGWU overwhelmingly reflected the longstanding aims of that body. Apart from diverting the government from its original goals regarding lightning strikes, O'Brien was successful in persuading the government of the need for a tribunal which would have the power to confer on certain unions exclusive rights of organisation in respect of specific categories of workers. This became the central feature of part III of the proposed legislation. Thus MacEntee's earlier preoccupation with the dual principles of making the trade unions responsible for the actions of its members, and of the community's entitlement to take retributive action against persons carrying out 'unjustifiable strikes', was in the former case diluted and in the latter case abandoned altogether.

When the minister introduced the second stage of the bill in the Dáil in June 1941, he emphasised that the multiplicity of trade unions was the greatest obstacle to industrial harmony.[123] MacEntee also demonstrated how he had allowed the multiplicity argument to override his own personal views on trade unions, views which he was keen to reconcile in his promotion of the bill: 'If trade union disputes in general and inter-union disputes in particular are to be of rarer occurrence in the future, it is necessary, in my view, to eliminate irresponsible unions, and to place greater responsibility on trade unions for the discipline and general conduct of their members and to increase the power of the trade union executives with this end in view.'[124] Of course MacEntee's characterisation of 'irresponsible unions' was entirely subjective. The task of defining who the guilty parties were would remain at the discretion of the minister. The tone of the government therefore towards the amalgamated trade unions became palpably hostile, MacEntee regarding the position of 'unions recorded here prior to 1922' as 'doubtful'. External trade unions were also required to maintain an office within the state and furnish the minister with information as to the rules, committee of management, trustees, secretary and other officers, such as is required for a registered trade union in this country. It was O'Brien's recommendations for part III of the bill that left these trade unions most vulnerable. It was intended to invest in a tribunal, consisting of members determined by the government, powers to grant negotiating licences to successful applicants that had succeeded in organising a majority of the workforce of a particular class and that had applied for a determination that it alone should have the right to organise members of that class. The tribunal, moreover, could grant or refuse such an application if satisfied that there were reasonable grounds in the public interest for so doing, and could determine that two or more specified trade unions alone should have the right to organise 'masters of that particular class'.[125] Despite these provisions, which clearly favoured larger and better organised unions and gave a clear advantage to those unions in Ireland who had better opportunities of recruitment, the minister maintained that the 'bill treats Irish and British trade unions alike in so far as it is possible to treat unions with headquarters outside this country and purely Irish trade unions alike'.[126]

In response to the minister's speech, Fine Gael deputies Dan Morrissey and

Richard Mulcahy moved an amendment which sought to divert the government from the matter in hand 'until such time as the report of the Commission on Vocational Organisation and the evidence presented to that commission have been presented to the Dáil so that the legislative proposals may be considered and discussed in the light of the evidence placed before the commission and the commission's report'.[127] Significant labour representation on the commission, which included Senator Seán Campbell, treasurer of the Dublin Typographical Society, Luke Duffy, general secretary of the Labour Party, Jim Larkin of the Workers' Union of Ireland – William O'Brien's longstanding nemesis – and Louie Bennett, general secretary of the Irish Women Workers' Union, may have indicated to the movers of the amendment that a more favourable approach towards the unions would be advocated by the commission. But the government had little intention of allowing the commission to become influential in any sphere of central policymaking and the notion of waiting for it to report before proceeding with important legislation was given short shrift by MacEntee, who suggested mischievously that the purpose of the amendment was 'to make the Dáil inferior to the Commission on Vocational Organisation'.[128] William Norton strongly rejected MacEntee's rather disingenuous claim that the bill would be 'welcomed by responsible trade union leaders', referring to the special confer-ence of executives of trade unions which had been called by the Trade Union Congress in May, and which had unanimously demanded the withdrawal of the bill. The government's *modus operandi*, Norton realised, was to be one of com-pulsion, not conciliation: 'At a time of emergency like this, when it is so neces-sary to promote national unity, why does the minister insist on throwing a bill of this kind into the public arena so that it may create all the disunity and all the dis-cord which this bill is certainly going to cause in the trade unions?'[129]

By indulging O'Brien and his union, the government's action was carried out with a guaranteed degree of support that had the secondary advantage of creat-ing a nationalist ascendancy within the trade union movement. This mutual accommodation was designed by O'Brien, flavoured by MacEntee and present-ed as the government's long-held desire to force the unions to clean up their act. Accordingly, MacEntee, in a strident defence of the measure, albeit in the more sober medium of a letter, regarded his bill as a 'compromise' between the pro-posals of the Irish trade unions as outlined in their memorandum to the ITUC commission, and the memorandum of the 'British' unions, because it left to each 'individual trade union the greatest possible liberty of action within the limiting condition that if any trade union was unable to comply with the requirements prescribed in the bill, it must merge or amalgamate with a kindred union'.[130] That is not to say that the minister did not see the benefits of playing the green card in justifying the necessity of the measure, nor that he broadly subscribed to O'Brien's proposed changes. He boldly asserted that the bill would 'bring order out of chaos', and would 'make the Irish Trade Union Movement what it ought to be, a source of pride and strength to Irish workers'.[131]

In spite of MacEntee's conduct, however, it is somewhat implausible to attempt to discern some Machiavellian plot to split the Labour Party on the minister's behalf.[132] It would also be wrong to regard MacEntee's 'red scare' election strategy in 1943 as an essential influence on the eventual split in the Labour Party.[133] In fact, suspicion of disruptive elements within the Labour Party, which in turn had exacerbated existing tensions, had been the source of problems for the party leadership in the run up to the 1943 general election and before, resulting in a number of notable expulsions, including that of Owen Sheehy-Skeffington.[134] MacEntee certainly manipulated an inherently fissile propensity in the labour movement, a susceptibility of which he would have been made acutely aware during his association with William O'Brien in the framing of the Trade Union Act; but he was by no means the architect of the rupture. Moreover, the red scare strategy was a moveable beast. O'Brien and the ITGWU duly adopted it when it disaffiliated from the Labour Party in 1944. Fianna Fáil, in turn, continued to pander to O'Brien by applauding the ITGWU's courage in forming a new National Labour Party – an act which seemed to vindicate MacEntee's approach of the previous year and which undoubtedly gratified his party's political aspirations. This was reciprocated by National Labour's refusal to attack Fianna Fáil during the 1944 general election, preferring instead to arraign its erstwhile comrades.[135] Again, a mutual accommodation was reached between O'Brien's wing of Labour and the government. This did not mean that they had 'played into MacEntee's hands',[136] merely that they used similar tactics for equally self-interested, if somewhat distinct, ends. Fianna Fáil's unimpeachable grip on government was restored by a snap election in 1944, thereby fulfilling MacEntee's fundamental aim while in turn accentuating the infirmity of the Labour Party, which was now severely damaged by a seemingly irrevocable split.

    Public demonstrations of opposition to the 1941 legislation were not slow to materialise. Although 'observers detected no unease in labour circles' when the terms of the bill were published on 30 April 1941,[137] the special conference called by congress in May suggested that antagonism to the bill was running high among the rank and file members. O'Brien himself was in the rather peculiar position of being unable to voice his support for the bill and the government given the inopportune timing of the Wages Standstill Order which was also discussed at the conference. In effect, the timing of Order 83, as outlined above, sealed the fate of the Trade Union Act at the conference. Notwithstanding the deep resentment of the government's measures among delegates, the resolution adopted by the conference, effectively assigning responsibility to the Labour Party to lead the fight, was symptomatic of O'Brien's deft handling of the issue. At the annual conference of congress in July, O'Brien suggested that governmental interference in the trade union movement was inevitable given the inability of the unions to carry out reform: 'As a consequence of the failure to meet the situation we have now governmental interference in our movement in a manner that is quite naturally resented but for which we ourselves in our affiliated unions are so largely responsible.'[138] And although he called for 'protests in the strongest possible fashion' against the order, this amounted to sending a deputation to meet the Taoiseach. O'Brien's own credibility within the movement had in fact been arousing suspicion for some time. On 31 May, *The Leader* reported that 'a good deal of opposition is being voiced in official labour circles to the Trade Union

Bill, but we happen to know that a considerable proportion of it is hollow and insincere.'[139] It was left to the Dublin Trades Council, from whom the ITGWU had disaffiliated following its decision to admit James Larkin's WUI, to mount an altogether more earnest campaign. The council established a Council of Action – of which Larkin's son became secretary – that, through its vigorously organised campaign of demonstrations and meetings, briefly recalled the heady days of 1913 in terms of effective trade union agitation. In keeping with this spirit, the campaign culminated in a large march to College Green on 22 June, at the end of which Jim Larkin theatrically 'swept a match from his pocket and torched a copy of the bill'.[140]

The presence of Big Jim Larkin invigorated union resistance to the bill. Norton, also on the platform at College Green, vowed to demonstrate his party's total opposition to the bill by not moving any amendments to it in the Dáil.[141] Larkin's supporters, moreover, were just as vituperative about O'Brien as they were about MacEntee and the government. On 26 July, Larkin's paper, the *Irish Workers' Weekly*, reported that: 'Calling to his aid statements of O'Brien, MacEntee forced through the final stages of the Trade Union Bill. Despite the large volume of opposition throughout the country to the bill the minister refuses to give way. Prime factor in urging him on with this employer-inspired measure is the existence at the top table of the Trade Union movement of one who is apparently in agreement with him.'[142] The paper laid much of the blame for the success of the bill at O'Brien's door: '[MacEntee] has an ally perched in the highest position inside the Trade Union movement who is frustrating the efforts of the movement to force the withdrawal of the bill.' The candour of this analysis must have made uncomfortable reading for the minister, whose preferred focus of vilification now became O'Brien's own *bête noire*: the amalgamated unions. Responding to what he regarded as a gratuitous attack on their conduct during the ITUC commission by MacEntee in the Dáil on 3 July, Sam Kyle of the ATGWU wrote to the minister to convey his objections, charging that MacEntee's reference to 'impertinent procedure' was 'unworthy of you and your high office, as it would lead the ordinary reader that we Irishmen were not capable of handling our own affairs'.[143] This followed a similar remonstration from J.T. O'Farrell of the Railway Clerks' Association of Great Britain and Ireland over MacEntee's comments about the amalgamated unions, which he felt constituted 'a grave injustice to a large number of organised workers in this country'.[144] The minister's response insisted that the condensed press reports of what he had said gave a misleading impression, but it concluded with the revealing aside that: 'It is unfortunate ... that [the cross channel unions] should have so unfavourably identified themselves with the attempts that have been made to reform the Trade Union movement in this country.'[135]

Underlying MacEntee's overall attitude to the trade unions was a reaffirmation of government control. His dismissive response to the Morrissey/Mulcahy amendment demonstrated his lack of conviction that the Commission on Vocational Organisation could provide an effective alternative to executive action.[146] Likewise, he regarded representative organisations as something of a hindrance, whose recourse to lobbying on issues of self-interest could, if regarded as antagonistic, potentially hamper the government's efforts to maintain public order during the Emergency. He also continued to express dubiety about the intentions of employers, particularly those in the 'sheltered trades', and as we have seen, was keen to see the government introduce a restriction of profits during the Emergency. There is also little reason to disbelieve MacEntee's avowed concern for the 'common people', whom he suggested were 'more to be regarded than either section' and who had 'suffered because of the evils with which the bill proposes to deal'.[147] That the bill changed so radically from MacEntee's original proposals to constitute an attack on British-based unions was conveniently and entirely compatible with de Valera's paramount concern for the enduring sovereignty of the state during the war. It can also be regarded as a compromise from within the cabinet which altered MacEntee's punitive measure to one that was far more likely to be accepted. Finally, that the government could resort to the central issue that had preoccupied successive trade union congresses for nearly a decade in order to justify its action made such a compromise all the more alluring.

The two years that MacEntee spent in the Department of Industry and Commerce were certainly eventful. The normal functions associated with the department were usurped, either by a critical lack of raw materials to sustain industrial enterprise or by the Department of Supplies, which assumed responsibility for key areas that would ordinarily have been associated with MacEntee's department. The gravity of the circumstances in which MacEntee was forced to operate produced an altogether uncharacteristic response. The pedantry and conservatism that defined his ministry of the Department of Finance were replaced by a vigorous stewardship of Industry and Commerce. And although he remained in many important respects a maverick in the cabinet, his acceptance of the need for the state to play a more active role in the economic and social business of the community was much more in line with Fianna Fáil policy since 1932.

NOTES

1. Éire was the official name of the country under the 1937 constitution.
2. For the dates of MacEntee's ministerial appointments, see Appendix B.
3. *Dáil debates*, vol. 77, col. 191, 27 September 1939.
4. *Irish Times*, 21 June 1938.
5. For example, see the debate on the statement of government policy, *Dáil debates*, vol. 77, 19 October 1939.
6. R. Fisk, *In Time of War: Ireland, Ulster and the Price of Neutrality* (Dublin, 1983), p.98.
7. Quoted in ibid.
8. UCDA P67/800, MacEntee to Michael McInerney, 1974.
9. A. McCarthy, 'Reacting to war: Finance and the economy, 1938–40', in D. Keogh and M. O'Driscoll (eds), *Ireland in World War Two: Neutrality and Survival* (Cork, 2004), p.48.
10. UCDA P67/800, MacEntee to Michael McInerney, 1974.
11. MacEntee does not name these 'influential persons' but de Valera was being advised by Professor Smiddy on economic matters at this time.
12. Fisk, *In Time of War*, p.98.
13. *Dáil debates*, vol. 77, col. 574, 29 September 1939.
14. UCDA P67/121. Handwritten letter to de Valera, n.d. MacEntee stated his unwillingness to continue in Finance and cited Industry and Commerce as his preferred destination.
15. Jacobsson had counselled MacEntee in October 1938 that during a European War it was preferable

that state borrowing should be limited as far as possible and as a consequence any excessive rise in prices and wages should be prevented. In a paper on 'War Finance' delivered at Queen's University in October 1938, MacEntee felt that the general monetary organisation would be better than in 1914. The government 'should be able, therefore, to employ more effectively the full power of the state in defence of the national economy; and what is perhaps even more important, we shall have no hesitation in using that power'. UCDA P67/563/6; see also *Irish Times*, 29 October 1938.

16. D. Nevin, 'Decades of dissension and divisions 1923–1959', in D. Nevin (ed.), *Trade Union Century* (Dublin, 1994), p.91.
17. Fanning, *Finance*, p.312.
18. NAI EHR/3/15/c2, *Record of Activities of the Department of Supplies*. This booklet was compiled to place a record of the department's functions which would be available if the need should ever arise again. The second reason given was that: 'During the Emergency the Department of Supplies had to exercise an unprecedented measure of control over a wide range of industry. The experience of the Department in this respect should be useful in connection with such control of economic activities as may be necessary in the post-war years.'
19. The deputy assistant secretary of the department was W. Maguire.
20. Farrell, *Seán Lemass*, p.53.
21. Horgan, *Seán Lemass*, p.96.
22. D. Roche, 'John Leydon', *Administration*, 27, 3 (1979).
23. K. O'Doherty, 'Working for Seán Lemass: reflections of a Private Secretary', paper presented to the Seminar for Contemporary Irish History, TCD, 15 October 2003.
24. In fact, nine officers including a principal, an assistant principal and six junior administrative officers were on loan to Supplies from Finance by August 1942. Shanagher transferred to Industry and Commerce at the end of the Emergency and subsequently became secretary of the department. See Fanning, *Finance*, p.551.
25. Although Leydon's loss to the department was significant, it should be pointed out that Ferguson was a highly qualified official who had been in the department longer than Leydon. See Roche, 'John Leydon'.
26. *Dáil debates*, vol. 79, col. 168, 6 March 1940.
27. For example, see E. O'Malley, *Industry and Economic Development: The Challenge for the Latecomer* (Dublin, 1989), pp.57–60.
28. Ibid. O'Malley's figures are based on the *Census of Industrial Production*, as adjusted by Kennedy (1971).
29. Ibid., vol. 77, col. 263, 27 September 1939.
30. *Dáil debates,* vol. 77, 2 September 1939.
31. Horgan, *Seán Lemass*, p.109.
32. *Dáil debates*, vol. 80, col. 731, 17 May 1940.
33. Quoted in Fanning, *Finance*, p.348.
34. *Dáil debates*, vol. 80, col. 1930, 7 August 1940.
35. *Dáil debates*, vol. 81, col. 275, 16 October 1940.
36. *Dáil debates*, vol. 84, col. 1412, 10 July 1941.
37. Which probably gave rise to the popular wartime ballad, 'Bless 'em all! Bless 'em all!/ The long and the short and the tall/ Bless de Valera and Seán MacEntee/ They gave us brown bread and a half ounce of tea!'; see J. Robins, *Custom House People* (Dublin, 1993), p.127.
38. *Dáil debates*, vol. 84, col. 1413, 10 July 1941.
39. Ibid., cols 1415–16.
40. *Dáil debates*, vol. 77, col. 834, 19 October 1939. The chairman of the committee was Hugo Flinn, parliamentary secretary to the Minister for Finance. The other members of the committee were: Arthur Codling, assistant secretary, Department of Finance; Commissioner Diarmuid O'Hegarty, Office of Public Works; Mr W.F. Nally, assistant secretary, Department of Lands; Mr P.J. Murray, assistant secretary, Department of Agriculture; Mr J. Keane, chief employment officer, Department of Industry and Commerce; and Mr J. Garvin, Department of Local Government and Public Health.
41. *Dáil debates*, vol. 77, col. 848, 19 October 1939.
42. *Dáil debates*, vol. 77, col. 854, 19 October 1939.
43. *Dáil debates*, vol. 77, col. 861, 19 October 1939.
44. *Dáil debates*, vol. 77, col. 866–7, 19 October 1939.
45. Daly, *The Buffer State*, p.283.
46. NAI DT S10927; Unemployment relief: labour corps.
47. Quoted in Daly, *The Buffer State*, p.282.
48. NAI DT S12262, Flinn to MacEntee, 21 April 1938.
49. Ibid.

50. NAI DT S11644; Notes of meeting of representatives of Trade Union Congress with MacEntee, 31 January 1940.
51. Ibid.
52. *Dáil debates*, vol. 81 cols 936–7, 28 November 1940.
53. Ibid., col 945. Regardless of the commitment of the government to establish the commission, endorsed later in the debate by de Valera, and the preliminary moves taken by MacEntee to carry this out, in October of the following year Lemass, on his return to Industry and Commerce, recommended to the government that the proposed commission be abandoned 'because conditions prevailing had become increasingly difficult; because of the difficulty in separating transient unemployment from causes continually operating; and because numbers of the unemployed had entered the army or had temporarily emigrated'. The item was subsequently removed from the cabinet agenda in December 1941.
54. Quoted in Fanning, *Finance*, p.344.
55. These were considered by the minister to be the departments of Supplies, Local Government and Public Health, Finance, Posts and Telegraphs, Industry and Commerce, the Office of Public Works together with representatives of the ESB and the Irish Tourist Board.
56. E. Delaney, *Demography, State and Society: Irish Migration to Britain, 1921–1971* (Liverpool, 2000), p.117.
57. Ibid., p.118.
58. NAI DT S11582 A: Industry and Commerce memorandum, 13 March 1941.
59. Ibid.
60. See M.E. Daly, *The First Department: A History of the Department of Agriculture* (Dublin, 2002), pp.239–41.
61. NAI DT S11582 A: Industry and Commerce memorandum: 'Recruitment of citizens of Éire for employment in Great Britain, 23 June 1941.' Between 1940 and 1945, Irish workers in Britain were given the official status of 'conditionally landed' and were obliged to return to Ireland after two years of work in exchange for exemption from conscription. See also James B. Wolf, '"Withholding their due": The dispute between Ireland and Great Britain over unemployment insurance payments to conditionally landed Irish wartime volunteer workers', *Saothar*, vol. 21 (1996).
62. NAI DT S11582 A: Memo from MacEntee to Government on 'Proposed embargo on the emigration of certain classes of agricultural workers', 23 June 1941.
63. Ibid., Flinn to MacEntee, 20 June 1941.
64. Ibid., MacEntee to Flinn, 23 June 1941.
65. NAI DT S11582 A.
66. Ibid. Cabinet decision of 1 July 1941.
67. B. Girvin, 'Politics in wartime: governing, neutrality and elections', in B. Girvin and G. Roberts (eds), *Ireland and the Second World War: Politics, Society and Remembrance* (Dublin, 2000).
68. NAI DT S11582 A. Extract from the *Standard* of 22 August 1941 reporting speech made by the bishop of Galway deploring the continuance of emigration. The bishop was Dr Michael Browne, chairman of the Commission on Vocational Organisation.
69. NAI Industry and Commerce file EHR /3/15/c2.
70. Delaney, *Demography, State and Society*, p.120.
71. NAI DT S11582 A: Memorandum from Industry and commerce to Government, 17 September 1941.
72. Ibid. Finance memorandum: 'Observations of the Minister for Finance on the memorandum submitted to the government by the Minister for Industry and Commerce on the subject of the employment of Irish workers in Britain, 19 October 1941.'
73. Delaney, *Demography, State and Society*, p.123.
74. Daly, *The Buffer State*, p.267.
75. Ibid., p.143.
76. See J. Deeny, *To Cure and to Care: Memoirs of a Chief Medical Officer* (Dublin, 1989), pp.76–7.
77. Ibid., p.77.
78. É.C. McKee, 'From precepts to praxis: Irish governments and economic policy, 1939 to 1952' (PhD thesis, UCD, 1997), p.23.
79. Daly, *The Buffer State*, p.283.
80. NAI DT S12865 Industry and Commerce memorandum, June 1942.
81. Quoted in Labour party, *Annual Report, 1940*, p.32.
82. NAI DT S11725 A: Finance memorandum, 27 June 1940.
83. The Labour party *Annual Report* of 1940 also reproduced statistics first published in the journal *Irish Industry* which showed that between 1926 and 1937 salaries, wages and earnings as a percentage of the net output of industry declined from 59.2 per cent to 56.5 per cent.
84. Ibid.

85. Such conciliation machinery that existed in 1940 had been inherited from British legislation preceding independence. Trade boards had been in existence since 1909 and were designed to regulate wages in certain trades. Joint industrial councils were also a legacy of the British administration but had a more limited scope than the British model, amounting to little more than negotiating committees for the discussion of wages. The chairman of the councils was normally an official of the Department of Industry and Commerce. Formal conciliation machinery was not set up until the passing of the Industrial Relations Act, 1946, among the provisions of which included the establishment of the Labour Court.
86. Quoted in McKee, 'From precepts to praxis', p.12.
87. NAI DT S11725 A: Memo by Industry and Commerce, 26 July 1940 relating to a proposed standstill order in respect of wages.
88. Ibid. Industry and Commerce memorandum to government for meeting, 5 October on proposed Stand Still order in respect of remuneration of employees and distribution of profits.
89. Industry and Commerce memorandum for the cabinet meeting of 12 November.
90. McKee, 'From precepts to praxis', p.14.
91. S. Cody, J. O'Dowd and P. Rigney (eds), *The Parliament of Labour: 100 years of the Dublin Council of Trade Unions* (Dublin, 1986), p.173.
92. Ibid.
93. *Seanad debates*, vol. 25, col. 1373, 27 May 1941.
94. Ibid.
95. Ibid., col. 1377.
96. Ibid., cols 1485–6.
97. See Cody et al, *The Parliament of Labour*, p.174. Such agitation was also immortalised in a ballad that was based on 'Who fears to speak of '98?' It was entitled 'Who fears to speak of '83' and the first verse gives a flavour of its tone towards the government: 'Who dares to speak of '83/ Nor blushes at the name? / O'Kelly, Dev and MacEntee / They bring their country shame / He's all a knave or half a slave / Who slights his country thus / So true men, like you, men / Come, take your stand with us!'
98. See K. Hannigan, 'British-based unions in Ireland: building workers and the split in congress', *Saothar*, vol. 7 (1981), pp.40–9. C. Lucey, 'Conciliation and arbitration in labour disputes', *Studies*, vol. XXIX (1940), pp.497–512.
99. S. Redmond, *The Irish Municipal Employees Trade Union, 1883–1983* (Dublin, 1983), pp.104–5. In addition to the IMETU, the strike involved members of the ITGWU, the Workers' Union of Ireland, the Irish Engineering and Industrial Union, the Irish Engineering and Foundry Union, Stationary Engine Drivers' Union, Builders Labourers' Union, the ATGWU, the Automobile Drivers' Union, the Plasterers and Paviors, the Fire Brigade and most significantly, considering the need to maintain supplies, the Irish Seamen and Port Workers' Union.
100. NAI DT S11750A, Memo submitted by Industry and Commerce 8 March 1940 for consideration of the government's meeting of same day.
101. UCDA P67/229 (13) MacEntee to R.C. Ferguson on draft heads of proposed bill, 17 March 1940. See also F.A. D'Arcy and K. Hannigan (eds), *Workers in Union* (Dublin, 1988), pp.200–6.
102. This earlier draft by the departmental secretary is not on file.
103. UCDA P67/229 (13) MacEntee to R.C. Ferguson, 17 March 1940.
104. Ibid.
105. I have been unable to find out who this individual was or his relevance; but that MacEntee had the address in his private papers and that he paid particular attention to it warrants its mention in this context.
106. UCDA P67/ 229 (14), Copy of presidential address to the commerce society of UCC by C.P. McCarthy, 11 March 1940, entitled 'Industrial disputes and wage levels in Ireland'.
107. Quoted in C. McCarthy, *Trade Unions in Ireland, 1894–1960* (Dublin, 1977), p.185.
108. Ibid., pp.184–5.
109. UCDA P67/229 (12), Copy of Industry and Commerce memorandum to cabinet, 2 April 1940.
110. Ibid.
111. NAI DT S11750A.
112. UCDA P67/229 (10), Observations of the Minister for Finance on the Memorandum circulated by the Minister for Industry and Commerce in connection with the proposed Bill to Regulate the Exercise of the Right to Strike, 12 April 1940.
113. Ibid.
114. Ibid.
115. E. O'Connor, *A Labour History of Ireland, 1824–1960* (Dublin, 1992), p.142.
116. See McCarthy, *Trade Unions in Ireland*, pp.142–73.

117. K. Allen, *Fianna Fáil and Irish Labour: 1926 to the Present* (London, 1997), p.66. Childers was general secretary of the Federation of Irish Manufacturers which represented industrialists who had benefited from the government's protectionist regime. It should be noted, however, that MacEntee, as detailed above, was less indulgent towards this group than was his predecessor, Lemass.
118. *Irish Trade Union Congress Annual Report, 1939*, p.153.
119. Quoted in O'Connor, *A Labour History*, p.142.
120. Quoted in K. Allen, 'Forging the links: Fianna Fáil, the trade unions and the Emergency', *Saothar*, vol. 16 (1991).
121. NLI, William O'Brien Papers, Ms. 13,974.
122. NAI, Department of Labour TIW 766, draft heads November 1940. See also O'Brien Papers, Ms 13,974, Industry and Commerce to William O'Brien, 21 June 1941. These measures were softened significantly in June in the face of O'Brien's continuing demurral.
123. *Dáil debates*, vol. 83, cols 1535, 4 June 1941.
124. Ibid., cols 1542–3.
125. Ibid., col. 1546.
126. Ibid., col. 1548.
127. Ibid., cols 1548–9.
128. *Dáil debates*, vol. 83, col. 1660, 5 June 1941. See also J. Lee, 'Aspects of corporatist thought in Ireland: the Commission on Vocational Organisation, 1939–43', in A. Cosgrove and D. McCartney (eds), *Studies in Irish History Presented to R. Dudley Edwards* (Dublin, 1979).
129. Ibid., col. 1557.
130. UCDA P67/235, Open letter to an Irish Trade Unionist concerning the Trade Union Bill 1941, c. June 1941.
131. Ibid.
132. Dunphy, *The Making of Fianna Fáil Power*, p.289.
133. See A. Murphy, 'Dissension and disunity: the story of the political and industrial split in the Irish labour movement', unpublished PhD thesis (University College, Dublin, 2000), pp.109–30.
134. A. Sheehy-Skeffington, *Skeff: The Life of Owen Sheehy Skeffington, 1909–70* (Dublin, 1991), pp.104–13. See also J.P Swift, *John Swift: An Irish Dissident* (Dublin, 1991), pp.111–19, and N. Puirséil, *The Irish Labour Party* (Dublin, 2007), pp. 91–95..
135. Murphy, 'Dissension and disunity', p.121.
136. Ibid., p.120.
137. O'Connor, *A Labour History*, p.143.
138. Quoted in McCarthy, *Trade Unions*, p.207.
139. O'Brien Papers, Ms. 13,974; *The Leader*, 31 May 1941.
140. E. O'Connor, *James Larkin* (Cork, 2002), p.105.
141. McCarthy, *Trade Unions*, p.209.
142. UCDA P67/236 (1), Cutting of the *Irish Workers' Weekly*, 26 July 1941.
143. NAI, TIW 766; Sam Kyle to MacEntee, 10 July 1941.
144. Ibid., J.T. O'Farrell to MacEntee, 4 July 1941.
145. Ibid., Ferguson to O'Farrell, 21 August 1941.
146. See also NAI DT S13552 for a full account of MacEntee's views on the commission.
147. *Dáil debates*, vol. 83, col. 1665, 5 June 1941.

5

Planning in the Custom House

'The many uncertainties of the first year and a half of the Emergency,' according to McKee, 'served to elucidate the preoccupations of three of the government's most senior members.'[1] MacEntee, in his judgement, remained primarily conservative 'though the prospect of social disruption had propelled him to propound contingencies which in any other situation would have been anathema to his whole outlook and his view of government as an unobtrusive adjunct to the operation of social forces'. Indeed on one occasion during the fraught early months of 1941, MacEntee, foreseeing little hope on the horizon, had suggested to the cabinet that: 'In the absence or shortage of industrial products there would be involved necessarily the principle of national control of all branches of non-agricultural production so that the population might ... be relieved to whatever extent was possible of the burden involved in the new situation.'[2] This clearly was a new departure for MacEntee from his days in Merrion Street. It was also 'an intriguing glimpse of the imaginative and ruthless mind that lay subsumed under the more characteristically conservative poise'.[3] It is, therefore, tempting to compare MacEntee's justification for such thinking with that of the contemporaneous social and economic developments in the United Kingdom, particularly in the form enunciated famously by Sir William Beveridge's report in December 1942. Both were reactions to wartime exigencies and both saw an entirely warranted role for the state in such exceptional circumstances. But MacEntee's reaction to these developments was laced with apprehension and doubt and his suspicions of Beveridge and his ilk were articulated in a characteristically hyperbolic manner.

Lemass, on the other hand, 'saw the vagaries of wartime unemployment as an irrefutable confirmation that the economy was embedded in a pre-developed stage and that it would take a strong heave on the part of an energetic and expansive government to realise the country's economic potential'.[4] De Valera was apparently also inclined towards this view. By June 1942, the cabinet had discussed 'the need for systematic planning not merely to meet the pressing problems of the moment but also to provide for the situation to be faced when the Emergency comes to an end'.[5] For the Taoiseach, necessity became the mother of invention and a cabinet committee on economic planning was duly set up in November 1942, consisting of de Valera, the Tánaiste and Minister for Finance, Seán T. O'Kelly, and Seán Lemass.[6] The committee thus constituted held forty-nine meetings from 2 December 1942 to 4 April 1945, when the government decided to enlarge it to include all members of the cabinet. That the committee had a dual remit, and that Emergency conditions continued to engage its thoughts, hampered the initial urge for long-term planning. By 1944 the committee decided that 'planning projects were to be deferred unless they could be shown to be urgently necessary'.[7] What was most important about the committee, however, was that its establishment constituted an acknowledgement by the government that any resolution of inveterate problems such as unemployment required a more coherent approach. Moreover, the original committee's exclusivity demonstrated where real cabinet authority lay.

Key figures such as MacEntee, Aiken and Ryan were all excluded from the original configuration. Clearly this was de Valera's attempt to ensure that the committee would be free from the paralysing vacillation that often attended government meetings. His overriding concern in appointing the committee was affirmative action, which could only be achieved through guaranteed consensus. What is more, O'Kelly, influenced no doubt by McElligott *et al* in Finance, had already made his opposition to additional large-scale public investment be known.[8] MacEntee's views were perhaps slightly less compliant to 'the Finance attitude' now that he had left that environment, but as Daly puts it: 'Lemass and de Valera may have regarded one opponent on the committee as enough.'[9] By this time, Lemass had been restored to his customary position in Industry and Commerce (as well as retaining Supplies for the remainder of the Emergency). This resulted in MacEntee, due to the resignation of P.J. Ruttledge on health grounds in August 1941, filling the vacancy at another large-spending department, Local Government and Public Health.[10] Not only did this mean that MacEntee was henceforth responsible for some key elements of Fianna Fáil's development programme, including housing and roads, but also for the party's chief social imperative, public health.

The new-found urgency on behalf of the government with regard to planning meant that in the early part of his tenure in the Custom House, MacEntee's department would often have to respond to, if not take the lead from, the cabinet committee on economic planning. Once he settled into his new role, however, MacEntee explicitly demonstrated to his departmental officials the authority he intended to exert. The flavour of the new minister's style is captured in a letter to the secretary of the department, James Hurson, in May 1942. The matter concerned one of MacEntee's *idées fixes*: emigration to Britain during the Emergency. He had learned that a reply had been forwarded by the department, devoid of his sanction, to a memorandum by Lemass. In order to ensure this did not happen again, MacEntee demanded that:

> All proposals to be immediately referred to my private office and as a matter of urgency brought to my personal attention, so that I may be aware at the earliest possible moment of proposals touching on my responsibility as a member of the Government or affecting the work of this Department.
>
> After I have seen them, the documents are to be issued to the general secretariat of the department for written observations and advice.
>
> When fully examined by all sections affected, written observations and recommendations to be submitted for my consideration.
>
> Where proposals affecting those sections of the Department under the

immediate control of the Parliamentary Secretary, the originating Department should be asked for a second copy – to be sent to the private office of the Parliamentary Secretary for observations and attention. The observations of officers of sections in question may then be submitted to me, either through the Parliamentary Secretary's private office, or through my office as the Parliamentary Secretary may find convenient.

Only when the procedure here outlined has been followed and views of the Department formulated to my approval and satisfaction may any observations be offered on a proposal which another Minister intends to submit for consideration by Government.[11]

Another senior civil servant in the Custom House, Tom Barrington, has also documented anecdotally MacEntee's methods, in an episode that not only reveals the mutual respect between the minister and his officials but also displays how intimately they came to be appreciated by advisers. It concerns a memorandum by John Collins, the assistant secretary, which MacEntee had requested to be ready on his return from a cabinet meeting.

MacEntee read down the ordered paragraphs and then said apologetically (for he respected Collins as much as the rest of us), 'This is a very good memo, Mr Collins, but it is completely against the line I want to take.' Collins, with an amused glint in his pale blue eyes, said gently, 'Turn over the sheet.' There, equally cogently argued, was, literally, the other side.[12]

Did MacEntee's highly personal style of command alter the already firmly established ethos of the department and were the strictures he adopted on scrupulous spending when Minister for Finance unburdened in this more improvident milieu?

PUBLIC EXPENDITURE

MacEntee's move to the Department of Industry and Commerce on the outbreak of the Emergency was his first taste of ministerial control of a traditionally high-spending department. As we have seen, however, his room for manoeuvre in terms of developmental initiatives was drastically restricted by the circumstances imposed by the war. Local Government and Public Health offered greater opportunities, particularly as the government had prioritised post-war infrastructural planning. Did the government's concern with such matters mean that it was embracing economic expansionism despite the inauspicious portents for the economy? The fate of the interdepartmental committee to consider economies in government expenditure, set up by O'Kelly in September 1939, proved to be symptomatic of the government's ambivalent attitude to the problem. Some of the economy committee's recommendations included the proposal that a ceiling of £1.2 million a year should be imposed on housing loans for 1940–2 and that new loans for public health works and hospitals should be frozen. The establishment of the cabinet committee on economic planning and the government's concomitant battle with wartime unemployment effectively meant that there would be a 'gap between what ... the economy committee deemed economically necessary and what the government deemed politically acceptable'.[13] Moreover, de Valera may well have been persuaded to probe the economy committee's reasoning by a memorandum he received from his economic adviser, Professor Timothy Smiddy, in September 1939. Smiddy contrasted the British government's need for economy, in order to channel resources into the munitions industry, with Ireland's converse need to maintain demand even if this meant a budget deficit.[14] He also counselled against a diminution of building activities, even if this necessitated substituting unattainable imported goods.

Deficiencies in essential materials made development schemes infinitely more difficult to realise. This impacted significantly on Local Government and Public Health expenditure during the war years. From 1939 to 1945, total government expenditure fell as a proportion of gross national product even though it rose in monetary terms from £48 million to £64 million.[15] This fall was particularly marked for capital expenditure.[16] The task for policymakers after this period was to return spending to pre-war levels. MacEntee claimed in his presentation of the 1946 estimates that the figure for housing of £658,000 was 'a very large sum'. It was, he contended, 'something more than 57 times the £11,500 which would have met Deputy Mulcahy's requirements in [his estimates for] 1932–33'.[17] Furthermore, the total expenditure of the proposals relating to post-war planning submitted by government departments was £86 million, of which the vast bulk had been presented by the Department of Local Government and Public Health. If 'Industry and Commerce responded quickly and ambitiously' to post-war planning, then this can equally be said of MacEntee's department.[18] Although the responsibility of overseeing this spending often tended to pass to Industry and Commerce, the wide scope of Local Government's plans was impressive.[19]

Table 1: Proposals for capital expenditure in the post-war years presented by the Department of Local Government and Public Health, May 1944.[20]

	Urban areas	Rural areas	Total
Hospitals	£2,846,000	£330,000	£3,176,000
Housing	£19,174,601	£4,196,867	£23,371,468
Water/Sewerage	£2,159,985	£1,339,300	£3,499,285
Swimming pools/Parks	£1,000,685	£329,400	£1,330,085
Roads	£5,000,000	£17,600,360	£23,600,360
Total	£30,181,271	£23,677,227	£53,858,498

Such ambitious schemes were liable however to remain hypothetical until normal conditions returned and necessary supplies were available. Perhaps a more accurate measure of the department's commitment to development was its performance between 1945 and 1948. In many ways expenditure undertaken by the government in these years was an attempt to cajole the economy back to its pre-war status. Thus public capital expenditure rose from an artificially low level of 0.5 per cent of GNP in 1945 to 3.8 per cent in 1948 when Fianna Fáil left office.[21] Thereafter, the public capital share increased markedly, reaching 10.4 per cent in 1951, mainly as a result of the availability of Marshall Aid funds. The government's commitment to increased expenditure was articulated by the white paper, *The Post-War Building Programme*, published by Industry and Commerce in 1945. This envisaged a total outlay of £99.5 million in the first five years after the war. Housing, roads, and water and sewerage costs accounted for half of this figure.[22] Yet scarcity of required materials continued to hamper the execution of these schemes. Daly asserts that the white paper, despite its promise of more funds, and contrary to the general view of the minister who authored it, 'showed a determination to keep the role of the state to a minimum'.[23] It proposed to give scarce building materials to private contractors and, notwithstanding the urgent need for houses in Dublin, its agenda continued to be dominated by job creation rather than allocation of resources due to utmost need. Investment levels therefore suffered accordingly, only truly recovering during Fianna Fáil's last year in government. This did not mean that efforts were not made by Local Government to facilitate local authorities in their petitions for greater investment. MacEntee gave a commitment during the 1945 estimates debate that local authorities that began house construction immediately would be given an extra subsidy to meet the costs incurred. He maintained that the government was 'determined, if we can, in our time to solve the housing problem, or at least to give local authorities every inducement to solve it'.[24] A Transitional Development Fund was established in the following year, providing additional grants to the tune of £5 million, made retrospective for work carried out during the 1945–6 financial year.[25] In June 1946, interest rates for Local Loans Fund loans were also reduced from 4.25 per cent to 2.5 per cent, providing the cheapest credit in the history of the state. Such incentives failed to yield expected results, however. Local authorities attributed the lack of activity to the enormous rise in building costs and claimed that subsidies advanced by central government were inadequate to cover these sharp increases.

HOUSING

One area where MacEntee's outlook was consistent with that of his new department was Local Government's habitual penchant for spending money on long-term improvements rather than on *ad hoc* job creation. Fortunately for both, the immediate concern of the cabinet committee on economic planning was to review departmental replies to a circular disseminated by de Valera in July 1942, which canvassed their collective observations on schemes for durable post-war development.[26] One such proposal that was considered by the committee at its inaugural meeting in December was the setting up of a planning board 'to consider and make recommendations regarding the technical and other problems involved in providing housing accommodation for the people in Dublin City and County'. Planning legislation had been framed by the Town and Regional Planning Act, 1934 and an amended version of the same act in 1939. The act enabled local authorities to make 'provisions for the orderly and progressive development' of cities and towns but did not oblige town or city councils to make a plan. The result was that the act was effectively ignored. By 1939, a mere fifteen local authorities had passed planning resolutions. Little, if any, pressure was applied by central government to change this. MacEntee, however, entered the Department of Local Government and Public Health with planning on his mind. In fact the planning board was MacEntee's idea. He first outlined his plans in a minute to Hurson in October 1942.[27] Although the board would deal with technical questions, the minister was at pains to suggest that it should not be 'solely composed of architects and engineers' but individuals with a 'wide knowledge of economic and social questions'. They would be 'men of outstanding ability and administrative capacity as well as of enterprise and vision'.

MacEntee forwarded a slightly modified proposal in an eleven-page letter on the housing problem to the Taoiseach on 30 November, which was duly considered by the committee on economic planning.[28] In it, he stressed that he had given much thought to the problem and to the post-war programme. He felt that Dublin constituted '9/10ths of the problem'. With this in mind, he had been trying to obtain the report of the Dublin housing commission of inquiry which had been set up in March 1939. Nevertheless, MacEntee had already concluded 'that there was no hope that a radical attack on our housing problem could be made through the medium of our existing machinery or organisation'.[29] He described the housing policy of the government as 'to ensure that every family within the state would be provided with decent housing upon terms which they could afford'.

There was a peculiar mixture of fantasy and expediency in the minister's plans. When he considered the actual form of the housing, he came to the conclusion that the 'suburban working class housing colonies with which Dublin is being surrounded ... belong to the pre-war age'.

> The common thing ... about them all is that they belong to a pre-war age, and the men who have been engaged in planning them have been thinking and are still thinking upon pre-war lines. In my view the advent of air power as a military factor will have as revolutionary effects on the evolution of our social and civic habits and organisations as the development of heat engines and electricity have had. And if we are going to have a rational and well-considered housing program [sic] for the future we must make our plans in the light of that fact. So far as the design and structure of our houses is concerned this may involve a radical departure from the principles upon which we have hitherto proceeded. If it does it will also involve equally far-reaching changes in all the ancillary services which serve urban habitations, e.g. roads, sewers, transport, gas, electricity, telephones, facilities for worship and education, shopping and amusements.

Such futurism, it should be said, was not unusual for MacEntee. Of course in his own professional training as an electrical engineer he demonstrated an aptitude for novel design. In the minister's view, the proposed planning board would satisfy the country's need for a more forward-looking housing project. Whatever de Valera thought of his minister's rather futuristic plans, it appears that Local Government officials were less than enamoured by his proposals. A further memorandum from the department on 20 February 1943 suggested that no administrative changes were required, therefore dismissing the need for the proposed board. In contrast to the minister's earlier submission, the memorandum also expressed no obvious dissatisfaction with the planning carried out by Dublin Corporation, and attributed problems to the punitive building costs and the continuing shortage of supplies. The prospects for local authorities to undertake new schemes was thus regarded as 'not encouraging' given the subsidisable limits fixed under the Housing Act, 1932. As to future policy, the department was of the view that, despite the high costs, 'it is proposed to allow house building to proceed in the four county boroughs as far as possible, and to proceed with the preparation of complete plans for new schemes in these areas to be undertaken when materials are available and building costs begin to fall; and that a detailed examination of surveys of housing needs in all other urban areas and towns is being made.'[30] In the meantime, MacEntee considered it necessary to continue making grants to private house builders. This recommendation was influenced by the fact that the number of new houses still required in urban areas was considerable.[31]

The apparent *volte-face* by the minister was most likely due to his fear that the proposed planning board would weaken his department's overall authority, a point that was no doubt laboured by his officials in their response to his plan. His sponsorship of the initiative, however, retains a certain degree of interest for the historian of his public life. As has been noted elsewhere, there was a distinct lack of any ministerial interest in planning during the first three decades of independence.[32] Indeed, it has been suggested that the administrative machine of the Department of Local Government and Public Health was singularly unenthused by planning. If, as Daly postulates, the department talked the minister out of the idea, it was a rare episode of divergence between their respective approaches to public policy.[33] Moreover, the episode again demonstrated, albeit fleetingly, MacEntee's imaginative response to problems afflicting his ministerial remit. The resolve of the department to maintain control of housing policy should be seen in the context of its difficult relationship with the cabinet committee on economic planning. Indeed a turf war had broken out between the department and the committee, personified by MacEntee and Lemass respectively. This manifested itself particularly in the early months of 1943 when MacEntee's department consistently failed to satisfy the demands of the committee.

The Taoiseach was also unimpressed with Local Government's response to his earlier request for planning projects and he again asked the department to collect 'such information as may be available in order to obtain a proper understanding of the country's post-war building requirements'.[34] He also complained that 'the picture is very incomplete and does not provide sufficient data for the working out of any sort of plan or programme of post-war building'.[35] The committee's exasperation was further compounded by a minute from the minister's private secretary, Brian Ó Nualláin (the writer Flann O'Brien), in October, intimating that the report of the Dublin Housing Commission would not be completed before March 1944.[36] By then, however, Lemass had already pressed ahead. During the summer, he and de Valera met a deputation from the National Council of the Building Industry in Ireland to discuss the post-war situation. In the autumn, the committee, which was increasingly dominated by Lemass and the

Taoiseach, decided to assign responsibility for detailed planning of post-war construction to a freshly created branch of an unspecified department.[37] The Department of Local Government and Public Health reacted with disquiet to this decision but could do little to alter the government's course. According to the historian of the department: 'Local Government [had] failed to grasp the opportunity and the initiative [had] passed to Lemass and Industry and Commerce.'[38] This is possibly a harsh assessment on the department as Lemass had seized the initiative as soon as the cabinet committee on economic planning had been established, something over which Local Government had no control.

MacEntee was finally invited to attend his first meeting of the cabinet committee in November 1943.[39] De Valera wished to ascertain the minister's views on the committee's proposed organisation for the planning of building activities, which had been approved earlier that month. The draft proposals were not intended to relate to building activities under normal conditions, but rather to such activities during a transition period in which, while it would be possible to resume building and construction activities on a relatively large scale, the available resources in personnel and materials would be likely to be inadequate to meet full requirements. Yet again MacEntee was in obstructionist mode, refusing to release any officer from his department to take charge of the proposed organisation, as the committee had wished. The committee's evident impatience with the department continued. In December, it asked Local Government's advice on possible legislation to make it mandatory for local authorities to adopt the Town and Regional Planning Acts. Local Government's advice was to preserve the *status quo*.

In May 1944, MacEntee furnished the committee with a progress report on the housing situation. It observed that 'had normal conditions existed since 1940 the housing problem would have been entirely solved in most parts of the country'.[40] As it was, the department had planned for the erection of 36,000 houses by local authorities; had prioritised conditions in Dublin and, to that end, were closely considering the Dublin Housing inquiry which had just completed 'a most exhaustive review of the subject'. MacEntee told the Dáil in the 1945 estimates debate that, despite the good work that had been carried out by the department, rising costs and delays in obtaining materials meant that 43,000 new dwellings were still required in urban areas.[41] By this time, however, the cabinet committee's patience had run out. Responsibility for the post-war building industry was invested in a new division of Industry and Commerce. Thus control of planning remained within the civil service, but alas not with Local Government. Despite the objectives of *The Post-War Building Programme*, real investment in housing only began once Fianna Fáil left office in 1948.[42]

MacEntee's exclusion from the cabinet committee on economic planning resulted in strained relations between his department and the committee. After its initial settling-in period, many of the committee meetings were, in fact, only attended by de Valera and Lemass, and this is reflected in the tenor of the minutes which reveal a recurring impatience with other ministers and departments for the poor progress being made on some of their recommendations.[43] It is also notable that some ministers, including MacEntee, were requested to provide explanations for the lack of progress on some desired projects, housing being a case in point. All in all, the committee's almost messianic optimism reflected certain elements germane to the Fianna Fáil economic outlook. Considering the conditions that prevailed, this approach was either incongruously sanguine or absurdly impractical. Moreover, despite its forward-looking title, the cabinet committee invariably concentrated on the relief of chronic unemployment as its principal desideratum. This imperative often ensured that the committee proposed what MacEntee believed were unremunerative schemes, his resistance to which was bound to be viewed reproachfully by the committee, which was now determining cabinet priorities.

ROADS AND RELIEF WORKS

One example of the flights of fancy that cabinet ministers were capable of during the Emergency years came from the Minister for the Coordination of Defensive Measures, Frank Aiken, in a letter to de Valera in February 1942. He suggested that 'we should start a national scheme of concreting all roadways in the country beginning first with the cul-de-sacs and then third class country roads and finally the main highways ... The order in which I suggest work should be undertaken is in accordance with the greatest social and economic needs. It is on these roads that people get their feet wet and that children suffer most hardships travelling to and from school.'[44] Given his general attitude towards such ideas and as the minister directly responsible for the state's road network, MacEntee was unlikely to indulge his cabinet colleague with a considered response. Instead, in the same month, a note from Local Government recommended visionary plans for fast roads around Dublin, permitting speeds of seventy-five miles per hour, with by-passes for other major towns.[45] What the committee was really looking for, however, were plans for today, not tomorrow. MacEntee's more imaginative outlook, allied to his dislike of short-termism, meant that his relationship with the committee would be continually tested throughout its brief existence.

In April 1943, the committee sought a report from the department on the position regarding construction plans of roads.[46] Local Government responded with a minute to the Taoiseach on 8 September 1943, informing the cabinet committee that an examination had been completed of the possibility of completing the Dublin–Bray road, one of the busiest in the country. The minister's focus in the minute exposes the gulf in priorities between members of the committee and the department. Whereas the committee hoped that the Bray road would absorb a considerable number of locals receiving unemployment assistance, MacEntee was of the opinion that the use of labour directly drawn from the unemployment assistance register was ill-advised and ultimately profligate. He argued that:

> [I]f the moneys made available for such works are to be related to the numbers of registered Unemployment Assistance recipients, resident locally, the employment of labour on the rotational basis and any restriction on the use of machinery, it will be evident that a considerable number of years

would elapse before the works are completed. The estimates of the cost of carrying out the Bray road scheme show that a considerable saving would be effected by having the work carried out on the basis of a free contract without any restrictions as to the use of Unemployment Assistance labour. … The Minister recommends that in considering large scale public works in connection with emergency or post emergency planning it be accepted that the financial provision to be made will not be subject to any of the conditions attaching to grants made available for the relief of unemployment and further that the moneys to be allocated will be made available in such amounts as to permit the work to be carried out in full within a period determined under contract conditions.[47]

The minister's views effectively condemned the project, making it and others like it prohibitive due to excessive cost – both in pecuniary and political terms – and to the committee's preference for schemes to absorb the unemployed. In one way, this approach made perfect sense as the conditions prevailing could be considered exceptional and transitory, but it also served to highlight the contradictory nature of the committee's remit. Prudent and comprehensive road development may have been deemed desirable for the post-war years, but while there was an overriding demand to provide employment, this aspiration could wait.

Other factors militated against a coherent roads policy during the Emergency. Income from the road fund had declined by about half from 1939–40 to 1941–2 due to petrol rationing. The number of licensed vehicles also dwindled considerably from the pre-war figure, 73,813 in 1939 to 26,188 in 1943. Moreover, the officials of the roads engineering section established in 1941 were promptly assigned to supervise local authority turf production, where they remained during the greater part of the Emergency.[48] Despite these inauspicious circumstances, the department was eager to fulfil the committee's original instruction. It duly submitted proposals for road improvements costing £6.5 million. In keeping with the minister's views the scheduled improvements valued efficiency and practicality over job creation. Indeed, a scheme was drawn up by the department's head engineer, Ted Courtney, which classified roads according to the anticipated volume of traffic in the 1990s. Clearly, futurism was infectious in the Custom House. Again, the travails of the Emergency probably condemned the scheme from the start. The minister was, however, requested by the cabinet committee in December to state the department's plans for the modernisation of major arterial routes from Dublin to Cork, Galway and Sligo, as well as circular roads around the capital city. In March, a progress report was submitted by MacEntee, which gloomily outlined that supplies were scarce, and despite repeated efforts by his officials to obtain tar and bitumen, 'these efforts have failed to meet with success'.[49] In an accompanying letter to Lemass, he attributed this lack of success to the amount of tar required in Britain for aerodrome construction and fuel.[50] A further progress report was prepared in May, which took into account the dual concerns of the committee. It separated post-war road expenditure into two categories: special schemes to provide short-term employment in the event of a sudden increase in the figures and investment which would serve the country's needs over the next fifty years.[51] In the short-term, the report drew attention to more pressing needs: 'It is estimated that in each of the five years following the Emergency, the maximum programme of road works that could be undertaken, having regard to the availability of men and materials, would be at the rate of £4,500,000, including maintenance works by local authorities. The first work urgently requiring to be undertaken would be extensive tarring, to make up for the absence of this essential maintenance during recent years owing to lack of tar.'[52] In the longer term, the department proposed to reconstruct nearly all the country's arterial highways.

In the summer of 1944, the cabinet committee decided to re-evaluate its primary function. At its meeting on 13 July, it was decided that 'in future the committee should aim at avoiding the consideration of matters of detail and should endeavour to concentrate on broadly reviewing the progress of departments in the advancement of their plans, in the preparation of necessary legislation and generally in bringing their preparatory measures to the most advanced stage practicable in existing circumstances.'[53] Notwithstanding this change, the committee's guiding principle remained the same. Daly notes that approximately 'half of the £13 million spent on employment schemes between 1932 and 1946 had consisted of low-grade road and footpath repairs, and from 1932 road expenditure had become little more than an appendage to the government's employment schemes'.[54] In the latter half of 1944 and the first half of 1945, the committee began actively to court proposals for employment creation. Lemass had been largely influenced by the British white paper on employment policy, published in May 1944. MacEntee was invited by the committee in December to contribute to an employment policy with particular regard to local authority schemes.[55] The minister duly informed the committee that it had been the policy of his department throughout the Emergency to urge local authorities to proceed with all classes of work likely to provide employment, and which could be undertaken with the available supplies of material and machinery. He gave particulars of a number of projects relating to public health, hospitals and roads, the plans for which had reached an advanced stage, but which could not be undertaken in the present supply position. Generally, it was his view that, unless the supply position eased, no appreciable expansion of work giving constructive employment could be undertaken by local authorities. He undertook to furnish the Department of Supplies with a statement giving particulars of materials and machinery for lack of which work undertaken by local authorities were not completed.

From the beginning of the cabinet committee's deliberations, Local Government and Public Health had made it clear that its chief interest lay in housing and road building, in turn drawing attention to the paradox of the committee's purpose, arguing that road schemes prepared to meet an abnormal increase in unemployment 'cannot properly be regarded as post-war planning as such planning is regarded as planning new forms of development rather than planning works for provision of employment'.[56] In September 1943 the committee asked the minister to submit to the government for decision the questions in regard to the financing of large-scale public works raised in a departmental minute of 6

September 1943.[57] The following month, the department was requested to draw up plans to provide employment for 10,000 unskilled workers in Dublin for up to three years after the Emergency. MacEntee's reply adverted to the difficulty of finding useful employment schemes, which would not compete with the normal programmes of the department for materials and workers.[58] A series of meetings then took place between de Valera and MacEntee wherein the minister contended that the committee had overestimated the number of labouring jobs required in Dublin. He also questioned the suitability of some of the unemployed – who were of the 'cuff and collar' class – to work on relief schemes.

To conclude, the cabinet committee on economic planning was a logical extension of the considerable powers appropriated by the government during the Emergency. No individual minister in government was more powerful than Seán Lemass who, as Minister for Industry and Commerce and Minister for Supplies, controlled imports, exports, transport, prices and wages. MacEntee's powers in Local Government and Public Health were not quite as extensive, but he was responsible for two sectors of building activity that were traditionally relied on by his party to provide significant employment – roads and houses. Construction of roads and houses was also fundamental to Fianna Fáil's tentative plans for the post-war world. Indeed the Emergency brought home to Irish policymakers the necessity of planning. During the war years, industrial output fell by one fifth, rationing was introduced and a turf development plan was initiated due to shortages in fuel. The concomitant fall in living standards focused minds on the need for some coherently thought-out solutions to the intractable difficulties facing the state.

Lemass also enjoyed a prominent position on the deliberately select cabinet committee on economic planning, a three-man apparatchik that dictated the pace and form of the government's plans. The committee's dual remit to provide employment and to consider future development plans resulted in a predictably confused response from a number of government departments. Initially Local Government was more than willing under MacEntee to engage in the planning process, as can be seen by the minister's proposal of the planning board. Moreover, the department's plans for road building and house construction were also far-seeing and ambitious. Planning for the post-war world, however, had to take second place to the exigencies of the Emergency or, as Lee has put it, 'the primacy of the political'. This approach valued job creation over durable planning. Many of these jobs were intended by the committee to come from relief works, which entailed hiring workers from the unemployment assistance register and prioritising projects that were labour intensive. Just as he had done as Minister for Finance, MacEntee questioned the wisdom of this approach; and, on more than one occasion, failed to cooperate with the committee by refusing to adopt these criteria in his own departmental plans. Lemass's place in the cabinet committee served to diminish the role of the Department of Local Government and Public Health and dictated that it was unable to 'assume a more central role in shaping the economy of post-war Ireland'.[59] Daly's assertion that if Seán Lemass had been Minister for Local Government and Public Health, this central role would have been fulfilled is clearly valid. As it was, given Lemass's role on the cabinet committee, and MacEntee's non-compliant attitude towards it, it was inevitable that Local Government would remain sidelined in the planning process.

A DICTATOR IN THE CUSTOM HOUSE?

Another area where MacEntee's commanding personality impacted on departmental business can be seen in his relationship with the local authorities. On assuming the role in August 1941, MacEntee inherited two pieces of legislation that would prove most unpopular with county councils: the County Management Act, 1940 and the Local Government Act, 1941. Both acts can be seen as symptomatic of the government's desire for greater control over local government administration, a wish that became pressing during the Emergency, notwithstanding the fact that both measures predated the coming of war. Given MacEntee's distaste for state intervention, and his neurotic concern about the spread of bureaucracy, it is worth assessing his contribution to the relationship between county councils and the government during the Emergency. It may also shed some light on the validity, or otherwise, of Whyte's argument that during the 1940s there existed a bureaucratic urge on the part of the government. Furthermore, he described MacEntee as one of 'the most determined defenders of the "bureaucratic viewpoint"'.[60]

The County Management Act, 1940 has been described as 'undoubtedly the most important piece of legislation relating to local government administration in the history of the state'.[61] The passing of the act was 'preceded by a decade of uncertainty about the reorganisation of rural administration'.[62] This uncertainty stemmed from the government's stated object of implementing change while doing little about it. Despite having paid lip service to the sanctity of local democracy when in opposition, Fianna Fáil was ambivalent about it once in government. No less than four county councils with anti-government majorities were dissolved in the summer of 1934 due to their refusal to collect rates.[63] Local elections, which were scheduled to take place every three years, were postponed twice by the government in 1937 and 1940. Such indifference to the system of local government was made explicit by the minister, O'Kelly, in 1934 when he was invited by the Executive Council to submit proposals for the amendment of the local government acts to provide for the adoption of a county managerial system. O'Kelly's initial memorandum to the cabinet anticipated 'further reforms at a later date with a view to acquiring central control and administration of all local affairs'.[64] Real impetus for altering the system came four years later and a bill was duly prepared in July 1939, which was approved by the cabinet in November. Under the bill, managers would be given a wide range of responsibilities including the executive functions of county councils, borough councils, urban district councils, mental hospital committees and public assistance boards. One opposition deputy accused the government of having a 'craze for centralisation' during the bill's second reading in the Dáil.[65] Another drew attention to the conflict between the imperatives of central government and those of the rank and file, suggesting that if Fianna Fáil had introduced the legislation four years earlier 'the whole party would have fainted away in sickened horror'.[66] Moreover, the confusion surrounding the appointment of the managers left the government vulnerable to allegations of cronyism.

In February 1942, the government decided to press ahead with the appointments of county managers while at the same time deciding to postpone scheduled local elections. The postponement was attributed to the logistical impediments to council meetings during the Emergency which, in turn, made the managerial system more desirable. Opposition to the deferral was so intense, however, that the government was forced into holding them in August. MacEntee shared his colleagues' indifference to the fate of the elections, not to mention their lack of confidence in them to make any appreciable difference: 'It is clear that the decision as between holding the elections and postponing them is a choice between two evils. Which of us will say with any conviction that one or other of these is the lesser evil?'[67] In August, the same month the elections were held, the County Management Act, 1940 and the Local Government Act, 1941 came into effect. The minister was given extended powers under the acts, including the authority to remove councillors without dissolving the entire council. 'The appointment of county managers,' according to Daly 'marked the beginning of a contentious new relationship between councillors and the administration, which reverberated for at least a decade.'[68] The department and the minister were continually criticised for their interventionist and authoritarian approach. The Labour Party, in particular, was keen to make political capital from the matter. Richard Corish told the Dáil, during the estimates debate in 1942, that 'People in the Custom House have not the same grasp of matters in the South or West of Ireland as the people there have.' James P. Pattison, also of Labour, impugned the minister's personal role in the department's conduct.[69] Another Labour deputy, William Davin, told the Dáil in October 1943 that councillors in his area regarded county managers as 'nothing more or less than the office boys of the minister'.[70] Was this the way MacEntee viewed them? And if so, did this constitute a bureaucratic imposition that reflected the political will of the minister?

In fact, MacEntee had moved to limit the powers of central government in relation to the staffing of local government offices with the introduction in January 1943 of the Local Government (Minor Offices) Order. This order removed a large number of minor positions, such as nurses, cooks, rent collectors and tradesmen from the detailed purview of the minister.[71] In the same year, the Local Government (Officers) regulations were made. These regulations stipulated that relations between the local officer and the local authority and the central authority would be normally governed by general regulations applicable to offices, and that intervention by the central authority in personal cases would be exceptional. Further steps were taken laying down rules for systems of grading, scales of remuneration, and methods of recruitment with the object of ensuring that the central authority would interfere less and less in the day to day administration of local authorities.[72] All of these developments were clearly designed to impose general regulations on local authorities which would make any intervention of the minister or his department unnecessary. According to one contemporary source, it would also ensure that 'cooperation between the state and the local bodies will ... remain on the higher

levels where the national interests must inevitably continue to link the central
and the local administrations closely together in all major public projects and in
matters of policy of principle affecting the well-being of the community and the
rights of the individual.'[73]

Although MacEntee continued to support government policy in regard to the
county managers, whom he publicly defended on a number of occasions, he was
keen to stress the scheme's efficiency and accountability, and certainly did not
regard it as a step on the road to intrusive bureaucracy. Indeed his dispassionate
attitude to the question might be instructive of his general attitude towards the
structure of local government. As agents of his administration, MacEntee certainly regarded the county managers' position as incontrovertible. But what the minister regarded as unforgivable was not merely the attitude certain councils adopted towards the managers, but what that attitude said about their relationship with
central government. Equally, he resented the conduct of some managers who were
deemed to have violated their authority. He told the Dáil during the estimates
debate in 1943 that he would not 'condone, nor expect members of an elected
body to tolerate, any incivility, lack of respect or act of usurpation on the part of
the manager'.[74] He expected correspondingly high standards of the councils:

> Elected bodies ... will be effective instruments of government only so long
> as their members recognise that the powers vested in them are of such far-
> reaching consequences that they must be exercised with good sense, dis-
> cretion and providence. Much damage, much hardship, may be occasioned
> by the misuse of such powers, and therefore, when the members of a local
> authority do misuse them, and in doing so manifest that as individuals they
> are not fit to be entrusted with them, there is no option, so far as the
> Minister who is responsible for the local government of the country is con-
> cerned, but to deprive them of their office and of the opportunities for
> injuring the community which that office affords.[75]

The minister's mutual ambivalence towards the councils and the managers
reflected his belief that as administrative agents the managers should be respected, but that they should also defer to the councils' democratic mandate.
Ultimately, what the minister wanted was that the system would serve the needs
of the local communities and would not impede unduly on the everyday business
of his department. A circular issued by MacEntee in 1944 to each local authority makes this clear:

> A loyal acceptance by the manager of the predominant position of the
> elected body will do much to elicit from them the support to which he is
> entitled in the discharge of his duties. The law gives the manager the right
> to take part in the discussions of local bodies. When he does intervene he
> should do so with tact and discretion. The manager must be prepared to
> give advice readily to members who are unacquainted with official routine
> and be obliging and courteous in his dealings with members of the local
> body and the public.[76]

Friction continued to exist between the managers and the councils, however.

MacEntee finally endeavoured to resolve the acrimony by publishing a white paper in April 1945, stating definitively the powers of local elected authorities. The minister continued to defend the new regime, notwithstanding the efforts of some to make personal representations to dissuade him. One such representation came from Aodh de Blacam, a member of Fianna Fáil's National Executive. He wrote to MacEntee in December 1946 exhorting him to produce 'some timely definition of the managerial position'.[77] De Blacam claimed that the structure was proving detrimental to the government as well as doing harm 'to the social well-being' of the community. The minister's response demonstrated the commitment of the government to the existing arrangement and, perhaps more significantly, its evident distaste for the old one. MacEntee regarded that system as wasteful and extravagant and one that failed to meet the demands of the community. Nevertheless, MacEntee's strictures to the managers continued. In February 1946, he advised them not to 'prejudice the council in its line of action' during meetings with local voluntary bodies. The minister's attempts to end the antagonism concluded in a proposal later that year that sought minor amendments to the act, including a stipulation that county managers could no longer administer two counties. The cabinet approved MacEntee's changes, but no bill was drafted before Fianna Fáil left office in 1948.

The perception that central government was becoming increasingly authoritarian was given full expression by an editorial in the *Irish Independent* in February 1946, just when MacEntee's attempts at appeasing managers and councils were reaching their climax. The editorial concerned the passage of the Local Government Bill, which gave authority to the minister to order each local authority to strike a higher rate or risk being dissolved. The concerns articulated undoubtedly reflected the views of many local authorities, but the vindictive tone adopted towards the minister was particularly unmerited. Under the headline 'Dictators at the Custom House', the article recalled MacEntee's caustic denunciation of the introduction of city management in Dublin in 1930, which he described as 'the very deification of bureaucracy'.[78] He continued: 'Under [the bill] not only the manager but the heads of the various administrative departments of the city are going to be placed in the position of so many Mikados.' Now, the *Irish Independent* claimed, MacEntee was to be 'the sole reigning Mikado'.[79]

The intemperate nature of the attack can probably be put down to an appeal to populism, reflecting an apprehension on the part of the electorate about bureaucratic interference in its affairs. Any fear that prevailed, however, was misdirected in this case. MacEntee's attack on the concept of bureaucracy in 1930 was certainly compatible with his party's instinctive grasp of opposition politics, but, as a member of government, he was not at liberty to play that card. Having witnessed at first hand the apparent difficulties with the previous system, Fianna Fáil dedicated itself to the modernisation of local government administration on efficient and economical lines. This enthusiasm for efficiency and economy was never as pronounced as it was during the Emergency. MacEntee, it is true, was incorrigibly opposed to bureaucracy, but he also recognised the state's obligation to nurture an efficient and modern administration. The lengths to which he went to smooth over the teething problems of the county management system also contradict an authoritarian motive. While it can be said that the tone MacEntee sometimes adopted towards would-be agitators was high-handed and rather disdainful, the equanimity he displayed in this case may have betrayed his belief that central government was in little danger of being discredited by its actions. And although recurring ill-feeling between local authorities and central government did not threaten social disruption, the minister was more than willing to allow his department to intervene to guarantee an enduring resolution.

BEVERIDGE AND CHILDREN'S ALLOWANCES

MacEntee's tenure as Minister for Local Government and Public Health, has received much critical attention from historians in the context of the evolution of social policy in independent Ireland. Inherent in the criticism of MacEntee's contribution to this area of public policy has been a concomitant hagiography of Seán Lemass and his more 'progressive' stance on social issues. Evidence is gleaned invariably from the two ministers' respective responses to developments in the social policy arena during the Emergency, including the publication in December 1942 of the Beveridge Report in the United Kingdom; the protracted debate surrounding the introduction of a scheme of children's allowances in Ireland from 1939–44, and the appearance of the Dignan Plan for the reorganisation of the health services in 1944. Bew and Patterson, in their summary of government reaction to the Beveridge Report, conclude that, compared to MacEntee, 'Lemass had produced much the more relevant response'.[80] Lee follows this line of argument when he considers the Dignan Plan, opining that: 'However different their sources of inspiration, Lemass and Dignan had more in common with each other than either had with MacEntee.'[81] Lemass was certainly more sympathetic to the ideals of the Beveridge Report but Bew and Patterson's contention that Lemass distinguished himself from MacEntee by adopting a stance based on 'hard-headed economic realism' does the latter's contribution to the debate a grave disservice.

   J.H. Whyte provided an alternative line of thought in his appraisal of the period that went beyond the personalities involved; he attested to a philosophical battle between two forms of government, one bureaucratic and one vocational. According to Whyte, MacEntee was among the 'most determined defenders of the "bureaucratic" viewpoint'.[82] McKee, writing sometime later, challenges this view. Defending the ministerial mindset characteristic of MacEntee, he described this philosophy of government as one which 'espoused restraint in the regulation of society, economy and family'. For MacEntee, 'intervention was based on the exigencies of running the country, not some self-interested perpetuation of bureaucratic control.'[83] As outlined below, MacEntee was willing to endorse government intervention when he deemed it justified, but was certainly not willing to interfere in the interests of bureaucracy. The spread of a social policy dogma based on increased state regulation and supervision, however, provided MacEntee with an altogether different problem.

   The Beveridge Report, or *Social Insurance and Allied Services* (1942), to give it its proper title, proposed a series of policies which would defeat the 'five giants on the road to reconstruction': want, disease, ignorance, squalor and idleness. MacEntee's initial response to the report was inextricably linked to the ongoing debate on the introduction of the government's proposed scheme of children's allowances.[84] Indeed Lemass had to postpone his perusal of the report due to the prioritisation of the government's plan.[85] De Valera, with Lemass's approval, had first mooted the idea of family allowances in 1939, when MacEntee, as Minister for Finance, opposed it on economic grounds. When MacEntee moved from Finance to Industry and Commerce later that year, he again urged the government to resist any inclination to introduce family allowances. This time he employed a more fitting critique of the scheme that was more compatible with his new responsibilities. He argued that the initiation of a scheme of children's allowances would 'drive the unfit into matrimony' and consequently 'drive the strongest, the most enterprising, the best educated of our young earners out of the country'.[86] What was at stake, maintained the minister, was not just a new public policy measure, but the entire edifice on which the state's social organisation was built.[87]

In keeping with the British response to the family allowances issue, which 'protected the integrity and superiority of male wages as a whole', and compatible with his contention that the unemployment assistance acts had subverted parental authority, MacEntee maintained that, in order to minimise the risk to the social order, payments of children's allowances should be made directly to the 'father of the family', but only on the proviso that 'his general character from the point of view of industry and sobriety warrants such payments'.[88] If any father was deemed unsuitable, payment should then go to the mother. That such a stipulation was deemed necessary demonstrated the minister's concluding point, which was articulated with a mandatory degree of overstatement: 'If the state subsidises parents to have children, it will be but a step to regulate the number of children, then to lay down who shall be permitted to have children and who shall not … until we shall have traversed the whole ground between the initiation of a state system of family allowances and the servile state.'[89]

Industry and Commerce was joined in opposition to the proposal by Finance and the Department of Local Government and Public Health. In response to more detailed proposals submitted by Lemass in April 1940,[90] the cabinet glossed over its differences, deciding to revert to the sanctuary of an interdepartmental committee consisting of representatives from the above-named departments and of the Department of Education.[91] MacEntee expounded further on the ideological basis to his opposition in a memorandum to the cabinet in November.[92] The Manichean climate of the war added a vivid colour to his invective, and saw him describe the measure as 'Communism for wives and children'. The interdepartmental committee had produced its report in October 1942.[93] It advocated a means-tested scheme to be paid to the father as the head of the family, to be administered by the Department of Industry and Commerce.[94] In December, de Valera allocated responsibility for the submission of a scheme for compulsory, contributory insurance to Industry and Commerce. Lemass wasted little time. Four days after the Taoiseach's invitation he circulated a memorandum proposing two children's allowances schemes – contributory and non-contributory – for all children after the first. In February 1943, he circulated the heads of a bill to that effect.

MacEntee's response to Lemass's plan was swift. Not only did he object to the proposals on the grounds that they were 'likely to be severely criticised by Catholic sociologists' but also because they transgressed the prerogatives of the Department of Local Government and Public Health.[95] MacEntee followed this up with a further memorandum in March that explicitly related it to the proposals put forward by Beveridge. Indeed his use of the appellation 'Beveridgeism' to depict all social policy initiatives that involved increased state bureaucracy became an indispensable rhetorical shorthand for the minister. He again drew the attention of the Taoiseach to a potential conflict with the clergy, and urged that 'the practical features of any scheme of children's allowances must be very carefully considered, so as to ensure that they are not patently in conflict with the fundamental principle laid down in [the papal encyclical] *Quadragesimo Anno*.'[96] Indeed the Catholic Church was integral to the debate on social welfare development in Ireland but its attitude was by no means as monolithic as MacEntee made out.[97]

Lemass's proposals of February 1943 contained one important difference to his earlier plan. The revised version included the provision of a non-contributory part of the scheme without a means test. This proved to be a contentious inclusion, for as Cousins observes, 'the change meant that, for the first time, a system of general support for families was being proposed as opposed to one focused on children in poor families.'[98] Lemass defended his new approach on the grounds that there was public disquiet at the idea of a means test, and that administrative costs would largely offset any economies accrued from it. MacEntee favoured a wholly contributory scheme, which would be compulsory for wage earners, and which would be inversely related to earnings. He also promised to submit a proposal based on voluntary contributions, but it is unlikely that this memorandum was ever drafted due to its unfeasibility, a point which was made to the minister by his departmental officials.[99] The question for the cabinet became simply which scheme to choose: MacEntee's or Lemass's. De Valera was personally inclined towards the latter, and circulated a memorandum on 23 February which suggested an entirely non-contributory scheme that would be financed by the exchequer.

In the light of this development, MacEntee again looked to the church for guidance. He forwarded de Valera an article by Peter McKevitt, Catholic priest and Professor of Sociology at Maynooth, which dealt with the Beveridge Report from an explicitly Catholic standpoint.[100] Of particular significance to MacEntee was McKevitt's warning of the dangers of creating an 'omnicompetent state'. Although the cleric's article was not without appreciation of Beveridge's ideas, this did not affect MacEntee's argument one bit.[101] Ultimately, as one of the foremost proponents of vocationalism in the state, McKevitt regarded the Beveridge plan as 'not for export', presumably because he had some faith in the ability of the Commission for Vocational Organisation, then sitting, to deliver the apposite response for Ireland. McElligott, who also received a copy of McKevitt's paper

from MacEntee, regarded it as 'the most informative statement in brief compass
that I have seen on the Catholic standpoint and I hope it gets widespread publicity'.[102]

Despite MacEntee's visceral antipathy to the scheme from the outset, his
memorandum of 16 March not only sounded a warning shot to the government
with regard to potential clerical censure, but also staked a claim on behalf of his
department to be the one to administer the scheme. With this end in mind, he had
instructed his officials in December 1942 to prepare proposals for a wholly contributory scheme.[103] Although he argued vigorously against the scheme in principle, he was more than prepared to take responsibility for its administration, particularly if it was at the expense of Lemass's department. Just as his efforts to
prevent the measure had failed, however, his petitions in this regard were also
rebuffed by the de Valera/Lemass nexus. On 13 April, the government approved
the drafting of a bill to provide for children's allowances, the cost of which was
to be borne entirely by the state.

MacEntee's appeal to de Valera's catholicism was motivated by political considerations as much as any ideological sympathy he may have felt towards
Catholic social teaching. On the children's allowances question, MacEntee was
well attuned to the fact that certain Catholic authorities, both in Ireland and on
the continent, regarded state assistance as savouring of socialism and state paternalism.[104] This was an argument that he undoubtedly found appealing when
opposing Lemass's scheme, but he would also have been aware that a leading
Irish Catholic intellectual, Cornelius Lucey, had in 1939 called for the principle
of family allowances to be accepted.[105] Catholic social thinkers also contributed
largely to the debate in France and regarded the introduction of family
allowances as a morally imperative gesture towards the '"patriotic" couples producing children for *la patrie*'.[106] Thus, MacEntee's own catholicism, and his
attendant abhorrence of totalitarianism, made him inimical to the state's invasion
of familial autonomy and the putative dilution of parental responsibility, but his
researches into Catholic social theory were selectively used for purely political
purposes. MacEntee was careful to alert the Taoiseach and his fellow ministers
to the relevant parts of the legislation that were disapproved of by the clergy, but
other articles more favourable to this type of social thought were ignored by him
due to their lack of political utility.[107] Moreover, the debate surrounding children's allowances again brought the MacEntee–Lemass rivalry into sharp focus.
While it may be going too far to suggest that Cowling's description of high politics in Britain in an earlier period exactly describes this rivalry, it certainly has
a resonance for the MacEntee–Lemass relationship, particularly during the
Emergency:

> Antipathy, self-interest and mutual contempt were the strongest levers of
> action, the most powerful motives in conflict, and they were so because no
> one knew what the outcome of conflict would be. It was the fact that they
> knew that they were fighting for an unknown future which explains the heat
> of the politics we are discussing and justifies the weight given to factors
> which politicians in retrospect prefer to forget. This would be true of any

historical period. It was particularly true when the future was as open, hope and fear as strong and the situation as new as the one we are discussing.[108]

The political impact of the Beveridge Report immediately caused concern in government circles. In December 1942 Hugo Flinn, parliamentary secretary to the Minister for Finance, conveyed its possible political ramifications, viewing the publication of the Beveridge report and the promise of its adoption in Northern Ireland as a '"god-send" for the Labour Party and, properly worked, worth quite a few seats'.[109] In the general election, due to be held the following summer, such issues were bound to be vote-winners, particularly in urban areas. At the Fine Gael West Cork convention in January 1943, the main opposition leader, W.T. Cosgrave, adumbrated his party's platform in the election by promising to introduce family allowances.[110] His party had decided that an overhaul of the social services was necessary in order to effect economies in their administration, and lessen any difficulties confronting recipients. If this speech had hastened de Valera's resolve to implement the children's allowances scheme, it may also have convinced MacEntee that its introduction had become a political necessity. Lemass also saw the Beveridge Report as a significant development for Ireland. He recognised implicitly that the ideals underpinning the provisions of the report elevated standards of public services irreversibly, and threw down a moral gauntlet to all governments that claimed to have a social agenda. In March, he conceded that Beveridge had made conditions in Ireland appear inadequate, something that would be ameliorated by the introduction of the new children's allowances bill.[111]

In April Lemass vowed not to get into a bidding war during the June general election and made it clear that the government would introduce children's allowances only if it returned to power. However, Cosgrave reiterated his intention to introduce family allowances, prompting Lemass to announce that the bill was almost ready for introduction in the Dáil.[112] Social policy was also an integral part of the Labour Party election programme. The party's election notes for MacEntee's constituency, Dublin Townships, contained strong echoes of Beveridgean ideas, offering the electorate 'a positive guarantee of real security based on freedom from want'.[113] To MacEntee, the Labour Party posed the greatest threat to Fianna Fáil's continuance in power.[114] His election speeches repeatedly stressed national security over other concerns, and he went to great lengths to associate the main opposition parties with wartime totalitarian belligerents. Thus, his audiences were constantly reminded of Fine Gael's Blueshirt past, as well as Labour's supposed communist credentials. Clann na Talmhan, a recently formed farmers' party that sought to capture Fianna Fáil's traditional support base, was not spared MacEntee's onslaught. It was a 'totalitarian party', a party of 'spalpeens', communist in its outlook.[115] The sustained virulence of MacEntee's attack was deemed counter-productive by the Fianna Fáil hierarchy. Lemass wrote to his ministerial colleague on 10 June advising that a 'number of our candidates have phoned me to suggest that we should modify our attack on Labour. They say that Labour is gaining from this and not the reverse.'[116] Lemass's intervention was bound to fail. MacEntee acknowledged the concerns of his fellow ministers but remained unrepentant and continued the attacks up to polling day.

There is no doubt that MacEntee wildly exaggerated any putative threat to the integrity of the state from Fianna Fáil's election rivals in 1943, and that he behaved in a histrionic manner when attacking the Labour Party – to the extent that, aided by some injudicious use of Special Branch reports, he could claim that 'Muscovites' were active in Dublin and had captured William Norton – but this was very much part of his belligerent political style. What is more, MacEntee's conduct during the 1943 general election was not wholly inexplicable. He had retained a residual disregard for labour, both organised and political, since the events surrounding the passage of the Trade Union Act in 1941, having been the object of much of that constituency's opprobrium during a particularly troubled enactment. He also claimed to have been the victim of systematic heckling by Labour party supporters throughout the campaign. Although Fianna Fáil was returned to power in 1943, the government party lost ten seats from its electoral high of 1938; its percentage share of the vote decreased by 10 per cent to 41.9. In the aftermath of the campaign, de Valera investigated MacEntee's conduct which, in turn, resulted in a humiliating admonition from the Taoiseach in front of the entire cabinet.[117] In a fifteen-page resignation letter dated 28 June, MacEntee refuted de Valera's criticism, suggesting that his motivation was never personal but was driven solely by concern for the Fianna Fáil party.[118] The letter tellingly disclosed MacEntee's apparent insecurity in the cabinet and his awareness of adversaries within the party. Whether the letter was ever sent, or whether de Valera dissuaded MacEntee from resigning, is not known.

In contrast to the 1943 general election campaign, when the government stressed its general dependability in the face of unrest over unemployment and the cost of living, the snap general election of 1944 produced a more positive campaign. Lemass referred to Fianna Fáil throughout as 'the worker's party' in an effort to regain some of the working-class support alienated by MacEntee in 1943. The 1944 campaign also saw MacEntee emphasising the government's unparalleled contribution to social policy reform. MacEntee's campaign literature boasted that 'since last July Fianna Fáil has introduced new legislation on housing, children's allowances, midwives and conditions of employment as well as the Local Authorities (Education Scholarships) Act, 1944.'[119] Fianna Fáil was again presenting itself as the natural champion of the underprivileged just as it had done in 1927 and 1932 and, at the very least, it appears that MacEntee acknowledged the strong political benefits accruing from social policy reforms, not to mention the moral authority it conferred on the benefactors of such measures.

Nonetheless, the debate about the introduction of children's allowances affords another opportunity of assessing the individual preoccupations of senior government figures. Lee has described the enactment of the measure as 'one of the few battles that the forces of resistance lost'. Moreover, the length of time between the measure's instigation and its realisation, argues Lee, 'provides eloquent corroborative testimony to the difficulty of actually getting anything done in the type of regime that had emerged after two decades of independence'.[120] This is somewhat ungenerous. The original examination of the question predated the

Emergency with the consequent ministerial and administrative restructuring it imposed.[121] Furthermore, as we have seen, the Emergency provided a plethora of other problems for the government to deal with and the enactment of legislation which, ordinarily, would have proved contentious within the cabinet was unlikely to remain at the top of its agenda for very long. A more benign interpretation might pay tribute to the fact that the measure was enacted as legislation before the Emergency was over. Lee's advertence to 'the forces of resistance' – his acerbic description of Messrs O'Kelly, McElligott and MacEntee – also does a disservice to the personalities involved. While it is unarguable that the Department of Finance continued to play devil's advocate to the government's interventionist instincts, MacEntee's inclusion in this group raises some obvious questions. Although he was ultimately unsuccessful in having his contributory scheme accepted by the cabinet, why, having consistently argued against the proposal, did he suddenly want to be the one to administer it? Also, why was the Department of Local Government and Public Health, under MacEntee, overtly amenable to a more *dirigiste* response to public policy development? The answer to the first question is, perhaps, contained in the proposal submitted by MacEntee. His contention that social security schemes should be developed, insofar as possible by those directly involved (employees and employers), with minimum state participation, was broadly consistent with the response of a number of Catholic thinkers to the Beveridge Report.[122] His disparagement of the model espoused by Beveridge was conditioned by this conviction. Furthermore, that MacEntee's desire to administer the scheme was first expressed after Lemass's department had taken the initiative cannot be regarded as coincidental. The answer to the second question requires consideration of MacEntee's reception of other important developments in the social policy arena.

THE DIGNAN PLAN

MacEntee's regular invocation of Catholic social principles, according to Lee, 'makes his bitter public dispute with Dr [John] Dignan, Bishop of Clonfert, in 1944–45, all the more curious'.[123] But, as Riordan has illustrated, while MacEntee proved himself adept at gauging the Catholic temperature on social issues, this was a secondary concern if it involved a diminution of ministerial authority.[124] Riordan's account of the affair is the most comprehensive, not only in describing MacEntee's conduct but also in assessing Dignan's agenda. In the main, this agenda has been sympathetically received by historians. Where Lee and Whyte have focused on the belligerence of MacEntee as representative of an authoritarian government with centralising tendencies, Riordan and McKee have identified an assertiveness to Dignan's behaviour as an outspoken proponent of vocationalism, which McKee has described as 'that vogue of Christian social teaching which often allowed vested interests to present themselves as a defence against "bureaucratic totalitarianism"'.[125] Dr Dignan was, in fact, Fianna Fáil's appointee in 1936 to the chairmanship of the committee of management of the National Health Insurance Society of Ireland (NHIS), a semi-autonomous body that functioned under the auspices of MacEntee's department. He was respected by the government as an opponent of the Treaty and supporter of Bunreacht na hÉireann, which he described as a 'second spring heralding the moulding of the nation as a truly Christian people'.[126] Relations had soured somewhat by 1943, however, when the committee of management, without seeking permission from the minister, had sanctioned bonus payments to staff, in direct contravention of Emergency Standstill Order no. 83 which, as we have seen, had been introduced with some difficulty by MacEntee.[127]

Dignan's paper, *Social Security: Outlines of a Scheme of National Health Insurance*, was read to the society on 11 October 1944.[128] It began by recognising the 'urgent necessity of reorganising and coordinating our health services'.[129] The plan envisaged a decentralised and unified health service, which would remove 'redundancy, duplication, over-lapping and anomalies', and which would be under the control of the National Health Insurance Society. It also proposed a 'special Minister for Social Services who would be responsible to the Dáil for their proper, efficient and economic working'. Dignan maintained that: 'In the new Society the stigma of poverty will be removed. All members and their dependants will have an equal right to its benefits irrespective of their wealth or their social position.'[130] What is more, 'Dignan's plan implemented the principle of subsidiarity, exalted the authority of the father of the family, and was contributory', ostensibly satisfying the arguments mobilised by MacEntee in the children's allowances debate.[131] The plan was warmly received by the national press when it was released to them the following week. It was soon realised, however, that media approbation for the Dignan Plan was simply a convenient way of arraigning the government for the existing state of the health services, much to the chagrin of the minister responsible. An editorial in the *Irish Independent* illustrated this point. Describing the bishop's proposals as 'important and far-reaching', it adverted to the 'chaotic and complex state of [the] social services'. Dignan's scheme was, the *Independent* stated, 'the Beveridge plan with modifications in accord with Christian and Catholic principles, and, with recognition of the fact that a relatively poor country like Ireland cannot afford the high standard of health and other social services that one expects to find in rich countries'.[132] Meanwhile, the *Irish Times* described the scheme as 'nobly comprehensive' and reported that it had been 'offered for the government's consideration'.[133]

Informing the government, however, was not the first thing on Dignan's mind. Three days after the scheme was released, he wrote to the Archbishop of Dublin, John Charles McQuaid, to apologise for not forwarding him a copy of the plan in the first instance.[134] Dignan's apparent discourtesy towards his clerical superior was surpassed by his failure to inform the minister of his intentions before the scheme appeared in the press to such fanfare. The day after its publication, Tom Barrington, MacEntee's private secretary, wrote to the press impugning the fundamental integrity of the plan: 'If by a scheme for an extension of social services is meant a proposal substantially worked out in detail, supported by factual argument and embodying estimates of the expenditure involved and concrete proposals for defraying the cost, the minister can categorically state that no such scheme has been submitted to him.'[135] For although the Department of Local Government and Public Health had been made aware of Dignan's intentions in April 1944, when he mentioned it to MacEntee's parliamentary secretary, Dr Conn Ward,[136] and Dignan had forwarded copies of the plan to both Ward and MacEntee at the same time as the press release, the minister took umbrage that Dignan had released it before ascertaining the department's considered opinion. MacEntee was also piqued by the complimentary tone and sympathetic treatment afforded by the radio and print media. Again through his private secretary, he contacted the Minister for Posts and Telegraphs, P.J. Little, to ascertain whether he was of the opinion 'that the matter was of such importance as to warrant such a full report on the radio and the devoting of so much broadcasting time to it'.[137] MacEntee also contacted the press to condemn it for its part in the scheme's positive reception.[138]

On the surface, this response appears unduly petulant but it was ultimately conditioned, not only by Dignan's apparent impertinence, but also by what MacEntee considered the uncritical and passive nature of the media commentary, with its affiliated willingness to admonish the government. That the scheme's positive reception was reinforced by an endorsement from a variety of interest groups, including the Labour Party, the ITGWU and ITUC, did little to recommend it to the minister.[139] The scheme also drew a response from the Medical Association of Éire (later the Irish Medical Association), which had been preparing its own plan, duly published in December 1944.[140] One of the authors of that proposal, Dr W.R.F Collis, wrote to Dignan to explain that while their respective schemes had similarities, the issue of control was fundamental to the doctors. In turn Dignan promised to 'join with the medical profession and do my utmost to get the Government to move'.[141] Dignan and Collis also agreed to meet with the president of the Medical Association, Dr John Shanley, with a view to discussing a coordinated approach.[142]

MacEntee went public on the Dignan scheme in answer to a Dáil question in January 1945 by Labour leader William Norton, describing it as impracticable 'under almost every heading',[143] and as far as the public debate was concerned, the minister deemed that closed. MacEntee's response to Dignan did not stem from the minister's 'inability to deal with the bishop's proposals on their merits', however.[144] In February 1945, the minister submitted his criticisms to cabinet 'which anatomised it with an almost sadistic attention to detail'.[145] This departmental dissection exposed a number of significant flaws in the cleric's plan, which were gleefully highlighted, notwithstanding Dignan's assurance to the minister that he 'realised the "several very complex fundamental difficulties" involved', of which he did his best to 'take due cognisance'.[146] MacEntee's principal criticism was that: 'There appears to be no answer to the proposition made that the exercise of functions, duties and rights affecting 90% of the population in relation to social services is already vested in the Oireachtas, whose authority devolved through the Government to Executive Ministers and is exercised by them through their staffs.' This, in itself, was probably enough to condemn the plan in the government's eyes, particularly as it had recently shelved the report of the Commission on Vocational Organisation for similar reasons.[147] In fact, both publications contained the defects which Whyte has identified as a too rigid application of Catholic social teaching. These included the paradox of combating bureaucracy with a centralised administrative structure; poor appreciation of costing and methods of finance; and the improbability that insurance could cover the 90 per cent of the population envisaged in the proposals, particularly as it disregarded how the self-employed and the destitute could be accommodated.[148] Furthermore, the figure of 90 per cent of the working population was fundamental to the scheme's success. Dignan naively believed that increased contributions would willingly be paid by both employers and employees 'when they realise the great value they receive'.

Dignan's plan was undoubtedly a 'sincere attempt to set out a new approach to the provision of social services in Ireland'. What the bishop did not know was that the Department of Local Government and Public Health was already in the process of addressing the question of social service reform.[149] The plan's enduring significance lay in its catalytic role in drawing the government's attention to the political desirability of a 'plan', and the cathartic effect it had on MacEntee to implement change. What is more, it convinced the minister that Dignan needed to be brought to heel and MacEntee declined to reappoint him to his post when it expired in August 1945. MacEntee's decision not to indulge the bishop by issuing a 'considered response' clearly contributed to the negative response the minister's conduct has routinely received. Needless to say, the spectacle of a government minister and a Catholic cleric at loggerheads was a peculiarly absorbing one both for the press and the public. It has been demonstrated conclusively elsewhere that Dignan's actions, in his use of the press to provoke the minister, were confrontational and unbecoming.[150] The bishop had articulated his grievances to a public meeting in Loughrea in March 1945, calling on the minister to 'state the grounds on which the scheme was declared "impracticable" … Under almost every heading I respectfully submit to him that his sweeping statement proves nothing and is not true.'[151] Dignan's timing was carefully contrived, as MacEntee was due to address a public meeting on the 'Coordination of the social services' in Dublin the following day. MacEntee's speech, reported widely in the press, included a hastily written addendum which denounced Dignan for attempting 'to engage him in public controversy'.[152] MacEntee also maintained that Dignan, in his role as chairman of the NHIS and the appointee of the minister, was not entitled to publish his recommendations without his prior consent. Dignan again responded provocatively. Two weeks later the *Irish Independent* published a speech given by the bishop which refuted MacEntee's contention:

> I repudiate the claim that I occupy the chair at 'his will and pleasure'. I am not 'the agent' of the minister, and when he says that I must not fail to observe my obligations to him 'in any regard', I consider this as tantamount to his claiming complete, almost autocratic, authority over the chairman and that I must consider myself if not a 'stamp-licking Irish serf', at least a rubber stamp serf.[153]

The bishop's efforts were in vain. For once, MacEntee preferred to keep his counsel private, and such was his determination that the spat be allowed to run out of steam, he was slow to respond to Dignan's private entreaties for some explanation of his criticism. Instead he drafted several responses which were never sent.[154] The drafts contain the kernel of the minister's disposition at this time: 'Your Lordship's proposition that the chairman of the committee of management is entitled to know why the minister considers certain proposals impracticable, would not be consistent with the position as I have defined it since it would make the minister accountable to his appointee for his decisions and policy.'[155]

Ultimately Dignan's proposals contained the serious defect of putting the administration of the health services into the hands of an unelected body. MacEntee was further irked by the inherent criticisms of his department's failure to provide adequate health services and the fact that any support for the Dignan proposals became a 'by-word for the inadequacy of Fianna Fáil's social policies'.[156] To conclude, as Lee does, that MacEntee's behaviour towards Dignan was all the more curious in view of his (MacEntee's) earlier invocation of Catholic teaching is to confuse two quite separate issues. The vagueness of Dignan's scheme was enough in itself to warrant the minister's assertion of authority; but the flagrant attempt by Dignan and the National Health Insurance Society to by-pass government, both in the publication of the proposals and in the plans for their administration, could never have been greeted enthusiastically by any responsible member of that government. That the scheme contained quite stinging criticism of the government department concerned literally added insult to injury.

THE DEPARTMENT OF HEALTH

The Dignan Plan was not the first time that a fundamental reorganisation of the state's social services was contemplated. Indeed the cleric had failed to acknowledge that the government had already begun to consider the future direction of the health services.[157] Perhaps this should not be surprising for, although the cabinet had instigated a tentative exploration of the matter in early 1939, little was done before Dignan's plan entered the public domain. This process was concurrent with the government's long-held desire to administer the social services in a more coherent and economical fashion. Duplication and overlapping in the administration of the social services was frequently criticised in the press and, as we have seen, media commendation of the Dignan Plan became a *quid pro quo* for his putative exposure of what was wrong with the health services.[158]

Having allowed the question of social services reform to lapse for almost two years, de Valera was forced to reconsider it in February 1942, when William Norton asked him in the Dáil whether he was 'prepared to consider the establishment of a department of social welfare to take over and co-ordinate the functions relating to social welfare now carried out by a variety of Government Departments and Ministers'.[159] De Valera's response, which had prior approval of the ministers concerned, conceded that the matter had been considered more than once by the government, but that 'such a step would be attended by many difficulties and it [wa]s not clear that it would result in any economy or increased efficiency in the administration of the services'.[160] Finance had, in fact, already dictated that the issue would be dominated by the dual concerns of economy and efficiency. In the same month as Norton put down his Dáil question, the parliamentary secretary to the Minister for Local Government and Public Health, Dr Conn Ward, met representatives of the national executive of the ITUC to discuss national health insurance. The unions expressed a desire for 'a comprehensive, all-inclusive scheme of social services, probably under a Minister of Social Services'.[161] Clearly, the matter was given renewed urgency by the publication of the Beveridge Report, which was circulated to all ministers on 16 December.[162] Moreover, the impetus which the Beveridge report gave to Ireland's intelligentsia to engage with the question of planning brought the government's inaction into sharper relief. A symposium of the Social and Statistical Inquiry Society of Ireland on 5 March 1943 examined in comprehensive detail the question of the Irish social services.[163] The following year was also notable for the cause of national planning. As well as the appearance of the Dignan Plan, a national planning exhibition was held in Dublin between 26 April and 5 May, organised by the national planning committee. On the day after the exhibition ended, a public meeting was held at the Mansion House in Dublin. Chaired by the editor of the *Irish Times*, R.M. Smyllie, it brought together a wide range of experts who had contributed to the planning debate in the pages of the newspaper in a weekly column known as 'Towards Tomorrow'. MacEntee was the guest speaker but, from the evidence of the editorial in the *Irish Times* the following day, he left the would-be planners less than satisfied. Smyllie regarded the minister's participation as designed to 'pour cold water on the entire enterprise' and to 'create a sense of disillusionment'.[164]

In September 1943, the cabinet decided that a committee consisting of MacEntee, O'Kelly and the Minister for Agriculture, James Ryan, should be set up to examine and report on the planning of a new Department of Social Services.[165] Despite the predictable failure of the committee to complete a report, MacEntee duly started the ball rolling with a memorandum for the government on 28 September which summarised his position thus: '[S]o far as the majority of social services administered by the Department of L[ocal] G[overnment] and P[ublic] H[ealth] or under its aegis are concerned there are very few which are so closely and essentially related to what may be generically described as Labour that it would be desirable to associate them either on psychological or administrative grounds with a Ministry of Labour.'[166] MacEntee was opposed to a significant diminution of the services under the control of his department, and was adamant that all cognate health services should not be removed from its remit. Norton raised the matter again in February 1944 but was met with a similar reply, de Valera regarding the present system as 'efficient and economical'.[167]

MacEntee's wish that all aspects of the public health services remain under the jurisdiction of his department was aided in March 1944 by formal delegation of public health to his parliamentary secretary, Dr Conn Ward. This was recognition of the fact that the task entrusted to Ward was one which required a more hands-on role than perhaps MacEntee's dual brief would allow. 'While I am strongly of the opinion that there should be a separate Ministry for Public Health,' MacEntee wrote to de Valera in January, 'I am convinced after two years' experience of the present position that there is no possibility that a joint ministry of Local

Government and Public Health will be made to work satisfactorily unless there is a comprehensive and effective delegation to a Parliamentary Secretary of the minister's functions in relation to one or other section of the joint department.'[168] Although Ward had undertaken similar delegation under O'Kelly, his formal appointment was a significant advance, which was further enhanced by the constructive working relationship he developed with the chief medical officer, Dr James Deeny. Deeny has recalled how they 'soon found a common interest, which was to create a good and effective health service'. The realisation of this aspiration, however, was ultimately contingent on the minister's patronage: '[Ward] had no money or power, save what his chief [MacEntee] could secure from the cabinet.'[169] The responsibilities delegated to Ward reflected the most urgent public health problems facing the government in the 1940s. MacEntee enumerated these problems in a memorandum to the cabinet in March, the most important of which were: codification and amendment of lunacy law; training of mental defectives; amendment of the public health law and its ultimate codification; control and treatment of venereal disease; and the growing tuberculosis problem.[170]

Legislation was duly enacted to address some of these areas in the form of the Mental Treatment Act, 1945 and the Tuberculosis (Establishment of Sanatoria) Act, 1945. Both acts were an attempt to modernise a set of inadequate and outdated provisions. The former act sought to 'substitute for the law at present ... a new code in harmony with modern views on the treatment of mental illness', while the latter proposed 'to provide, as far as possible, the most up-to-date methods of diagnosis and treatment' of a disease whose prevalence had resulted in the number of deaths in the state increasing from 1.23 per thousand population in 1937 to 1.46 in 1942.[171] This act was the culmination of MacEntee's resolve to see it reduced significantly, a determination which was first outlined in a letter to the Archbishop of Dublin in March 1943.[172]

By 1945 there were three proposals for overhauling the state's health services on the table. In October 1944, the Medical Association of Éire had submitted a scheme for a national medical service to MacEntee. The minister informed the cabinet in March 1945 that the association had 'been pressing for an opportunity to discuss their proposals and have appointed a very large and representative deputation'.[173] The prime instigator of the association's scheme was Dr John Shanley, who also acted as chairman of the association from 1942–4. Shanley had experience as a poor law medical officer in Dublin and was uniquely placed to witness the damage to health caused by deprivation and malnutrition.[174] He was also a member of Fianna Fáil and on good terms with MacEntee and Ward. Notwithstanding this, MacEntee felt it judicious to expose the scheme to the scrutiny of the same departmental committee set up to examine the outlines of the Dignan scheme.[175] 'Criticism of the doctors' plan by the Department of Local Government and Public Health,' as McKee has noted 'was nothing if not comprehensive.'[176] It concluded that the plan had been 'carelessly thrown together' with 'far too much emphasis on the working conditions of the general practitioner'.[177] As with Dignan's proposals, what ultimately made the plan unworkable from the department's point of view was that it involved 'the passing of executive control of national health services and insurance into the hands of the medical profession'.[178] Again, to quote McKee, 'neither Dignan nor the Medical Association (nor any other interest group) had rights to claim health policy without a commensurate burden of responsibility. It was not a question of bureaucracy but of power and responsibility.'[179]

As it turned out, the departmental committee established by MacEntee to review the non-governmental approach to the reorganisation of the health services produced by far the most relevant response. Manned by a group that consisted of the aforementioned Dr James Deeny – who had been appointed by Ward and was an expert in links between nutrition, poverty and ill-health – John Collins, assistant secretary of the department, John Garvin, principal officer, P.J. Keady, deputy controller of the national health insurance department, and Desmond Roche, the committee's draft report was issued in September 1945. It envisaged:

> [A] public medical service which will aim at conserving health as well as remedying ill-health. The service would be at two levels – local and regional and is estimated conservatively at £7 millions annually, as compared with the current annual expenditure of £3½ million on public health services. The service would extend to about two million persons. It was proposed that the general control and direction of the medical services would be under a minister for public health who would be assisted by an expert advisory council.

The departmental committee held seventeen full meetings and eleven sub-committee meetings before producing its report. It had studied schemes considered at that time the most enlightened social security and health schemes anywhere, including those of New Zealand, Canada, the United Kingdom and Australia. From this broad sweep, Deeny and his associates anticipated a scheme that would see the entire population covered without charge: 'The ideal to be aimed at is a national health service embracing all classes within its scope, recognising no limitation of effectiveness on mere economic grounds, and treating the people from the health point of view as a unit.'[180] Taking the peculiarities of Irish social conditions very much into account, the plan was to be 'approached in stages and was to be, as in Canada, partly financed by insurance contributions and partly by state funds both central and local'.[181] According to Barrington, the 'departmental committee's recommendations were radical by any standards'.[182] She also makes the pertinent point that this was all the more surprising given the status of their authors: 'Deeny, Garvin, Collins and Keady were not in the position of Beveridge, independent of the system and free to toss ideas into the political and administrative court.'

MacEntee, conscious of the need to come to some decisions in the light of developments in Britain, and mounting criticism closer to home, recommended that the committee's report be accepted by cabinet and that it should serve as the basis for a white paper.[183] MacEntee, in Deeny's view, was well capable of convincing the cabinet of the report's worth: 'He had a marked commonsense, was politically very able and had an immediate grasp of what the public would "buy".'[184] Moreover, 'his approach was almost exclusively political, whether government, party, public or personal. It was not so in any cheap vote-getting sense and one had to admire him for his wisdom, practicality and indeed courage. Sometimes it was of supreme importance to know whether a thing was practically feasible, and if he could sell it to the cabinet, to the party or the public. On such matters he was superb.' The minister circulated a memorandum to cabinet in March 1946 proposing 'free medical treatment detached from public assistance administration'. Unsurprisingly, there were reservations expressed, most notably by the Department of Finance, which maintained that the proposals 'would amount in effect to the socialisation of medicine and would entail an extension of benefit at the expense of individual liberty'. Despite this, MacEntee duly secured the cabinet's support for the measure, agreeing in principle to the proposals on 10 May when the minister was also authorised to submit a white paper to government. Perhaps the 'forces of resistance' that Lee has referred to were outdone on this occasion. The Health Services Act, 1947, the culmination of Deeny's committee, sought to expand the health services by taking the financial burden away from local authorities and passing it to central government. The legislation would consolidate twenty-six previous statutes, codify infectious diseases, and map out a new role in local public health with a distinctly preventive focus.[185]

In tandem with the cabinet's decision to pursue a reorganisation of the health services, it also resolved to create two new departments.[186] Indeed it was MacEntee who persuaded the Taoiseach of the importance of establishing separate departments of Health and Social Welfare. In February 1945, an interdepartmental committee consisting of Finance, Industry and Commerce and Local Government was set up to examine the organisation of the social services.[187] MacEntee's initial response was defensive. He reminded the Taoiseach that the setting up of the committee was at variance with his statements in the Dáil on 17 February 1944 in response to Norton's inquiry. The minister did not regard the position as being in any way different from then, and resubmitted his memorandum of 28 September 1943, which had stressed that 'the essential relationship between labour as a generic category and many of the social services may be very tenuous indeed.' MacEntee felt that this was particularly the case in most of the social services under his control.[188] Moreover, MacEntee wanted more than one representative from his department on the committee (as suggested by cabinet) if it was to be representative of the many social services administered by his department.

The government, as it often did, duly struck a compromise, deciding that the committee would be under the auspices of Finance, and that the departments involved would retain the prerogative to nominate one or two members. Having met for eight sessions, the committee produced a majority and a minority report in June 1945, the latter being signed by the representatives of MacEntee's department, Deeny and Garvin.[189] It deviated from the majority report's findings insofar as it concentrated on the impact of the proposals on the administration of the public health services, and not the social services in general. The signatories of the minority report stressed 'the necessity of retaining health insurance in close association with the medical services supervised by the department of L[ocal] G[overnment] and P[ublic] H[ealth]' and considered that the 'most important development of the social services ... will be the reorganisation of the health service throughout the country and the placing of better facilities for medical services at the disposal of those who out of their own resources are unable to provide such services'.[190] They argued, *apropos* of Beveridge, that 'the development of health insurance must play an important part and it should be associated with a department of state entrusted with the supervision of medical and public health services.' In doing so, however, the minority report concurred with the spirit of the majority report's important conclusion that 'the Government should have available to it a centre of informed opinion, abreast of modern trends and capable of formulating a policy which will maintain a satisfactory balance between modern developments and our domestic problems, needs and resources.'[191] Both Finance and Industry and Commerce endorsed the majority report; Finance, in particular, saw the advantages of a dedicated income maintenance department in the interest of efficiency and economy.

The question rose to the top of the cabinet's agenda in November in response to a motion put down in the Dáil by National Labour deputies James Everett and James P. Pattison requesting the government to 'introduce proposals for the establishment of a scheme of social security, in which all the existing social services shall be unified and co-ordinated under a ministry of social services, and all persons in gainful employment brought under the provisions of a comprehensive scheme of social insurance'.[192] De Valera's response to the motion was decidedly cautious. He concurred with the majority report's conclusion that 'if future developments of social services ... are to be envisaged and adequately planned, supervised and coordinated the Government should have at its disposal the specialist advice of a Minister and a Department established for that purpose.' He was keen to stress, however, that 'no further considerable expansion of the social services will be possible without an appreciable expansion of our actual wealth.'[193] Nevertheless, the heads of a bill to create two new departments of state were finally circulated in October 1946. In November, the government, after an informal discussion, decided the title of the new department specifically concerned with income maintenance would be Social Welfare, not Social Services. MacEntee explained to the Dáil that social welfare was a more accurate description of the new department, which was only one of a number concerned with social services in the wider sense.[194]

In the same month, MacEntee introduced the Ministers and Secretaries (Amendment) Bill to provide the legal framework for the new department. In preparation for the bill, MacEntee submitted a memorandum on income-maintenance services. He intended his memorandum to 'stimulate thought and provoke discussion'.[195] He also brought up the question of the extent to which further redistribution of the national income was desirable but acknowledged that it was impractical to make it an issue at that time. During the second reading of the bill, MacEntee quoted at length from an address he had given to the UCD medical society in February 1944, which outlined the criteria on which any new department would be considered, and contemplated the difficulties the government faced in framing the new legislation. The essential point he made, and perhaps the issue that most informed his response to the Dignan Plan, was one of control:

> The setting up of such a Ministry ... will require a great deal of careful thought, a great deal of preparatory work, and, therefore, quite a significant time before it can be undertaken. For we have so entangled our public health services with our general civic administration that it is going to be a difficult task to disentangle them and to provide for our public health services an administrative system which will give us effective service and yet conform to sound principles of financial and democratic control.

Whyte goes too far in his summation of the Department of Local Government and Public Health under MacEntee: 'It showed a readiness to concentrate authority, a lack of interest in the maintenance of autonomous groups, a reluctance to consult outside groups that made a sharp contrast with "vocational" principles.'[196] Like much of the commentary on public policy during this time, Whyte demonstrates a readiness to assume that any scheme which was thwarted by government was beyond reproach. Furthermore, his analysis ignores the work of Deeny's committee, which did consult other interests. His point about the centralisation tendencies of the department is more difficult to refute. That this was not done in the interests of an extension of bureaucracy must admit an alternative explanation. MacEntee was consistently protective of his department's workload, be it from vocational organisations or from other departments of government. Lee suggests that this was endemic to the Fianna Fáil governments of the 1940s, but it is clear that few other government departments resented encroachment on its powers to the same degree as did the Department of Local Government and Public Health (save perhaps the Department of Industry and Commerce, whose powers at this time were considerable). If the evil of centralisation was not a wholesome prescription for the overall health of the state, it was, according to MacEntee, essential for the viability of the Department of Local Government and Public Health. Centralisation also ensured that control would be invested in the government and the Oireachtas. This was not only important in principle, but perhaps constitutes a further indication of MacEntee's lack of faith in local authorities to deal adequately with such issues as the effective administration of health services.

BEVERIDGEISM

How can MacEntee's actions as Minister for Local Government and Public Health in overseeing one of the most momentous administrative changes in the history of the state be reconciled with his stated views on the centralist thesis that lay at the core of the Beveridge Report? Was his attitude to the introduction of children's allowances and his sponsorship of comprehensive health reforms which drew a hostile response from many Catholic figures incompatible? In attempting to come to some understanding of these issues, it is worth considering a speech MacEntee delivered on the future of the social services to the Tomás Ó Laoghaire Fianna Fáil cumann in March 1945.[197] It is also impossible to ignore the political context in which this speech was given, for the minister's critique of 'Beveridgeism' was much more than merely an academic response to Britain's blueprint for post-war reconstruction. His agenda in scrutinising Beveridge can be looked at from many different angles; his description of the book as 'slick, shallow and superficial' possibly points to his exasperation with advocates of Beveridge who had not read a single line of his recommendations. More pertinently, it can also be read as an indirect response to supporters of Beveridge within the Fianna Fáil cabinet. Therefore, the audience to whom the minister chose to impart his views was carefully chosen. A few weeks prior to MacEntee's speech, Lemass had circulated his memorandum on 'full employment' to the committee on economic planning.[198] The Lemass document, which amounted to a response to the British white paper published in 1944 – itself largely based on Beveridge's work – was littered with references to modern economic research and its chief proselytisers, Keynes and Beveridge. If MacEntee's voice was being ignored within the cabinet room, it is tempting to conclude that by attacking the fundamental thesis central to that document in such a public fashion he was guaranteeing it would not remain unheard for long. In effect, MacEntee's real invective was probably being directed at his government colleague and, since cabinet disunity was never made public, attacking Sir William Beveridge was the most convenient way of demonstrating his dissent.

The speech itself is worthy of inspection, not only for what it reveals about the minister's tactical position on the subject, but also for its vivid illustration of MacEntee's proclivity for savage political invective. As officials in his department were busy examining the feasibility of the various social security schemes under consideration, including those pioneered by Beveridge and Dignan, MacEntee used the occasion to deliver his own considered verdict on 'Some recent proposals for the co-ordination of our social services'. MacEntee decided to deconstruct Beveridge's follow-up report *Full Employment in a Free Society* (1944) for the apparent edification of his audience, in a manner that could not be described as disinterested. As noted above, the minister prefaced this rigorous inquisition of the Beveridge document with his first public admonishment of Dignan's methods, and it was this part of the talk which drew subsequent comment in the press. The main body of the address was instructive, however, as an articulation of MacEntee's most extravagant fears of what 'Beveridgeism' would mean for society.

The ostensible subject of MacEntee's talk, Beveridge's *Full Employment*, was more than a sequel to his original 1942 report. It not only saw the social insurance plan as an iceberg tip of a much more ambitious and far-reaching programme of social reconstruction, but also looked to the social and economic readjustment required to facilitate his earlier design.[199] MacEntee began by denouncing the inevitable bureaucratic intrusiveness arising from 'Beveridgeism', and the limits on freedom that it would impose. Beveridge had adverted to four problems that faced society's efforts to create full employment. They were that changes of government invariably brought different economic policies; that the right to strike prevented wages and prices from being kept under control; that efficiency suffered from easy job availability; and that demand could not be guaranteed. Beveridge had grappled with these problems for some time, as his biographer has noted: '[his] central concern in his full employment inquiry was not merely how unemployment could be abolished, but how it could be abolished without infringing "basic freedoms" – which he defined as freedom of speech, worship and association, freedom to choose an occupation and freedom in spending a personal income.'[200] MacEntee allowed the expression of these fears to become an opportunity to make an overtly political point; for it is clear that his attack on Beveridge was also aimed at other targets of closer propinquity: 'There is scarcely a page of his book in which these freedoms are not referred to, and referred to, only to be by innuendo disparaged and decried. For these freedoms, so sweet and precious to the ordinary man, make things too complicated for Sir William Beveridge.'[201]

Another problem that Beveridge referred to in his text concerned the government's relative inability to enforce on the peacetime population what could be accepted by a community during wartime. The war, by exposing the wider community to equal risks of life and death and by inculcating a collectivist spirit, proved that reform could be enacted for the greater good if the general will existed. Beveridge's universalist social insurance continued and extended this wartime insight to the everyday risks of post-war existence. Again, MacEntee chose to see something insidious in the design:

> What a paltry sophism is Beveridge's suggestion that in war men and women have a value beyond the ordinary, when the one thing that the general experience of the last five years has proven beyond doubt or question is that in wartime men and women have less value than a tank ... what a sinister purpose is revealed in the statement that the problem is to persuade the people to do deliberately in peace what they are forced to do in war.[202]

Having attacked the Beveridge text on humanistic and civil libertarian grounds, MacEntee then turned his attention to the specific economic proposals contained therein. He questioned the perceived wisdom of the insurance concept and estimated its cost to the community as something far greater than had been previously admitted. This of course did not stop him from endorsing Deeny's inclusion of insurance contributions as part of his health plan, as detailed earlier in this chapter. The emphasis for Beveridge and his economic advisers centred on the significance of public expenditure financed out of taxation, on state replenishment of capital equipment and provision of social services. MacEntee's argument against this approach was a familiar one: 'When the state takes from a citizen by way of taxation the cash which he might otherwise spend on a new pair of shoes, or a new hat, it may spend it and create employment in one direction, but it also tended to create unemployment in another.'[203]

The context supplied by the minister's public falling out with Bishop Dignan undoubtedly provided MacEntee's analysis of Beveridge with a more malignant tone than it might otherwise have had. No doubt influenced by the arguments (not to mention the metaphor) employed by F.J. Hayek in his classic critique of centralised planning, *The Road to Serfdom*, MacEntee assured his listeners that the government, of which he was a member, would 'ensure that whatever be the consequences the state that will function here will be constituted of free men and women, whom the state will exist to serve, and not they to serve the state'. That MacEntee delivered his speech in such a hyperbolic style was perhaps not surprising. Like his former private secretary, Brian Ó Nualláin, MacEntee recognised the 'corrupting influence of language'.[204] Indeed in summarising the minister's overall attitude to social policy development, it is necessary to re-evaluate Ó Nualláin's influence. At this time, Ó Nualláin was the acting principal officer in the Department of Local Government and Public Health and in this capacity not only had direct access to MacEntee but was responsible for drafting some of the minister's speeches. He was also the author (as Myles na gCopaleen) of a polemical and often hilarious column in the *Irish Times*, 'Cruiskeen Lawn'. By the middle of 1943, there was strong evidence that Ó Nualláin was using the everyday business of his civil service role as raw material for his journalism.[205] According to MacEntee's daughter, a good relationship between the two men, forged during Ó Nualláin's tenure as MacEntee's private secretary from August 1941 to April 1943, was based on a shared temperament and a consistency of political views. Moreover, Ó Nualláin's skills as a speechwriter were particularly appreciated by the minister.[206] Such was the conflation of ideas enunciated regularly in 'Cruiskeen Lawn' with MacEntee's speech that it is not unreasonable to assume that it may have been written by the official. Ó Nualláin also had his own targets closer to home. His editor at the *Irish Times*, R.M. Smyllie, was an indefatigable advocate of social service reform and used the paper to promote its cause at every opportunity. This often led to criticism of the government in general, and MacEntee in particular. Smyllie's most outspoken critic was Ó Nualláin. Often, in his column, 'he sustained a line of often virulent opposition to the ideas espoused by his editor.'

Responding to the general fervour for planning among Ireland's literate establishment, Ó Nualláin identified the reliance of planners such as Dignan and Beveridge on 'pseudo-technical language and jargon as destructive to informed and critical evaluation'.[207] Likewise, MacEntee announced to a gathering of the Literary and Historical Society of UCD on 8 May, convened to debate the motion 'Should Éire plan for full employment?', that he was afraid that the phrase 'full employment' was little more than a catch-phrase like 'social credit' used to be: 'a phrase which caught the imagination and enabled those who desired to exploit the public commercially or politically to sell their wares'.[208] Once again, MacEntee reiterated his concern about the regulation of planning and its relationship to democracy: 'We should have to face the question who are to be the planners, how the planners are to be directed and controlled, which will inevitably lead to the question as to what is to be the relation between the economic planners, their planning organisations and the political organisation of the state.'[209] Similarly, Ó Nualláin's response to Dignan's proposals utilised the language of propaganda – 'jack-booted secret police', 'neo-fascism' and one of MacEntee's old favourites 'regimentation' – to associate the scheme with totalitarianism and the atmosphere of the fascist state.[210]

On 16 March 1945, three days after MacEntee's speech to the Tomás O'Laoghaire cumann, the *Irish Times* published an editorial on 'Beveridgeism', almost certainly written by Smyllie. It criticised MacEntee's lack of initiative as Minister for Local Government and Public Health and urged the government to 'make every conceivable effort to maintain their social services on as high a level as those of Great Britain and Northern Ireland'. It also drew attention to the possible repercussions of this inaction on the tradition of high emigration in the country. It asked: 'Must Mr MacEntee devise these flamboyant phrases to apologise for the fact that Great Britain is making an honest attempt, which has been applauded by nine-tenths of the world, to bring some order into the chaotic condition of her social services?'[211] MacEntee was certainly a thoughtful and uncompromisingly intelligent government minister but the point is well made that if he had been more adept at publicising the efforts of his department rather than indulging in gratuitous political point-making, his reputation would be considerably more favourable. This, however, was simply not his style. As a contemporary profile acknowledged, his political combativeness was not only unique in the government but was regarded by the minister as a distinct badge of honour:

> Whether it is by set purpose or accident, he invariably draws on his head a barrage of interruptions from all the Opposition parties. And most of his colleagues manage to escape this when addressing the house. He seems to revel in it, hitting hard and taking, sometimes in good humour, sometimes with poor grace, the barbed and almost merciless retorts flung back from the Fine Gael and Labour benches. Once started on a reply which he considers pertinent and effective, however, there is scarcely any power, other than physical force, capable of restraining Mr MacEntee.[212]

NOTES

1. McKee, 'From precepts to praxis', p.31.
2. NAI DT S12296, MacEntee memorandum, 22/2/41.
3. McKee, 'From precepts to praxis', p.29.
4. Ibid.
5. Quoted in ibid., p.46.
6. NAI DT S13026A, cabinet committee on economic planning, 2/12/42 to 17/4/44.
7. J.J. Lee, *Ireland 1912–1985: Politics and Society* (Cambridge, 1989), p.230.
8. Ibid.
9. Daly, *The Buffer State*, p.286.
10. Lee, *Ireland 1912–1985*, p.238.
11. Quoted in Daly, *The Buffer State*, pp.250–1.
12. Robins, *Custom House People*, p.122.
13. Fanning, *Finance*, p.321.
14. NAI DT S11466, Smiddy to de Valera, 25 September 1939.
15. Daly, *The Buffer State*, p.272 and Lee, *Ireland 1912–1985*, p.226.
16. O'Hagan, 'An analysis of the relative size of the government sector', p.24.
17. *Dáil debates*, vol. 101, col. 1717, 12 June 1946.
18. Ibid.
19. NAI DT S12882 A, Planning for post-war situation.
20. Source Daly, *The Buffer State*, p.294.
21. O'Hagan, 'An analysis of the relative size of the government sector', p.30.
22. Government white paper, *The post-war building programme*.
23. Daly, *The Buffer State*, p.326.
24. *Dáil debates,* vol. 97, col. 1200, 29 May 1945.
25. Daly, *The Buffer State*, p.325.
26. NAI DT S13026A.

27. NAI DT S13059 A, Minute from MacEntee to Hurson, 16 October 1942.
28. Ibid., MacEntee to de Valera, 30 November 1942.
29. Ibid.
30. NAI DT S13059 A, Local Government memorandum, 20 February 1943.
31. The breakdown being: Dublin county borough – approximately 19,000 for slum clearance; Cork county borough 3,500; Limerick 2,280 and Waterford 1,144. This totalled 38,054 new houses, and when other urban areas were included, the cost was estimated at a prohibitive £23,452,002.
32. K.I. Nowlan, 'The evolution of Irish planning', in M. Bannon (ed.), *Planning: The Irish Experience, 1920–1988* (Dublin, 1989).
33. Daly, *The Buffer State*, p.288. This was not the first time that Local Government officials had objected to far-reaching plans of the minister. During the 1930s they had been hostile to O'Kelly's proposal to establish a powerful housing board.
34. NAI DT S13059A, Taoiseach's department note, 23 March 1943.
35. Quoted in Daly, *The Buffer State*, p.288.
36. NAI DT S13026A, Minutes of the twenty-third meeting of the cabinet committee on economic planning, 25 October 1943.
37. Unsurprisingly, responsibility for planning was later given to Industry and Commerce.
38. Daly, *The Buffer State*, p.288.
39. NAI DT S13026 A, Twenty-fifth meeting of the cabinet committee on economic planning, 15 November 1943.
40. Ibid., Progress report on housing by MacEntee to the Taoiseach, 13 May 1944.
41. *Dáil debates*, vol. 97, col. 1128, 29 May 1945.
42. Growth in public expenditure on housing was particularly apparent between 1947 and 1951, when there was an abundance of capital in the economy at large. See F. Kennedy, 'Public expenditure on housing in the post-war period', *Economic and Social Review*, 3, 3 (1971–2).
43. Also present was the official, Maurice Moynihan.
44. Quoted in McKee, 'From precepts to praxis', p.43.
45. NAI DT S12900, Department of Local Government and Public Health note, 14 February 1942.
46. NAI DT S13061 on roads.
47. Ibid., Minute to the Taoiseach, 8 September 1943.
48. Daly, *The Buffer State*, p.394.
49. NAI DT S13061, MacEntee to de Valera, 24 March 1944.
50. Ibid., MacEntee to Lemass, 24 March 1944.
51. Daly, *The Buffer State*, p.395.
52. NAI DT S13061, Progress report on road planning submitted by Department of Local Government and Public Health, May 1944.
53. NAI DT S13026A, Thirty-sixth meeting of the cabinet committee on economic planning, 13 July 1944.
54. Daly, *The Buffer State*, p.395.
55. NAI DT S13026A, Forty-second meeting of the cabinet committee on economic planning, 6 December 1944.
56. Quoted in Daly, *The Buffer State*, p.290.
57. NAI DT S13026A, Nineteenth meeting of the cabinet committee on economic planning, 22 September 1943.
58. NAI DT S11916A.
59. Daly, *The Buffer State*, p.295.
60. J.H. Whyte, *Church and State in Modern Ireland* (2nd edition, Dublin, 1981), p.118.
61. Daly, *The Buffer State*, p.297
62. E. O'Halpin, 'The origins of city and county management', in *City and County Management, 1929–1990: A Retrospective* (Dublin, 1991), p.13.
63. Ibid., p.15.
64. NAI DT S6466, Local Government memorandum, 1 March 1934.
65. *Dáil debates*, vol. 78, col. 191, 5 December 1939.
66. *Dáil debates*, vol. 78, cols 1009–10, 7 December 1939.
67. Quoted in D. Ferriter, *Lovers of Liberty: 100 years of Local Government* (Dublin, 2001), p.66.
68. Daly, *The Buffer State*, p.312.
69. *Dáil debates*, vol. 87, col. 903, 3 June 1942.
70. Quoted in Daly, *The Buffer State*, p.312.
71. See J. Garvin, 'Nature and extent of central control over local government administration', in F.C. King (ed.), *Public Administration in Ireland* (Dublin, 1949).
72. Ibid.

73. Ibid.
74. *Dáil debates*, vol. 91, col. 1353, 28 October 1943.
75. Ibid., cols 1348–9.
76. Quoted in Daly, *The Buffer State*, p.313.
77. UCDA P67/282, de Blacam to MacEntee, 4 December 1946.
78. *Irish Independent*, 9 February 1946. See also Ferriter, *Lovers of Liberty*, pp.65–6.
79. *Irish Independent*, 9 February 1946.
80. P. Bew and H. Patterson, *Seán Lemass and the Making of Modern Ireland 1945–66* (Dublin, 1982), p.29.
81. Lee, *Ireland 1912–1985*, p.286.
82. Whyte, *Church and State in Modern Ireland*, p.118.
83. É. McKee, 'Church–State relations and the development of Irish health policy: the mother-and-child scheme, 1944–53', *Irish Historical Studies*, xxv, 98 (1989), p.164.
84. See M. Cousins, 'The introduction of children's allowance in Ireland 1939–44', *Irish Economic and Social History*, vol. XXVI (1999), pp.35–53.
85. NAI DT S13026A, third meeting of the cabinet committee on economic planning, 16 December 1942.
86. NAI DT S11265A, notes by MacEntee on the proposal to institute a state system of family allowances, 28 October 1939. Also see Lee, *Ireland 1912–1985*, pp.283–4.
87. Ibid. Quoted in Lee, *Ireland 1912–1985*, p.283.
88. Ibid. For a full account of the British and French attitude to family allowances see S. Pedersen, *Family, Dependence and the Origins of the Welfare State: Britain and France, 1914–1945* (Cambridge, 1993).
89. Industry and Commerce memo on Family Allowances, 28 October 1939, quoted in Lee, *Ireland 1912–1985*, p.284.
90. NAI DT S12117A, Outline of proposals for the payment of family allowances to children under 14 years, 8 April 1940.
91. NAI DT S12117B, GC 2/207, 4 October 1940.
92. Quoted in Lee, *Ireland 1912–1985*, p.284.
93. NAI DT S12173, Interdepartmental committee on family allowances, 14 October 1942.
94. MacEntee had by this time moved to Local Government and Public Health.
95. NAI DT S12117B, Local Government memorandum on Children's allowances, 18 February 1943.
96. NAI DT S12117B, Local Government memorandum on 'Children's allowances, "Beveridgeism" and the Catholic church', 16 March 1943.
97. A. Kelly, 'The Catholic Church and the welfare state in modern Ireland', *Archivium Hibernicum*, vol. LIII (1999), pp.107–17.
98. Cousins, 'The introduction of children's allowance', p.44.
99. Ibid. See also NAI LG IA 129/53F.1.
100. McKevitt published widely on the Catholic attitude to welfareism, and in 1944 the Catholic Truth Society published his collected ruminations, *The Plan of Society*.
101. UCDA P67/261; Rev. P. McKevitt, 'The Beveridge plan reviewed', in *Irish Ecclesiastical Record*, vol. LXI (March 1943).
102. UCDA P67/261, McElligott to MacEntee, 27 March 1943.
103. NAI IA 129/53F; See also Cousins, 'The introduction of children's allowance', p.43.
104. For an Irish version of this view see E.J. Coyne, 'Irish social services: a symposium', *Journal of the Social and Statistical Society of Ireland*, vol. 17 (1942–3).
105. C. Lucey, 'Family allowances', *Irish Ecclesiastical Record*, vol. 54 (1939), p.481. Lucey held the chair of philosophy and political theory in Maynooth from 1929 to 1950, after which he became the bishop of Cork.
106. Pedersen, *Family, Dependence and the Origins of the Welfare State*, p.421.
107. UCDA P67/261. Catholic opinion on the Beveridge plan was less than clear-cut. Extracts from the *Catholic Herald* from February 1943 which linked the Beveridge report to the children's allowances debate were in MacEntee's possession. Under a headline of 'Catholics may support Beveridge', the paper reported 'That everyone realises that a critical decision lies before us was demonstrated by the intense interest taken in a lecture in Belfast on the subject by the Rev. Dr Lucey, the well known champion of the family allowance system.' See also Kelly, 'The Catholic Church and the welfare state in modern Ireland', pp.107–17.
108. M. Cowling, *The Impact of Labour, 1920–24* (Cambridge, 1971).
109. NAI DT S13053A, Flinn to de Valera, 13 December 1942.
110. *Cork Examiner*, 18 January 1943.
111. *Irish Press*, 2 March 1943.

112. Ibid., 18 June 1943.
113. UCDA P67/362 (9).
114. There was some credibility to MacEntee's analysis. Labour party branches grew from 174 in 1941 to 750 in 1943.
115. M. Manning, *James Dillon: A Biography* (Dublin, 1999), p.186.
116. UCDA P67/363 (6), Lemass to MacEntee, 10 June 1943.
117. UCDA P67/364. Drafts and texts of speeches made by MacEntee in the 1943 campaign were sent to Miss O'Connell.
118. UCDA P67/366 (1), draft letter from MacEntee to de Valera, 28 June 1943. Again it is impossible to say whether this letter was ever sent.
119. UCDA P67/367, general election leaflet for Dublin Townships, 1944. See also *Irish Press*, 26 and 27 June 1944.
120. Lee, *Ireland 1912–1985*, p.277.
121. The first official government discussion took place in the early summer of 1939 and the cabinet requested the Department of Local Government to examine the question in July.
122. Cousins, 'The introduction of children's allowances', p.50. See also articles by McKevitt and Lucey cited above.
123. Lee, *Ireland 1912–1985*, p.285.
124. S. Riordan, '"A political blackthorn": Seán MacEntee, the Dignan Plan and the principle of ministerial responsibility', *Irish Economic and Social Hist*ory, vol. XXVII (2000), pp.44–62.
125. McKee, 'Church–State relations', p.163.
126. J. Cooney, *John Charles McQuaid: Ruler of Catholic Ireland* (Dublin, 1999), p.196.
127. UCDA P67/257.
128. The paper was not published until March 1945.
129. UCDA P67/257, paper read to the committee of management of the National Health Insurance Society of Ireland by Dr John Dignan, 11 October 1944.
130. Ibid.
131. Lee, *Ireland 1912–1985*, pp.285–6.
132. *Irish Independent*, 18 October 1944.
133. *Irish Times*, 18 October 1944.
134. Dignan to McQuaid, 21 October 1944, quoted in Cooney, *John Charles McQuaid*, p.196.
135. Quoted in Riordan, '"A political blackthorn"', p.45.
136. Ward had been formally delegated responsibility for public health services in January 1944.
137. UCDA P67/257, Barrington to Posts and Telegraphs, 19 October 1944.
138. Ibid., MacEntee to the editor, *Irish Press*, 19 October 1944.
139. *Irish Press*, 16 November 1944 and UCDA P67/257, Cathal O'Shannon to MacEntee, 8 January 1945. It also received a positive review after its official publication in summer 1945 from Dignan's fellow Catholic social thinker, Cornelius Lucey. See *The Leader*, XCI, 21 (15 December 1945).
140. *Journal of the Medical Association of Éire*, December 1944.
141. UCDA P67/258 (1), Dignan to Collis, 23 October 1944. It is interesting to note that this correspondence ended up in MacEntee's private papers.
142. UCDA P67/258 (2) Collis to Shanley?, 25 October 1944. See also Lee, 'Aspects of corporatist thought', p.340: '[Michael] Browne's [Chairman of the committee on vocational organisation] pathological hatred for the civil service was matched only by his pathological veneration for the professions, above all for the medical profession, which he persuaded himself placed public above private interest.'
143. *Dáil debates*, vol. 95, cols 1488–9, 24 January 1945.
144. Riordan, '"A political blackthorn"', p.46.
145. Riordan, '"A political blackthorn"', p.48. NAI DT S13570, 'Summary of some departmental criticisms of Most Rev. Dr Dignan's Paper', by John Collins, John Garvin and P.J. Keady, 12 February 1945. See also UCDA P67/257 (2), 'Observations on a paper entitled "Outlines of a scheme of national health insurance"' [n.d.].
146. UCDA P67/257, Dignan to MacEntee, 26 January 1945.
147. Lee, 'Aspects of corporatist thought'. See also Brian Ó Nualláin's (of Local Government) critique of both the report and the plan in the *Irish Times*, 26–8 October 1944, in his journalist guise Myles na gCopaleen. This is explored in S. Curran, '"Could Paddy leave off copying just for five minutes": Brian O'Nolan and Éire's Beveridge plan', *Irish University Review*, vol. 31 (2001).
148. See Whyte, *Church and State in Modern Ireland*, pp.104–5 and Riordan, '"A political blackthorn"', p.48.
149. M. Cousins, *The Birth of Social Welfare in Ireland, 1922–52* (Dublin, 2002), p.135.
150. See Curran, '"Could Paddy leave off copying just for five minutes"'.

151. *Irish Times*, 13 March 1945.
152. *Irish Times*, 14 March 1945.
153. Quoted in Curran, "'Could Paddy leave off copying just for five minutes'".
154. UCDA P67/257.
155. UCDA P67/257, Dignan to MacEntee, 26 January 1945 and MacEntee's draft reply [n.d.].
156. Riordan, "'A political blackthorn'", p.50.
157. Deeny, *To Cure and to Care*, p.104.
158. The responsibilities of the Department of Industry and Commerce in regard to social services included unemployment assistance and insurance, family allowances and food vouchers. The Department of Lands was responsible for rural housing grants and Gaeltacht housing grants. The Office of Public Works (OPW) was responsible for turf production and special employment schemes. The majority of the social services, however, were under MacEntee's direct jurisdiction in the Department of Local Government and Public Health. These included, *inter alia*: national health insurance, widows' and orphans' pensions, old age pensions, blind pensions, public assistance, housing, maternity and child welfare, free milk, school meals, public health and treatment of tuberculosis.
159. *Dáil debates*, vol. 85, col. 1818, 18 February 1942.
160. Ibid.
161. Annual report of the ITUC, 1941–42, quoted in Cousins, *The Birth of Social Welfare*, p.130.
162. NAI DT S13026A, third meeting of the cabinet committee on economic planning, 16 December 1942.
163. *Journal of the Statistical and Social Inquiry Society of Ireland*, vol. XVII (1942–3).
164. See Curran, "'Could Paddy leave off copying just for five minutes'", and *Irish Times*, 8 May 1944.
165. NAI DT S11109A. Indeed the issue of centralising the social services had been occupying the British government and the result of this was observed with interest from Dublin. Extracts of *The Times* of 8 and 9 October 1943 which reported that a cabinet committee was considering the improvement of the machinery of government were among the papers in the Department of the Taoiseach.
166. Ibid. Memorandum from the Department of Local Government and Public Health, 28 September 1943. See also UCDA P67/261.
167. *Dáil debates*, vol. 92, col. 1237, 17 February 1944.
168. UCDA P67/251, MacEntee to de Valera, 3 January 1944.
169. Deeny, *To Cure and to Care*, pp.66–7.
170. UCDA P67/253, 'Urgent problems relating to public health which must be dealt with', 22 March 1944.
171. *Dáil debates*, vol. 95, cols 1082–3, 29 November 1944 and vol. 95, col. 1869, 31 January 1945. See also R. Barrington, *Health, Medicine and Politics in Ireland, 1900–1970* (Dublin, 1987), p.139.
172. J. Horgan, *Noel Browne: Passionate Outsider* (Dublin, 2000), p.36.
173. UCDA P67/261, Local government memorandum on the Irish Medical Association's scheme for a national health service, 4 March 1945.
174. Barrington, *Health, Medicine and Politics in Ireland*, p.153.
175. NAI DT S11109A.
176. McKee, 'Church–state relations', p.162.
177. Quoted in ibid.
178. NAI DT S13444 B, Report of the departmental committee on health services, September 1945.
179. McKee, 'Church–state relations', p.165.
180. NAI DT S13444 B, Report of the departmental committee on health services, para. 189.
181. Deeny, *To Cure and to Care*, pp.110–11.
182. Barrington, *Health, Medicine and Politics in Ireland*, p.159. Barrington's analysis is all the more reliable because she was able to conduct a wide range of interviews with the personalities involved, including Deeny, Garvin, Ward and Shanley. Her comments on MacEntee are also significant because she was privy to her father's recollections about his period in the department and as MacEntee's private secretary in 1945–6.
183. See McKee, 'Church–state relations', p.165.
184. Deeny, *To Cure and to Care*, pp.67–8.
185. See A. McCarthy, 'Aspects of local health in Ireland in the 1950s', in D. Keogh, F. O'Shea and C. Quinlan (eds), *The Lost Decade: Ireland in the 1950s* (Cork, 2004).
186. Ibid., p.177.
187. Representatives from the Department of Posts and Telegraphs were added some time later.
188. NAI DT S11190A, Local Government memorandum on the social services, 28 September 1943. Also see UCDA P67/261.
189. The majority report was signed by L.M. Fitzgerald (Finance), W. Maguire (Industry and

Commerce), A.P. Ward, T.R. Price, F.T. McHenry and J.A. Scannell. For further analysis of this committee and its deliberations see Cousins, *The Birth of Social Welfare*, pp.138–41.

190. UCDA P67/261(14), Local Government memo.
191. UCDA P67/261, majority report of the interdepartmental committee on social services, 2 July 1945.
192. *Dáil debates*, vol. 98, col. 1144, 14 November 1945. The motion had originally been read a year earlier in November 1944.
193. *Dáil debates*, vol. 99, cols 171–2, 30 January 1946.
194. Cousins, *The Birth of Social Welfare*, p.142.
195. NAI DT S11109 A.
196. Whyte, *Church and State in Modern Ireland*, p.130.
197. UCDA P67/270, text of lecture by MacEntee, 13 March 1945.
198. UCDA P67/ 264 (4), Industry and Commerce memo on 'full employment', 16 January 1945.
199. J. Harris, 'Beveridge's social and political thought', in J. Hills, J. Ditch and H. Glennerster (eds), *Beveridge and Social Security* (Oxford, 1994), p.29.
200. J. Harris, *William Beveridge: A Biography* (Oxford, 1977), p 436.
201. UCDA P67/270.
202. Ibid.
203. Ibid.
204. See Curran, '"Could Paddy leave off copying just for five minutes"'.
205. For a full account of Ó Nualláin's journalistic writings on the Dignan Plan, see ibid.
206. Ibid.
207. Quoted in ibid.
208. *Irish Times*, 9 May 1945. See also UCDA P67/570 for transcript of MacEntee's speech on full employment to UCD L&H.
209. Ibid.
210. Curran, '"Could Paddy leave off copying just for five minutes"'.
211. *Irish Times*, 16 March 1945.
212. UCDA P67/ 791, *People's Weekly*, September 1946, profile of MacEntee by Paddy Hogan.

6

Indian Summer?

No chancellor of the exchequer is worth his salt who makes his own popularity either his first consideration, or any consideration at all, in administering the public purse. In my opinion, the Chancellor of the Exchequer
is the trusted and confidential steward of the public. He is under a sacred
obligation with regard to all that he consents to spend.[1]

William Ewart Gladstone, 1879

Fianna Fáil returned to office in 1951 after three years in opposition when an
unlikely assortment of political opponents introduced the concept of coalition
government to Ireland, unified by the desire, in the words of the sloganeers, of
'putting them out'.[2] The first inter-party government had offered the electorate three
years of economic expansionism – Keynes, in Patrick Lynch's phrase, had come to
Kinnegad – facilitated predominantly by the proceeds of Marshall Aid and the
deployment of external assets for capital development. Unfortunately, this proto-
Keynesian phase helped to accelerate an inflationary spiral caused by the knock-on
effects of the devaluation of the pound sterling by the British government in 1949
and the advent of the Korean War a year later.[3] This policy was also deficient in
other respects: namely, that it 'did not provide any direct encouragement to
exports'.[4] Cumulatively, this had grave consequences for Irish trade, which revealed
itself in a current account deficit of £61.6 million in 1951, representing 14.7 per cent
of GNP, the largest ever recorded in the state.[5] Thus Seán MacEntee's reappointment as Minister for Finance – a portfolio he had last held twelve years previously
– was a deliberately orthodox choice that, it was thought, would deliver the necessary correctives to an economy that was palpably in trouble.[6]

His reappointment to Finance has generally been seen as an Indian summer
for MacEntee when his star was sufficiently high within the cabinet to subdue
the importunate demands of Lemass and his department for greater governmental action regarding the economy.[7] This approach, however, overestimates the
role of the MacEntee–Lemass dialectic and tends to ignore other significant factors such as the enduring omnipotence of de Valera within the cabinet in spite of
his regular enforced absences; the Taoiseach's characteristic caution in economic matters; the critical nature in which the economic situation was viewed by all
within the cabinet and the consequences for Ireland of the actions of the British
government in its economic and monetary policy. Bew and Patterson, for example, have dismissed the role that de Valera played in economic matters, but that
he still had the casting vote in terms of government policy certainly dictated the
pace and form of its overall strategy.[8] That strategy has also come in for some

severe criticism; indeed one commentator has viewed it as having 'strong claims to be considered the worst de Valera government'.[9] The apparent 'morass' has been attributed to the failure of the party to remobilise after its embittered experience of opposition when MacEntee and Lemass again proved to be Fianna Fáil's most aggressive and effective Dáil performers. MacEntee's presence in the Finance portfolio did prove an accurate barometer of the new government's priorities but there is little real evidence that this occasioned an elevation within the party above the Tánaiste, Lemass. That Lemass deputised for de Valera for four-and-a half months during 1951 while the latter was undergoing eye treatment, moreover, manifestly impugns the credibility of this thesis.[10]

Indeed, the key event in the life of the government – the budget of 1952 – has been regarded as MacEntee's darkest hour and it was he that ultimately bore the responsibility for its lasting effects both on Fianna Fáil and on the electorate. That the budget revisited many of the recommendations of the much maligned Central Bank Report of 1951 ensured its political utility for the opposition, who condemned it as reactionary and extreme. It should be said that the adoption of a partially restrictive budgetary strategy did not result in the same macroeconomic emergency that occurred after a comparable strategy in 1955–6. A more approved line for curbing consumption, coupled with the maintenance of considerable investment, was followed in 1952, aided by an upturn in the trade balance which ensured that it never threatened to become what the later crisis developed into: 'the defining event of post-war Irish economic history'.[11] Again to quote Lynch: 'The Fianna Fáil answer to the Inter-Party commitment to capital investment in 1950 and 1951 as a solution of Irish economic ills was a plausible one … they took the view that it did not apply to Ireland at that particular time when, it seemed to them, the community was living beyond its income and consuming more than it was currently producing.'[12] The ruling party's approach was less defined than Lynch's comment would have us believe. It continued to uphold a similar level of investment; the significant difference lay in the financing of that investment.[13]

What perhaps ultimately characterised Fianna Fáil's diffident approach to the dilemma was a combination of severe economic impositions with tentatively applied social reform. This uncertainty reflected what Lemass later suggested was a lack of appetite on the part of the party to deal with the problems of post-war Ireland: 'I did not welcome the prospect of coming back into government in the conditions of 1951 at all … we had not really got down to clearing our minds on post-war development.'[14] The euphemism 'clearing our minds' is undoubtedly an allusion to the lack of unity within the party on the direction that development would take; and it was de Valera's attempt to square that particular circle which resulted largely in the compromise offered by Fianna Fáil in 1951–4. This chapter will outline that compromise by examining closely the economic context in which the government's measures were undertaken; the role played by MacEntee – on his return to his first departmental home – in the formation of an economic solution to the balance of payments crisis; how his economic philosophy dictated the nature of that solution; how this was received by his party and the electorate and, lastly, how his adherence to an almost Gladstonian mission to preserve sound finance, despite the currency and increasing popularity of new economic and monetary ideas in Ireland, led to eventual political disaster for Fianna Fáil and enduring notoriety for him personally.

THE CENTRAL BANK REPORT

The 1951 general election campaign was notable for its unusual concentration on the economic performance of the state under the different post-war administrations, a development which reflected the fact that the language of political conflict was now being colonised by economic terms and complex monetary theories rather than the traditional vocabulary of nationalist dogma. If 'the first three decades of Irish independence witnessed the ruthless subordination of economic imperatives to the more compelling imperatives of Irish nationalism', the realisation of the Republic of Ireland in 1949 now shifted the emphasis of political debate [15] and was seen by many as a fundamental advance in the evolution of Irish political discourse.[16] On the eve of the election, MacEntee outlined what he saw as the economic imperative: 'It must be the first task of the new government to grapple vigorously with, and provide a solution for, the problem of the soaring cost of living, which is menacing the economic life of the State and the happiness of the people ... All other considerations must under present conditions be subordinated to the over-riding necessity of reducing the cost of living and increasing the value of the people's income.'[17] Fianna Fáil published a seventeen-point economic programme to be implemented on taking office, the first point of which summarised its all-embracing ambition: 'To take appropriate measures to secure the fullest utilisation of national credit and capital resources so as to achieve a rapid expansion of agricultural and industrial production, to increase opportunities of employment and to rectify the present adverse position affecting the country's external trade'.[18] Grappling with inflation, however, would continue to be the primary consideration in framing fiscal policy.[19]

The establishment of the Central Bank, under the 1942 act, added another layer of financial orthodoxy to the economic policymaking apparatus of the state, albeit in a largely advisory capacity. This orthodoxy brought it gradually more to the centre of political controversy, as Dáil deputies became increasingly critical of its forebodings on the economy. Such criticism was expressed in its most virulent form in the aftermath of the bank's report for the year ending 1951, which was presented to the new Fianna Fáil government in September, but was not published until 24 October.[20] The *Irish Times* editorial accurately summarised its general tenor: 'The Report of the Central Bank of Ireland ... is a dismal document, inasmuch as it lays unusual stress on the national position in respect of balance of payments.'[21] The controversy that surrounded the report has been attributed to various reasons, including that 'political leaders were sensitive following the recent transfers of power and partly because the report was so rich in phrases that could be used with damaging effect by persons who were predisposed to regard bankers as lacking in concern for social welfare'.[22] A further reason for the enduring nature of the tumult over the report was the 'real conflict of opinion', according to the historian of the bank, Maurice Moynihan, 'between those who sincerely believed that Ireland could be stirred out of economic stagnation only by massive public investment, for which adequate resources could be found only by borrowing, and those, in the Central Bank and elsewhere, who believed with equal sincerity that such a policy was bound eventually to defeat its own ends.'[23] The opposition – whose main cheerleaders for the expansionist case were Seán MacBride and the former Taoiseach John A. Costello (heavily influenced by his son-in-law and sometime economic adviser, Alexis Fitzgerald) – immediately went on the offensive for the twin purpose of pinning the report to the government and also in order to refute the anticipated charge that it was the opposition that bore responsibility for the crisis.

Indeed it was the inter-party government's apparent misuse of funds such as Marshall Aid which provided Fianna Fáil with one of the core planks of its election strategy in 1951. De Valera claimed that the net effect of its spending was to increase the total capital liability of the state from £100 million to £192 million.[24] MacEntee attacked the 'vainglorious megalomania' of certain ministers, and said extravagant borrowing to provide for extravagant spending had given an illusion of prosperity, but the 'rake's progress' was now at an end.[25] When Fianna Fáil took power, however, the main source of revenue available to the previous administration had dried up. In October 1948, the Inter-Party government had approved the European Recovery Programme (ERP) Long Term Programme, incorporating Fianna Fáil's post-war capital development plans and its own plans relating to investment in agriculture, fuel and power, tourism, shipping, mineral development, fishing, reafforestation, housing and health.[26] A substantial portion of the funds was allocated to land reclamation and drainage, as well as to the government's capital programme, with housing the largest beneficiary. By March 1952 the fund was exhausted. A total of £40.5 million had been invested in the exchequer. This amounted to nearly 50 per cent of government capital expenditure of £81.93 million for the years 1949–52.[27] Moreover, the percentage share of public sector expenditure devoted to capital expenditure increased from 3.8 in 1948 to 10.4 in 1951.[28]

The Inter-Party government, however, did not heed the counsel of the Department of Finance, nor of the Central Bank, to sterilise the funds for repayment of the sums loaned through ERP.[29] As a result of the economic climate facing the new Fianna Fáil government, Finance officials warned in June 1951 of the consequences of the deteriorating terms of trade; the growing deficit in the balance of payments position; the increased consumption of non-essential items and the inadequacy of savings to meet capital expenditure. The memorandum concluded that 'the public and the government between them are spending more than the nation can afford.' This view was reaffirmed by department officials throughout the autumn, by which time a crisis in the sterling area was beginning to emerge due to the sharp drop in dollar and gold reserves.[30] Among the 'remedies' suggested by Finance was that consideration should be given immediately 'to curtailing or abandoning the more uneconomic or wasteful elements in the capital programme' because of the low level of personal savings and public take-up of issues and the imminent exhaustion of the loan counterpart fund. The Land Reclamation Project initiated by the previous regime was an obvious target.

Along with schools, houses and hospitals, investment in drainage and reclamation was regarded by Finance officials as non-productive. There was no obvious or immediate increase in agricultural output and therefore no immediate return to the exchequer.[31] This analysis was largely endorsed by the Central Bank Report.

Opposition attempts to pin the Central Bank Report to the government, however, proved more elusive than would have first seemed. A day before the report was published the government presented its own white paper, which carried a similar message to that outlined in the Central Bank document, albeit in more politic terms. In fact, both publications coincided with a new session of the Dáil, which traditionally offered political observers an opportunity to second guess the government's probable objectives. Furthermore, MacEntee and an unlikely *socius criminis*, Lemass, had already given most such commentators a hint of what was to come by stressing the gravity of the trade situation.[32] Fianna Fáil was, at the same time, also attempting to placate the small group of independents who had given the party its support. By drawing attention in the strongest possible terms to the balance of payments shortfall and the likely budgetary correctives, the party was bracing that group for the worst. One of those independents, Noël Browne, rather conveniently for the government, 'chose to ignore those policies disagreeable to [him] in order to concentrate on the issue of the health services'.[33] The others, it was probably felt, would only stomach such stern measures under the premise that the government was amending a situation that was caused exogenously and that required urgent and drastic attention.[34] Certainly this was the thrust of the argument being put forward by MacEntee and Lemass, and was given greater credence by the stark warnings contained in both the white paper and the Central Bank report. The white paper described the lack of balance in the state's external trade as 'unique in Europe' and hinted that a supplementary budget might be required.[35] The adverse trade balance was expected to reach £70 million, more than 15 per cent of GNP – a figure that was overestimated but not to the outrageous extent that those who accused the government of using scare tactics claimed.

The most instructive debate on the Central Bank Report took place on the occasion of the second reading of the Supply and Services (Temporary Provisions) Act, 1946 (Continuance) Bill, 1951. Lemass immediately distanced the government from the report while at the same time refusing to diminish the warnings contained therein.[36] Lemass also expressed his 'almost complete agreement' with the response of the Irish Trade Union Congress to the Central Bank Report. This response was highly critical of the measures advocated by the governor, Joseph Brennan, and his colleagues. The minister had his own reasons for embracing the union view, a constituency to which he had always been close politically; but the differences that separated him from their report proved more salient in anticipating the government's strategy. He rejected the idea that a special tax should be levied on luxury items and also dismissed the report's suggestion of increasing the food subsidies. In fact he went so far as to float the idea of abolishing the subsidies altogether.[37] Lemass also followed the Finance line by lamenting the low level of savings, pointing out its inadequacy for a soundly based expansionist policy, and the dangers of depleting the external reserves further: 'If we reach that situation, in which the reserves upon which we are now drawing to finance our present level of consumption and our present level of new investment are exhausted, we shall be forced to cut down our standard of living whether we like it or not and to experience the unemployment and the other unpleasant consequences to which the Trade Union Congress Executive referred in their statement.'[38] He continued by issuing a warning that was becoming increasingly heard in the corridors of Merrion Street: that Ireland's economic independence would be lost if the present crisis was not dealt with appropriately.[39]

The apocalyptic warnings of the government were not well received by the opposition, who angrily rejected its message as damaging to public confidence and unwarrantably pessimistic. Some opposition deputies interpreted Lemass's warnings as confirmation that 'those who control our money and our credit reign supreme over ... the Government'.[40] Counted among the Central Bank's plethora of sins were the charges that it had deliberately restricted credit and that it had failed to invest any of its assets in Irish securities. Both of these accusations proved difficult to refute and Lemass's response betrayed a confidence in the institution that was considerably less than absolute: 'I have said that in the fulfilment of the programme upon which we decide we expect to get and, I think, will get, the co-operation of the banks, the Central Bank and the commercial banks. If we do not get that co-operation then we will have to do something about it.'[41] The programme to which Lemass referred involved considerable investment. His pledge to maintain the construction of housing and hospitals mirrored the Inter-Party administration's commitment to social capital expenditure. He outlined that the government was preparing a ten-year electricity programme and contemplated that an investment of £40 or £50 million over that period would be required. Further expenditure was also planned for turf development and the expansion of the merchant shipping service. Lemass also stated the government's intention of stimulating 'investments by private enterprise in the expansion of cement production, textile output, and various other industries'. The wide-ranging programme also envisaged an expansion of the output of sugar, investment in industrial development in the congested areas, and investment in agricultural efficiency. 'Over and above all that,' he concluded, 'we have the continuing need to find capital to maintain the housing programme, the extension of health services, the construction of hospitals, and the provision of water schemes and sewerage services, all of which are necessary.'[42]

If pinning the report to the government proved elusive, the government's own attempt to rid itself of the association with the Central Bank also proved difficult, despite Lemass's protestations. His case was scarcely helped by MacEntee, who continued to mention the white paper in the same breath as the Central Bank Report, and for all intents and purposes treated them as the same document. He described the former as 'a strikingly objective document [that] is based upon statistics which have been computed on the surest foundation of known facts available'.[43] On the subject of the bank itself, the minister was careful to stress its independence from the government. He maintained that it was 'free to judge the policies of the politicians ... It is free to express its unfettered opinion on these policies and on the developments which in its view may affect the purchasing power of the currency and endanger its stability.'[44] The suspicion that MacEntee was sympathetic to the analysis provided by the Central Bank was further rein-forced when he mounted a strong defence of the bank's actions: 'They sit and meet as responsible citizens and they are charged by the statute with the supreme public duty of doing everything which they may deem advisable towards safe-guarding the integrity of the currency and ensuring that in what pertains to the control of credit, the constant and predominant aim shall be the welfare of the people as a whole.' 'These men are,' he continued 'in a sense, the watchdogs of the people.' De Valera, ever alert to subtle public divisions in the cabinet, endeavoured to put the matter to an end when he rose to speak, asserting that: 'The report is the report of the Central Bank. It is a public document. It is intend-ed to give information to the public from the point of view of the Governor and Board of the Central Bank.'[45]

Meanwhile Brennan was less than gratified by the impression gleaned from the various ministerial statements and prepared a memorandum for the govern-ment conveying his deep disquiet at its public response.[46] He explained that he had met MacEntee on 3 October and had 'expressed a desire to explain or amplify any matters in the report that might occasion difficulty to the minister or his col-leagues. The minister mentioned that he had read the report twice and did not see anything in it at the moment that he would controvert.'[47] MacEntee, in turn, had informed him that he had not had time to consult with the rest of the cabinet, but Brennan was not told of any opposition to the report until he read Lemass's Dáil statement and the views of de Valera at the party's árd fheis the previous day, which stressed that the report 'need not be accepted'. Brennan regarded the lack of communication and the statements themselves as a 'gross affront to the bank'. He went on to criticise Lemass for making what he maintained was a false dis-tinction between the government's proposed strategy and the strategy promoted in the bank's report. Brennan argued that it was a misrepresentation of the Central Bank's position to merely concentrate on the cutting down of consumption: 'Apart from the fact that the remedies indicated by the bank cover much more than consumption the implication that the bank unlike the government is not con-cerned about increasing production is clearly wrong.'[48] Although this point was subsequently deleted by Brennan, the memo patently revealed his acute annoy-ance at what he regarded as Lemass's imprudence. What worried Brennan above all was what his remarks promised in terms of future government policy.

The memorandum is all the more remarkable for highlighting the conflict within Fianna Fáil on the appropriate economic path to follow. In Brennan's account the party's thinking appears indecisive and incoherent, with MacEntee apparently finding little objectionable in the report and Lemass and de Valera hav-ing evident misgivings about it. In fact MacEntee's memorandum to his govern-ment colleagues on 13 October was preoccupied with amplifying the untold mis-ery envisaged by the bank's investigation.[49] Among the passages he underlined for particular consideration was its contention that 'for the time being the nation is living beyond its means', combined with its criticism of increased government expenditure, especially on public works and food subsidies. He also urged the government, through the warnings of the report, to adopt 'fiscal measures to curb inflation, balance the budget and restrict improvident spending' as well as 'restraint in wage policy and restriction of bank credit'.[50] Notwithstanding the fact that MacEntee had long been regarded as something of an economic Cassandra within the cabinet, subsequent direction of government policy was determined by Fianna Fáil's attempt to deny the existence of an emerging schism between MacEntee's endorsement of the report's findings and Lemass's desire for the extension of the proposed development programme.

MacENTEE AND WHITAKER

In tandem with the emergence of economics as the chief weapon in political debate was a concurrent battle to educate and convince the public of the proper strategy required to secure economic prosperity. 'Trade recession has replaced the weather as a topic of conversation. Everywhere one goes there is a continuous questioning as to the reasons creating the slump in consumer purchasing power', opined a correspondent to the *Irish Times*, illustrating the point rather extravagantly.[51] The Supply and Services Bill debate was as much about instructing the public as to the nature of the difficulties facing the policymakers as it was about political point scoring. Presenting the harsh facts to the community was also emphasised by Finance officials who, in turn, were more than agreeable to the task of edifying their political masters. Dr Brendan Menton, the department's economist and the official largely responsible for the white paper, hoped that the government's decision to publish it thus would achieve 'the object of instructing public opinion'.[52] Similarly, in a twenty-three-page memorandum to the government in October, prepared by deputy assistant secretary T.K. Whitaker, which forcefully stated the case for urgent remedial action, there was a separate section devoted to the importance of presenting this message as candidly as possible to the public. This amounted to a simple, if unpalatable, choice:

> What is needed is a realisation that if houses, electricity development, afforestation and all the other forms of capital expenditure are desired by the community, the desire should be expressed in the form of preferring these things to others – of turning over to the State some of the money now being spent on non-essential consumer goods so that the State can carry on with its capital programme without causing too much inflation. If the public wish to spend now largely on works that confer social benefits or whose economic fruits are slow to appear, the result must be that which our balance of payments deficit shows – purchasing power spilling over and being absorbed by surplus consumer imports … Our ability to maintain social services and to await the fruition of long-term development schemes is being imperilled. The position would be corrected if State expenditure – current and capital – were curtailed and a much greater proportion of it financed from taxation.[53]

Despite the great lengths to which the government had gone to prepare the public for such a scenario, Lemass's refusal to endorse the Central Bank's proposals only served to obscure the message further. It was interpreted in some quarters, for example, as confirmation that: 'There is to be no reversion, as the opposition had feared, to deflation. The present Government's mentor is to be Lord Keynes and not Montague Norman. The task will not be easy but, at least, the general line of advance has the agreement of all political parties in the state.'[54] Alas, such a cosy consensus, even within the governing party, proved illusory.

That such confusion still prevailed was testament to the government's desire to implement its intended development programme while at the same time demonstrate its ability to manage the economic crisis.[55] Nevertheless, that the Menton memorandum was sanctioned by the cabinet and published as a white paper indicated where its interim priorities lay.[56] It was also attentive to the tough curative measures counselled by Whitaker's memorandum. This analysis, which was an updated version of the memorandum prepared for the incoming government in June, and which 'served as a blueprint for the 1952 budget',[57] conceded that: 'There is still plenty of room for capital investment of the right kind in this country; but, even if there were not, it would still be impossible to approve of our external assets being wasted, as they are at present, in excessive imports of consumer goods for current consumption.'[58] Whitaker's judgement was corroborated not only by his departmental secretary, J.J. McElligott, but also by the Director of the Central Statistics Office, M.D. McCarthy, who added that a 'reduction in the standard of living must be faced and to achieve it there must be some control of increases in employee remuneration and distributed profit',[59] an observation which Whitaker felt 'should be emphasised'. Most interestingly, Tom Murray, assistant secretary in the Department of Industry and Commerce, also endorsed these measures.[60] Murray's comments on Whitaker's memorandum were volunteered on a confidential basis, and included an insight into how it could best be presented to the government, which Whitaker advised McElligott was 'valuable':

> To my mind the most important single achievement lies in the admission (if it is fair to call it that) that the Department of Finance is not fundamentally opposed to capital expenditure, even if the objectives are mainly social or even where the expenditure involves repatriation of our sterling assets ... I feel very strongly that, if the presentation of the problem is not prefaced by some *positive* [original emphasis] statement of policy on these lines, the memorandum will be dismissed as just 'another moan from the Department of Finance'.[61]

It is clear that whatever impression this advice made on McElligott, it was as nothing compared to the imprint it made on his ever watchful junior colleague. It was not long after this that Whitaker described, with a fair degree of self-justification, what he called 'the finance attitude', an exercise that was just as much about attempting to gain acceptance on the part of other government departments for what he viewed as the innate reasonableness of the Finance position, and to summarily dismiss the notion that it was just 'another moan'.[62]

Indeed the relationship between departmental officials and the minister during MacEntee's stewardship was particularly strong and the quality of the advice proffered does not bear an overtly dissimilar philosophy to that underpinning the

much lauded *Economic Development* six years later.[63] When MacEntee and
McElligott considered Whitaker's analysis, which was a 'personal viewpoint', so
completely did they endorse it that they made no substantive changes other than
including a suggestion that subsidies be eliminated and making a reference to the
inadvisability of import controls. They did spice it up with some short and characteristically pungent sentences, adding, for instance, that 'no nation can consume its capital without reducing itself to poverty and need and losing its economic independence' or stridently asserting that the gap between external disinvestment and domestic capital formation indicated a pure 'waste of national capital'.[64] Indeed Whitaker has recounted that it was his job to see that the minister's
labours, in preparation for the budget, were tempered and given official
approval:

> When it came to the budget of 1952 which [MacEntee] intended to be
> rather severe and saw as a necessary corrective, he was dashing away draft-
> ing, drafting and McElligott would say 'he has so many pages written and
> we don't know what he is saying, can you get hold of him and tell him to
> stop or wait until we have submitted something from the official side' ... I
> think that delicate operation was performed reasonably well. He did slow
> down and he did take on board the draft prepared for him.[65]

Moreover, the relative success of this rapport in alleviating the worst effects of
the balance of payments crisis directly contradicts Lee's contention that: 'One
could not have predicted, on the basis of the intellectual performance of Finance
in the early fifties, that before the end of the decade it would prove capable of
producing as impressive a document as *Economic Development*.'[66] It is also the
case, as has been noted elsewhere, that it is 'too easy to see Finance always in
the role of villain and to read too much wisdom into the views of anyone brave
enough to oppose the prevailing orthodoxy' whether inside or outside government.[67]

However constructively the department submitted its findings, the facts it presented fully exposed the grim magnitude of the difficulties before the minister:

> Trade returns for the first eight months of 1951 show a trade deficit of
> £91.6 million as compared with £59.9 million for the corresponding peri-
> od of 1950 – an increase of £31.7 million. The quantity imported is 7½%
> greater than in 1950 and 58% greater than in 1938. The increase in the vol-
> ume of imports over last year accounts for 10.6 million of the total increase
> in imports of £36.1 million; the remaining £25.5 million is the result of
> increased prices. On the other hand, we exported 3% less this year than in
> the same eight months of 1950 and the meagre increase in the value of
> exports of £4.4 million is entirely the result of increased prices which,
> however, lagged behind import prices.[68]

Whitaker was precise in his detection of the principal root of the disruption to the
nation's finances: 'There can be no doubt that the method of financing state capital outlay, coupled with the character of that outlay, has been mainly responsible for the recent serious deterioration in the financial situation.'[69] Among the

correctives advanced was 'a substantial increase in taxation, sufficient not only to avoid the glaring abuse of a deficit in the "current" budget, but also to cover a sizeable fraction of capital expenditure and thus reduce its excessively inflationary effect as evidenced by the heavy realisation of external assets for consumption purposes'.[70] If the promise of a substantial increase in taxation made some members of the government uneasy, MacEntee's request in December to make 'an interim announcement that a further increase in food subsidies cannot be afforded' must have been even more difficult to contemplate given the expected political consequences.[71] 'The minister,' he continued, 'is very conscious of the difficult problems which he will be called upon to face in connection with the 1952 Budget and he desires that every possible step should be taken to lighten his task in advance.' Indeed the question of what to do about the food subsidies – originally introduced in 1941 with the intention of stabilising wages and the cost of living index – was being actively considered by the government, which appointed an inter-departmental committee in October to investigate alternative methods of relief 'in respect of the burden of the cost of living'.[72] The committee submitted a summary of conclusions in February which can be briefly condensed to the following: 'There is no real justification for continuing this policy and in principle it would be desirable to abolish the food subsidies, provided arrangements are made to ensure that the weakest sections of the community do not suffer as a consequence.'

MacEntee was keen to see his task lightened in other ways too. He responded to proposals for reform of social welfare schemes under the government's talismanic Social Welfare Bill – which would have increased the burden on the public purse by an estimated £7.25 million a year – in a similar manner by recommending 'in the most emphatic manner possible' that 'before consideration is given to the proposals of the Minister for Social Welfare the Government should first consider the steps to be taken to deal with the serious budgetary position.'[73] Further demands were being made on the exchequer by the Department of Industry and Commerce, which submitted proposals on the enhancement of the burgeoning tourist industry. MacEntee expressed his recognition of 'the importance of tourism in the national economy and in particular the significance of tourist income in the balance of payments', and was prepared 'to increase within reason the amount of public funds committed to the promotion of tourism'.[74] There was one important stipulation: 'It is imperative, he emphasised, 'that state aid should not be given without the strictest regard to economy and to the probable effectiveness of the expenditure in producing early and substantial results'. As well as dealing with the demands of government to meet new commitments, MacEntee was also confronted with an altogether different problem and one that threatened to have an equally sober effect on the budgetary position.

THE STERLING AREA CRISIS

If MacEntee's tone in the above entreaties to government sounded increasingly desperate it was manifestly due to the perilous state of the sterling area, on which he was informed personally by the British Chancellor of the Exchequer, R.A.

Butler, on 14 December.[75] Butler was seeking the cooperation of the Irish government 'in dealing with the very grave economic crisis which faces the sterling
area'. The communiqué between the chancellor and his Irish equivalent emanated from a paper entitled 'Objectives and General Policy' compiled by the
Treasury Working Party for an emergency Commonwealth Finance Ministers
conference[76] scheduled for January 1952 which revealed four main objectives:

> First, to convince the members that the sterling area was good for them and
> that the UK was determined to earn a balance of payments surplus for the
> area after being in deficit over the past few years. The second was to get an
> undertaking from members that they would adopt internal and external
> measures to correct their economies and cease being drains on the dollar
> reserves. The third objective was to organise longer-term plans for closer
> economic cooperation and the last objective was to draft a strongly word-
> ed communiqué expressing the area's resolve to strengthen sterling.[77]

Sterling area gold and dollar reserves had lost almost $900m or 10 per cent in the
second half of 1951 as the value of exports fell against import expenditure.
Butler duly informed MacEntee of the measures undertaken towards reversing
that trend:

> As an emergency measure the cutting of import programmes is an unfortu-
> nate necessity. But I know very well that it is not a policy in itself and that
> our real task is to hold back inflation at home and to prove that our econo-
> my is basically sound and our currency worthy of confidence. To my mind
> this means the establishment of a surplus on overall account as a normal
> feature of the United Kingdom economy. As a first step to this end we have
> restricted credit by monetary action and intend to make further cuts in our
> investment programme. We have also set up a committee of senior
> Ministers under my Chairmanship to consider as a matter of urgency the
> other measures that we must take to restore the health of our economy.[78]

If the difficulties facing the sterling area left MacEntee with an even larger problem than he had before the British call for assistance, at least Butler's subscription to policies already advocated by Finance served to strengthen the minister's
hand in his dealings with his own cabinet. If nothing else, MacEntee had further
justification for pursuing a deflationary route and in employing that policy *sine
mora*: 'In these circumstances,' wrote the chancellor, 'I venture to hope it may
be possible for your Government, without waiting for the inter-Governmental
discussions which I have suggested, to consider as a matter of urgency any measures that can be taken towards improving your balance of payments with the
non-sterling world and so helping to stop the drain on the sterling area central
reserves, and if it is at all possible to do so, to put the measures into effect without delay.'[79]

    In January MacEntee stressed to the government the reciprocal nature of the
problem and the interdependence of the British and Irish economies, arguing that
Ireland's balance of payments difficulties were impossible to relieve without the
cooperation of Britain. Indeed if something were not done to relieve the situation

and the international system of sterling collapsed completely, 'the immediate consequences for this country would be disastrous, with far-reaching effects on our standard of living, on the possibility of economic development, and on our demographic problem.'[80] The memorandum reiterated in the most explicit form possible what it expected the government to do: 'The redressing of the basic disequilibrium in our balance of payments is our most immediate and vital problem ... no alternative to budgetary measures exists which would even be partially effective.' Notwithstanding the general indifference of the cabinet to the British predicament – most clearly reflected in its decision to appoint an inter-departmental committee 'to examine the respects in which British policy in matters concerning Ireland's economic interests (for example, in relation to the supply of coal) has been detrimental to those interests' – it accepted Finance's appeal for greater control mechanisms over imports embodied in an exchange control committee. The aforementioned inter-departmental committee, chaired by Whitaker, reported to the government on 7 February and again recommended the acceptance of the proposals for a restrictive economic policy contained in Butler's letter and drew attention to the arguments of previous memoranda on the subject of government expenditure. On the question of British policy concerning Irish economic interests, the committee concluded that that policy had not been inimical to those interests and that where there were instances of unexpected decisions made unilaterally 'these do not constitute a genuine cause of grievance'.

The inter-governmental talks took place in London on 18–19 February 1952. MacEntee and Lemass headed the Irish delegation, accompanied by six officials, including McElligott, Hogan and Whitaker from Finance. Lemass's inclusion was apparently at the request of the Irish government, which viewed the willingness of Finance to support British demands with considerable suspicion.[81] Thus Hogan, replying to Tom Murray on 16 February 1952: 'As to your hypothetical worries [about British pressure], I do believe that the Department of Finance is well able, in the matters which concern it, to counter adequately any incorrect statements or allegations by Perfidious Albion and has no need or inclination to be reminded of the Yankee apostrophe on patriotism [sic].'[82] Evidently, the Finance–Treasury link was still looked on with much dubiety within government. MacEntee's performance during the talks, however, belied any undue obligation he may have felt under this special relationship. Early in the negotiations he established the two guidelines of the Irish approach: that his government's position in parliament 'was somewhat precarious and they did not want to make it an election year in Ireland'; and that corrective measures that resulted in increased unemployment and emigration would not be considered.[83] Consequently, Butler's request for a reduction in the Irish deficit in the balance of payments with the non-sterling world from the estimated £25 million for the first six months of 1952 to £10 million was rejected. And despite his repeated willingness to cooperate with measures designed to strengthen sterling, MacEntee desired to 'give primary attention to positive measures, particularly in regard to exports, which would enhance Ireland's capacity to deal with her balance of payments deficit and avoid any kind of economic or social dislocation'.[84] 'The difference between the two sides,' in the words of the historian of the

Department of Finance, 'was about means rather than ends.' 'The Irish delegation refused to commit themselves to a specific figure by which they would
reduce the deficit but indicated, as an earnest of their determination, their intention of introducing a particularly early budget, while continuing to stress (in a
phrase of the Minister for Finance to the Chancellor) "that our interest in sterling
is only second to your own".'[85]

The subsequent press release agreed by both sides concluded rather noncha-
lantly that: 'Ireland's external reserves would, as far as possible, only be used to
improve living standards permanently by promoting an increase in domestic capital development beyond that for which normal current savings would provide.'[86]
The rather untroubled tone probably provided the Irish government with an alibi
in the likely event of domestic criticism, and facilitated a $16 million cut in the
imports of sugar and tobacco already licensed by the Exchange Control
Committee which the government approved on 7 March 1952. At the same meeting a request by MacEntee for permission to reassure the British of the good
intentions of the government was approved in the light of a letter received from
Butler on 5 March requesting an annual balance of payments deficit with the
non-sterling world of £30 million, of which the dollar element would be no more
than £12 million.[87] MacEntee duly informed the Dáil of these developments on
12 March, an announcement which drew a caustic riposte from the former
Taoiseach, John A. Costello. Not only did he allege that there was a clear gulf
between 'the restrictionist policy of the Minister for Finance and the expansionist policy of the Minister for Industry and Commerce', he also charged MacEntee
of being 'suckled in a creed outworn since the day when Gladstone died'.[88]
Costello also made much of the travel arrangements of the two ministers who
had made their way to London separately. Lemass's presence at the London
talks, if anything, converted him, however temporarily, to the necessity of parts
of the Finance strategy. That is not to say that he abandoned completely his own
economic convictions. As Fanning has acknowledged, 'it is indisputable that the
government strongly supported the policy advocated by Finance at the height of
the 1952 crisis'; but what is also incontestable is that despite the stringent rhetoric of the budget, its adverse reception by its political opponents and its application of some deflationary instruments, the government was not willing to compromise its capital programme, resulting in an unsystematic approach to overall
fiscal policy in the budget.[89]

PYRRHIC VICTORY: THE 1952 BUDGET

MacEntee continued to press the cabinet to come to a resolution on fiscal policy
but had little success. In January, he advocated a cut in the capital programme as
the most realistic way of balancing the budget.[90] But a decision on those proposals
was postponed at no less than seven government meetings in February and on nine
occasions in March. Such irresolution was inevitably reflected in a budget that had
the modest aim of a 'restoration of a reasonable budgetary balance', thus leaving
the door open for additional capital expenditure.[91] Government rhetoric, however,
revived the distressed tone that had characterised Finance's pronouncements since

June of the previous year and was most clearly identifiable as the work of the minister. Introducing the earliest budget in the history of the state on 2 April, he explained the necessity of the timing by stressing that it was 'due to the urgent need to restore order in the public finances and in our general economy'.[92] He delineated the main features of that economy by restating the poor levels of national production and the failure of Irish industry to develop adequate export markets: 'There are others [Irish firms] who have not yet risen to the occasion, who appear content in the enjoyment of the home market. It is time for them to bestir themselves, first, to meet all the demands of our own people and second-ly, to extend their activities abroad.'[93] When it came to divulging the details of the budget, however, capital commitments showed a remarkable continuity with the budget of the previous year prepared by Patrick McGilligan, notwithstanding MacEntee's description of the cost of public services as 'a highly disturbing ele-ment in our economy'.[94] The division of the budget into capital and current account was also maintained despite MacEntee's reservations 'because of their political background and because of the doubtful quality, in his view, of some of the components'.[95]

Indeed those public services (capital and current) had cost central govern-ment £123.5 million in 1951–2 compared to £71.1 million in 1947–8, and a rel-atively modest £34.6 million in 1938–9, the year of MacEntee's last budget.[96] 'Social services, health services, education, superannuation, subsidies and the service of debt between them now account for roughly three-fifths of the current outlay of public authorities,' reported the minister. Just how interventionist the state had become was also revealed rather pointedly by MacEntee's observation that 'Public finance ... has become predominantly concerned with redistributing national income', a development which MacEntee failed to identify as being positive or negative, but the inference was quite clear.[97] Total current expenditure for 1952–3 amounted to £101.7 million (compared to an actual figure of £90.6 million the year before), including a provision of £3 million for the cost of the Social Welfare (Insurance) Bill, 1951, and was to be met from estimated revenue of a robust, if inadequate, £86.6 million (compared to £70.5 million in 1951).[98] 'There is a gap of £15.1 million to be bridged,' MacEntee explained. 'This can be closed only in two ways – by cutting down expenditure and by putting on additional taxation.'[99] Cutting expenditure was, however, patently not on the agenda. Tellingly, MacEntee chose to cite public opinion as the reason for the government's unwillingness to choose the former option.[100]

The exception was food subsidies which, in the view of the government, would be tolerated by public opinion and was, according to MacEntee, the 'largest item of current expenditure in which significant economies are [sic] readily pos-sible and fully defensible'.[101] Furthermore, the government was satisfied that as 'incomes had advanced more than the cost of living and that essential foodstuffs were no longer scarce', there was no 'economic or social justification for a poli-cy of subsidising food for everybody'.[102] From 1 July, tea, butter and sugar were to be charged at their real cost; the price of bread and flour would also be raised but not to their unsubsidised level and rationing of all foodstuffs was to be abol-ished. Congruent with the interdepartmental committee's suggestion in February that reductions in the food subsidies should be attended by arrangements 'made to ensure that the weakest sections of the community do not suffer as a consequence', the government introduced compensatory increases in social welfare benefits,[103] measures that prompted the Labour Party leader William Norton to suggest that it was 'a cod relief giving the old age pensioner 1/6 whilst at the same time increasing the price of the commodities upon which the old age pensioner mainly lives'.[104] The minister's answer to these charges was that bread subsidies applied to all, not merely to old age pensioners.

Estimated gross savings from the subsidy reductions of £6.67 million was partly offset by the cost of the increased benefits which totalled £2.75 million. For the remaining £11.2 million required to balance the current budget, MacEntee's only recourse was to substantially increase both direct and indirect taxation with the greater part coming from the latter category. Staples such as tobacco, beer, spirits and petrol were all hit. Revenue from the increases in customs duties amounted to £10.38 million, the remaining £800,000 covered by a rise in the standard rate of income tax by one shilling to 7/6 in the pound. Again the government attempted to assuage this burden by introducing new bands of income tax with the objective of lessening the tax payable on lower taxable incomes. The total effect of net tax yields was a surplus on the current budget of a rather negligible £90,000. 'Budget cuts [in food subsidies] therefore only contributed one fourth of the amount needed to balance the current budget leaving the balance to be financed by measures which would have an impact on consumption as well', hence fulfilling Finance's principal budgetary purpose.[105]

An interrelated purpose was to encourage an upsurge in savings, something that was vital, the minister stressed, to financing the capital commitments of the government. Savings bank deposits and purchases of savings certificates, by a rather optimistic evaluation, indicated a yield of £6 million; the gap of £28 million was to be provided, again in an assessment that favoured sanguinity over reality, by a national loan, notwithstanding the fact that the average subscription to the three national loans launched since 1948 had been £9 million out of a target of £13 million.[106] That the success of the government's capital programme was predicated on such unrealistic expectations served to amplify the limits of its budgetary strategy. MacEntee's final statement of almost Churchillian confidence in the Irish people betrayed a minister searching for an unlikely *deus ex machina*: 'We shall rely on our own people to provide by their industry and thrift the capital necessary to build up the nation. We relied on them before during stringent and terrible days. They did not fail us then and they will not fail us now.'[107]

The electoral potential of the budget was not lost on the opposition. Reduction of the food subsidies became the principal stick with which to beat the government, but it could be said that they were spoiled for choice.[108] McGilligan described it rather pungently as 'butchery of the taxpayer' and castigated the minister's relative apathy towards the twin evils of emigration and unemployment. He hoped that 'the minister and his colleagues will give us an opportunity soon of getting a decision from the people in these matters'.[109] The apparent anxiety on the government benches was also referred to by Norton, who had witnessed 'more enthusiasm in a morgue'. He also suggested that 'there will be very few chapel-gate meetings next Sunday to extol the virtues of this budget. If Fianna Fáil was 100 years old next Sunday, you would not get the boys to come to a cumann meeting to debate [it].'[110] Norton also echoed McGilligan's view that there would 'be rejoicing over it in Foster Place this evening and in other places where the governors of banks meet'. Seán MacBride also made the association between the budget and the Central Bank Report, alleging that the budget had been 'conceived in the minds of the people who wrote the Central Bank Report', and mordantly asked: 'Who represents the views of the government in this House – MacEntee or Lemass?'

The answer to that question on the strict evidence of the budget is that both ministers had a significant input. What is more, by solely emphasising the deflationary aspects of the budget – for wholly different reasons – both the opposition and the Minister for Finance were being somewhat disingenuous. In this light, the remark by MacEntee that 'we have done what is essential to put the public finances in order and to revive confidence in the credit and stability of the state' was an exaggeration if purely based on the merits of his preceding analysis. As Andersen has persuasively concluded:

> In real terms, public expenditure – current and capital – rose slightly, compared to the previous year. That is not to say that the increase in indirect taxation did not have a curbing effect on personal consumption. The response by the public to the launch of a new national loan proved otherwise, but the deflationary elements were not strong enough to explain an improvement in the balance of payments of the size that occurred in 1952 … Thus the most important contribution of the 1952 Budget was probably indirect, as it caused no actual harm to the economy through either severe deflationary measures, or greatly expanded public spending. At the same time the public was persuaded to save more. It could be said that the lack of an overall fiscal policy, by coincidence, helped to relieve the balance of payments difficulties.[111]

Lee's contention that 'the 1952 budget probably contributed significantly to both the reality and atmosphere of depression' discounts the trade position.[112] In fact, trade improved markedly for the following year, and in July 1953 Whitaker reported that 'the £62 million deficit for 1951 was reduced in 1952 to a mere £9 million' and the deficit with 'the non-sterling area as a whole … from £62½ million to £37½ million'.[113] However, by reducing the deficit, unemployment rose and economic activity fell, fuelling the perception that Lemass's efforts to overcome the forces of darkness in Finance were being vainly pursued. It also resulted in some party members transferring their allegiance to Lemass's Dublin South-Central constituency.[114] Indeed, according to one authority, the budget had 'a seismic effect on Fianna Fáil' and resulted in other party members leaving altogether.[115]

The party was forced to embark on a damage limitation exercise in advance of the June by-elections.[116] In the June edition of the party's monthly bulletin,

Gléas, edited by Michael B. Yeats, commentary on recent events naturally focused on the passing of the Social Welfare Bill rather than the effects of the budget.[117] Mention of the budget was confined to stressing the measures designed to offset the effects of the food subsidies. As an indicator that activists were determined to perceive the glass half full, this analysis was exemplary: 'Unlike the food subsidies which were only temporary, these benefits will be permanent.'[118] Newspaper editorials on the day after the budget also contributed to the atmosphere of despair. The *Irish Times* editorial was entitled *Dies Irae* or 'days of wrath'.[119] It, too, considered the electoral implications, opining: 'If there is not a general election within the next six months or so, it certainly will be a miracle.' It was, it continued, 'by far the most severe [budget] that has ever been opened in Dáil Éireann', and even postulated that the minister was peculiarly equipped to be the one to present it: 'Mr MacEntee never lacked courage, and yesterday's budget certainly proves that he has shown it to an almost incredible degree … he has thrown political discretion to the winds. A more unpopular Budget could hardly be imagined.'

The 1952 budget, it has been argued, should have promoted an expansionary fiscal policy inspired by Keynesian theory. Kennedy and Dowling, for example, have advanced a popular view that 'a reasonable rate of growth of demand led by an expansionary fiscal policy could have been safely sustained had there been a less restrictive view of the balance of payments constraint and less concern about increasing the national debt.'[120] An increase in the input of capital is generally assumed to inevitably lead to higher total output. There are valid reasons, however, to question this notion. Irish consumers were scarcely expected to respond enthusiastically to an enlarged supply of Irish-produced commodities for consumption, as a widespread complaint heard at that time related to the inferior nature of domestic produce. An expansionary fiscal policy would, furthermore, have had to be financed either by foreign direct investment or repatriation of foreign assets or by borrowing from abroad. The government, as we have seen, was unanimously opposed to depleting foreign assets further while the political implications of courting foreign direct investment could not yet be contemplated. Nor was the prospect of borrowing any more favourable. Whitaker has recounted 'the difficulty of raising even a few million pounds on a short-term basis in London in 1956'.[121] By accentuating the lack of direction and, indeed, imagination of Irish politicians – the protagonist inevitably being MacEntee – critics of the budgetary measures have overestimated the impact of policy on economic reality, thereby cheapening the importance of long-standing structural constraints, and have also tended to disregard the compromise struck within government. Indeed key elements within Fianna Fáil opposed implicitly any notion of structural change. Only recidivistic use of nationalist rhetoric and appeals to patriotism made it possible to gradually overcome this resistance in a later age.[122] Other factors limited the prospect of structural change and inhibited a more innovative budgetary strategy. Andersen notes that: 'The gathering of statistics had not yet reached a stage where it was possible to contemplate accurate economic forecasting. Neither had the mathematical models become an inevitable part of economic policy. Thus it was hardly surprising that the government concentrated on the short-term aspects of the balance of payments difficulties instead of the need for a structural transformation.'[123]

The government had ignored MacEntee's requests to reduce capital investment, despite the restraints put on domestic credit by the commercial banks and the discouraging prospects of a national loan. Unsurprisingly, the government – like governments all over Europe – found it more convenient to raise taxes than cut public expenditure. Improved expectations of consumption and employment among populations after the war meant that politicians were instinctively anathema to applying economic measures that would result in hardship, however short-lived. Such considerations were tellingly revealed by MacEntee in the February discussions on the sterling area: 'It was doubtful,' according to the Minister for Finance, 'if the Irish public fully appreciated the seriousness of the balance of payments problem; they did not like talk of hardships. It was, therefore, all the more necessary to recognise that the social and economic considerations [unemployment and emigration] ... severely limited the choice of corrective measures.'[124]

Austerity promised electoral disaster, so the government chose increasing taxation and tampering with the food subsidies to maintain a significant level of investment as the lesser of two evils. Personal differences within the government complicated things further and made a compromise even more attractive. Such tensions certainly existed between Lemass and MacEntee, reflecting the clash of two opposing attitudes to fiscal policy. MacEntee was probably a deliberately conservative choice for Finance, made against the wishes of Lemass, but that it was in the interests of the Tánaiste to hold the bogey of fiscal conservatism responsible for the subsequent electoral failings of the party is not an unreasonable assumption to make. The ageing de Valera thus kept a more characteristically secure grip on his governments – *pace* Bew and Patterson – than is often presumed. Sustaining this grasp for the remainder of the party's time in office would prove to be an equally onerous task even for a leader as redoubtable as de Valera. For MacEntee, the budget would haunt him for the remainder of his political career and irretrievably made him synonymous with the stringency it imposed. It also ended any designs he may have had on the party succession but his cavalier disregard of enduring popularity probably had condemned any notion of that some time before he introduced his infamous budget.

If the 1952 budget exemplified the conciliation at the heart of the *immobiliste* Fianna Fáil minority government, the next two years of office extended this 'Augustinian procrastination' and led inevitably to further compromise.[125] In the aftermath of the budget, and with its counsel apparently having some success, Finance endeavoured to consolidate its authority on the economic position by urging restraint in expected wage negotiations with trade union leaders who sought recompense for the inflationary aspects of MacEntee's budget such as the reduction of food subsidies.[126] The outcome of the talks between the Federated Union of Employers and the Labour congresses gave rise to a permissible increase of 10 per cent for the lower wage groups, which Finance maintained was unjustifiable. McElligott was first out of the blocks in forewarning his minister. In mid-May he sent MacEntee correspondence with his opposite number in the Department of Industry and Commerce, John Leydon, as well as press cuttings of that day's date signalling the imminent pay talks. 'It is very desirable that you should urge restraint' was his rather succinct advice to the minister.[127]

Leydon's reply was altogether more sympathetic to wage demands and revealed the habitually antagonistic relationship between the two departments: 'We must realise what is happening and I think another round is imminent. It will be a matter for your department to siphon off as much as possible of the increases by way of savings if the consequences you fear are to be avoided.'[128] Whitaker rejected this criticism by deflecting the responsibility back to the spending departments who, he maintained, were culpable for the 'excessive expenditure which is at the root of the trouble'. Leydon also pointed out that the campaign for a new round of wage increases was launched long before the 1952 budget, and that Lemass had informed the unions that the government should not be involved directly in the discussions. He encouraged more Finance indignation with his observation that the 'standard of living of the working classes has been reduced by the budget whilst that of the better-off classes has been improved'. Whitaker repudiated Leydon's analysis, describing it as 'a Rip Van Winkle comment'.[129] Just how much discord existed between Finance and Industry and Commerce was further exposed by Leydon's admission that his department did not support Finance's contention that there should be no compensatory wage increases for the reduction of the food subsidies: 'The fact that the subsidies were withdrawn in the budget does not, in my opinion, uphold the view that a relief, even by way of wage increases, was not justified.'[130] Whitaker duly prepared a reply for McElligott on 29 May which contended that:

> [F]ull compensation is not justifiable in the present state of the economy. A temporary reduction in living standards must be accepted until higher output provides a support for the consumption level established in recent times. Unless there is restraint, the influence, slight as it is, which the budget might have in reducing the waste of external capital for consumption purposes will, as I have said before, be offset by the inflationary effects of increases in wages and in money incomes generally.[131]

Retrenchment remained Finance's guiding principle for the rest of the year despite the general amelioration of the external trade figures. It submitted a two-part review of the exchequer position in November and December which had mixed news for the government.[132] Inexplicably, given the punitive tax increases and food subsidy reductions, the national loan proved an unprecedented success, attracting a 'record number of investors, including many people of small and modest means' as MacEntee cheerfully informed the Dáil in his budget statement the following May.[133] The minister chose to see this response as a salutary reminder that 'while the activities of the state have a considerable influence, they are not of predominant importance in our economy.'[134] A large inflow of small savings, the sale of sterling securities of departmental funds and favourable assistance from the banks supplemented the capital from the loan and gratified the minister that his policies in 1952 had been well determined. Notwithstanding this, the review warned that 'the total amount of finance obtainable for state capital purposes … from sources other than the banks and the sale of sterling securities was £15 million below the cost of the capital programme': £26.7 million as against £42 million. The review concluded by emphasising 'that prospective resources fall substantially short of what is required to maintain the capital programme on its present scale. [The minister] again asks the Government to set up a Committee of the Cabinet to review the capital programme as a whole in relation to the prospective availability of savings and a reasonable rate of external disinvestment as reflected in balance of payments deficits.'[135] McElligott learned that the above proposal, which was commended to the government in a further memorandum in February, had been withdrawn from the cabinet agenda on the day before MacEntee was to deliver his 1953 budget speech. The notion of a committee specifically designated to review the capital programme was patently Whitaker's idea but that the idea foundered in yet more procrastination possibly indicates Lemass's disapproval. The committee was also evidence of a more proactive outlook on behalf of the Department of Finance in framing overall economic policy, as opposed to its more customary tactic of challenging initiatives from the traditional spending departments.[136] Further, and most significantly, it was reflective of Whitaker's more prevalent influence in the department, something that became more obvious after the departure of J.J. McElligott to the Central Bank in March 1953.

Further differences between Finance and Industry and Commerce were revealed in their respective responses to the Report on the Industrial Potentialities of Ireland carried out by the IBEC technical services corporation. More commonly labelled the Stacey May Report, it was commissioned by Industry and Commerce as part of the ECA Technical Assistance Programme on 1 June 1951 to undertake a preliminary survey of Ireland's industrial development potential. Once submitted to the government in October 1952, Lemass immediately sought its publication, but before doing so he enquired from the departments of Finance, Agriculture and External Affairs whether they would have any objections to publication on the lines suggested by him. MacEntee felt 'it would be preferable that the question of the report should be deferred until the Government is in a position to furnish considered replies to the question as to Government policy on various aspects of the report to which its publication would undoubtedly give rise.'[137] The ability of the government to furnish such a considered and coherent reply was apparently in some doubt.

A more comprehensive statement was issued from Finance on 27 October which outlined the principal cause of the minister's discomfiture:

> Although the report contains some helpful comments on financial matters, it also contains quite a number of statements based on misconceptions and misinterpretations. In particular, the allegation is repeated several times in the report that the Irish banking system (and the Government) are channelling Irish savings into the British Capital market in preference to retaining them in Ireland for domestic investment. It is obviously undesirable that this fallacy should be given a spurious respectability and a renewed currency by publication of the Stacy May Report.[138]

MacEntee also maintained that 'in letters to the Minister for Industry and Commerce in September', he had shown 'that the allegation is unwarranted and is invalid as a basis for policy'. De Valera intervened to request a copy of the letters. Despite a frantic search of the Department of Finance, only one of MacEntee's letters (29 September) was located. The letter in question was a direct response to a draft speech written by Lemass. The first point where MacEntee diverged from Lemass's analysis was on the point of financing the capital programme: 'It is not true that Irish resources, in the form of current savings, are adequate to support the present level of investment in Ireland. The fact that we have had to draw so heavily on external resources for years past is proof of that.'[139] The more substantive point, on the often-heard allegation that the Central Bank wilfully redirected its assets to the British capital market, was also refuted. MacEntee hoped that 'what I have written will lead you to reconsider the subject matter of your speech':

> It seems to me that in any discussion of the problem of capital development in Ireland the matters for emphasis are rather: (1) the need for a great improvement in personal and corporate savings in order to support the present high level of investment; (2) the desirability of raising the proportion of directly productive projects in the national investment programme; and (3) the desirability of continued, voluntary repatriation of external assets for fruitful domestic development. In regard to (3), sudden or large-scale movements are not to be expected. We must, therefore, so arrange our capital programme that we shall be able to sustain it for many years to come.

This explanation failed to persuade the Taoiseach, however, and at a meeting of the cabinet on 14 November 1952 the government decided that the IBEC report should be published.

What is significant about the case outlined by MacEntee in his correspondence with Lemass is its striking resemblance to some of the conclusions made by Whitaker's seminal paper to the Statistical and Social Inquiry Society of Ireland entitled 'Capital formation, saving and economic progress' in May 1956 – a paper in which, according to Fanning, 'one may … detect in embryo many of the ideas that were to be elaborated during the coming months and, particularly, within the pages of *Economic Development*'.[140] That he was prepared to admit the desirability of 'voluntary repatriation of external assets for fruitful domestic development' was also consistent with Whitaker's thesis. Indeed MacEntee sought an altogether different approach to the matter of development, ruffling feathers within the cabinet by explicitly questioning the wisdom of important cornerstones of government policy. Despite paying lip service to the abilities of domestic industry to provide 'the capital to build up the nation' in his 1952 budget speech, he submitted a memorandum in 1954 suggesting that the Control of Manufactures acts should be repealed or modified, a proposal which was opposed by Industry and Commerce:

> In view of the recent dearth of current savings an increase of foreign capital would lead to the more rapid development of our national resources and

thus provide additional employment opportunities and help to reduce emigration. [There would be political resistance to repeal and] the need for [the acts] is a first article of faith with the Federation of Irish Manufacturers which has in recent years unsuccessfully sought to have even tighter restrictions imposed on the entry of foreign capital into Irish industry.[141]

MacEntee was realistic enough to foresee difficulties in attracting such investment, noting that: 'Any investor looking at the state of our economy in 1951, for example, could only conclude that this was a country to keep well away from'; but his heretical probing of such measures at least merited full governmental contemplation. Alas such soul searching on the part of the government was not carried out until some time later.

MacEntee's advice was ignored again when the cabinet decided at a meeting on 12 August 1953 that a fund 'to be entitled the National Development Fund [NDF]' (Aiken's suggestion) and to be administered by the Minister for Finance, should be established as soon as possible.[142] It also decided that 'the initial amount of the fund should be £5,000,000'; 'a far cry from Lemass's figure of £20m or £30m'.[143] Finally, and in keeping with Lemass's objectives, it was determined that the money should be used for 'financing desirable projects of development of a public character'. Finance duly responded to the government's decision after soliciting the views of McElligott, now in the Central Bank.[144] Among an exhaustive list of observations were: 'The initiation of another series of spending projects – particularly if they are of a non-productive character – must necessarily diminish the Government's borrowing potential even for inescapable existing commitments ...' and that 'The programme of State expenditure is already extended to the danger point where an unfavourable movement on external account such as higher imports or a decrease in export prices would seriously affect our capacity to sustain the programme to completion. Such a sustained and comprehensive attack on the proposals proved fruitless, however, as de Valera put his faith in the Tánaiste's assessment, with Aiken's involvement no less important. The National Development Committee was duly established under MacEntee's seal on 3 September, and the National Development Fund Bill became law in March 1954.[145] The election of the second Inter-Party government in June 1954, however, saw Finance renew its efforts to curb public spending. The NDF was a casualty of these efforts. Although it was not terminated officially until March 1957, 'it became dormant from the summer of 1954', and expenditure reached a mere £5.255 million.[146]

MacEntee's resolve to oppose the proposed National Development Fund was dulled significantly at this time as personal matters intruded on his political life. During the late summer of 1953, he had undergone a series of tests for suspected cancer. According to his daughter's memoir, this was a particularly traumatic time for the family; her father had 'made his peace' with the Church 'and, paradoxically, seemed to us to have become much less compulsively devout'.[147] In October, MacEntee wrote to de Valera, informing him that he was to go into a 'Nursery Home' and that he 'should not defer surgical treatment any longer'. He finished the handwritten note by thanking the Taoiseach for 'the kind inquiries which you have been making regarding my condition and the consideration that you have always shown me' and added that he 'had hoped to be able to carry on here until the Dáil adjournment for the Xmas recess' but found it 'physically and indeed mentally impossible'.[148]

By 1955 his recovery was complete and he was back on fighting form, as can be gauged by his reception of a comprehensive memorandum prepared by Lemass for the party committee in April.[149] The party's period of opposition between 1948 and 1951 had come as such a shock that little was done to prepare itself for a return to power. The widely held belief within Fianna Fáil was that its policies had had little to do with its defeat and did not require substantive revision.[150] It was unreceptive to new blood and new ideas as evidenced by Michael B. Yeats's anecdote about a suggestion he made at a committee meeting being dismissed by Frank Aiken with the words 'tá tú óg' (you are young). As Puirséil has dryly noted, Fianna Fáil 'was no party for young men'.[151] But, according to one of Lemass's biographers, the 'lessons of 1948–51 had been learnt. Next time around, Fianna Fáil needed both policies and organisation to win back office. Lemass was given the job of providing the former and, despite internal opposition, increasingly arrogated to himself the latter.'[152] Thus, Lemass's memorandum, not to mention MacEntee's reception of it, was strongly conditioned by that political imperative. Accordingly, MacEntee noted that Lemass's proposals involving increased expenditure 'will be god-sends to Fine Gael'. Lemass's eleven paragraphs dealt specifically with the party's financial policy and contained conclusions that were undoubtedly affected by the 1951–4 experience. His first paragraph dealt with budgetary strategy. He noted that the 'primary aim of Fianna Fáil's policy has been in the past, and should be in the future, to increase the nation's wealth and to improve the living conditions of its people, and it should be stated again that these aims override all other considerations'. MacEntee's note acidly questioned whether these aims should override 'economic stability and political independence'. Lemass's document was equally concerned with the need to increase the nation's productive power, the need to achieve full employment and to reduce to a minimum all other forms of waste of economic resources. In response, MacEntee asked rhetorically 'what is full employment?' and suggested that over-employment was the most fruitful source of waste.

In a clear reference to the *modus operandi* of the Department of Finance, Lemass suggested that 'Fianna Fáil should make clear its belief that the desire to avoid increasing taxation at all costs is likely to be productive of false economies, and would restrict the ability of the Government to use the budget as a flexible instrument of economic policy and, when circumstances require it, as a stabilising influence in the nation's economic life.' The one point that secured MacEntee's wholehearted assent was his contention that 'Fianna Fáil should stress its intention of insisting on the efficient and economical performance of its functions by every branch of public administration.' Lemass, who, it should be said, was always more radical in opposition, believed that Fianna Fáil should declare its intention of revising the whole system of taxation and that the number of separate taxes should be kept as low as possible. In this respect he felt that

the party should indicate its intention of eliminating all taxes which yield insufficient revenue to justify the public inconvenience or higher prices which they
involve, such as the present excise duties on tyres and tubes, matches and mineral waters, and the customs duties on a number of commodities where no element of protection is involved; and to review the large number of stamp duties
and fees and on licences with a view to the removal of those which no longer
serve any other than a revenue-yielding purpose. MacEntee countered by noting
that all such revenue streams were easy to collect and queried what would
replace the lost revenue. Lemass believed that Fianna Fáil should announce its
acceptance in principle of the desirability of introducing a Pay-as-You-Earn system of taxation of personal incomes. MacEntee opposed this recommendation on
the grounds that a PAYE system was 'inflationary and discouraging'. The final
point made by the Lemass memorandum concentrated again on budgetary strategy. He wanted the party to 'accept that, over a reasonable period, the budget
must be balanced but not that it is necessary to adjust tax rates in every year to
meet fluctuations of revenue and expenditure'. MacEntee's response was again
that of the sound and prudent financier dedicated to fiscal rectitude. He noted
that the budget had never been balanced 'regardless of the consequences' but that
'unless the consequences are taken into account and faced up to the budget will
never be balanced.'

By then, Lemass had made his own doubts about the viability of the protectionist structure public, thus countering Finance's censure made in the July memorandum. In November 1953, not long after the government's decision to proceed with the National Development Plan, he warned that it intended to conduct
a review of industrial efficiency and the current effects of protective tariffs.[153]
And in a speech in January 1954, which would have been more characteristic of
his ministerial colleague in Finance, he argued that 'a far more extensive development of Irish industry can be secured by means of private business enterprise
than by any system of socialised industry.'[154] The task of fully challenging this
system would have to be deferred, however, as two by-election defeats in March
1954 made a general election unavoidable; a consequence which afforded the
electorate the opportunity of passing judgement on the economic record of the
government.

Unfortunately for MacEntee, the 1952 budget would play a dominant role in
the election campaign. The effects of the budget were not felt immediately, however, and Fianna Fáil won two out of the three by-elections in 1952. But a momen-
tum of distrust gathered against the government in 1953 and 1954. De Valera, in
his last radio broadcast before the election, attempted to stem this unwelcome tide
by expressing it in terms that would be appreciated by his audience:

Our aim in the 1952 budget was the simple one of making ends meet – of
balancing current expenditure by current revenue, as any prudent person
would do in his own private affairs. We had to bridge the immense gap of
£15 million by which estimated revenue was short of estimated expenditure. It has been said that the Government instructed the banks to restrict

credit. This, too, is without foundation. There is no evidence that the banks did restrict credit, but, if they did, it was certainly not on Government instructions. On the contrary, I myself made it clear on many occasions in Dáil Éireann and outside it, and so did the Tánaiste and other members of the Government, that we did not desire any restriction of credit ... The first achievements to our credit as a Government have been that we have faced up to these two serious problems of an unbalanced current budget and an unprecedented and alarming deficit in the balance of payments, and solved these problems.[155]

The verdict delivered by the electorate resulted in defeat for Fianna Fáil and served to further discredit MacEntee.[156]

Overall, the fiscal policy of the government has been depicted as 'a battle between MacEntee and Lemass which MacEntee won'.[157] As well as being a wholly reductive thesis, it is also a fatally flawed one in other respects. As the above analysis demonstrates, MacEntee, far from winning, was mollified to a degree by acute taxation increases in the face of the government's renewed commitment to extensive capital expenditure. Having been gratified somewhat by the amelioration of the worst effects of the balance of payments deficit, he was again defeated at cabinet by its announcement of further commitments under the National Development Plan and its willingness to entertain trade union demands for higher wages; evidence that baldly contradicts the notion that MacEntee was in any way victorious or that he was successful in sidelining Lemass. Ultimately the Fianna Fáil government of 1951–4 was handcuffed by the trade position it had inherited on coming to office. Its somewhat incoherent approach to relieving this problem, as well as its impatient desire to fulfil the programme upon which it had been elected, resulted in apparent obfuscation of its priorities as perceived by the electorate and contemporary commentators alike. This confusion has extended to the historical analysis which has typically preferred to depict it as evidence of the ongoing conflict between Finance and Industry and Commerce. To an extent this is true, but such analysis does not admit the genuine points of convergence between the departments, as well as the ministers' respective attitudes. Likewise, it tends to overlook the enduring validity of the Finance argument, an argument that was to have a much greater potency when advocated in *Economic Development* in 1958. For MacEntee, the term was an unmitigated failure and although he was relatively successful in achieving his department's aims, it came with the costly price of near political ruin and resulted in him being held in perpetual disrepute by some elements within his party.

NOTES

1.   Quoted in an address by G.A. Duncan to the Dublin Chamber of Commerce, 24 May 1950; NLI Brennan Papers Ms. 26,428.
2.   J.A. Murphy, '"Put them out!": Parties and elections, 1948–69', in J.J. Lee, *Ireland 1945–70* (Dublin, 1979). For a more recent survey of post-war electoral politics, see N. Puirséil, 'Political and party competition in post-war Ireland', in B. Girvin and G. Murphy (eds), *The Lemass Era: Politics and Society in the Ireland of Seán Lemass* (Dublin, 2005).
3.   P. Lynch, 'The Irish economy since the war', in K.B. Nowlan and T.D. Williams (eds), *Ireland in the War Years and After* (Dublin, 1969).

4. K.A. Kennedy and B.R. Dowling, *Economic Growth in Ireland: The Experience since 1947* (Dublin, 1975), p.201.
5. Ibid., p.203.
6. Longford and O'Neill, *Éamon de Valera* (Dublin, 1970), p.439. MacEntee accepted the interpretation of Longford and O'Neill that he was a consciously conservative choice in 1951. This is apparent from later correspondence with Brian Farrell. He also declared himself a monetarist in an interview with the *Irish Independent* on 13 December 1979.
7. See, for instance, Bew and Patterson, *Seán Lemass and the Making of Modern Ireland* and G. Murphy, 'The politics of economic realignment: Ireland 1948–64' (unpublished PhD thesis, Dublin City University, 1996) for examples of this interpretation.
8. Bew and Patterson, *Seán Lemass and the Making of Modern Ireland*, p.62.
9. Lee, *Ireland 1912–1985: Politics and Society*, p.321.
10. Horgan, *Seán Lemass*, p.150.
11. For a full analysis of the 1955–6 crisis see Kennedy and Dowling, *Economic Growth in Ireland* and P. Honohan and C. Ó Gráda, 'The Irish macroeconomic crisis of 1955–56: how much was due to monetary policy?', *Irish Economic and Social History*, vol. XXV (1998).
12. Lynch, 'The Irish economy since the war'.
13. 'Indeed the rise in the borrowing requirement between 1950 and 1951 was probably more expansionary than in a normal year because of the small proportion financed by domestic savings: roughly £34 million was raised by use of Marshall Aid funds and sales of foreign reserves held in departmental funds. Bank credit also expanded rapidly … The rise in 1950 was 15.2 per cent and in 1951 12.4 per cent.' Kennedy and Dowling, *Economic Growth in Ireland*, p.207. Borrowing increased from £2.8 million in 1945 to a peak of £49.3 million in 1951. In 1952 it was cut to £36.1 million. See O'Hagan, 'An analysis of the relative size of the government sector'.
14. Quoted in Bew and Patterson, *Seán Lemass,* pp.61–2.
15. See R. Fanning, 'The genesis of economic development', in J.F. McCarthy, *Planning Ireland's Future: The Legacy of T.K. Whitaker* (Dublin, 1990).
16. See *Irish Times*, 5 November 1951.
17. Ibid., 16 May 1951.
18. *Irish Press*, 5 June 1951.
19. In his budget speech in 1951 McGilligan also highlighted the potential dangers of continuing inflation and balance of payments difficulties: See *Dáil debates*, vol. 125, 2 May 1951.
20. Moynihan, *Currency and Banking*, p.374: 'The draft Report was submitted to the Board in instalments over a period from May to September 1951 and the final text was approved and sealed on 25th September. The rules of Cabinet procedure required that it should be presented to the Government by the Minister before being presented to each House of the Oireachtas in compliance with section 36 of the Currency Act, 1927. Following a practice designed to save time, the Minister placed the Report before the Government in printed copies marked "Proof". Later there was a suggestion that, having received the document in proof copies, the Government had an opportunity of requesting the Central Bank to alter it and therefore had a share in the responsibility for its contents.'
21. *Irish Times*, 24 October 1951.
22. Moynihan, *Currency and Central Banking*, pp.377–8
23. Ibid.
24. D. McCullagh, *A Makeshift Majority: The First Inter-Party Government, 1948–51* (Dublin, 1998), p.241.
25. Ibid.
26. B. Whelan, 'Ireland and the Marshall Plan', in *Irish Economic and Social History*, vol. XIX (1992), pp.49–70.
27. Ibid.
28. J.W. O'Hagan, 'An analysis of the relative size of the government sector'.
29. Whelan, 'Ireland and the Marshall Plan'.
30. NAI S13831C, Finance memorandum to the government, June 1951.
31. B. Whelan, *Ireland and the Marshall Plan, 1947–57* (Dublin, 2000), p.277.
32. Lemass had strongly attacked the economic policies of the inter-party government. Responding to the 1951 budget (which Fianna Fáil inherited and implemented) on behalf of his party, he took particular exception to the burden of debt produced and blamed them directly for the balance of payments problem: 'Whatever expansion there has been in the consumption of luxury goods, which added unnecessarily to our imports, was deliberately encouraged by the government's policy but, over and above any such expansion, the wasting of assets and resources accumulated by good management in the past is to be attributed mainly to the reckless and thriftless policy which the Government pursued during that period.' See *Dáil debates*, vol. 125, col. 1914, 2 May 1951.

33. N. Browne, *Against the Tide* (Dublin, 1986), p.211.
34. McGilligan had also anticipated the likely necessity of budgetary correctives if the problem did not improve. In his budget statement on 2 May 1951, he warned that: 'The present position on external account is by no means satisfactory and if it continues to develop unfavourably the application of corrective measures will be called for.' *Dáil debates*, vol. 125, col. 1883, 2 May 1951.
35. *Irish Times*, 30 October 1951.
36. *Dáil debates*, vol. 127, cols 299–300, 7 November 1951.
37. Ibid., cols 304–5.
38. Ibid., cols 306–7.
39. Ibid., col. 307.
40. Ibid., col. 316.
41. Ibid.
42. Ibid., col. 310.
43. *Dáil debates*, vol. 27, col. 723, 14 November 1951.
44. Ibid., col. 738.
45. Moynihan, *Speeches and Statements*, p.549.
46. NLI Brennan Papers, Ms. 26, 240. Draft memorandum by Brennan for the government, 9 November 1951. It is not clear whether this document was sent, but it is noteworthy for the views expressed by the author.
47. Ibid.
48. Ibid.
49. Fanning, *Finance*, p.470.
50. Ibid.
51. *Irish Times*, 2 November 1951.
52. Fanning, *Finance*, p.473.
53. NLI Brennan Papers Ms 26, 428. Finance memorandum, 16 October 1951; see also NAI F200/18/51.
54. *Irish Times*, 9 November 1951.
55. *Dáil debates*, vol. 127, col. 310, 7 November 1951; *Irish Times*, 8 November 1951.
56. I have been unable to determine whether there was any internal cabinet dissent relating to the publication of the white paper. That the government had the Central Bank report for over a month before publishing its own white paper suggests that it had ample time to consider its position before both documents were released for public consumption.
57. Fanning, *Finance*, p.483.
58. NAI F200/18/51, draft Finance memo, 16 October 1951.
59. Ibid., McCarthy to Whitaker, 24 September 1951.
60. One well placed authority has described Murray as the official in the Department of Industry and Commerce who habitually displayed independence and moral courage. 'Tom did not hesitate in conference or committee to express, sometimes forcibly, dissent from the line taken by his Secretary [Leydon] – a practice rare enough among senior civil servants who still retain hopes of advancement.' See Roche, 'John Leydon', *Administration*, 27, 3 (1979).
61. Ibid., Murray to Whitaker, 21 September 1951.
62. *Administration*, vol. 1 (1953–4), pp.60–8.
63. Interview with Dr T.K. Whitaker, 21 July 2003. See also McElligott to MacEntee, 11 March 1954, UCDA P67/224; and Whitaker to MacEntee, 2 June 1954, UCDA P67/227.
64. McKee, 'From precepts to praxis', pp.325–7.
65. Interview with Dr T.K. Whitaker, 21 July 2003.
66. J.J. Lee, 'Economic development in historical perspective', in McCarthy (ed.), *Planning Ireland's Future*.
67. B.M. Walsh, review of *The Irish Department of Finance 1922–58* by R. Fanning in *Irish Economic and Social History*, vol. VII (1980), pp.121–4.
68. NLI Brennan Papers, Ms. 26, 428.
69. Ibid.
70. Ibid.
71. Ibid. Finance memo on food subsidies, 31 December 1951.
72. NLI Brennan Papers Ms. 26, 428. Interdepartmental committee on food subsidies, 12 February 1952. The committee was comprised of J. Williams from Industry and Commerce (chairman), J.C. Nagle (Agriculture), T.K. Whitaker (Finance), P.J. Keady (Social Welfare), T.J. Barrington (Local Government) and Dr M.D. McCarthy from the CSO.
73. Ibid. Summary of observations of Department of Finance on proposals for reform of social welfare schemes [28 December 1951], 5 January 1952.
74. Ibid. Finance memorandum to the government on the proposals of the Minister for Industry and Commerce regarding the tourist industry, 5 January 1952.

75. UCDA P67/218, Butler to MacEntee; letter marked 'Top secret and Personal', 14 December 1951.
76. C.R. Schenk, *Britain and the Sterling Area: From Devaluation to Convertibility in the 1950s* (London and New York, 1994), p.70.
77. Ibid., pp.70–1.
78. UCDA P67/218.
79. Ibid.
80. Quoted in Fanning, *Finance*, p.474.
81. *Irish Times*, 18 February 1952.
82. NAI DT S14192 B.
83. McKee, 'From precepts to praxis', p.330.
84. NAI F 17/1/52.
85. Fanning, *Finance*, p.479.
86. *Irish Times*, 20 February 1952.
87. NAI DT S13831 C.
88. *Dáil debates*, vol. 129, col. 1954, 12 March 1952.
89. Fanning, *Finance*, p.481.
90. NAI DT S15253, Budget 1952: preview, finance memorandum, 31 January 1952.
91. For a similar view on the budget see H. Lundgaard Andersen, 'The 1952 Financial Budget: Rhetoric and Reality' (unpublished MA thesis, UCD, 1996).
92. *Dáil debates*, vol. 130, col. 1113, Budget statement, 2 April 1952.
93. Ibid., col. 1117.
94. Ibid., col. 1121.
95. T.K. Whitaker, *Interests* (Dublin, 1983), p.86.
96. There were two budgets in the year 1939–40, one introduced by MacEntee and a supplementary budget by his successor Seán T. Ó Ceallaigh.
97. *Dáil debates*, vol. 130, col. 1122, 2 April 1952.
98. A supplementary estimate was required to meet the additional costs arising under the social welfare legislation of 1952 of £4,754,810.
99. *Dáil debates*, vol. 130, col. 1136.
100. He elaborated on this point in his budget statement of 1953 which he prefaced with a staunch defence of the 1952 budget: '[Current expenditure] was fixed for us by the commitments we had inherited and by the obligation of fulfilling the pledges to expand and improve the social services which had been given by all parties during the [1951] general election.' See *Dáil debates*, vol. 138, col. 1186, 6 May 1953.
101. *Dáil debates*, vol. 130, col. 1136, 2 April 1952.
102. Ibid., col. 1138.
103. Old age pensions were augmented by 1/6 a week and the weekly payment for third and subsequent children under the children's allowances scheme was increased to 4/–.
104. *Dail debates*, vol. 130, cols 1163–4.
105. Andersen, 'The 1952 financial budget'.
106. Budget statement, 2 April 1952, cols 1154–5.
107. Ibid., col. 1155.
108. *Irish Times*, 2 April 1952. An editorial on the day of the budget suggested that Fine Gael was not unanimous in its opposition to the anticipated reductions in the food subsidies.
109. *Dáil debates*, vol. 130, cols 1158–60.
110. Ibid., col. 1162.
111. Andersen, 'The 1952 financial budget'.
112. Lee, *Ireland, 1912–85*, p.325.
113. Quoted in Fanning, *Finance*, p.482.
114. Horgan, *Seán Lemass*, p.158.
115. Ibid.
116. The electoral implications of the budget were not immediately apparent. Fianna Fáil won two out of three by-elections in June 1952. See Appendix A.
117. UCDA P67/436.
118. Ibid.
119. *Irish Times*, 3 April 1952.
120. See Kennedy and Dowling, *Economic Growth*, pp.214–18.
121. Whitaker, *Interests*, p.89.
122. S. Baker, 'Nationalist ideology and the industrial policy of Fianna Fáil: the evidence of the *Irish Press* (1955–1972)', *Irish Political Studies*, vol. 1 (1986).
123. Andersen, 'The 1952 financial budget'. Interview with Dr T.K. Whitaker.

124. NAI F 17/1/52, Appendix A: discussions on sterling area position, 18 and 19 February 1952.
125. Whitaker, *Interests*, p.87.
126. NAI F121/6/52. Finance was also heartened by the report on the internal financial situation in member countries of the OEEC published in July. Whitaker endorsed publication of the report and MacEntee endeavoured to have it circulated to cabinet. Whitaker informed Biggar in External Affairs on 24 July that: 'The principles enunciated in the report are not merely unexceptionable: they provide the only basis for rational and orderly progress.'
127. NAI F29/1/52, McElligott to Leydon, 8 May 1952.
128. Leydon to McElligott, 24 May 1952 in ibid.
129. Notes by Whitaker on ibid.
130. Leydon to McElligott, 24 May 1952.
131. Draft reply, prepared by Whitaker, 29 May 1952.
132. NAI F13/5/52, Finance review of the exchequer position prepared by Whitaker, November 1952.
133. *Dáil debates*, vol. 138, col. 1192, 6 May 1953.
134. Ibid., col. 1181.
135. NAI F13/5/52, Finance memorandum on position of the exchequer, November 1952. The committee sought by Finance was eventually set up in 1956 under MacEntee's successor, Gerard Sweetman, as the Capital Advisory Committee.
136. Indeed a more general appraisal of the role of the public servant was underway among policymakers and the intelligentsia. The best expression of this can be found in Patrick Lynch's challenge to the civil service to 'be organised so that its officers not merely are models of probity and integrity, but possess also an enlightened approach to problems, flexibility of mind and an awareness of contemporary trends in informed thought ...' See P. Lynch 'The economist and public policy' first published in *Studies*, Autumn 1953; republished in B. Chubb and P. Lynch (eds), *Economic Development and Planning* (Dublin, 1969), pp.5–24.
137. D/T S15389; Industrial potentialities of Ireland: report by the IBEC technical services corporation (The 'Stacey May' report).
138. Finance to Industry and Commerce, 27 October 1952 in ibid.
139. Ibid., MacEntee to Lemass, 29 September 1952.
140. Fanning, *Finance*, p.503.
141. UCDA P67/223, 1954. There is also evidence that Lemass had had doubts about the merits of these acts. These doubts were expressed as early as 1942 in a lengthy memorandum prepared by Ferguson following a directive from Lemass: 'While it is not possible to anticipate the changes in the post war period to the extent of being able to forecast what changes, either in the direction of tightening up or loosening the terms of these Acts in respect of foreign participation in industry ... it is very necessary to reconsider, as a matter of general policy, the principles contained in these Acts.' Quoted in Horgan, *Seán Lemass*, p.112.
142. Minutes of cabinet committee, 12 August 1953.
143. Daly, *The Buffer State*, p.416.
144. UCDA P67/221, National Development Fund, August 1953. Finance memo on the Cabinet Committee on the provision of employment, 25 August 1953. The original date on this memo is 18 August but is crossed out and replaced with 25. The later date may be due to MacEntee receiving the views of McElligott at the Central Bank. McElligott to MacEntee, 22 August: 'My dear Minister, I promised to let you see in advance a copy of what we proposed to say.'
145. Fanning, *Finance*, p.498.
146. Daly, *The Buffer State*, p.420.
147. Cruise O'Brien, *The Same Age as the State*, p.206.
148. UCDA P67/222, MacEntee to de Valera, 29 October 1953.
149. UCDA P67/468, Memorandum by Lemass for the party committee with annotations by MacEntee, 15 April 1955; see also Horgan, *Seán Lemass*, pp.163–4.
150. Puirséil, 'Political and party competition in post-war Ireland', p.14.
151. Ibid.
152. Horgan, *Seán Lemass*, p.159.
153. Ibid.
154. Speech at Kilkenny, 20 January 1954, quoted in ibid.
155. Election broadcast, 14 May 1954 in Moynihan, *Speeches and Statements*, pp.566–70.
156. See Appendix A.
157. Horgan, *Seán Lemass*, p.158.

7

The Lemass Dispensation

Fianna Fáil swept to power with an overall majority in the general election of 1957, winning more seats (seventy-eight) than the party had ever done before.[1] De Valera put together his last cabinet, consisting of several new ministers and several of the old faithful.[2] MacEntee was among a group of party elders that had been in ministerial office since 1932. As well as MacEntee, this core group comprised Lemass, Ryan and Aiken. As for some of the others, Lee rather mordantly observes, 'Death, disability and calculation were at last beginning to take their toll.'[3] The fortitude of the former group had an almost Darwinian aspect to it. It would not be an overstatement to say that it was this group that had exerted most influence on the shape of public policy in all the years of government occupied by Fianna Fáil. That men of lesser ability were simply 'eased out', as Gerry Boland was in 1957, suggests that their continuing presence had less to do with familiarity and all to do with performance and dependability. That Ryan and MacEntee ultimately 'swapped places' in the new cabinet – Ryan taking up Finance while MacEntee moved to Health (Social Welfare was later added to his responsibilities) – also suggests an effortless interchangeability within this group, despite individual proclivities and political sensibilities.

MacEntee's move from Finance was deemed necessary given the political fallout of his previous tenure there and the fact that he had become synonymous with the stringent budgetary measures imposed during that period. A similar fate also befell his immediate successor in Finance, Gerard Sweetman, whose budgetary policy met with considerable hostility from within Fine Gael. MacEntee's move should not, however, be read as a determination on behalf of the government to change financial policy. In fact the economic circumstances that greeted the party in 1957 were much worse than had prevailed in 1951 and ultimately encouraged a change of emphasis in the management of economic activity, coming, not from the new government, but from the civil service. In 1956 the second Inter-Party administration had introduced three deflationary budgets designed to redress the balance of payments deficit, a crisis 'that prompted a fundamental shift in economic policy'.[4] The new government's instinctive response to this crisis was conditioned largely by the Department of Finance's reaction – itself a response to the setting up of the Capital Investment Advisory Committee in late 1956[5] – which was to redirect public expenditure from ostensibly 'social' to 'productive' investment. Health expenditure fell into the 'social' category and therefore was not a priority for the government.[6]

If MacEntee's most immediate concern in his new portfolio was the excessive cost to the exchequer of the services under his control, the abiding themes of his second stint in the Custom House were twofold: firstly, the open hostility between his department and the Irish Medical Association and secondly, the importunate calls for the existing health services to be streamlined, with cost and efficiency being the dominant imperatives. The first issue had its roots in the enduring enmity between Fianna Fáil and the doctors, which had first manifested during the mid-1940s with Dr Conn Ward's initiatives for reform. The second matter became a politically sensitive area for the government following the 1961 general election campaign, when the opposition parties focused on health as their principal desideratum. Faced by a rigorous opposition, which included MacEntee's predecessor in Health, T.F. O'Higgins of Fine Gael and Dr Noël Browne, again an independent,[7] the minister decided in November 1961 to appoint a select committee of the Dáil to examine the health services. That the committee failed to produce a substantive report after nearly three years in session only contributed to the political pressure on the minister and may have been a factor in his retirement from the cabinet before the general election in 1965.

One lasting testament to MacEntee's legacy in Health was his Health (Fluoridation of Water Supplies) Act, 1960. This measure met with stringent opposition both inside and outside the Dáil because, it was argued, it violated 'personal bodily integrity' and involved 'mass medication'. The minister's declared distaste of state interference was now set aside under the apprehension that the fluoridation of public water supplies was the right and responsible thing to do. That MacEntee sternly resisted opposition to the act should be regarded as symptomatic of his complex political outlook. Generally, this amounted to a staunch defence of *laissez faire* government but there were particular issues which MacEntee sponsored that illustrated how far he believed the state could go in regulating society. Fluoridation was a measure which was conferred benevolently on the community in the general interests of public health and hygiene. Before considering these developments however, it is important to acknowledge the economic imperatives of the government and how they affected MacEntee's department.

ECONOMIC DEVELOPMENT

It is reasonable to conclude that the allocation of the new ministries in 1957 reflected Lemass's stature as leader-in-waiting. MacEntee returned to the Custom House to take up the Health brief, while James Ryan was given the apparent object of MacEntee's desire, Finance. This was not surprising as the Tánaiste was closer to Ryan, both politically and personally, than he was to the new Minister for Health.[8] It would be wrong, however, to see it as a portent of what has been described as the '*demarche* into Keynesian expansionism',[9] or to suggest that that direction would not have been possible with MacEntee at the helm in Finance. Lee has rationalised it in this very way, proposing that de Valera would have made the change without the presumed pressure from Lemass because he 'would have wanted no repeat of the electoral consequences of a MacEntee performance of 1951–4 vintage'.[10] If this was part of the Taoiseach's calculations, it owed more to political expediency than to any lack of faith in MacEntee. As we have seen, the 'MacEntee performance of 1951–4 vintage' was conditioned by many factors, not least the need to maintain consensus within the cabinet. Lee is not the only historian of twentieth-century Ireland to form this conclusion. Fanning, in his survey of the genesis of *Economic Development*, argues that de Valera's decision not to reappoint MacEntee to Finance was a 'straw in the wind of change': 'This erosion of the old orthodoxies was marked by the fact, recorded in his diary on 8 March by a disappointed MacEntee, that de Valera "had seen Ryan and Aiken before me. He was apparently committed to both".'[11] This quotation only reveals half the story. MacEntee had in fact suggested Lemass for Finance, telling de Valera that he 'was not anxious to be Minister for Finance'. When the Taoiseach informed him that he had already offered Ryan Finance and Agriculture and that he had earmarked Local Government for MacEntee, the latter responded by saying the only ministry he would consider was External Affairs. De Valera wanted Frank Aiken for External Affairs and 'pressed [MacEntee] gently to take Local Government'. MacEntee resorted to brinkmanship by telling the Taoiseach he was not interested and would prefer to stay out of the cabinet.[12] Using all his persuasion de Valera eventually got MacEntee to think it over and in the meantime came up with the compromise of Health.

The speculation that de Valera's decision to overlook MacEntee for Finance was a 'straw in the wind of change' is also inconsistent with some pertinent evidence. For one thing, MacEntee's performance of 1951–4 was heavily influenced and supported by Finance officials, most notably the assistant secretary, T.K. Whitaker, author of the seminal white paper, *Economic Development*, and the official regarded as the prime instigator of the new direction. Moreover, the prescription advocated by Whitaker in *Economic Development* was not altogether unlike the advice he had proffered MacEntee during the 1951–4 period. A salient difference, however, was that Finance now played the role of principal director of policy. Having, for years, with varying degrees of enthusiasm, implemented initiatives that routinely emanated from the Taoiseach's department or more often from the Department of Industry and Commerce, Whitaker minuted Ryan in May 1957 in order to seek a directional, as well as an intellectual, shift: 'It is ... desirable that this department should do some independent thinking and not simply wait for Industry and Commerce or the I.D.A. to produce ideas.' Whitaker felt that the 'central position of the Department of Finance gives us a special responsibility for studying how economic progress can be promoted'.[13] Furthermore, ideological obstacles to implementing a fresh departure, firmly entrenched heretofore and politically impossible to dismantle, now largely disappeared as the Fianna Fáil leadership finally accepted that the protectionist model could not guarantee long-term economic growth.[14] That MacEntee would have resisted the course advocated by Whitaker discounts not only the mutual respect each had for the other, but presupposes that MacEntee was incapable of looking beyond the latest economic crisis. In fact MacEntee had already advocated a similar doctrine in response to the preferred remedial devices of Industry and Commerce at the height of the 1951–4 cabinet deliberations on future economic policy. He had maintained that 'export possibilities [we]re considerable but, because of indiscriminate and excessive protection, Irish industries, with

some notable exceptions, [we]re neither willing nor able to exploit the possibilities.' 'There is a dim future for Irish industry,' the memorandum proclaimed, 'if
its prospects are mainly or exclusively dependent on an increase in population in
the Twenty-Six Counties.'[15] A further memorandum for the government in
October 1951 on Financial Policy, prepared by Whitaker and approved and presented to the cabinet by MacEntee, had emphasised 'the need for a better choice
of State capital projects or a better balance between productive works and those
of mainly social benefit'.[16]

Economic rehabilitation was not altogether apparent in 1957, however, and
the new government was immediately forced to effect economies in the administration of the public services. One area where the government targeted potential economies was in the health services, the cost of which had risen sharply
in large part due to the generous provisions of the Health (Financial
Provisions) Act, 1947 which undertook to increase the exchequer's share of the
cost of the health services to 50 per cent of the total.[17] In his budget speech of
1957, Ryan told the Dáil that: 'At a time when national production is not
increasing and when ordinary revenue is not keeping pace with current expenditure the rising deficits in voluntary hospitals and the growing cost of health
services are a cause of concern.'[18] Commitments under the hospital-building
programme and the cost of specialist services placed greater demands on
health expenditure to which MacEntee responded by raising hospital charges
for specialist consultations and x-rays for the middle-income group at outpa-
tient clinics.[19] He defended this policy in the Dáil, contending that it was 'only
right, just, fair and equitable that those who could afford to contribute something should do so'.[20] This of course was very much in keeping with
MacEntee's general philosophy; a philosophy which anticipated John F.
Kennedy's famous dictum regarding the relationship between individual and
state. Moreover, when introducing the Health and Mental Treatment Bill in the
Dáil shortly after taking office, the purpose of which was to 'permit certain
moderate increases' in the charges fixed for institutional (hospital) services,
MacEntee's listeners could have been forgiven for thinking that, psychologi-
cally at least, he remained the Minister for Finance:

> It is imperative in our present circumstances that all available savings
> should be used for productive capital investments; and any diversion of
> such savings to meet expenditure which should properly be met out of
> revenue means deferring much-needed capital projects and postponing
> still further the expansion in production which is fundamental to our
> prosperity.[21]

The minister's emphasis on productive capital expenditure was entirely compatible with the government's adopted *modus operandi* as outlined in the introduction to Whitaker's report:

> There is no conflict between what are termed 'socially desirable' and 'eco-
> nomic objectives'. 'Socially desirable' objectives will not be permanently
> realised merely by increasing 'social' investment. The erection of houses,

schools and hospitals – socially desirable in themselves – will, of course, provide employment but the employment ceases once the period of production is over and the unemployed man is left with facilities which, if he remains unemployed, will contribute but little to his standard of living.[22]

Consequently, Ryan urged his cabinet colleagues to switch 'capital outlay from non-productive to strictly productive purposes'.[23] Continuity between Ryan's approach and that of MacEntee (as Minister for Finance) was also evident in the removal of food subsidies in the 1957 budget, and in their shared preference for low taxation levels; a desire which was revealed in December by the Minister for Finance in a series of personal letters to his colleagues that exhorted them to 'economise in every possible way, including costs of administration', in order to 'reduce the heavy burden of taxation' which was 'the greatest fillip that could be given to economic development and progress'.[24] Even Lemass was forced to concur that the new approach was the responsible one, regardless of the unpopularity it was likely to engender. He told the Dáil during the budget debate of 1957 that:

> It would be far too much to expect that we can get out of this very serious situation without having some troubles to deal with. That is what Governments are for, but it will be well worth while if at the end of it all we can feel we have put the freedom of the country upon an economic foundation which is sound and have the certain prospect that employment will increase and that emigration will begin to decrease, the prospect that the living standards of our people will be made more secure than they have been in the recent past.[25]

Furthermore, during the budget debate in 1960, Lemass, now Taoiseach, implied that any improvements in Health and Social Welfare were contingent upon increases in productivity across the economy: 'The aim of Government policy – and I want to say this without any possibility of ambiguity whatsoever – is to keep on expanding our social welfare services in accord with increases in national income *as they are brought about* [emphasis added].'[26]

Thus the government's immediate priorities, and indeed the prerogative that would be afforded primacy throughout the life of the *First Programme for Economic Expansion*, relegated health and social welfare spending to the more pressing needs of satisfying the government's ability to finance productive capital investment, as far as possible, out of its own resources. Between 1957 and 1958, current expenditure on health fell by 8.1 per cent.[27] Hospital building slowed due in part to the fact that the assets of the Hospitals' Trust Fund, which was the main source of finance for capital purposes, had been exhausted by 1957.[28] Although MacEntee broadly agreed with the government approach, he was unwilling to see Health completely neglected. In fact, when *Economic Development* was circulated by Ryan to cabinet ministers for their observations in the summer of 1958, MacEntee, far from criticising the emphasis on long-term productive investment, sought broader definition of this term to include the services under his control. His observations are worth quoting as they demonstrably reveal his ambitions for Health:

1. The impression received from the study is that social services are regarded as constituting a brake on economic progress and are to be tolerated only because they represent a *fait accompli*, and that any significant improvement in them should not be permitted on the ground that it might retard material prosperity. The Minister for Health cannot support this thesis.

2. Expenditure on health services is not non-productive. Expenditure on the prevention and treatment of illness will avoid and minimise losses to the economy.

3. Emigration is not entirely due to monetary inducements of living abroad. In the case of Britain particularly, the comprehensive social services are a very important factor. While it will probably never be possible to have similar services here, it should be a long-term aim to ensure that the services supplied here will be such as to assure workers that old age, illness or unemployment will not create undue hardship for themselves or their dependants. *Accordingly, whilst it is realised that there can be no considerable extension of these services at present, the acceptance of the aims outlined in this study by the government should not imply a bar to the further extension and improvement of the social services as economic circumstances permit* [my emphasis].

4. Though the non-capital expenditure on the health services increased substantially in post-war years, it only represented 2.8% of the gross national product in 1957. The figure is expected to remain fairly static and may even tend to fall in the future. Accordingly, modest extensions and improvements of the services could be carried out without any great strain on the economy, provided the national income continues to increase. This is borne out by the British experience.

5. There is at present about [£]1½ million available each year for capital purposes from the Hospitals Sweepstakes Fund, which merely enables a slow rate of progress on hospital construction and improvement. The Minister does not propose that the State should subvent the fund to accelerate the rate of hospital construction, but if the economy improved appreciably the matter might be reopened.[29]

Thus the Minister for Health accepted the premise of the *First Programme* that social services could only be financed once productivity and national income levels increased, but he was keen to have this principle explicitly approved by the cabinet. FitzGerald has noted that the pattern of public investment during the life of the *First Programme* did not depart significantly from the principles laid down in the white paper.[30] Kennedy has also shown that 'social expenditure fell to 13.7 per cent of GNP in 1962 compared with 14.8 per cent in 1952'.[31] The social share of public spending fell from 45.1 per cent in 1957 to 41.8 per cent in 1961.[32] This left the minister responsible for the health and welfare services in an invidious position, as the clamour for more efficiency and greater accessibility to the services grew; and to make matters worse, was forthcoming not only from the opposition, vigorously supplied by T.F. O'Higgins and Noël

Browne, but also from MacEntee's fellow delegates at successive party árd fheiseanna.

For his part, MacEntee remained obedient to the thrust of government policy and continued to defend the legislative embodiment of that approach: the Health Act of 1953. That the 1953 act had a singularly prolonged gestation, having such a protracted and troubled passage from its original form, contained in the proposals advanced by Deeny's committee in 1945, to its eventual operation by Ryan in May 1954, calcified Fianna Fáil's defence of it and made the party's resistance to change all the more strident. Accordingly, it was a full five years before the government decided to consider the prospect of change in the health services. To complicate matters further for the minister, there was a recurrence of the government's difficulties with the medical profession; difficulties that engaged the minister's attention for his first term in the Health portfolio and that cast a rather ominous shadow over the general business of the department. As ever, MacEntee proved a most formidable opponent, and the Irish Medical Association was forced into an accommodation with the Department of Health in 1964 that ultimately gratified and vindicated his position.

THE IMA

Fianna Fáil's Health Act of 1953, which had its genesis in the departmental committee established by MacEntee in 1945, was strongly resisted by the medical fraternity. This was, perhaps, not surprising, given that the provisions of the act threatened the status and income of the profession. The party's defeat in the 1954 general election meant that implementation of the act was left to T.F. O'Higgins, Minister for Health in the second Inter-Party government. The Irish Medical Association, which represented 90 per cent of the country's doctors, constituted the vanguard of opposition to the state's increasing role in the organisation of the health services. O'Higgins's tenure, however, paved the way for a *rapprochement* between the department and the IMA, through his friendly relations with some of the younger members of the association.[33] Accordingly, he secured its agreement to the introduction of a revised mother and child scheme for the lower income group as part of the 1953 act. The thaw in relations between the profession and the department did not last very long. A recrudescence of the conflict coincided with Fianna Fáil's return to power in 1957.

Conflict first emerged over the wording of certain contractual obligations of doctors taking up local authority health posts. One such obligation gave the minister authority to inspect a patient's medical records in cases where a complaint was made against a dispensary doctor. The IMA was also dissatisfied about the pay and conditions of doctors employed by local health authorities, but the association's requests for consultation with the minister were met with MacEntee's refusal to discuss such issues because it was not registered as an excepted body under the terms of the 1941 Trade Union Act.[34] Medical staffs in local authority hospitals were, according to the minister, officers of the particular local authority concerned and, consequently, any negotiations had to be with the local authority rather than with him. The association responded by inserting an 'Important

Notice' in the *Journal of the Irish Medical Association* and in the *British Medical Journal*, which advised doctors who contemplated applying for local authority posts not to do so without previously consulting the secretary of the IMA. This ensured that all doctors would be informed of the official view of the association on the particular duty to which the association took exception.[35] The duty as stated was regarded by the association as incompatible with the basic principles of medical secrecy.[36] In turn, the minister and his department considered the 'Important Notice' as a proscription of the posts that would cause a serious impediment to the successful development of the health services. They insisted that its publication should cease as a prerequisite to any discussions on matters at issue.

The spat was compounded by the minister's refusal to consult the profession on the terms of the Health and Mental Treatment Act, 1958 which increased the income limit for entitlement to hospital and specialist services from £600 to £800 a year.[37] On 23 May 1959 the association, far from withdrawing the ban on the posts already covered by its earlier announcement, published a notice seeking to extend the ban to include recruitment to all medical posts in all local authority hospitals. The association's journal also directed the government's attention to what it saw as a devaluation of health posts which was leading to widespread emigration of young doctors.[38] When pressed by James Dillon in the Dáil in June 1959 to meet a deputation of the association, MacEntee insisted that the 'only obstacle to the restoration of good relations [with the IMA] ... is the entirely arbitrary action which the executive of this association have taken and which I am firmly convinced their members deprecate just as much as I do'.[39] Two days after MacEntee's Dáil speech, the association issued a statement disclaiming the existence of any ban.[40] MacEntee mistakenly interpreted this statement as a withdrawal of the existing ban and consequently intimated his willingness to receive the proposed deputation. He was invited to be the guest at the association's annual dinner in Killarney on 1 July.[41] MacEntee attended the annual dinner with his wife and senior departmental officials. The minister subsequently maintained that his decision to attend the dinner was indicative of his 'warm desire for the friendliest relations with the association and the great profession which it represents', and manifested his readiness to enter into discussion with the association, though strictly on the basis of its declaration 'that, there is not, and never has been, any ban or boycott of these posts organised by the association either in public or private'.

Fine Gael was all too willing to highlight the potentially injurious effect the affair was having on the administration of the health services. O'Higgins argued in the Dáil in November that he did 'not think it is possible to have a continuance of any cold warfare between the Minister for Health and the Irish Medical Association'. 'If that is to continue,' he maintained, 'then the only result will be a stultifying of efforts which were being made to improve the standard of health services.'[42] Moreover, he impugned MacEntee personally for his role in the affair and contrasted the minister's conduct with the cordial relations prevailing during his own tenure.[43] Notwithstanding O'Higgins's incontestable claim that relations had suffered under MacEntee relative to his time in the department, the IMA's tactics were undeniably provocative. When the notices continued to appear in the association's journal, the minister duly sent the association £5 to cover the cost of the hospitality extended to him and Mrs MacEntee in Killarney. The association's brinkmanship reached a new level in November when, seemingly aware of tension between Lemass and his Tánaiste on the issue, it sent an 'open letter' to the Taoiseach which was published in the national press.[44] MacEntee reacted furiously to the implication that his behaviour did not meet with the approval of the Taoiseach and the cabinet. He wrote to four salaried public service doctors whose names appeared on a published list of those who authorised the letter, condemning their actions in no uncertain terms.[45]

Before long, the dispute had assumed an unsavoury and distinctly personal tone. Later that month the editor of the association's journal, William Doolin, published a blistering attack on the minister which has been described by a past president of the IMA as 'an appalling outpouring of vitriol'.[46] Accusing MacEntee of duplicity and disingenuousness, he concluded his editorial by deprecating the minister's apparent impertinence and, in so doing, offended MacEntee's wife, a lady of 'generous proportions': 'That a Minister of State should be so far forgetful of the dignity of his high office as to have sent the Hon[orary] Treasurer of a professional association his personal cheque for £5.0.0 to cover the expense of the entertainment of himself and his *formidable escort* [my emphasis] ... was an incredible gesture on his part.'[47] Unsurprisingly, Doolin's comments led to a total breakdown of communications between the Minister for Health and the body that represented the medical profession in the country.[48]

Just how far relations had deteriorated since MacEntee's assumption of the Health portfolio is demonstrable by the fact that it wasn't until February 1964 that the *Journal of the Irish Medical Association* could announce the 'end of the affair'.[49] Indeed the course of events had disillusioned many members of the association who openly questioned the tactics of their representative body. Discussions on the possibility of establishing a formal negotiating organisation became more frequent during 1961 and a proposal to form a trade union, under the control of the association, was passed at that year's annual general meeting. The formation of the Irish Medical Union placated MacEntee to a degree and led to a reestablishment of communications which was officially recognised by the minister's attendance at the annual dinner of the association in 1963.[50] The substantive issue of access to medical records was also resolved by the agreement of the IMA to a new formula which obliged doctors against whom complaints were made, to release the case notes to a medical officer nominated by the minister. If the patient objected to the release of the notes, the matter ended there.

This rather bizarre and protracted affair is not one of intrinsic importance; on one level it revealed MacEntee's apparent invulnerability to public conflict and on another and more fundamental level it once again reaffirmed his belief in the eminence of the ministerial prerogative. That he could put the efficient operation of the health services at risk by allowing the dispute to persist for over five years illustrated inflexibility and obduracy that was rooted in his conviction that the government could not be held to ransom.[51] Moreover, his attitude to the IMA was entirely consistent with the suspicion in which he held such interest groups generally, and as confirmed by his dealings with the trade unions when he was Minister for Industry and Commerce. Despite the evident dangers involved in the spat, that the affair ended to the minister's obvious satisfaction was not only a chastening experience for a professional group that had enjoyed considerable freedom before the state's encroachment into its sphere, but also inaugurated a new set of principles that would underpin future dealings between it and central government.

PUTTING POLITICS BACK INTO HEALTH: THE SELECT COMMITTEE

If it was John A Costello's specific instruction to T.F. O'Higgins, when he asked him to become Minister for Health in the second Inter-Party administration, to 'take health out of politics', MacEntee's accession to the position coincided with it becoming an intense political issue once again.[52] The impetus for this development came predominantly from the opposition parties, who published their proposals for the reform of the health services in the lead up to the 1961 general election.[53] During that campaign, MacEntee responded to criticism of Fianna Fáil's apparent inaction on the issue by espousing his party's fundamental guiding principle towards the social services: 'Fianna Fáil stands on the firm conviction that it is our duty to foster the spirit of independence and self-reliance in our people. In our social policy we reject all excesses of paternalism, believing that to the best of his ability a man should provide for his own needs. We also recognise, however, that there are many who are unable to fulfil this obligation; and these, we hold, must be helped to the extent that our resources will allow.'[54] The minister strongly rejected the need for new legislation with a view to restructuring those services. He was of the opinion that the Health Act of 1953 provided everything that the opposition was proposing under new legislation. And in response to another of its demands, MacEntee regarded as impossible the notion that everyone could be provided with medical care and a free choice of doctor.[55]

Fianna Fáil's return to office as a minority government after the election did not dull opposition demands. O'Higgins sponsored a new scheme designed to cover 85 per cent of the population through insurance contributions. Also included in this scheme was a free choice of dispensary doctor, free hospital and specialist services and abolition of medical cards. O'Higgins's plan captured the essence of the contrasting priorities of government and opposition towards the health services: these related to the means of financing the services and the provision of choice to a wider constituency.[56] In November 1961, O'Higgins brought this scheme to the attention of the Dáil in the form of a motion that claimed that the 'existing health services have been proved to be inadequate'.[57] He specified what the chief defects of the 1953 act were and especially vilified the dispensary system which he considered a 'pauperisation of the health services'.[58] MacEntee responded to the Fine Gael motion by proposing the establishment of a select committee of the Dáil to examine whether 'the existing system of health services does not meet in a reasonable way and at reasonable cost the essential needs of the various sections of the population for medical care' and 'to make recommendations on these matters and such other matters related to the health services and their operation as the committee think fit'.[59]

The committee reflected the previous political difficulties regarding health and, as such, constituted a wish on the part of the government to gain cross-party support for any new approach. The terms of the committee also amounted to a tacit recognition by the government that there was room for improvement both in the financing and in the administration of the services. In fact the system that prevailed in 1962 was considered by many to be unwieldy and inefficient.[60] The cost of these services was borne by a combination of central government, local authorities and the hospitals' trust fund; the health authorities defrayed half the cost from the rates, with the other half coming from the exchequer. Since the Department of Health was established in 1947, the exchequer had assumed an increasingly greater responsibility for the cost of the services. State grants accounted for a mere 16 per cent of the total in 1947 but had grown to 50 per cent under the 1953 act.[61] Under Fianna Fáil, the cost of health expressed as a percentage of Gross National Product had remained reasonably stable at 2.7 per cent since 1957, an increase of 70 per cent on the 1947 figure and one that compared favourably with other European states.[62]

Despite MacEntee's apparent recognition that an investigation of the sort now envisaged was necessary, he continued to defend the existing services and the level of expenditure on them.[63] This did not preclude the department from enacting some change however. The Health Authorities Act, 1960 provided for the unification of health services in Dublin, Cork, Limerick and Waterford, and for the setting-up of a new health authority in each area. The number of local authorities responsible for the health services was thus reduced. This was the culmination of a trend towards having fewer and bigger local authorities responsible for the services, which culminated in the setting up of health boards under the Health Act, 1970.[64] MacEntee believed that the 'administration of the services must be integrated and simplified; and the readiest way of doing this is to set up the new authorities'.[65] It also provided for a more economical and efficient approach. Of the total expenditure of £16.5 million on local authority health services in 1959–60, about £7.5 million, representing nearly half the expenditure for the country as a whole, was spent in Dublin, Cork, Limerick and Waterford.[66] In 1961, the minister introduced the Health (Corporate Bodies) Bill, in order to invest control of a variety of ancillary health services, which could not be readily operated by existing statutory bodies, in corporate bodies. Several new bodies were set up under the act, including the Medico-Social Research Board, the National Drugs Advisory Board and the Health Education Bureau.[67] The new corporations complemented the most important statutory advisory body, the National Health Council, which continued up to 1968.

The minister's apparent willingness to prepare 'to submit [him]self to the judgment of other people', via the select committee was, according to one authority, 'uncharacteristically and superficially accommodating'.[68] Opposition deputies, meanwhile, interpreted it as a ploy 'to put [health policy] into the political limbo of forgotten things'.[69] Both analyses, however, overlook the minister's preference for technocratic solutions to problems of public policy.[70] Having said that, it was clear that the minister did not seek comprehensive change and that he believed the government 'must proceed empirically in organising and developing the [health services]'. 'That,' he said, 'appeals to my temperament. I trust that approach will also appeal to the House.'[71] This declaration can be interpreted as a statement of limited ambition; but again this ignores the political sensitivity of the issue. Having staunchly defended the existing provisions during the election campaign, it was highly unlikely that the minister could announce such a radical restructuring so soon after. The establishment of the select committee also paralleled events in the United Kingdom, where the Porritt Committee was evaluating in some detail the much trumpeted National Health Service.[72]

Furthermore, MacEntee was of the opinion that the Health Act, 1953 was being unfairly maligned due to inconsistent administration by different health and local authorities. He was also keen to ensure that any new proposals would be congruent with the specific structure of Irish society and would not merely imitate the seemingly generous services obtainable in other countries. Accordingly, MacEntee stipulated that it pay 'particular regard to our own circumstances, our own way of life, the particular form of our economy, our social organisations and the relationships within it and, of course, the scale of resources available to all our people'.[73] The committee's creation, though largely welcomed as a positive step, did expose the minister to some damning criticism, most belligerently expressed by Richie Ryan of Fine Gael who regarded its establishment as 'amounting to nineteen backbenchers of the House sitting down to do the work of the Minister for Health and his Department'. 'Never,' he continued, 'in the history of democratic government, has any Minister had the cheek of the Minister for Health to abdicate his responsibilities while holding on to the crown and the throne and the profits of office.'[74] Others viewed it as an indication 'that the government accepts the possibility of an alternative method of financing and administering the health services based on insurance rather than on taxation'.[75]

The committee adopted a working programme in October 1962, and the government set out its attitude early in the committee's deliberations, submitting a memorandum in November, a month before formal hearings began.[76] This memorandum was intended as a preliminary indication of the minister's views on the general medical services. He did not suggest that the committee should make any conclusions on the issues considered by the memorandum before they had heard evidence from the appropriate bodies, but it was quite clear what was expected of it.[77]

> In developing the services ... the government did not accept the proposition that the State had a duty to provide unconditionally all medical, dental and ancillary services free of cost for everyone, no matter what their individual need or circumstances might be. On the other hand, the services are not designed so that a person must show dire need before he can avail himself of them.[78]

Having met on twenty occasions, the committee reported to the cabinet late in 1964. Its findings provided a trenchant endorsement of the department's position in regard to the general medical services.[79] Indeed the nature of the changes contemplated by the committee either had already been considered by the department itself – as in the case of providing a choice of doctor in the dispensary service – or modifications that could easily be accommodated by minimal interference with the existing legislation.[80] The department also noted with evident satisfaction that in only one submission was there a demand for an extension of hospital and specialist services to those earning over £1,100 a year.[81]

There were dissenting voices, however. In March 1963, on the presentation of the committee's second interim report, Noël Browne, despite acknowledging the 'substantial progress' made 'in the [general medical services]', was critical of the 'dilatory' nature of the proceedings and suggested that it had turned out 'to be the classic device used since Victorian times, and probably long before that, by a conservative government in office anxious to resist change and to resist progress'.[82] On 12 March 1964, the committee submitted a draft third interim report. It suggested that the report on the general medical services and on the general institutional and specialist services should be submitted before outlining 'its consideration of the system of health services as a whole in its final report'. Consideration of the subsequent report on the services specified was postponed during April and May. Alas, the delay proved fatal to the committee's labours. In the interim, T.F. O'Higgins submitted a memorandum outlining his proposed scheme in detail. MacEntee interpreted the timing of O'Higgins's submission as an indictment of the committee which questioned its competency to proceed. This view was based on O'Higgins's proposal 'to urge the Committee not to permit its work to be done in a piecemeal fashion but rather to consider now the full problem of whether a General Medical Service on a comprehensive basis is desirable, and if so to what extent can it be provided'. The minister also construed O'Higgins's comments to mean that the committee should effectively ignore the many witnesses who had endorsed the present services as satisfactory. Accordingly, MacEntee submitted that in deference to this cumulative testimony and 'in fulfilment of its responsibility to Dáil Éireann, the select committee must proceed to the close and detailed consideration of such memoranda and evidence. This is an inescapable obligation which, in my opinion, the members of the Committee cannot ignore.'

MacEntee's own rebuttal of O'Higgins's suggestions was nothing if not comprehensive. He submitted a counter-memorandum to the Taoiseach on 17 June 1964, which he wanted to be considered by the government 'at the earliest possible meeting', and wished to submit it to the select committee 'as soon as possible'. Thus, the minister was, despite his own misgivings, prepared to consider the insurance method in order to solve the spending conundrum to which the government had committed under *Economic Development*. Lemass agreed to have the memorandum considered before the next meeting of the government, but a number of weeks later MacEntee requested the Taoiseach to withdraw the issue from the agenda pending the views of the Fianna Fáil members of the committee. Extending to ninety-eight pages, his four-part memorandum not only outlined the conclusions reached by the committee on the general medical services but deconstructed the assumptions that underpinned Fine Gael's proposals. MacEntee regarded his fundamental approach, as a member of the select committee and as Minister for Health, as investigative rather than defensive. He

maintained that: 'If changes for the benefit of the patient are shown to be desirable and, in their financial and other aspects, practical, I am prepared to support
them.' However, he rejected out of hand Deputy O'Higgins's purpose, which he
interpreted as a call for an entirely new system, 'unless the present one was
proven to be fundamentally unsound'. He also felt that the committee should not
accept responsibility for the 'medicare' of any group 'unless the need to do this
had been firmly established'.[83] Furthermore, MacEntee pointed out that additional expenditure of the order envisaged by O'Higgins (£6 million for the general
medical services), which he regarded as an underestimate, would bring the ratio
of GNP well over 3 per cent 'and thus higher than in any of the EEC countries'.
'Expenditure of this magnitude,' the minister insisted, 'whether met by special
taxation, in the guise of insurance contributions, or, as now, by straight and open
taxation, cannot ... be justified at this particular stage of our economic evolution.'

According to Barrington, the department's cautious attitude towards spending in the early 1960s illustrated three things: 'a distrust of the capacity of local
authorities to spend money wisely, a belief that additional funds would be made
available to improve health services and an assumption that it was the most
responsible body to decide how this money would be spent'.[84] The following
statement, included in a departmental memorandum submitted to the select committee, supports this analysis:

> In the provision of the health services, there is very considerable scope for
> extravagance and unless the authority which is responsible for day-to-day
> decisions in the operation of the services is governed by a sense of financial
> responsibility which arises from having to contribute a considerable part of
> the rise in expenditure which might result from its actions, then there is the
> possibility that expenditure might rise unnecessarily and wastefully.[85]

It also illustrated the limits of this method of financing the health services as the
taxable capacity of the local authorities had been at stretching point for some
time. It may also explain why spending in health lagged behind that planned in
the first and second programmes of economic expansion.[86]

Barrington's analysis is worth considering because it confirms what we know
of MacEntee's views on the position of local authorities and with his assumptions
in respect of the government's own ultimate supremacy. Accordingly, the minister's avowed concern for the national resources was possibly overstated. In reality, MacEntee was far from immune to challenging the restriction of health spending by the government. This was most clearly expressed in his repeated requests
for extra funding to be made available towards improving hospital accommodation by an increase in the capitation rates for voluntary hospitals.[87] In January
1964, he submitted a memorandum for the government explaining his position in
this regard.[88] MacEntee's rejection of O'Higgins's scheme also had an ideological
dimension regarding the principle of insurance contributions. He argued that the
insurance principle was incompatible with the mitigation of distress caused by ill
health. Insurance, according to the minister, could not be applied to the administering of schemes for medical care because: 'The State simply cannot refuse medical aid to a sick person merely because the person concerned, or his employer on

his behalf, has failed to make certain payments.' He affirmed that it was 'the duty of the State to provide medical care, either full or partial, for all those of its citizens whose circumstances so require' and that because the state was bound to do this, 'must eliminate completely the practical possibility of administering and financing state systems of medical care according to insurance principles'.

By the middle of October, Lemass was pressing MacEntee for some definite answers in relation to the committee. Responding to criticism from the Labour Party over the length of time it was taking to publish any concrete proposals, he wrote to his Minister for Health inquiring as to the 'estimate of the time it will take to complete the work of the committee' and suggesting 'if this is likely to be prolonged and if the prospect of an agreed report is not very good', that Fianna Fáil withdraw from the committee and announce its intention to go ahead with the revision of the health acts in accord with its ideas as communicated to the committee.[89] In response, MacEntee indicated that he hoped to be in a position 'very soon' to ask for the restoration of this item to the cabinet agenda. He also blamed the unfortunate timing of O'Higgins's submission for the delay and attached the interim report which was to have been considered at a meeting in April.[90] Dismissing Lemass's suggestion of withdrawing from the committee, MacEntee argued: 'To withdraw now would suggest that we had no answer to Deputy O'Higgins's submission, whereas … we have many good answers, and the weight of evidence before the Committee is in favour of the lines of policy set out in my draft submission.' Lemass gave MacEntee the benefit of the doubt by accepting his conclusions but felt that it was desirable that an interim report on the progress made should be submitted to the Dáil before, or soon after, its resumption on 3 November.[91] Despite the item being restored to the agenda of the cabinet a week later on 27 October, no compromise was reached and in March of the following year, prompted by a carefully choreographed remark by Lemass a month before the general election proclaiming that the Fine Gael proposals were 'unacceptable', the opposition deputies formally withdrew from the committee. In sum, its legacy consisted of two interim reports of minor importance. The committee had met on forty-seven occasions, the last of which was in May 1964.[92] The original intention of conducting an expeditious but thorough examination had been defeated by the sheer volume of submissions admitted as evidence and by its inability to agree to publish its recommendations in a manner that gratified both the government and the opposition.[93] But the thing that had the greatest bearing on its fate was Lemass's impatience with the lack of progress being made and his desire for the government to be seen to be forcing the agenda.

Inevitably, the committee's demise dictated how the health issue was treated during the subsequent general election campaign. The opposition used it as evidence of the government's indecision, as well as confirmation of apparent friction between its two most senior figures. O'Higgins, speaking in March, said that the health committee 'fiasco' clearly showed a rift between Lemass and MacEntee. 'The Taoiseach had shown his total disregard for his Minister for Health, when he condemned out of hand the Fine Gael health proposals,' he argued, 'without even consulting Mr MacEntee or giving him a chance to put forward counterproposals on which he had the officers of his department working.'[94] O'Higgins was overstating things. MacEntee had, in no uncertain terms, made his views on O'Higgins's proposals known to the Taoiseach. Lemass's decision to go public with his denunciation of the proposals, however, was indicative of his lack of faith in the committee to reach any satisfactory conclusions despite his Minister for Health's optimism in this regard.

The Taoiseach's announcement that MacEntee would not be considered for a cabinet portfolio in the event of Fianna Fáil returning to government also provided him with an exit strategy in the face of the committee's failure to produce anything substantive. Lemass's determination to disarm the opposition on the issue was further explicated by his promise to introduce new provisions as soon as the election was over if Fianna Fáil returned to office. Lemass's determination to expedite the party's health proposals was further invigorated by the language and rhetoric of the Fine Gael electoral programme, *The Just Society*, published in March 1965. This document was based on the assumption that the government was vulnerable on welfare issues and that the ideological context provided by Catholic social teaching was favourable to a more overtly social agenda.[95] By the eve of the election, as Bew and Patterson have noted, Lemass had been forced to move on to opposition terrain, claiming that it would be possible to draw up a 'social development programme not dissimilar to and linked with the Economic Development Programme'.[96]

MacEntee, for his part, came out fighting, attributing the committee's demise to Fianna Fáil's opponents. In a letter to the *Irish Independent* in April, rejecting the paper's suggestion that the establishment of the committee was an implicit condemnation of the existing services by the Taoiseach, he maintained that the 'Select Committee was set up on [his] motion'. Furthermore, its 'aim was to make Fine Gael spokesmen prove the wild charges which they had flung around during the 1961 General Election'. He also accused Fine Gael and Labour of deliberately wrecking the committee 'in order to prevent it from presenting its report' which was, in the main, an endorsement of the existing system.[97]

It has been suggested that MacEntee's failure to 'contemplate changes in the health services may have contributed to his undignified departure from the Custom House'.[98] This view requires some qualification, however. For one thing it neglects the consistency between MacEntee's approach and that taken by his successor, Donogh O'Malley. Where one can detect differences between the O'Malley and MacEntee approach, however, is in the level of spending carried out under their respective regimes. In fact, an upsurge in health spending reflected the general trend in 'social' spending after 1963 due to the more favourable economic situation. Social expenditure grew from 13.7 per cent of GNP in 1962 to 16.6 per cent in 1966.[99] O'Malley, who was also a member of the select committee, was certainly of a different temperament to his senior party colleague and may have made a dramatic impact on the department in his one year as minister, but the white paper that his department published in January 1966, *The Health Services and their Further Development*, based many of its conclusions on the evidence submitted to the committee. The one significant extension of the established service that it recommended was to ensure those in the middle-income group would be entitled to state assistance towards the cost of obtaining expensive medication.[100] MacEntee, in his counter-memorandum to O'Higgins's scheme, had in fact acknowledged that 'there was general agreement that this should be done notwithstanding the fact that substantial additional expenditure may be involved.'[101] Interestingly, the white paper was described by the *Journal of the Irish Medical Association* as being 'pragmatic rather than radical', and was assured of 'strong support from the medical profession'.[102]

Lemass was not prepared to indulge MacEntee's faith in the all-party approach and recognised that there was political capital to be gained by unilateral health service reforms. On the other hand, MacEntee wanted the government's fundamental approach publicly vindicated by the committee's findings. MacEntee's departure from the cabinet will be considered more fully below, but it is stretching the point to attribute this to his performance in the health portfolio. Lee's rather glib observation that MacEntee's contention in 1965, 'that the Irish health service was the best in the world, on the simple grounds that it was not state controlled', and his subsequent assertion that Lemass appointed O'Malley 'to make up for lost time', not only fails to take into account the fact that MacEntee's assertion was based on a thorough (if dogmatic) examination of the health services available in other countries but also disregards the continuity between the respective approaches of O'Malley and MacEntee.[103] The investigations carried out by the select committee not only formed the basis of the 1966 white paper, but also contributed to further reforms such as the establishment of area health boards, regional hospital boards and Comhairle na nOspidéal, following the Health Act, 1970.

FLUORIDATION

Apart from the disappointing results of the select committee, there were notable innovations during MacEntee's tenure in Health. As well as the administrative changes noted above, the first poliomyelitis vaccines were administered in the country in 1957.[104] Another significant advance was made in 1964, when the first public water supplies in the country were fluoridated as a public health measure to prevent premature decay of children's teeth. Indeed the fluoridation issue became one of the most protracted policy measures introduced during the 1960s. The initiative had originated in the Department of Health under Dr James Ryan, who in 1952 requested the Medical Research Council of Ireland to undertake a survey 'to ascertain whether there were significant differences in dental condition amongst school children living in different areas of the country and whether such differences, if they existed, could be related to differences in the dietary intake of the children'.[105] This survey was based on the Irish National Nutrition Survey which MacEntee, as Minister for Local Government and Public Health, had initiated in 1944, and which began in 1946. The information obtained by the nutrition survey formed the basis of the survey into dental conditions.[106]

In May 1956, O'Higgins appointed a consultative council of experts to examine the matter.[107] This council produced its report in June 1958, which met with the approval of his successor.[108] In an address given by MacEntee on 12 June 1958 to the members of the Fluorine Consultative Council to mark the presentation of the council's report, he praised 'the judgment and discrimination with which [his] predecessor selected the men for the task'.[109] He also assured his audience that he was sufficiently aware of potential difficulties in implementing its recommendations: 'Seasoned mariner as I am on the stormy waters of public life, paragraph 37 of the report is a fair warning that there may be breakers ahead,' he warned. The paragraph in question concerned the ethical nature of adding fluorine to public water supplies. Two of the signatories of the final report had, in fact, dissented from the inclusion of this particular paragraph because they thought it to be a matter that the council should not comment upon.[110] Apart from this contentious inclusion, the findings of the report were unanimous. The main grounds for objection to fluoridation were that it was mass medication, a usurpation of parental rights by the public authorities and interference by the public authority with the integrity of the human body. These objections were carefully considered and advice was sought by the council. It was satisfied, however, that there was no ethical objection to the fluoridation of public water supplies within the margin of safety recommended in its report, which amounted to the fluoridation of public water supplies to the level of one part per million.

The Department of Health duly accepted the council's report in full, but under Irish law, local authorities had power to supply 'pure and wholesome' water to members of the public. This right did not include the addition of fluoride salts to water for the purpose of making children's teeth more resistant to dental decay, a point that had given rise to litigation in Ontario and New Zealand.[111] MacEntee, therefore, decided with the approval of the government to introduce special legislation to legalise the addition of fluoride to piped public water supplies. There followed a meeting between Health and Local Government on 21 November on the specific points that would be required to be included in any proposed legislation. The remaining sticking point that was discussed at the November meeting was whether the legislation should impose a statutory obligation on local authorities to fluoridate public water supplies or whether to leave it to the authorities' individual discretion. Supported by both the assistant secretary and the secretary of his department, MacEntee regarded compulsion as the only practical way of implementation. A draft scheme of the bill was submitted to government in the summer of 1959, and in February 1960 it came before the Dáil as the Health (Fluoridation of Water Supplies) Bill, 1959.

MacEntee introduced the bill in early April, observing that dental caries was 'one of the most prevalent and widespread disabling diseases in the world' and that its prevalence in Ireland was 'appalling'.[112] This point was illustrated by not only the findings of earlier surveys in Ireland, but was also supported by the evidence of a Commission of Inquiry carried out in New Zealand.[113] The minister also cited the conclusions of a report by a committee of experts set up by the World Health Organisation to study the question of water fluoridation, which included the assertion that 'the effectiveness, safety, and practicability of fluoridation as a caries-preventive measure has been established'. Thus, the case for prophylactic action was strong. MacEntee regarded the weight of scientific evidence as incontrovertible, but acknowledged caustically that 'there are some individuals who even to-day would contend that the earth is flat.'[114] Accordingly, the minister went on to give some consideration to the arguments put forward by the opponents of fluoridation who, in Ireland, were represented by a body known as the Pure Water Association. Its principal objection to the compulsory implementation of the measure was that it violated individual rights. In considering this question, the minister carefully outlined the philosophy with which he approached the issue:

> It is highly germane to the argument to point out that the public water supplies do not belong to the individual; they belong to the community … As an individual he has no right of veto over the decisions of the community, though of course he has the right to dissent from them. Where these decisions are made for the common good by the appropriate authority, he must abide by them for so long as he may wish to enjoy the advantages which membership of the community gives to him…

Fine Gael did not oppose the bill in principle but argued strongly that it should be left to the representatives of each local authority to decide whether or not they wished to fluoridate their water supplies. O'Higgins indicated the example of New Zealand in support of this approach.[115] One member of the party, however, Richie Ryan, opposed the bill vigorously, alleging that it would introduce a poisonous substance into the human system which could help to cause or aggravate numerous ailments including cancer, rheumatism, arthritis, kidney and liver diseases and mental illness. He also alleged that fluoridation of public water supplies was a violation of constitutional and fundamental rights and even suggested that it had the 'smell of dictatorship about it'.[116] His argument was largely based on anti-fluoridation literature that had been circulated in Ireland by the Pure Water Association about the possible dangers to health associated with the long-term ingestion of fluoridated water. The Labour Party did not take any policy stand for or against fluoridation but allowed individual members to express their own opinions on the subject, a policy which produced votes for and against the measure largely dictated by their views on the compulsion issue. For MacEntee, the crux of the question came down to that old ministerial paradigm: responsibility. With regard to the mandatory nature of the bill, his abiding rationale was 'to carry responsibility for [the state's] health services'; therefore, he asked:

> Am I going to shoulder that responsibility: am I going to try to make these findings effective, or am I going to pass the buck to county councils and some obscure district councils and say: 'You are responsible; you will be responsible for defying the sort of demagogy which will be hurled against you. You will be told that you will be responsible to the people if you put this "deadly poison" into their pure water. You will be responsible for defying the ethical principle involved in this matter.'[117]

Despite the vociferousness of Deputy Ryan's objections, both houses of the Oireachtas signed the bill into law on 28 December 1960. Opposition to the measure did not end there, however. After the Senate had passed the bill, the Pure Water Association wrote directly to the Council of State expressing objections to the bill, which they alleged infringed their constitutional rights. Some individuals also wrote directly to the president asking him not to sign the bill but to refer it to the Supreme Court for a decision on its constitutionality.[118] A recommendation in favour of fluoridation by the Dublin City Medical Officer was discussed by the city council in May 1961. After a discussion lasting several hours, the City Medical Officer's report was adopted by sixteen votes to twelve. A further attempt was made later by some members of the Dublin City Council to hold up fluoridation of the Dublin Corporation water supply by refusing to approve the expenditure to purchase the necessary equipment but this attempt was also defeated.[119] MacEntee expressed his disgust at the nature of the opposition from the council, and stated before its meeting in October 1962: 'Where the public health is concerned, a partisan majority in a subordinate authority cannot be allowed to flout the law and defy the Oireachtas.'[120] Richie Ryan responded somewhat hysterically to the passing of the proposal by shouting at its proponents: 'Let them stand up and be counted with the murderers of the children of Dublin.'[121] Strong resistance to the proposed fluoridation of public water supplies was also raised at meetings of Cork City Council which, in April 1962, adopted a motion, by eleven votes to seven, stating that they wished to have no part in the scheme to add fluoride to the Cork city water supply. The local branch of the Irish Dental Association and the Professor of Dental Surgery at University College, Cork urged the City Council to reconsider their decision on this important matter. It was only after the High and Supreme Courts had held, in 1963 and 1964 respectively, that the fluoridation of public water supplies was not unconstitutional that Cork City Council agreed to proceed with fluoridation. Likewise, fluoridation of the Dublin city water supply did not commence – although the equipment had been installed in early 1963 – until after the Supreme Court judgment was announced in July 1964.[122]

These rulings had been prompted by an action taken against the state by Gladys Ryan, a Dublin housewife, who was legally represented by the ubiquitous Richie Ryan (no relation). She sought a declaration that the Health (Fluoridation of Water Supplies) Act, 1960 was repugnant to the constitution. In his judgement, Mr Justice Kenny said that he was 'satisfied that the fluoridation of public water supply in the manner proposed and in [the] country's climate was not dangerous to anybody'.[123] The plaintiff argued further that the act was a violation of the imprescriptible rights guaranteed to the family by Article 41 of the constitution; and that it was a violation of the inalienable rights of parents to provide, according to their means, for the religious, moral, intellectual, physical and social education of their children, under Article 40 of the constitution.[124] However, Mr Justice Kenny interpreted the right to bodily integrity rather narrowly as a right 'not to have to undergo any mutilation of body or limb', a view that was upheld two years later by the Supreme Court under appeal.

The fluoridation episode is worthy of consideration in light of the objections raised against the measure and, indeed, in light of the standard interpretation of MacEntee's political outlook provided by historians such as McKee and Lee. In fact, the minister's response revealed just how far he was willing to see the state go in order to provide what he considered a necessary service. That the opponents of the measure saw in it an undesirable and potentially dangerous level of state encroachment into the community's everyday lives not only paradoxically recalled MacEntee's own exaggerated fears of what 'welfareism' would bring during the 1940s but, ultimately, must qualify any assessment of him based on those inflated fears. It is also possible to reconcile both of these views in light of the relative pre-eminence of MacEntee's role in formulating the respective policies. In the earlier case, MacEntee was reacting not only to developments coming from Britain which were being heralded as the answer to Ireland's social problems, but also to schemes from other departments of state, and from non-governmental agencies. Fluoridation, on the other hand, had been promoted by the Department of Health from the outset, was inherited by MacEntee at an inchoate and rudimentary stage of the policy process and was supported by very credible scientific evidence.[125]

ENDGAME

Seán MacEntee's long and distinguished ministerial career expired with the seventeenth Dáil. It has been suggested that Lemass used the opportunity of the demise of that administration 'for the political retirement of MacEntee', a charge to which MacEntee subsequently took particular exception.[126] This *dénouement* of the MacEntee–Lemass dialectic is wholly seductive to those who regard the coming of economic success in the 1960s as some sort of climacteric which vindicated the Lemass approach and undermined that of his critics, chief among whom was MacEntee. In reality, political changes were taking place across the political divide that reflected the demographic demise of the post-revolutionary leaders. De Valera, on his accession to the presidency, made way for his heir apparent in 1959; James Dillon succeeded Richard Mulcahy as leader of Fine Gael in the same year, and Brendan Corish followed William Norton as leader of the Labour Party in 1960.[127] The changes wrought by Lemass to his early cabinets, however, owed more to electoral exigencies than to any putative desire to 'surround himself with bright, energetic, young ministers'.[128] According to Lee, 'he was in no position in party political terms to make immediate sweeping changes.'[129] Lemass was also disposed to defer to seniority, something which ultimately influenced his choice of Tánaiste and which he rationalised thus: 'MacEntee was the senior minister. It would have seemed a rebuke to him if I did not appoint him as Tánaiste so I did appoint him. It is far more important to maintain goodwill and harmony than seek a more effective distribution of responsibility.'[130]

Unsurprisingly, MacEntee always maintained that the decision to end his ministerial career was his alone. The dissolution of the Dáil had been caused by a by-election defeat for the government in Cork in March 1965. Lemass had promised that if the Fianna Fáil candidate were unsuccessful, a general election would be called.[131] Early in the campaign, the Taoiseach announced that MacEntee would not be considered for ministerial office if the party returned to power. Responding to this announcement, the *Irish Times* suggested that MacEntee 'in all decency' should have retired altogether from politics, to which the Tánaiste responded by inviting the paper to 'go dance on another grave'![132] MacEntee's own recollections of events, however, suggest that he was ready to retire, only to be persuaded otherwise by electoral considerations:

The facts in this case are that on the afternoon of the 11th March 1965 when all the information obtainable indicated that the Fianna Fáil candidate would be heavily defeated [in Cork], I asked to see the Taoiseach in his room in Leinster House. He saw me at about 4.30 p.m. We discussed the unfavourable news from mid-Cork and whether he should ask for a dissolution of Dáil Éireann. I then told him that I wished to let him know that I had decided that if there were an election I would not be a candidate, that being over 75 years of age I wished to retire from active political work. He seemed surprised that I did not wish to stand again …[133]

MacEntee subsequently changed his mind owing to the rearrangement of the boundary of the constituency of Dublin South-East, which provided Fianna Fáil with the opportunity, 'providing that its panel were well-chosen', of winning two seats out of three. As it happens, this is exactly what occured: MacEntee and Seán Moore were elected at the expense of Noël Browne, now a Labour Party candidate.[134]

MacEntee's recollection may well have been governed by concern for his reputation. The slightest suggestion that such an enduringly significant role in government would come to an end at someone else's will clearly discomfited the Tánaiste. Lemass's announcement was unquestionably resented by him, and was, furthermore, deemed unbecoming by some of MacEntee's former colleagues.[135] Barrington has even described his departure from the government as 'undignified and ignominious' but again this is an overstatement.[136] His tenure in Health may not have produced the reforms that he regarded as so necessary in the 1940s but his appointment of the select committee was, at the very least, a willingness to consider how best to proceed with the financing and administration of the health services. Moreover, at seventy-five, 'old mischief' was well aware that his time at the coalface of Irish politics was at an end. Notwithstanding this, he retained an admirable appetite for the task, which was exemplified by his robust defence of his decision to stand for election in 1965. At the beginning of that campaign, MacEntee provided election workers in Rathmines with a fitting valediction: 'I have looked death in the eye for Ireland; I have been in penal servitude for Ireland and many times in prison. I have served my country without self-seeking. I have devoted all my powers – and they are not inconsiderable – to that service. I can look back on almost fifty years of an active and arduous public life. Yet no man can say, no man nor colleague of mine, no member of our organisation, not the humblest of the constituents whom I have had the honour to represent, can ever say that I did not serve them honourably and well.'[137]

MacEntee did not stand for re-election in 1969 but remained a member of the Fianna Fáil National Executive, serving as vice-president of the party until his retirement in 1978, sixty years after his election as an MP for South Monaghan.[138] After his retirement from public life he settled down to a quiet domesticity with his wife, Margaret. In 1970 they moved to 'Montrose', Trimelston Avenue in Booterstown, having decided to leave their home of thirty-four years in Leeson Park. Domestic life was punctuated occasionally by requests to relate his experiences to television and

radio as well as for the historical record. He still had time for his business interests, for his occasional duties as a member of the Council of State and to corre-
spond with the newspapers, which he did on a regular basis, giving his opinion
on a wide range of issues.[139] He died in Dublin on 9 January 1984, at ninety-four
years of age.[140]

NOTES

1. This figure is somewhat misleading due to the low turnout. It can also be argued that Fianna Fáil's victory was less an endorsement of its policies than a rejection of the second inter-party administration, which had been discredited by the economic crisis of 1955–6.
2. The new ministers were Jack Lynch, Neil Blaney and Kevin Boland.
3. Lee, *Ireland 1912–1985*, p.329.
4. Daly, *The Buffer State*, p.434. See also P. Honohan and C. Ó Gráda, 'The Irish macroeconomic crisis of 1955–56: how much was due to monetary policy?', in *Irish Economic and Social History*, vol. XXV (1998), pp.52–80.
5. See Lee, *Ireland: Politics and Society*, p.343 and Fanning, *Finance*, p.507. Lee argues that the establishment of the Capital Investment Advisory Committee came 'as a nasty surprise for Finance'. The bulk of the committee was nominated without reference to Finance and contained two economists, Louden Ryan and Patrick Lynch, who had been vocal in their advocacy of change. Moreover the chairman of the committee, John Leydon, as has been documented in this book, was one of Finance's enduring antagonists.
6. F. Kennedy, 'Social expenditure of public authorities and economic growth 1947–66', *Economic and Social Review*, vol. 1 (1969–70). Health expenditure expressed as a percentage of GNP in 1955 was 3.1 per cent; this figure was reduced to 2.8 per cent by 1961.
7. UCDA P67/469, MacEntee to Blaney, 13 February 1957. MacEntee rejected Browne's nomination to the Fianna Fáil ticket in his own constituency of Dublin South-East in 1957, a fact that undoubtedly added extra spice to their sparring over health in the Dáil.
8. See, for example, Farrell, *Seán Lemass*, p.102.
9. R.F. Foster, *Modern Ireland 1600–1972* (London, 1988), p.577.
10. Farrell, *Seán Lemass*, p.102.
11. R. Fanning, 'The genesis of economic development', in J.F. McCarthy, *Planning Ireland's Future: The Legacy of T.K. Whitaker* (Dublin, 1990). See also UCDA P67/815.
12. See UCDA P67/815 (4). Diary entry for 8 March 1957. It is interesting to note that MacEntee's desire to become Minister for External Affairs coincided with his daughter Máire being a member of the Irish delegation to the General Assembly of the United Nations.
13. Quoted in S. Lalor, 'Planning and the civil service 1945–70', *Administration*, 43, 4 (1995), pp.66–7.
14. See S. Baker, 'Nationalist ideology and the industrial policy of Fianna Fáil: the evidence of the *Irish Press* (1955–1972)', *Irish Political Studies*, vol. 1 (1986) and M. Morrissey, 'The politics of economic management in Ireland 1958–70', in ibid., pp.79–95.
15. NAI DT S15551A, Observations of Finance on Industry and Commerce memorandum for cabinet committee on employment, 31 July 1953.
16. NAI F200/18/51, Finance memorandum for the government, 16 October 1951.
17. MacEntee was reported in the press on 21 November as stating that government spending on health had increased from £5 million in 1947 to £16 million ten years later. See *Dáil debates*, vol. 164, cols 1266–7, 28 November 1957. Before 1947 local authority rates were accepted as the main source of finance for the services, with central government providing 16 per cent of the cost through state grants.
18. *Dáil debates*, vol. 161, col. 941, 8 May 1957.
19. Barrington, *Health, Medicine and Politics*, p.253. He justified the increases with the observation that the net cost of providing these particular services to the exchequer and local authorities had risen by 54 per cent since 1952–3.
20. Quoted in ibid. See *Dáil debates*, vol. 163, col. 131, 26 June 1957.
21. *Dáil debates*, vol. 162, col. 28, 29 May 1957. Also see Fanning, *Finance*, p.511. MacEntee acted as Minister for Finance in Ryan's absence during the autumn of 1957.
22. Quoted in Fanning, *Finance*, p.510.
23. Ibid., pp.510–11.
24. Ibid., p.513.
25. *Dáil debates*, vol. 161, cols 1151–2, 8 May 1957.
26. *Dáil debates*, vol. 181, col. 472, 3 May 1960.
27. F. Kennedy, *Public Social Expenditure in Ireland*, ESRI Broadsheet, no. 11 (Dublin, 1975), p.13.

28. NAI DT S13444 P/95, Department of Health memorandum for the government on 'Financing of Hospitals Building Programme, June 1957.
29. NAI DT S16474A, Finance memorandum summarising the views of government ministers on the paper *Economic Development*, 4 July 1958.
30. G. FitzGerald, *Planning in Ireland* (Dublin, 1968), p.44.
31. Kennedy, *Public Social Expenditure in Ireland*, p.12.
32. Ibid., p.6. Although it should be noted that despite persistent recommendations by the Capital Investment Advisory Committee and in the reports of the Central Bank, the social share did not fall below 40 per cent.
33. See T.F. O'Higgins, *A Double Life* (Dublin, 1996), pp.165–9.
34. *Dáil debates*, vol. 175, col. 1477, 11 June 1959.
35. For a brief outline of the affair see *Journal of the Irish Medical Association*, vol. LIV (February, 1964).
36. NAI DT S16374B/95.
37. Barrington, *Health, Medicine and Politics*, p.255.
38. *Journal of the Irish Medical Association*, vol. XLV (January, 1959).
39. *Dáil debates*, vol. 175, col. 1478, 11 June 1959.
40. UCDA P67/322, Copy of statement issued on behalf of the Minister for Health, 1 December 1959.
41. Ibid.
42. *Dáil debates*, vol. 177, col. 1178, 12 November 1959.
43. Ibid.
44. See UCDA P67/320, Conn Ward to MacEntee, 17 October 1959. See also M.P. Flynn, *Medical Doctor of Many Parts* (Mullingar, 2002), pp.174–5. A personal letter was sent to Lemass at the same time as the open letter was published in the press.
45. Flynn, *Medical Doctor*, p.175.
46. *Journal of the Irish Medical Association*, vol. XLV (December, 1959); Flynn, *Medical Doctor*, p.176.
47. *Journal of the Irish Medical Association*, vol. XLV (December, 1959).
48. Doolin died in April 1962. For an account of his career, see *Journal of the Irish Medical Association*, vol. L (May, 1962).
49. *Journal of the Irish Medical Association*, vol. LIV (February, 1964).
50. Flynn, *Medical Doctor*, p.177.
51. UCDA P67/324. This conviction was reinforced by a personal and confidential letter from Michael Moran, Minister for Lands, on 1 March 1960, giving details of attempts by the IMA to dissuade representatives of county physicians and county surgeons from entering into negotiations with the county managers with regard to their pay and conditions of employment, in the context of the disagreement between the minister and the association.
52. O'Higgins, *A Double Life*, p.156.
53. For example, see the Labour party, *Policy Document on Health*, 1959.
54. UCDA P67/400, general election broadcast, 22 September 1961.
55. In fact his department had given serious consideration to this proposal but its report was not available to the minister until February, 1962. See Deeny Papers, Mercer's library, for report of the study group on the general medical service, February, 1962.
56. On the financing of the health services see P.R. Kaim-Caudle, 'Paying for the health services', *Administration*, vol. XIII (1965).
57. *Dáil debates*, vol. 192, cols 720–1, 23 November 1961.
58. Ibid., cols 721–3.
59. Ibid., cols 746–7.
60. It divided the population into lower, middle and higher income groups for the purposes of deciding who should pay for health benefits; but the dividing line between the lower income and the middle income group was far from definite and was often contingent on where the individual lived, as the groups were defined by the relevant health authorities. The lower income group was entitled to free medical services with the exception of a number of small charges; the middle income group had to pay for general practitioner care, as well as a modest maintenance charge in hospital; but the higher income group was not afforded any such concessions.
61. M.M. Wiley, 'Irish health policy in perspective', in F. Ó Muircheartaigh (ed.), *Ireland in the Coming Times: Essays to Celebrate T.K. Whitaker's 80 Years* (Dublin, 1997).
62. UCDA P67/336. The department's own investigations revealed that for 1960 the percentages of GNP represented by public expenditure on health care were as follows: Belgium 2%; France 2.6%; Germany 3%; Italy 2.6%; Luxembourg 2.2%; Netherlands 1.8% and Ireland 2.9%.
63. *Dáil debates*, vol. 192, cols 752–3, 23 November 1961.
64. B. Hensey, 'The health services and their administration', in F. Litton (ed.), *Unequal Achievement: The Irish Experience 1957–82* (Dublin, 1982), p.149.

65. *Dáil debates*, vol. 177, col. 668, 4 November 1959.
66. Ibid., col. 666.
67. Hensey, 'The health services and their administration'. See also *Dáil debates*, vol. 191, cols 1585–1601, 20 July 1961.
68. Barrington, *Health, Medicine and Politics*, p.257.
69. *Dáil debates*, vol. 192, col. 853, 23 November 1961.
70. See D. Keogh, *Ireland and Europe 1919–1948* (Dublin and New Jersey, 1988), p.113.
71. *Dáil debates*, vol. 192, col. 762, 23 November 1961.
72. The Porritt report recommended the unification of most of the NHS under area health boards, see J. Carrier and I. Kendall, *Health and the National Health Service* (London, 1998), p.107.
73. Ibid.
74. *Dáil debates*, vol. 192, col. 853, 23 November 1961.
75. *The Journal of the Irish Medical Association*, L, 295 (January, 1962).
76. The committee was chaired by the Fianna Fáil deputy Michael Carty and comprised deputies Lionel Booth, Noel C. Browne, Philip Burton, Patrick Byrne, Jim Carroll, Frank Carter, Mark A. Clinton, Liam Cunningham, Patrick Hogan (South Tipperary), Brian Lenihan (parliamentary secretary to the Minister for Lands), Celia Lynch, Patrick McAuliffe, Seán MacEntee (Minister for Health), John W. Moher, Michael Mullen, Thomas F. O'Higgins, Donogh O'Malley (parliamentary secretary to the Minister for Finance), Gerard Sweetman and Seán Dunne.
77. NAI DT S13444/P/95. See MacEntee memorandum on the select committee, 17 June 1964 with enclosures of memorandum submitted to the committee in November 1962.
78. Quoted in Barrington, *Health, Medicine and Politics*, p.257.
79. MacEntee reported that the 'weight of evidence elicited at the hearings would not support a suggestion that the existing system of general medical services was in any way radical or significant way defective. On the contrary, the hearings confirmed that the services in question meet "in a reasonable way and at reasonable cost the essential needs" of those sections of our people for whose benefit they have been organised.' DT S13444/P/1/95, four-part memorandum of Minister for Health on proposals submitted by T.F. O'Higgins. See also UCDA P67/336, select committee on the health services [n.d.]
80. See Barrington, *Health, Medicine and Politics*, pp.254–5.
81. Ibid., p.258.
82. *Dáil debates*, vol. 200, col. 1135, 13 March 1963.
83. Ibid.
84. Barrington, *Health, Medicine and Politics*, p.259.
85. Quoted in M. Wiley, 'Financing the health services: from local to centralised funding and beyond', in J. Robins (ed.), *Reflections on Health: Commemorating Fifty Years of the Department of Health, 1947–1997* (Dublin, 1997).
86. Kennedy, *Public Social Expenditure in Ireland*. The limits of this method of financing the health services were recognised in the government white paper, published in 1966.
87. NAI H34/8a, Health memorandum, June 1957; DT S13444 P/95, Health memorandum to government, 13 January 1964.
88. NAI DT S13444 P/95.
89. NAI DT S13444/P/95, Lemass to MacEntee, 15 October 1964.
90. Ibid. MacEntee to Lemass, 19 October 1964. 'I should mention that, practically since the commencement of the committee's work, I had been endeavouring to pin the deputy down to presenting his proposals in concrete form, as they are presented in this document.'
91. Ibid. Lemass to MacEntee, 20 October 1964.
92. Fourteen meetings of the committee were held between March and December 1962; fifteen were held from January to July 1963; and a further eight were held between February and May 1964.
93. Interestingly, this was not the end of the select committee in the consideration of Irish health policy. Notwithstanding the lack of success of MacEntee's committee, in 1977 the Labour party Minister for Health, Brendan Corish, introduced a similar body in the Dáil which was met with approval by Fianna Fáil. See *Dáil debates*, vol. 297, col. 999, 9 March 1977.
94. *Irish Independent*, 22 March 1965.
95. P. Mair, 'Ireland 1948–1981: issues, parties, strategies', in I. Budge, D. Robertson and D. Hearl (eds), *Ideology, Strategy and Party Change: Spatial Analyses of Post-War Election Programmes in 19 Democracies* (Cambridge, 1987). Mair's analysis points to Fine Gael's increased attention to welfare issues in the early 1960s.
96. Bew and Patterson, *Seán Lemass*, p.161.
97. UCDA P67/338, MacEntee to editor *Irish Independent*, 5 April 1965. See *Irish Times*, 30 March 1965 for a report of speech by MacEntee in Rathfarnham.
98. Barrington, *Health, Medicine and Politics*, p.260.

99. Kennedy, *Public Social Expenditure in Ireland*.
100. Ibid.
101. UCDA P67/336, select committee on the health services [n.d.].
102. *Journal of the Irish Medical Association*, LVIII, 344 (February, 1966).
103. Lee, *Ireland, 1912–1985*, p.364. See also P.R. Kaim-Caudle, *Social Policy in the Irish Republic* (London, 1967), p.30.
104. UCDA P67/618.
105. *Dáil debates*, vol. 180, cols 1743–4, 5 April 1960.
106. Ibid., col. 1744.
107. For a full chronology of events see UCDA P67/304.
108. UCDA P67/301, copy report of the Fluorine Consultative Council, June 1958.
109. UCDA P67/302.
110. See UCDA P67/310 for text of a lecture given by Michael Stanley, assistant principal officer, Department of Health, read at a seminar on fluoridation in Rutgers University, New Jersey, USA, on 1 December 1965.
111. Ibid.
112. *Dáil debates*, vol. 180, col. 1743, 5 April 1960.
113. Ibid., col. 1748.
114. Ibid., col. 1762.
115. Ibid., col.1768.
116. *Dáil debates*, vol. 184, col. 174, 26 October 1960.
117. *Dáil debates*, vol. 184, cols 286–7, 27 October 1960.
118. UCDA P67/310.
119. UCDA P67/312, J.J. MacWeeney to MacEntee, February 1969 on the success of fluoridation reported in the press that day (22/2/69). He was in city hall when the subject was debated on a night the *Irish Times* called the 'most stormy night in city hall for 50 years'.
120. Quoted in F. Tobin, *The Best of Decades: Ireland in the 1960s* (Dublin, 1984), p.59.
121. Ibid.
122. UCDA P67/310.
123. UCDA P67/308, copy judgement of High Court on 31 July 1963.
124. *Irish Times*, 1 August 1963.
125. UCDA P67/730. The minister's deep personal interest in the issue was recognised by his induction as an honorary life member of the Irish Dental Society in 1965.
126. See B. Farrell, *Chairman or Chief: The Role of the Taoiseach in Irish Politics* (London, 1971), pp.63–4 and UCDA P67/788 for MacEntee's response. Professor Farrell defended his conclusions in a letter to MacEntee on 9 February 1981 in which he wrote: 'The original drafts of the essay in *Chairman or Chief* were based on a number of interviews with participants. These included an interview you kindly gave in the Dáil on 16 December 1968 and a long and helpful telephone call on 3 October 1970. Access to the series of recorded interviews between Mr Lemass and Dermot Ryan Ryan was also most helpful. The statements of Mr Lemass's opinions were strengthened by two particular interviews with him on 14 April 1970 and 16 February 1971.
127. R. Fanning, *Independent Ireland* (Dublin, 1983), p.196.
128. Farrell, *Seán Lemass*, p.102.
129. Lee, *Ireland, 1912–1985*, p.388.
130. Farrell, *Seán Lemass*, p.101.
131. Lee, *Ireland*, 1912–1985, p.366.
132. UCDA P67/403.
133. UCDA P67/788, MacEntee to Professor Brian Farrell [Draft].
134. See Appendix A for all MacEntee's election results.
135. UCDA P67/403. See letters to MacEntee from Gerry Boland (19 March 1965) and Seán T. O'Kelly (23 March 1965).
136. Barrington, *Health, Medicine and Politics*, p.260.
137. *Irish Times*, 27 March 1965.
138. *Irish Times*, 4 March 1978.
139. MacEntee held directorships in Irish Life and Braids Ltd.
140. See *Irish Times*, 10 January 1984 for obituary.

Epilogue

Is it not ample proof of the statement which I made that I am an empiricist and that I am prepared to change my mind if the facts show me to be wrong?[1]

Seán MacEntee, 23 November 1961

Seán MacEntee was not only a highly influential political personality who served the independent Irish state for more than forty years; he was a profoundly complex one. Far from the one-dimensional conservative caricature that has been hitherto presented, this research shows him as a more thoughtful and less inflexible politician than some have suggested. Which begs the question: is it possible to neatly define his political philosophy? The short answer must be no. As I have attempted to show, there were notable inconsistencies in his career, concomitant with, and typically conditioned by, prevailing political and economic considerations. For example, on Fianna Fáil's accession to office in 1932, MacEntee, like his party colleagues, was still in thrall to the language of political opposition and his speeches at that time anticipated wide-ranging and fundamental reforms in the functioning of the state. Reform did come, most notably in the social and economic policy arenas and in constitutional matters. But as the 1930s drew to a close, it is clear that MacEntee envisaged a more limited role for the state in areas such as employment creation and that he resented the government's ambivalent attitude to established fiscal structures. The onset of the Emergency, however, served to reignite MacEntee's capacity to conceive of the state as more than just a mere adjunct to conventional social and economic forces. Emergency Powers legislation facilitated a more interventionist and diagnostic governmental approach. MacEntee was often at the forefront of the government's efforts in this regard. The Trade Union Act of 1941, the wages standstill order and the facilitating of emigration to Britain all typified an assertive response to a manifestly exigent set of circumstances.

Moreover, MacEntee's faith in state action was not altogether discarded when the Emergency was over. As Minister for Local Government and Public Health (1941–8), he oversaw a department with strong centralising tendencies. That this was the case, as we have seen, did not amount to a commitment to bureaucratic dominion on MacEntee's part, as J.H. Whyte has suggested. Rather it was reflective of his desire to see a more efficient, as well as a more dynamic, administration in place. It also indicated his acknowledgement that the wartime experience had significantly altered society's expectations in a number of ways. Welfare was now on the agenda, and although MacEntee distrusted the proponents of schemes which promised to cure society's ills overnight, he took the message on board in the context of his own departmental remit. In 1944, MacEntee announced his intention to recreate a public health system 'commensurate with modern requirement'.[2] This decision would have far-reaching consequences, both socially and politically, and constituted a radical response to the needs of the community in relation to public health provision. As Lindsey Earner-Byrne has noted, this aspiration 'signalled a fundamental shift in state health and welfare policy'. It resulted in a 'more secular approach to the rights of citizenship', and led to a more official and legislative approach to health care which 'had been left largely to private practitioners, local authority initiative and charitable endeavour'.[3]

After Fianna Fáil's period in opposition between 1948 and 1951, MacEntee returned to Finance and to a balance of payments crisis. Lee has described that government as de Valera's worst, and it is clear that a coherent approach to the problems it faced was thwarted by disharmony and indecision. MacEntee not only became synonymous with that government's response to the fiscal crisis, predominantly through the corrective measures introduced in his 1952 budget, but he also carried the burden of culpability for subsequent electoral failings. Accordingly, some have viewed this administration as bearing the hallmarks of MacEntee's putatively rigid political philosophy and have perceived it as a straight fight between Lemass and MacEntee which the latter won. This verdict is patently incompatible with the evidence presented. In fact, the budget of 1952 was an exercise in consensus. Nevertheless, MacEntee keenly felt the legacy of the 1952 crisis. Apart from almost losing his own Dáil seat at the 1954 general election, his prospects of ever leading the party suddenly evaporated. He would always be 'the third man'. It also resulted in his not being considered for the Finance role when Fianna Fáil returned to office in 1957. This, of course, denied him the opportunity of finishing the job he had started in 1951–4, when he had worked closely with T.K. Whitaker, whose approach at that time anticipated many of the curative measures he was later to advance in *Economic Development*. Instead, MacEntee had to make do with Health, a portfolio he had done much to establish during the 1940s. His time there, despite being restricted by the stringent code of public spending outlined in *The First Programme*, led to a number of important changes in the administration of the health services, and was marked by an investigative process – the select committee – that eventually led to further reforms in 1966 and 1970.

If an expedient and unambiguous definition of MacEntee's political philosophy is impossible, perhaps a better and more equitable way of providing a *précis* of MacEntee's career would be to construct a balance sheet of his most obvious and enduring qualities. The justification for such an approach used by the biographer of MacEntee's most redoubtable nemesis, Noël Browne, could equally apply to the subject of this biography because, like Browne, MacEntee has been portrayed as seeing 'things in such, stark, black and white terms'. The balance sheet method, moreover, allows for the 'necessary complexities of human character', not to mention inconsistencies of political philosophy.[4] Firstly, although MacEntee's Catholicism should not be discounted – particularly in the light of correspondence between Archbishop John Charles McQuaid and Bishop Michael Browne of Galway in 1959, that suggests that they looked to MacEntee as the man in Fianna Fáil 'most disposed to upholding the interests of the Catholic Church'[5] – his approach to public policymaking was undoubtedly secular. Certainly, MacEntee was sensitive to Catholic opinion on a wide range of political issues, but he remained fundamentally wedded to the separation of church and state in legislative and executive matters.[6] We have seen how he contemptuously rejected the Dignan Plan and the Report of the Commission on Vocational Organisation, both of which sought to arrogate greater powers to vocational interests. What conditioned his response to both was his absolute conviction that the state should retain its pre-eminence in the legislative field. Moreover he 'liked to consider himself detached from the conservative aura which hovered over Fianna Fáil during de Valera's leadership and he opposed censorship and the ban on divorce in the 1937 Constitution'.[7]

Another prevalent theme of his lengthy political career was MacEntee's residual predilection to play politics on every conceivable issue. This not only informed his attitude to public policy, as we have seen in his confrontations with Dignan and the medical profession, but was perhaps best demonstrated by his conduct on the hustings and in the Dáil. In stark contrast to his erudite and genteel private manner, MacEntee the politician was often caustic, sardonic, uncompromising, sharp and, at times, spiteful. This often led to fiery exchanges in the Dáil. Following the 1943 general election campaign, the Labour Party leader, William Norton, denounced MacEntee on the occasion of his nomination as a minister in the ensuing government. Norton's contribution to the debate on the government's nominees was notable for the ferocity of its ill-feeling towards MacEntee:

> I think it is well known even to the decent minded Ministers and members of the Fianna Fáil Party that Deputy MacEntee is a specialist in throwing election muck. That is his only qualification for inclusion in the Fianna Fáil Government. Everybody knows that the Minister indulged in the most deliberate misrepresentation of his political opponents in the last election, and particularly of the Labour Party, which seems to annoy Deputy Seán MacEntee to an almost limitless extent.[8]

He concluded by proclaiming that he regarded 'that Minister [MacEntee] as the greatest liability that this country could have'. The general election of 1943 was not the only occasion that MacEntee attacked political opponents in a virulent and histrionic fashion. In fact, MacEntee's election campaigning was not only habitually unrestrained but could also be wounding on a personal level. During his frequent jousts with Noël Browne, MacEntee, it has been claimed, vilified his opponent 'up and down the constituency'. Moreover, this vilification included ungracious references to Browne's father who had been in the Royal Irish Constabulary.[9] In the 1948 general election, just as he had done to Clann na Talmhan and the Labour Party in 1943, MacEntee accused Browne's party, Clann na Poblachta, of being communists. This led to the *Irish Times* describing him as a 'political Don Quixote tilting gaily at Communist windmills and smelling Bolsheviks behind every bush ...'[10] When asked in later life about his perceived anti-communism, MacEntee sought to qualify the charge:

> Well now, you see, I doubt if I'm on record as an anti-Communist '*simpliciter*', but rather as against those who have used the concept of a society in which men would be free and equal and in individual rights and possessions, to justify the organisation and propagation of helotry. I don't believe in a regimented society, I don't believe in authoritarianism, though I do believe that authority, discipline and order are essential for the preservation of a liberal and progressive society. One must distinguish between the ideal, the utopian ideal, which the early propagators of communism sought to realise, and the manifestations of aggressive statism to which the name has been applied in the modern world. The fact is, of course, that not Marx's theories, but the principles of Marx-Leninism, which markedly deviates from them, have shaped the social structure and the role of the Government in the most repressive and aggressive police-state in the world, and it is against this type of tyranny that I have been opposed. It is because I think that Marxism in practice is contrary to the spirit of freedom that I oppose it.[11]

On the other side of the balance sheet, it must be noted that MacEntee 'had a capacity, rare in Irish politics, for divorcing the personal from the political'. This was exemplified on a number of occasions, most notably on polling day in 1948 when he offered Noël Browne his hand in a conciliatory gesture which the latter refused to acknowledge.[12] MacEntee's overriding concern with party politics was also evident in the 1954 election when Browne shared the Fianna Fáil platform with him. On this occasion, MacEntee was magnanimous to the point of almost surrendering his seat. As we have seen, largely due to the fallout of the 1952 budget, MacEntee's seat was less than secure in this election. Notwithstanding this, he allowed Browne to distribute personalised election literature, the only proviso being that his own name be included on the leaflets. MacEntee's election organiser, Eddie McManus, was 'aghast at such unselfishness towards somebody who, he feared, might threaten his candidate's seat'.[13] In the event, his fears were very nearly realised, MacEntee winning the third seat by a mere 108 votes from Browne. After the election, MacEntee again displayed his chivalric side, paying a handsome and heartfelt tribute to his running mate. MacEntee also made many friends among Dáil opponents; Desmond FitzGerald was a close friend during his early career and latterly he was friendly with Jim Doogue, a Fine Gael senator and fellow engineer. It is difficult to ascertain, however, whether MacEntee was ever particularly close to any of his own party colleagues. His daughter did not remember any particular alliances made by her father when a cabinet minister.[14] And despite his partisanship in the Dáil, he was also more amenable than many of his colleagues to the notion of an alliance with Fine Gael. Indeed, during the 1943 election campaign James Dillon wanted the Taoiseach to invite the other parties in the Dáil to form a national government.[15] MacEntee, for one, was prepared to acknowledge that the differences between the two main parties were small. He recognised that the principal distinguishing feature between them was 'now merely a matter of personality' and called on Fine Gael to unite with Fianna Fáil under de Valera on the grounds of national unity: 'I am sure that in their hearts many of the Fine Gael leaders rejoiced at what under [de Valera's] leadership this nation had accomplished.'[16]

A third recurring theme of MacEntee's political life was his pedantic adherence to propriety in public office and his fastidious attention to ministerial, as well as cabinet, responsibility. Indeed his concern with ministerial responsibility led him to object to the government's decision to publish the white paper, *Economic Development*, revealing its civil service authorship.[17] While James Ryan and de Valera recognised the political advantages of such an unprecedented move, MacEntee regarded it as an abdication of responsibility on the government's part. His concern for the integrity of high office, however, was never meant to demean the efforts of the civil servants who worked under his ministerial seal. In each department he headed, he established strong working relationships with senior staff. His most enduring relationship of this kind was formed with J.J. McElligott in Finance although they never met outside the office.[18] Together they formed a team as redoubtable as the one made up of Lemass and John Leydon in Industry and Commerce. That their paths first crossed in Easter week 1916 probably helped cement a professional bond that proved as formidable as any other in the history of the state.[19] The esteem in which MacEntee was held by McElligott was disclosed in a personal letter to the minister in March 1954, the purpose of which was to wish MacEntee well after an enforced absence from departmental business due to illness:

> I cannot adequately express in words the feeling of pleasure I had when learning last night of your return to business and to good health. I did not care to trouble you with inquiries when you were away, and therefore I can see nothing for you in the months ahead but hard work, plain living and high thinking, I feel you will prove equal to the burden, and will acquit yourself with honour and integrity. In any case you carry now, as always, my respect for your ingenuity and courage and my admiration for the single-minded manner in which you have served your country ever since I came to know you, nigh forty years ago and in slightly different circumstances! If all Ireland's sons were so devoted to her service how different would be her recent history! May your days be long in the land and may all good fortune attend you and yours is my heartfelt wish.[20]

Another regular feature of his political style was his frequent resort to brinkmanship. This was exemplified again in his dealings with Noël Browne. In February 1957, Browne was added to a panel of candidates at a Fianna Fáil National Executive meeting. After much discussion about Browne's candidature among the deputies present, it was realised that he had some significant support but there were also those who regarded him as a 'loose cannon' that Fianna Fáil could do without. MacEntee was firmly in the latter camp. He 'delivered the *coup-de-grâce*' by threatening to withdraw his own candidacy unless Browne's name was removed from the panel. According to Browne's biographer, de Valera's evident preference for his minister led to a steady collapse of support for

Browne.[21] MacEntee had already outlined his tactics in a letter to Neil Blaney. He believed that if Browne were added to the panel there were indications 'that many members of the organisation in Dublin S.E. will flatly refuse to work for him'. More pertinent was MacEntee's observation that: 'The addition of his name will be taken by the country as an endorsement by the National Executive of everything he has said, since Cara Fáil, with National Executive funds, afforded him a personal platform and gave him exceptional facilities to ... put over his own socialistic views.'[22] MacEntee also informed Blaney of his willingness to deliver the fatal blow to Browne or face the ultimate consequence: 'I know I represent the views of the vast majority of our workers and supporters in Dublin South-East and I have a feeling that these are views also of very many of our people throughout the country. I am determined, therefore, to go through with it or "bust".'

MacEntee's resort to brinkmanship was also routinely evident in cabinet, especially on occasions when his views were not being given the attention he felt they deserved. His resignation letters in 1938 and 1939 were products of his being overruled at the cabinet table. Despite these fits of petulance, MacEntee does seem to have accepted with considerable solemnity the principle of collective ministerial responsibility.[23] During the Anglo-Irish negotiations of 1938, for example, he impugned the attitudes of two ministers (Gerry Boland and Oscar Traynor) which he maintained had 'destroyed the only basis on which a cabinet can last: that upon agreement on the essentials of policy and a pervading confidence that the policy having been stated will be accepted by all'.[24] Notwithstanding MacEntee's frequent differences 'on the essentials of policy' with the rest of the cabinet and his 'outsider status', he appears to have afforded due respect to de Valera's consensual manoeuvrings during government meetings and, furthermore, was prepared to submit to the majority verdict even when it constituted a fundamental departure from his own position.

What does all this say about the party that MacEntee served for so long? From the beginning, Fianna Fáil was a distinctly populist organisation. But despite MacEntee being very much to the forefront in eloquently articulating the party's protest politics, his personal style was never populist. The Fianna Fáil governments of the 1930s, much more so than Cumann na nGaedheal during the 1920s, exhibited an enormous faith in what government could achieve – something that Daalder has recognised as common to nationalist leaders in new states.[25] But the politics of protest, evident before 1932, was soon replaced by the rhetoric of responsibility. That is not to say that Fianna Fáil's achievement in government during the 1930s was not impressive. In fact, the party's success was notable in a number of different areas. Its activism in the field of legislation was unprecedented. It also firmly established the rule of law, defeating the twin threats of the Blueshirt movement and the IRA. Furthermore, Fianna Fáil's 'economic policy during the 1930s helped to shape the face of Irish society: the protected national bourgeoisie grew in numbers and in political weight, and Fianna Fáil's organic links with that class – in terms of party finance, policy consultation, direct and indirect political influence and ideological integration – grew also'.[26]

This outcome was not as predetermined as Dunphy implies, however.

Girvin's point that 'Fianna Fáil was never fully united behind the radical economic and social policies identified with Lemass' is true, but only so after 1936.
Despite notable differences in the emphasis of the early speeches of Lemass and
MacEntee, both were committed to a full-scale transformation of Irish social and
economic life on Fianna Fáil's accession to power. I have already noted how
Lemass's speeches during the 1930s showed an increasing appreciation of the
limits of politics. Perhaps MacEntee's avowed empiricism, not to mention the
influence of his civil servants in Finance, made him more conscious, at an earlier date, of the disadvantages of the government's strategy. By the outbreak of
war in 1939, MacEntee was openly questioning the merits of the government's
long-term commitment to protectionism and its interventionist role in other
spheres. This did not mean that MacEntee had completely lost faith in the power
of the state. In fact, during the Emergency, MacEntee was perceptibly more committed to governmental action than at any time during the 1930s. His reaffirmation of faith in this principle can best be explained by the sense of catastrophe
the war wrought in Irish policymakers.

MacEntee was more often than not at the forefront of any internal dissent in
government, a nonconformist among an otherwise compliant Fianna Fáil cabinet.[27] In many ways, he was untypical of the conventional Fianna Fáil minister.
On the surface this was reflected in his lifestyle. Tod Andrews has recorded how
he liked the 'good life'; how he cultivated 'a certain style of living'; and how he
indulged in 'dandified dress'.[28] In other words, he liked to entertain, enjoyed
good food and fine wine. This not only went against de Valera's espousal of anti-
materialistic values but was scarcely consonant with the party's identification
with 'the plain people of Ireland' who presumably had little time for fine wine
or good food. On a less superficial level, although he shared the party's devotion
to the creed of republicanism, which he unselfconsciously wore on his sleeve,
MacEntee could be heretical to the point of churlishness on occasions. To many
party members, the election victory of 1932 constituted a retrospective vindication of republicanism and a concomitant repudiation of the Treaty. De Valera certainly interpreted it as a mandate to dismantle that document. MacEntee, like
Lemass, was a pragmatist, however, and he preferred to concentrate on the material well-being of the community over any due regard for the minutiae of the
constitutional position. Privately, this was evident in his opposition to the
Economic War and his differences with de Valera over partition, revealed during
the Anglo-Irish negotiations in 1938.[29] MacEntee, dismayed that de Valera was
evident stalling on the signing of the agreement until some solution was reached
on partition, wrote: 'I feel that the partition problem cannot be solved except
with the consent of the majority of the northern non-Catholic population. It certainly cannot be solved by their coercion. Hitherto we as a government have
done nothing of ourselves to secure a solution, but on the contrary have done and
are doing things which have made a solution more difficult. The demand which
we make continuously that the British should compel the Craigavonites to come
in with us, had only had the effect of stiffening them against us.'

MacEntee's enduring prominence within Fianna Fáil might be the most per-
suasive evidence that it was a broad-church party. He clearly had his rivals,

Lemass being the most obvious and most robust. As the latter's most recent biographer has acknowledged, however, any view of the history of Fianna Fáil 'that is presented principally as a Lemass–MacEntee conflict … is reductionist in the extreme'.[30] Any such view is also immune to the changing priorities and evolving philosophies of de Valera's two most outspoken lieutenants. Each played his part in a political struggle that Cowling described as 'the continuous process by which politicians created personalities for themselves in order to claim the right to play a part in reducing political problems to a form suitable for governmental decision'.[31] If Lemass liked to see himself as 'the left wing of Fianna Fáil', MacEntee probably saw himself more as the party's watchdog.[32] Although the climacteric of Lemass's accession in 1959 and the subsequent economic growth spurt experienced by the state in the immediate aftermath have been routinely used as a vindication of Lemass's dynamic style and his greater managerial acumen, it should be noted that in achieving this Lemass came closer to the MacEntee position than he had done in over thirty years of sharing a common party platform. This is not to discredit or lessen the Lemass achievement in any way but merely to point out that the prescription advanced by *Economic Development* was advocated in government circles before 1958 but was not heeded by the then Minister for Industry and Commerce. Differences between ministers in de Valera's governments, however, never threatened to become as pronounced as the faction fighting that dogged the party after the retirement of the post-independence leaders and which continued up until recent times. Perhaps, as Garvin has argued, the sense of comradeship that existed between the veterans of the old IRA and Sinn Féin outweighed any ideological differences between them.[33] The lack of any public dissent in de Valera's cabinets, I would argue, can also be attributed to a more acute sense that politics was less about personal ambition than about the serious business of nation-building.

Despite this, rivalry within Fianna Fáil in de Valera's Ireland retains a certain fascination for the historian of the independent state. What makes it even more intriguing is the scarcity of material that explicitly reveals the exact nature of such relationships. Oblique examples of MacEntee's evident remoteness to Lemass are therefore seized upon to support the theory. One such example occurred in the aftermath of Paddy Smith's resignation from the government over his own differences with Lemass. MacEntee wrote to Smith to convey his feelings on the affair. From Smith's reply it is clear that MacEntee was in an invidious position in regard to what he could say publicly in Smith's defence. Smith wrote: 'Many thanks for your letter and all the nice things which I know you feel for quite a while. "Everyman Seán who is alone is wrong" or words to that effect. I do not want to discuss here things that have been so often debated but Seán I could not expect you to say I was right in the course I took. I may not be and seriously hope time will prove I was not.'[34] Seán T. O'Kelly and Gerald Boland also implied an appreciation of MacEntee's difficulties with Lemass on the occasion of his resignation from the cabinet in 1965.[35] Another former member of Lemass's cabinet, Dr Paddy Hillery, also attested to the 'guarded' nature of their relationship: 'Lemass sometimes referred to a quotation which described MacEntee as "a minor poet". Lemass just said it without a smile or a laugh.

MacEntee liked language ... and polished his speeches. I think when MacEntee exercised his role in government to debate against proposals brought to government the Taoiseach [Lemass] would support the minister bringing forward policy proposals.'[36]

Perhaps the most explicit evidence of the strained nature of the MacEntee–Lemass relationship was provided by MacEntee himself in a speech to the Fianna Fáil parliamentary party on the occasion of Lemass's retirement in November 1966. MacEntee's contribution to proceedings shocked and confused his party colleagues in equal measure. He was scathing in his criticism of Lemass's decision and the timing of his departure,[37] an action which he argued had done irreparable damage to the party: 'Today ... the organisation which did so much is at its lowest ebb; and in the minds of the general public appears to be riven apart. Responsibility for this situation in my view rests mainly with the Taoiseach.' He continued: 'The devious course which he has pursued not only in relation to his leadership and the succession but to other questions as well, have confounded the members of our organisation, so that none of them know where we stand on any issue.' MacEntee's attack also extended to the policies pursued by Lemass since the party's re-election in 1965: 'The policies which the Government has formulated and pursued since then have been peculiarly the Taoiseach's own. They are still working themselves out. In fact they have reached the truly crucial stage of their development. Within a few months, most probably by the date of the next Budget, the country will know whether the modest resources of the nation have matched the cost of these policies.'

MacEntee's absence from the cabinet undoubtedly contributed to the unreserved nature of his condemnation of Lemass but there may also be detected an element of regret that an era of Irish politics, in which he had played a significant role, was finally coming to an end: 'The members of Fianna Fáil throughout the country pinned their faith on him and persuaded hundreds of thousands to do likewise. Now he is preparing to let us all down, and by his manner of doing so do what Costello, Dillon, Cosgrave could not do, gravely weaken our whole organisation.' Underpinning MacEntee's extended critique was the strong feeling that Lemass had forsaken his party for purely personal reasons:[38] 'The journalists who profess to know so much of what passes in the Taoiseach's mind overlook the genetic fact that those who under de Valera founded and built up Fianna Fáil intended it to serve the nation and not the personal interest of any individual ... The restoration of that unity, the healing of the divisions which this miserable controversy has created, is to my mind the supreme need of this party.'[39]

It is not known whether MacEntee regretted his intemperate attack on Lemass when he later realised the true extent of the latter's illness but he did pay his rival a heartfelt and generous tribute on his death in May 1971. Whatever of the malevolence of MacEntee's speech, his contention that Fianna Fáil had been damaged by Lemass's departure was certainly accurate, as subsequent events would demonstrate. These events also proved that Lemass, in choosing his successor, did have the best interests of the party at heart. Unfortunately he did not live long enough to exert any influence on the internal politics of Fianna Fáil in the early

1970s. MacEntee, on the other hand, was still at large and was anxious to impart his considerable experience on the difficulties facing the party. These difficulties have been sufficiently described elsewhere but it is worth considering briefly MacEntee's views during this time.[40] His description of Lemass's 'devious course' in relation to his leadership and the succession stemmed from the fact that MacEntee, along with other senior figures in the party, supported the candidature of George Colley for the leadership in 1966. Lemass had other ideas, preferring Jack Lynch – who he had made Minister for Finance after the 1965 election – as his successor. Despite MacEntee's respect for Colley, the new Taoiseach never had to question MacEntee's loyalty in what was a singularly rebellious period for the party. The rebellion was caused by the 'Arms Crisis', the biggest calamity to befall the party since its foundation and the outbreak of the Troubles in Northern Ireland. At the infamous 1971 árd fheis, MacEntee faced down his former cabinet colleague Kevin Boland, one of the rebels, but found that the general audience was not receptive to his views. One reporter recalled the ensuing scene with incredulity:

> [MacEntee] came to the rostrum while a section chanted 'Boland, Boland' and amid boos: he spoke amid cheers and boos and down under me I saw comparative youngsters go berserk in their shouting as they sought to drown him. It was a naked moment – and an astonishingly sad moment, too. For here was a man, in the wintering days of a long life in which he had, to one degree or another, put that life on the hazard for the right to live and speak freely, being drowned out by a section of the party of which he was, and is, an elder statesman. Men half his age stood and brandished their fists at him and while he was still fighting to make his case, the platform ambushed him from the wing by gonging him for time. He looked astonished and having appealed for more time, went on. Flushed of face, and chopping the air with this hand, he tried to make himself heard. Then the platform disconnected the amplification and with the place in an uproar he went flailing on, unheard and becoming more and more excited. In the end it took a marshal and Joe Groome to get him reluctantly off the rostrum. Only then did Erskine Childers lift his shamed head off the table; Joe Brennan, who stoically faced the audience and betrayed no emotion, reached for his pipe, as part of the audience rose to give MacEntee a standing ovation and the others rose to boo him.[41]

Indeed Boland's advocacy of a hawkish response to the Troubles allowed MacEntee to publicly recapitulate some of his most cherished principles. In a letter to the *Irish Times* in June 1970, MacEntee considered the effects of Boland's stated desire to arm the nationalist minority in Belfast, opining that: 'Mr Boland carries moral responsibility for the fires and killings which occurred in Belfast last weekend. Before the killings become mutual carnage and the fires general conflagrations, he should strive to quench the passions, the sectarian passions which, blaspheming Wolfe Tone, his wilful words have helped to kindle.'[42] Boland's description of MacEntee as 'a 1916 contemptible' on an RTÉ television programme in September 1971 also prompted a written response which sought to outline the differences, as MacEntee perceived them, between the republicans of 1916 and those of 1971: 'The men of 1916 did not plant bombs in public places, caring not whom these might kill or maim, whether men, women or children. Neither did they fan sectarian hatred, as neither did they turn their guns on each other in furtherance of personal or organisational rivalries. They were true soldiers and fought a clean fight.'[43] MacEntee's divergence from elements within his party who continued to embrace the entrenched nostrums of republicanism was also conveyed privately. At a National Executive meeting in January 1974, MacEntee drew a clear distinction between republican prisoners in the North and his own contemporaries: political prisoners like Thomas Ashe and Terence MacSwiney were 'imprisoned for advocating their principles' while IRA prisoners in the North 'were guilty of or attempted to commit mass murder of innocent non-belligerent people. No assassins should not expect to be treated otherwise than as murderers.' Two days later he met Jack Lynch, then in opposition, and spoke to him about 'amending Article 3 of the Constitution to provide that Northern Ireland would not be integrated with the Republic except with the consent of a majority of the inhabitants'.[44]

MacEntee's belief in the principle of consent was not merely a reaction to events in the North in the late 1960s and early 1970s. In fact, throughout his political career he had been consistent on this point. Indeed on receiving the first printed draft of the constitution, Finance's response, written by McElligott but endorsed by MacEntee, dealt most extensively with Articles 1–3, pointing to an important contribution from the minister. McElligott argued that it was 'not usual in a Constitution to define the national boundaries' and warned that the claim of sovereignty over Northern Ireland would 'give offence to neighbouring countries with whom we are constantly protesting our desire to live on terms of friendship'.[45] McElligott's arguments presaged much of what MacEntee had to say about partition during the Anglo-Irish negotiations of the following year. During the war, MacEntee again gave his views on partition. He said on that occasion that the partition problem 'might be solved after the war, not by force, but by the people on both sides of the border living in amity and as good neighbours, and cooperating on issues which affected the peace and progress of their respective communities and the country as a whole'.[46] MacEntee frequently reiterated his concerns over partition and claimed during a by-election in Cork in June 1946 that 'nobody was more concerned than he with the problem of partition … He had a deeper concern about the problem than almost any man, except the Taoiseach.' Responding to a suggestion by the War of Independence veteran, Tom Barry – standing as an independent – that a separate ministry be set up for the recovery of the six counties, MacEntee maintained that the only way to solve the problem was to proceed with the policy of 'national reconstruction, social progress, industrial development and letting people in the North see what would be their lot if they came in with us'.[47]

MacEntee's views on the 'Ulster question' probably hampered his chances of ever leading Fianna Fáil and may have compromised his relationship with de Valera. For although MacEntee had an enduring respect and admiration for de Valera, respect that was reciprocated by his appointment to every one of the latter's cabinets, he was not an intimate of the party leader in the same way as were Seán T. O'Kelly, Frank Aiken and P.J. Ruttledge.[48] At their very first meeting during the summer of 1916 in the workshop of Dartmoor prison, what impressed MacEntee most about de Valera was 'how little he knew' about Ulster politics.[49] De Valera in turn expressed his surprise that MacEntee had retained an admiration for Joseph Devlin. That MacEntee remained outside de Valera's inner circle was also a product of their frequent divergence on issues of public policy. It could also be attributed to his political indiscretions and the fact that de Valera liked to think of MacEntee as someone he could count on to 'always say the wrong thing but do the right thing'.[50] Not that this bothered MacEntee unduly. Indeed he seems to have enjoyed his maverick status. It could be said that it provided him with a certain leeway in his political battles and allowed him to cross lines that would have been balked at by some of de Valera's less outspoken associates.

NOTES

1. *Dáil debates*, vol. 192, col. 758, 23 November 1961.
2. MacEntee to the editor, 16 March 1944, in the *Journal of the Medical Association of Éire*, 14, 82 (April, 1944), p.40.
3. See L. Earner-Byrne, 'In respect of motherhood: maternity policy and provision in Dublin city, 1922–1956' (Unpublished PhD thesis, University College, Dublin, 2001), p.148.
4. Horgan, *Noel Browne: Passionate Outsider*, p.292.
5. Quoted in Cooney, *John Charles McQuaid*, p.332.
6. This also applied to the relationship between the Church and his private conscience, as has been recorded by his daughter in her recent memoirs. See Cruise O'Brien, *Same Age as the State* (Dublin, 2003), pp.122–3.
7. McMahon, *Republicans and Imperialists*, p.17.
8. *Dáil debates*, vol. 94, cols 44–7, 9 June 1944.
9. See Horgan, *Noel Browne*, pp.2–3.
10. Quoted in D. McCullagh, *A Makeshift Majority*, p.21.
11. UCDA P67/795, transcript interview by Tony Meade in the *Kerryman* newspaper, 29 March 1969.
12. Horgan, *Noel Browne*, p.55. See also O'Higgins, *A double Life*, p.288.
13. Horgan, *Noel Browne*, p.178.
14. Dr Patrick Hillery endorsed this view, describing MacEntee as an 'independent personality'. Information supplied to the author by Dr Patrick Hillery.
15. NAI DT S13240 B, on proposals of national government.
16. UCDA P67/364, speech at Harold's Cross, 7 June 1943.
17. Interview with Dr T.K. Whitaker.
18. Cruise O'Brien, *Same Age as the State*, p.126.
19. Whitaker, *Interests*, p.287.
20. UCDA P67/224, handwritten letter McElligott to MacEntee, 11 March 1954. MacEntee had had a gall bladder removed in October 1953.
21. Horgan, *Noel Browne*, p.185.
22. UCDA P67/469, MacEntee to Neil Blaney, 13 February 1957 regarding the proposed candidature of Noel Browne.
23. See Robins, *Custom House People*, pp.130–2.
24. UCDA P67/155.
25. H. Daalder, 'Government and opposition in the new states', *Government and Opposition*, vol. 1 (1965–6), p.223.
26. Dunphy, *The Making of Fianna Fáil Power*, p.313.
27. See *Irish Press*, 30 August 1975. Despite MacEntee's claim, in his obituary of de Valera, that 'de Valera's governments were not composed of yes-men. In our discussions no punches were pulled, no argument – however unpalatable – unuttered, but all were listened to patiently and all were pondered by the Taoiseach to whom they were addressed', it is clear that there was a considerable proportion of the cabinet that was intimidated by 'the Chief' and which was not as forceful or assertive during cabinet meetings.
28. C.S. Andrews, *Man of No Property* (Dublin, 1982), p.58.

29. See UCDA P67/179 and UCDA P67/155. MacEntee to Margaret MacEntee (n.d.); MacEntee to de Valera, 17 February 1938.
30. Horgan, *Seán Lemass*, p.353.
31. M. Cowling, *The Impact of Labour, 1920–24* (Cambridge, 1971).
32. *Irish Times*, 12 May 1971.
33. T. Garvin, 'The growth of faction in the Fianna Fáil party, 1966–1980', *Parliamentary Affairs*, vol. 34 (1981).
34. See UCDA P67/335, Smith to MacEntee, October and November 1964.
35. UCDA P67/403. See letters to MacEntee from Gerry Boland (19 March 1965) and Seán T. O'Kelly (23 March 1965).
36. Information supplied to the author by Dr Patrick Hillery.
37. Dr Patrick Hillery, for one, was perplexed by the harsh tone of MacEntee's speech: 'I was puzzled at MacEntee's speech and felt he was wrong. It seemed inappropriate to attack a man who was leaving. I did not understand it.'
38. Lemass had resigned on medical grounds.
39. UCDA P67/734, handwritten text of a speech [intended for a meeting of the FF parliamentary party] 11 November 1966 critical of Lemass's decision to resign. Whether MacEntee's speech to the parliamentary party was quite as stinging as this version of the speech is unknown. This draft, however, certainly reveals MacEntee's unvarnished view.
40. See, for example, S. Collins, *The Power Game: Ireland under Fianna Fáil* (Dublin, 2001).
41. *Irish Times*, 22 February 1922.
42. *Irish Times*, 30 June 1970.
43. *Irish Times*, 25 September 1971.
44. UCDA P67/815 (8), diary entries for 14 and 16 January 1974.
45. NAI DT S9715B, response of Department of Finance to the first draft of the Constitution, 23 March 1937. For a full discussion see D. Keogh and A. McCarthy, *The Making of the Irish Constitution, 1937* (Cork, 2007), pp.124–36.
46. *Irish Times*, 22 April 1944.
47. *Irish Times*, 8 June 1946.
48. MacEntee's letters to de Valera were seldom informal. His tone was always respectful to the point of being deferential but did not convey companionship or undue familiarity.
49. UCDA P67/479, 'De Valera: the man I knew', by Seán MacEntee, published in *Iris Fianna Fáil* (party journal) in winter 1975 edition.
50. Information supplied to the author by Ann de Valera.

Appendix A[1]
Election Results of Seán MacEntee

Election	Party	Constituency	First Preferences	Highest polling candidate	Quota	Assembly
1918	Sinn Féin	Monaghan South	7,524	7,524	n/a	House of Commons, Westminster
1921	Sinn Féin	Belfast West	2,954	13,298	10,691	Northern Ireland Parliament
1923	Sinn Féin	Dublin Co.	2,350	20,821	6,374	Dáil Éireann
By-election 1924	Sinn Féin	Dublin Co.	10,623	16,456	21,082	Dáil Éireann
June 1927	Fianna Fáil	Dublin Co.	4,238	15,918	7,788	Dáil Éireann
September 1927	Fianna Fáil	Dublin Co.	5,954	15,462	8,023	Dáil Éireann
1932	Fianna Fáil	Dublin Co.	10,496	11,332	8,965	Dáil Éireann
1933	Fianna Fáil	Dublin Co.	15,644	15,644	10,051	Dáil Éireann
1937	Fianna Fáil	Dublin Townships	10,124	10,124	9,245	Dáil Éireann
1938	Fianna Fáil	Dublin Townships	10,903	10,903	8,901	Dáil Éireann
1943	Fianna Fáil	Dublin Townships	11,336	11,336	9,650	Dáil Éireann
1944	Fianna Fáil	Dublin Townships	10,034	10,034	9,155	Dáil Éireann
1948	Fianna Fáil	Dublin South-East	7,371	8,473	7,407	Dáil Éireann
1951	Fianna Fáil	Dublin South-East	8,334	9,222	7,336	Dáil Éireann
1954	Fianna Fáil	Dublin South-East	5,971	11,305	6,705	Dáil Éireann
1957	Fianna Fáil	Dublin South-East	5,916	6,918	6,091	Dáil Éireann
1961	Fianna Fáil	Dublin South-East	7,222	7,222	6,184	Dáil Éireann
1965	Fianna Fáil	Dublin South-East	7,823	8,056	7,204	Dáil Éireann

NOTE

1. B.M. Walker (ed.), *Parliamentary Election Results in Ireland 1918–92* (Dublin, 1992).

Appendix B
Ministerial Positions Held

Ministerial Office	From	To
Minister for Finance	9 March 1932	16 September 1939
Minister for Industry and Commerce	16 September 1939	18 August 1941
Minister for Local Government and Public Health	18 August 1941	18 February 1948
Minister for Finance	14 June 1951	2 June 1954
Minister for Social Welfare	27 November 1957	11 October 1961
Minister for Health	20 March 1957	21 April 1965

Select Bibliography

PRIMARY SOURCES

National Archives of Ireland, Dublin
Bureau of Military History Witness Statements
Cabinet Minutes
Department of Finance Files
Department of Health Files
Department of Local Government and Public Health Files
Department of Industry and Commerce Files
Department of the Taoiseach Files

National Library of Ireland, Dublin
Joseph Brennan Papers
Frank Gallagher Papers
William O'Brien Papers

University College, Dublin, James Joyce Library
Colonial Office Files

University College, Dublin, Archives Department
Frank Aiken Papers
C.S. Andrews Papers
Ernest Blythe Papers
Fianna Fáil Party Papers
Denis McCullough Papers
Seán MacEntee Papers
Eoin MacNeill Papers
Richard Mulcahy Papers
Éamon de Valera Papers

NEWSPAPERS AND PERIODICALS

Administration
Capuchin Annual
Catholic Bulletin
Christus Rex
Cork Examiner
Crane Bag

Dublin Opinion
Economist
Hibernia
Irish Ecclesiastical Record
Irish Independent
Irish Monthly
Irish Press
Irish Times
Irish Worker
Irish Workers' Weekly
Journal of the Medical Association of Éire
Journal of the Social and Statistical Society of Ireland
Manchester Guardian
Round Table
Standard
Statist
Studies
Sunday Independent
Sunday Press
Tablet
The Bell
The Leader
The Torch
Thom's Directory

OFFICIAL PUBLICATIONS

Dáil debates
Seanad debates
Report of the Commission of Inquiry into Banking, Currency and Credit (1938)
Report of the Dublin Housing Inquiry (1943)
Report of the Committee on Vocational Organisation (1944)
Report of the Departmental Committee on Health Services (1945)
The Post-War Building Programme (1945)
Outline of Proposals for the Improvement of the Health Services (1947)
Economic Development (1958)
First Programme for Economic Expansion (1958)
The Health Services and their Future Development (1966)

SECONDARY SOURCES

Theses

Andersen, H.L. 'The 1952 financial budget: rhetoric and reality' (MA thesis, UCD, 1996).

Banta, M.M. 'The red scare in the Irish Free State, 1929–37' (MA thesis, UCD, 1982).

Buckley, P. 'The electoral policies of Fianna Fáil, 1927–32' (MA thesis, UCD, 1984).

Earner-Byrne, L. 'In respect of motherhood: maternity policy and provision in Dublin city, 1922–1956' (PhD thesis, UCD, 2001).

Feeney, T.M. 'Fianna Fáil and the civil service, 1927–37' (MA thesis, UCD, 1999).

Hay, M. 'Bulmer Hobson: the rise and fall of an Irish nationalist, 1900–16' (PhD thesis, UCD, 2005).

McKee, É.C. 'From precepts to praxis: Irish governments and economic policy, 1939 to 1952' (PhD thesis, UCD, 1997).

Magner, E. 'Seán Moylan: some aspects of his parliamentary career' (MA thesis, UCC, 1982).

Murphy, A. 'Dissension and disunity: the story of the political and industrial split in the Irish labour movement' (M.Litt thesis, UCD, 2000).

Murphy, G. 'The politics of economic realignment: Ireland 1948–64' (PhD thesis, Dublin City University, 1996).

Murphy, W. 'In pursuit of popularity and legitimacy: the rhetoric of Fianna Fáil's social and economic policy, 1926–34' (M.Litt. thesis, UCD, 1998).

Reynolds, B. 'The formation and development of Fianna Fáil, 1926–1932' (PhD thesis, Dublin University, 1976).

PUBLISHED WORKS

Articles and chapters

Allen, K. 'Forging the links: Fianna Fáil, the trade unions and the emergency', *Saothar*, vol. 16 (1991).

Baker, S.E. 'Orange and Green: Belfast, 1832–1912', in H.J. Dyos and M. Wolff (eds), *The Victorian City: Images and Realities* (London, 1973).

Baker, S. 'Nationalist ideology and the industrial policy of Fianna Fáil: the evidence of the *Irish Press* (1955–1972)', *Irish Political Studies*, vol. 1 (1986).

Cody, S., O'Dowd, J. and Rigney, P. (eds), *The Parliament of Labour: 100 Years of the Dublin Council of Trade Unions* (Dublin, 1986).

Colbert, J.P. 'The banking commission in general', *Irish Monthly* (May, 1939).

Cousins, M. 'The introduction of children's allowances in Ireland 1939–44', *Irish Economic and Social History*, vol. XXVI (1999).

Coyne, E.J. 'Irish social services: a symposium', *Journal of the Social and Statistical Society of Ireland*, vol. 17 (1942–43).

Coyne, E.J. 'The Third Minority Report', *Irish Monthly* (February, 1939).

Cronin, M. 'Golden dreams, harsh realities: economics and informal empire in the Irish Free State', in M. Cronin and J.M. Regan (eds), *Ireland: The Politics of Independence, 1922–49* (Hampshire, 2000).

Curran, S. '"Could Paddy leave off copying just for five minutes": Brian O'Nolan and Éire's Beveridge plan', *Irish University Review*, vol. 31 (2001).

Daalder, H. 'Government and opposition in the new states', *Government and Opposition*, vol. 1 (1965–6).

Daly, M.E. 'An Irish-Ireland for business? The Control of Manufactures Acts, 1932 and 1934, *Irish Historical Studies*, vol. xxiv, no. 94 (1984).

Daly, M.E. 'The employment gains from industrial protection in the Irish Free State during the 1930s: a note', *Irish Economic and Social History*, vol. XV (1988).

Daly, M.E. '"An atmosphere of sturdy independence": the state and the Dublin hospitals in the 1930s', in G. Jones and E. Malcolm (eds), *Medicine, Disease, and the State in Ireland 1650–1940* (Cork, 1999).

Daniel, T.K. 'Griffith on his noble head: the determinants of Cumann na nGaedheal economic policy, 1922–32', *Irish Economic and Social History*, vol. III (1976).

Dunphy, R. 'The enigma of Fianna Fáil: party, strategy, social classes and the politics of hegemony', in M. Cronin and J.M. Regan (eds), *Ireland: The Politics of Independence, 1922–49* (Hampshire, 2000).

Fanning, R. 'The impact of independence', in F.S.L. Lyons (ed.), *Bicentenary Essays: Bank of Ireland 1783–1983* (Dublin, 1983).

Fanning, R. 'Economists and governments 1922–58', in A. Murphy (ed.), *Economists and the Irish Economy from the Eighteenth Century to the Present Day* (Dublin, 1984).

Fanning, R. 'Alexis Fitzgerald', in P. Lynch and J. Meenan, *Essays in Memory of Alexis Fitzgerald* (Dublin, 1987).

Fanning, R. 'The genesis of economic development', in J.F. McCarthy, *Planning Ireland's Future: The Legacy of T.K. Whitaker* (Dublin, 1990).

Farrell, B. 'De Valera: unique dictator or charismatic chairman?' in J.P. O'Carroll and J.A. Murphy (eds), *De Valera and his Times* (Cork, 1983).

Ferriter, D. 'Local government, public health and welfare in twentieth-century Ireland', in M.E. Daly (ed.), *City and County Management: One Hundred Years of Local Government in Ireland* (Dublin, 2001).

Gallagher, T. 'The dimensions of Fianna Fáil rule in Ireland', *West European Politics*, vol. 4 (1981).

Garvin, J. 'Nature and extent of central control over local government administration', in F.C. King (ed.), *Public Administration in Ireland*, vol. II (Dublin, 1949).

Garvin, T. 'The destiny of the soldiers: tradition and modernity in the politics of de Valera's Ireland', *Political Studies*, vol. 26 (1978).

Garvin, T. 'The growth of faction in the Fianna Fáil party, 1966–80', *Parliamentary Affairs*, vol. 34 (1981).

Garvin, T. 'Theory, culture and Fianna Fáil: a review', in M. Kelly, L. O'Dowd and J. Wickham (eds), *Power, Conflict and Inequality* (Dublin, 1985).

Geary, R.C. 'Irish economic development since 1921', *Studies*, vol. 40 (December, 1951).

Girvin, B. 'Political culture, political independence and economic success in Ireland', *Irish Political Studies*, vol. 12 (1997).

Girvin, B. 'Politics in wartime: governing, neutrality and elections', in B. Girvin and G. Roberts (eds), *Ireland and the Second World War: Politics, Society and Remembrance* (Dublin, 2000).

Hannigan, K. 'British-based unions in Ireland: building workers and the split in congress', *Saothar*, vol. 7 (1981).

Honohan, P. and Ó Gráda, C. 'The Irish macroeconomic crisis of 1955–56: how much was due to monetary policy?' in *Irish Economic and Social History*, vol. XXV (1998).

Jessop, W.J.E. 'Health services: a critical appraisal', *Journal of the Statistical and Social Society of Ireland*, XXI, 1 (1963).

Kaim-Caudle, P.R. 'Paying for the health services', *Administration*, vol. 13 (1965).

Kelly, A. 'The Catholic Church and the welfare state in modern Ireland', *Archivium Hibernicum*, vol. LIII (1999).

Kennedy, F. 'Social expenditure of public authorities and economic growth 1947–66, *Economic and Social Review*, vol. 1 (1969–70).

Kennedy, F. *Public Social Expenditure in Ireland*, ESRI Broadsheet, no. 11 (Dublin, 1975).

Keynes, J.M. 'National self-sufficiency', *Studies* (June, 1933).

Lalor, S. 'Planning and the civil service 1945–70', *Administration*, 43, 4 (1995).

Lee, J.J. 'Economic development in historical perspective', in J.F. McCarthy (ed.), *Planning Ireland's Future* (Dublin, 1990).

Lucey, C. 'Family allowances', *Irish Ecclesiastical Record*, vol. 54 (1939).

Lucey, C. 'Conciliation and arbitration in labour disputes', *Studies*, vol. 29 (1940).

Lynch, P. 'The economist and public policy', *Studies*, vol. 42 (1953).

Lynch, P. 'The Irish economy since the war', in K.B. Nowlan and T.D. Williams (eds), *Ireland in the War Years and After* (Dublin, 1969).

Lynch, P. 'The years of readjustment, 1945–51', in K.B. Nowlan and T.D. Williams (eds), *Ireland in the War Years and After* (Dublin, 1969).

Mair, P. 'Ireland 1948–1981: issues, parties, strategies', in I. Budge, D. Robertson and D. Hearl (eds), *Ideology, Strategy and Party Change: Spatial Analyses of Post-War Election Programmes in 19 Democracies* (Cambridge, 1987).

McCarthy, A. 'Michael Collins – Minister for Finance 1919–1922', in G. Doherty and D. Keogh (eds), *Michael Collins and the Making of the Irish State* (Dublin, 1998).

McCarthy, A. 'Aspects of local health in Ireland in the 1950s', in D. Keogh, F. O'Shea and C. Quinlan (eds), *The Lost Decade: Ireland in the 1950s* (Cork, 2004).

McKee, É. 'Church–State relations and the development of Irish health policy: the mother-and-child scheme, 1944–53', *Irish Historical Studies*, xxv, 98 (1989).

McKevitt, P. 'The Beveridge plan reviewed', *Irish Ecclesiastical Record*, vol. LXI (March, 1943).

McMahon, D. 'A transient apparition: British policy towards the de Valera government, 1932–5', *Irish Historical Studies*, vol. 22 (1981).

McPolin, J. 'Public Health Bill', *Christus Rex*, 1, iii (1947).

MacRae, D. 'Populism as an ideology', in G. Ionescu and E. Gellner (eds), *Populism: Its Meanings and National Characteristics* (London, 1969).

Mitchell, A. 'William O'Brien, 1881–1968, and the Irish labour movement', *Studies*, vol. 60 (1971).

Morris, C. 'In the enemy's camp: Alice Milligan and *fin de siècle* Belfast', in N. Allen and A. Kelly (eds), *The Cities of Belfast* (Dublin, 2003).

Morrissey, M. 'The politics of economic management in Ireland 1958–70', *Irish Political Studies*, vol. 1 (1986).

Mulcahy, R. 'The Irish Volunteer Convention, 27 October, 1917', *Capuchin Annual*, 1966.

Murphy, J.A. '"Put them out!": parties and elections, 1948–69', in J.J. Lee (ed.), *Ireland 1945–70* (Dublin, 1979).

Neary, P. and Ó Gráda, C. 'Protection, economic war and structural change: the 1930s in Ireland', *Irish Historical Studies*, xxvii, 107 (1991).

Nevin, D. 'Decades of dissension and divisions 1923–1959', in D. Nevin (ed.), *Trade Union Century* (Dublin, 1994).

Nowlan, K.I. 'The evolution of Irish planning', in M. Bannon (ed.), *Planning: The Irish Experience, 1920–1988* (Dublin, 1989).

O'Donoghue, F. 'Reorganisation of the Irish Volunteers, 1916–1917', *Capuchin Annual*, 1966.

O'Driscoll, F. 'Social Catholicism and the social question in independent Ireland: the challenge to the fiscal system', in M. Cronin and J.M. Regan (eds), *Ireland: The Politics of Independence, 1922–49* (Hampshire, 2000).

O'Hagan, J.W. 'An analysis of the relative size of the government sector: Ireland 1926–52', *Economic and Social Review*, vol. 12 (1980).

O'Halpin, E. 'The civil service and the political system', *Administration*, 38, 4 (1991).

O'Halpin, E. 'The origins of city and county management', in E. O'Halpin, *City and County Management, 1929–1990: A Retrospective* (Dublin, 1991).

O'Halpin, E. 'Fianna Fáil on the high wire of foreign policy', in P. Hannon and J. Gallagher (eds), *Taking the Long View: Seventy Years of Fianna Fáil* (Dublin, 1996).

O'Halpin, E. 'Parliamentary party discipline and tactics: the Fianna Fáil archives, 1926–32', *Irish Historical Studies*, xxx, 120 (1997).

O'Halpin, E. 'The system of city and county management', in M.E. Daly (ed.), *County and Town: One Hundred Years of Local Government in Ireland* (Dublin, 2001).

O'Loghlen, P.J. 'The papal encyclicals and the Banking Commission', *Irish Monthly* (May, 1939).

Patterson, H. 'Fianna Fáil and the working class: the origins of the enigmatic relationship', *Saothar*, vol. 13 (1988).

Pratschke, J.L. 'The establishing of the Irish pound: a backward glance', *Economic and Social Review*, vol. 1 (1969–70).

Puirséil, N. 'Political and party competition in post war Ireland', in B. Girvin and G. Murphy (eds), *The Lemass Era: Politics and Society in the Ireland of Seán Lemass* (Dublin, 2005).

Riordan, S. '"A political blackthorn": Seán MacEntee, the Dignan plan and the principle of ministerial responsibility', *Irish Economic and Social History*, vol. XXVII (2000).

Wall, M. 'Partition: the Ulster question, 1916–26', in T.D. Williams (ed.), *The Irish Struggle, 1916–26* (London, 1966).

Whitaker, T.K. 'The Finance attitude', *Administration*, vol. 1 (1953–4).

Whiteker, T.K. 'Capital formation, saving and economic progress', *Journal of the Statistical and Social Inquiry Society of Ireland* (May, 1956).

Wiley, M.M. 'Financing the health services: from local to centralised funding and beyond', in J. Robins (ed.), *Reflections on Health: Commemorating Fifty Years of the Department of Health, 1947–1997* (Dublin, 1997).

Williams, T.D. 'De Valera in power', in F. MacManus (ed.), *The Years of the Great Test, 1926–39* (Cork, 1967).

Williams, T.D. 'Public affairs, 1916–1966', *Administration*, vol. 13 (1965–6).

BOOKS

Allen, K. *Fianna Fáil and Irish Labour: 1926 to the Present* (London, 1997).

Allen, N. and Kelly, A. (eds), *The Cities of Belfast* (Dublin, 2003).

Andrews, C.S. *Man of No Property* (Dublin, 1982).

Augusteijn, J. *From Public Defiance to Guerrilla Warfare: The Experience of Ordinary Volunteers in the Irish War of Independence, 1916–1921* (Dublin, 1996).

Bannon, M. (ed.), *Planning: The Irish Experience, 1920–1988* (Dublin, 1989).

Barrington, R. *Health, Medicine and Politics in Ireland, 1900–1970* (Dublin, 1987).

Bew, P. and Patterson, H. *Seán Lemass and the Making of Modern Ireland 1945–66* (Dublin, 1982).

Boland, K. *The Rise and Decline of Fianna Fáil* (Dublin, 1982).

Bowman, J. *De Valera and the Ulster Question, 1917–1973* (Oxford, 1989).

Brennan, R. *Allegiance* (Dublin, 1950).

Browne, N. *Against the Tide* (Dublin, 1986).

Canning, P. *British Policy towards Ireland, 1921–1941* (Oxford, 1985).

Chubb, B. and Lynch, P. (eds), *Economic Development and Planning* (Dublin, 1969).

Collins, S. *The Power Game: Ireland under Fianna Fáil* (Dublin, 2001).

Cooney, J. *John Charles McQuaid: Ruler of Catholic Ireland* (Dublin, 1999).

Cousins, M. *The Birth of Social Welfare in Ireland, 1922–1952* (Dublin, 2003).

Cronin, M. and Regan, J.M. (eds), *Ireland: The Politics of Independence, 1922–49* (Hampshire, 2000).

Crowe, C., Fanning, R., Kennedy, M., Keogh, D. and O'Halpin, E. (eds), *Documents in Irish Foreign Policy: Volume V, 1937–1939* (Dublin, 2006).

Cruise O'Brien, M. *The Same Age as the State* (Dublin, 2003).

D'Arcy, F.A. and Hannigan, K. (eds), *Workers in Union* (Dublin, 1988).

Daly, M.E. (ed.), *County and Town: One Hundred Years of Local Government in Ireland* (Dublin, 2001).

Daly, M.E. *Social and Economic History of Ireland* (Dublin, 1981).

Daly, M.E. *The Buffer State: The Historical Roots of the Department of the Environment* (Dublin, 1997).

De Valera, T. *A Memoir* (Dublin, 2004).

Deeny, J. *To Cure and to Care: Memoirs of a Chief Medical Officer* (Dublin, 1989).

Delaney, E. *Demography, State and Society: Irish Migration to Britain, 1921–1971* (Liverpool, 2000).

Doherty, G. and Keogh, D. (eds), *Michael Collins and the Making of the Irish State* (Dublin, 1998).

Dooley, T. *Inniskeen, 1912–1918: The Political Conversion of Bernard O'Rourke* (Maynooth, 2004).

Dunphy, R. *The Making of Fianna Fáil Power in Ireland* (Oxford, 1995).

Dyos H.J. and Wolff, M. (eds), *The Victorian City: Images and Realities* (London, 1973).

Fanning, R. *The Irish Department of Finance, 1922–1958* (Dublin, 1977).

Fanning, R. *The Four-Leaved Shamrock* (Dublin, 1983).

Fanning, R. *Independent Ireland* (Dublin, 1983).

Farrell, B. *Chairman or Chief: The Role of the Taoiseach in Irish politics* (London, 1971).

Farrell, B. *Seán Lemass* (Dublin, 1981).

Feldman, G.D. *The Great Disorder: Politics, Economics, and Society in the German Inflation 1914–24* (New York, 1997).

Ferriter, D. *Lovers of Liberty: 100 Years of Local Government* (Dublin, 2001).

Ferriter, D. *The Transformation of Ireland, 1900–2000* (London, 2004).

Ferriter, D. *Judging Dev: A Reassessment of the Life and Legacy of Éamon de Valera* (Dublin, 2007).

Fisk, R. *In Time of War: Ireland, Ulster and the Price of Neutrality* (Dublin, 1983).

FitzGerald, D. *Desmond's Rising: Memoirs 1913 to Easter* 1916 (Dublin, 1968).

FitzGerald, G. *Planning in Ireland* (Dublin, 1968).

FitzGerald, G. *All in a Life* (Dublin, 1992).

Fitzpatrick, D. *Harry Boland's Irish Revolution* (Cork, 2003).

Flynn, M.P. *Medical Doctor of Many Parts* (Mullingar, 2002).

Foster, R.F. *Modern Ireland 1600–1972* (London, 1988).

Gallagher, M. *Political Parties in the Republic of Ireland* (Dublin, 1985).

Garvin, T. *Preventing the Future: Why was Ireland so Poor for so Long?* (Dublin, 2004).

Gaughan, J.A. *Alfred O'Rahilly: Academic* (Dublin, 1986).

Girvin, B. *Between Two Worlds: Politics and Economy in Independent Ireland* (Dublin, 1989).

Girvin, B. *From Union to Union: Nationalism, Democracy and Religion – Act of Union to EU* (Dublin, 2002).

Girvin, B. and Murphy, G. *The Lemass Era: Politics and Society in the Ireland of Seán Lemass* (Dublin, 2005).

Girvin, B. and Roberts, G. (eds), *Ireland and the Second World War: Politics, Society and Remembrance* (Dublin, 2000).

Hannon, P. and Gallagher, J. (eds), *Taking the Long View: Seventy Years of Fianna Fáil* (Dublin, 1996).

Harris, J. *William Beveridge: A Biography* (Oxford, 1977).

Hensey, B. *The Health Services of Ireland* (Dublin, 1972).

Hepburn, A.C. *A Past Apart: Studies in the History of Catholic Belfast, 1850–1950* (Belfast, 1996).

Horgan, J. *Seán Lemass: The Enigmatic Patriot* (Dublin, 1997).

Horgan, J. *Noel Browne: Passionate Outsider* (Dublin, 2000).

Jones, G. and Malcolm, E. (eds), *Medicine, Disease, and the State in Ireland 1650–1940* (Cork, 1999).

Kennedy, K.A. and Dowling, B.R. *Economic Growth in Ireland: The Experience since 1947* (Dublin, 1975).

Kennedy, L. *Colonialism, Religion and Nationalism in Ireland* (Dublin, 1996).

Kennedy, M. and O'Halpin, E. *Ireland and the Council of Europe: From Isolation towards Integration* (Strasbourg, 2000).

Keogh, D. *Ireland and Europe 1919–1948* (Dublin and New Jersey, 1988).

Keogh, D., O'Shea, F. and Quinlan, C. (eds), *The Lost Decade: Ireland in the 1950s* (Cork, 2004).

King, F.C. (ed.), *Public Administration in Ireland*, vol. II (Dublin, 1949).

Laffan, M. *The Resurrection of Ireland: The Sinn Féin Party, 1916–1923* (Cambridge, 1999).

Lee, J.J. (ed.), *Ireland 1945–70* (Dublin, 1979).

Lee, J.J. *Ireland 1912–1985: Politics and Society* (Cambridge, 1989).

Litton, F. (ed.), *Unequal Achievement: The Irish Experience 1957–82* (Dublin, 1982).

Lynch, P. and Meenan, J. (eds), *Essays in Memory of Alexis Fitzgerald* (Dublin, 1987).

Lynch, R. *The Northern IRA and the Early Years of Partition, 1920–1922* (Dublin, 2006).

Lyons, F.S.L. *Ireland since the Famine* (London, 1971).

Lyons, F.S.L. (ed.), *Bicentenary Essays: Bank of Ireland 1783–1983* (Dublin, 1983).

MacDermott, E. *Clann na Poblachta* (Cork, 1998).

MacEntee, S. *Episode at Easter* (Dundalk, 1966).

MacManus, F. (ed.), *The Years of the Great Test, 1926–39* (Cork, 1967).

McBride, L.W. *The Greening of Dublin Castle: The Transformation of Bureaucratic and Judicial Personnel in Ireland, 1892–1922* (Washington, 1991).

McCarthy, C. *Trade Unions in Ireland, 1894–1960* (Dublin, 1977).

McCarthy, J.F. (ed.), *Planning Ireland's Future: The Legacy of T.K. Whitaker* (Dublin, 1990).

McColgan, J. *British Policy and the Irish Administration, 1920–22* (London, 1983).

McConville, S. *Irish Political Prisoners 1848–1922: Theatres of War* (London, 2003).

McCullagh, D. *A Makeshift Majority: The First Inter-Party Government, 1948–51* (Dublin, 1998).

McMahon, D. *Republicans and Imperialists: Anglo-Irish Relations in the 1930s* (London, 1984).

Manning, M. *James Dillon: A Biography* (Dublin, 1999).

Meenan, J. *The Irish Economy since 1922* (Liverpool, 1970).

Mitchell, A. *Revolutionary Government in Ireland: Dáil Éireann, 1919–1921* (Dublin, 1994).

Moynihan, M. *Currency and Central Banking in Ireland, 1922–60* (Dublin, 1975).

Moynihan, M. (ed.), *The Speeches and Statements of Éamon de Valera, 1917–1973* (Dublin, 1980).

Nevin, D. (ed.), *Trade Union Century* (Dublin, 1994).

Nevin, D. *James Connolly: A Full Life* (Dublin, 2005).

Nowlan, K.B. and Williams, T.D. (eds), *Ireland in the War Years and After* (Dublin, 1969).

Ó Broin, L. *No Man's Man* (Dublin, 1982).

Ó Broin, *Just Like Yesterday* (Dublin, 1986).

O'Carroll, J.P. and Murphy, J.A. (eds), *De Valera and his Times* (Cork, 1983).

O'Connor, E. *A Labour History of Ireland* (Dublin, 1992).

O'Connor, E. *James Larkin* (Cork, 2002).

Ó Gráda, C. *Ireland: A New Economic History 1780–1939* (Oxford, 1994).

O'Hagan, J.W. and Foley, G.J. *The Confederation of Irish Industry: The First Fifty Years 1932–1982* (Dublin, 1982).

O'Hagan, J.W (ed.), *The Economy of Ireland: Policy & Performance* (Dublin, 2000).

O'Higgins, T.F. *A Double Life* (Dublin, 1996).

Ó Muircheartaigh, F. (ed.), *Ireland in the Coming Times: Essays to Celebrate T.K. Whitaker's 80 Years* (Dublin, 1997).

O'Neill, T.P. and Lord Longford, *Éamon de Valera* (Dublin, 1970).

Patton, M. *Central Belfast: A Historical Gazetteer* (Belfast, 1993).

Plunkett Dillon, G. *All in the Blood: A Memoir of the Plunkett Family, the 1916 Rising and the War of Independence* (Dublin, 2006).

Powell, F.W. *The Politics of Irish Social Policy, 1600–1990* (New York, 1992).

Puirséil, N. *The Irish Labour Party, 1922–1973* (Dublin, 2007).

Quinlivan, A. *Philip Monahan: A Man Apart: The Life and Times of Ireland's First Local Authority Manager* (Dublin, 2006).

Redmond, S. *The Irish Municipal Employees Trade Union, 1883–1983* (Dublin, 1983).

Robins, J. *Custom House People* (Dublin, 1993).

Robins, J. *Reflections on Health: Commemorating Fifty Years of the Department of Health, 1947–1997* (Dublin, 1997).

Schenk, C.R. *Britain and the Sterling Area: From Devaluation to Convertibility in the 1950s* (London and New York, 1994).

Skinner, L. *Politicians by Accident* (Dublin, 1946).

Tierney, M. *Eoin MacNeill: Scholar and Man of Action, 1867–1945* (Oxford, 1980).

Tobin, F. *The Best of Decades: Ireland in the 1960s* (Dublin, 1984).

Townshend, C. *Easter 1916: The Irish Rebellion* (London, 2005).

Walker, B.M. (ed.), *Parliamentary Election Results in Ireland 1918–92* (Dublin, 1992).

Walsh, D. *The Party: Inside Fianna Fáil* (Dublin, 1986).
Whelan, B. *Ireland and the Marshall Plan, 1947–57* (Dublin, 2000).
Whitaker, T.K. *Interests* (Dublin, 1983).
Whyte, J.H. *Church and State in Modern Ireland* (Dublin, 1971).

Index